The Politics of Commonwealth
Citizens and Freeme

The Politics of Commonwealth offers a major reinterpretation of urban political culture in England during the sixteenth and seventeenth centuries. Examining what it meant to be a freeman and citizen in early modern England, it also shows the increasingly pivotal place of cities and boroughs within the national polity. It considers the practices that constituted urban citizenship as well as its impact on the economic, patriarchal, and religious life of towns and the larger commonwealth. The author recovers the language and concepts used at the time, whether by eminent citizens or more humble tradesmen and craftsmen. Unprecedented in terms of the range of its sources and freshness of its approach, the book reveals a dimension of early modern culture that has major implications for how we understand the English state, economy, and 'public sphere'; the political upheavals of the mid-seventeenth century; and popular political participation more generally.

PHIL WITHINGTON is Lecturer in Cultural History at the University of Aberdeen. He is the co-editor of *Communities in Early Modern England* (2000).

Cambridge Social and Cultural Histories

Series editors:

Margot C. Finn, *University of Warwick*
Colin Jones, *University of Warwick*
Keith Wrightson, *Yale University*

New cultural histories have recently expanded the parameters (and enriched the methodologies) of social history. Cambridge Social and Cultural Histories recognises the plurality of current approaches to social and cultural history as distinctive points of entry into a common explanatory project. Open to innovative and interdisciplinary work, regardless of its chronological or geographical location, the series encompasses a broad range of histories of social relationships and of the cultures that inform them and lend them meaning. Historical anthropology, historical sociology, comparative history, gender history, and historicist literary studies – among other subjects – all fall within the remit of Cambridge Social and Cultural Histories.

The Politics of Commonwealth

Citizens and Freemen in Early Modern England

Phil Withington

University of Aberdeen

CAMBRIDGE
UNIVERSITY PRESS

CAMBRIDGE UNIVERSITY PRESS
Cambridge, New York, Melbourne, Madrid, Cape Town, Singapore, São Paulo, Delhi

Cambridge University Press
The Edinburgh Building, Cambridge CB2 8RU, UK

Published in the United States of America by Cambridge University Press, New York

www.cambridge.org
Information on this title: www.cambridge.org/9780521826877

First published 2005
This digitally printed version 2008

A catalogue record for this publication is available from the British Library

ISBN 978-0-521-82687-7 hardback
ISBN 978-0-521-10036-6 paperback

For Cathy and Ellen

Contents

Figures

Tables

Acknowledgements

My first debt is to Keith Wrightson. If this book achieves half his craft and insight then it will have been worth writing. By recent, RAE-driven standards it is a book with a somewhat convoluted history. Although its genesis can be traced to my Ph.D. thesis, the final product is (thankfully) very much removed from its origins. Along the way, Peter Borsay, David Ditchburn, Elizabeth Hallam, Andrew Mackillop, John Morrill, Jane Ohlmeyer, Cathy Shrank, Micheal O'Siochru, and David Rollison read early (in some cases foetal) drafts of chapters and made valuable comments. Its writing has also benefited from the conversation and support of other friends and colleagues, whether they know it or not. They include Geoff Baldwin, Dermot Cavanagh, Alan Cromartie, Isabel Davis, Adam Fox, Henry French, Andy Gordon, Steve Hindle, Jean Howard, Tim Ingold, Joanna Innes, Mark Knights, Peter Kirby, Mary Morrissey, Ed Muir, Craig Muldrew, Tom Nichols, Arlene Oak, Alan Orr, Markku Peltonen, Sarah Rees-Jones, David Scott, Alexandra Shepard, Paul Slack, Naomi Tadmor, Robert Tittler, John Walter, Andy Wood, and Steve Zwicker. Mary Laven and Jason Scott Warren kindly let me stay with them while finishing my research in York, as did Jennifer Richards and Dermot Cavanagh in Newcastle. Especial thanks go to Jennifer Richards and David Clemis, whose friendship and enthusiasms reminded me at regular intervals why I was writing the book in the first place. David Ditchburn read half of the final draft and Cathy Shrank and Keith Wrightson read it all. The final result is, of course, entirely of my own making.

There are institutional debts. A research fellowship at Jesus College, Cambridge gave me the initial space to gather my thoughts; and the University of Aberdeen has subsequently provided invaluable support – in particular, the time and money to test chapters at seminars and conferences, and its commitment to both Cultural History and the Centre for Early Modern Studies. Even then it is doubtful the book would have been written without an AHRB Research Grant in 2002–3. As important have been the many librarians and archivists who have helped me on my sometimes tortuous way. Sue Hubbard in the Herefordshire County Record Office and Claire Welford at Cambridge University Library helped with particular references. The staff at the Shropshire Archives in

Shrewsbury have always been extremely helpful and friendly on my numerous visits. So, too, have those at the Berkshire Record Office, Borthwick Institute of Historical Research, British Library, Brymor Jones Library, East Sussex Record Office, Corporation of London Record Office, Cambridgeshire County Record Office, Devonshire Record Office, Huntingdon Record Office, North Yorkshire County Record Office, Post Office Record Office, Public Record Office in Kew, Sheepscar Library, and Tyne and Wear Archives. However, my biggest thanks go to where it all started – with Rita Freeman and the staff and volunteers at the York City Archives, a unique and wonderful institution. I'd like to thank Elizabeth Howard at Cambridge University Press for trusting me with a contract and the series editors for advising her to do so. I'd also like to thank Isabelle Dambricourt, Jackie Warren, Jo North and Val Howard and all the other people involved in the production of this book for their skill and patience. Alison Sandison drew the maps and Neil Curtis, curator of the Marischal Museum, introduced me to the unusual Commonwealth coin in his care.

I'd like to thank, finally, my family: Lynda and Barry Withington for their continual support; Lucy and Alan Shrank for their generosity, hospitality, and interest, especially on my research trips to Shropshire; and the Turons for living near Huntingdon. The last debt is the greatest. Whether providing references and translations, discussing ideas, or reading yet another draft of a chapter, Cathy Shrank has shared in this project from the outset.

All dates and spellings have been modernised.

Part I

Introductions

1 Urbanisation and political culture in early modern England

Urbanity and urbanisation

The word 'urbanity . . . being derived of the Latin word Urbanus' is 'not common amongst us'. So wrote Angel Daye in 1586.[1] Until quite recently, historians of early modern England would have probably agreed. The Italian city-states; the free cities of Germany; the imperial and provincial capitals of Spain and France; and the ports and walled towns of the Low Countries: these are traditionally recognised as centres of urbanity in pre-modern Europe. Whether the civic republicanism of Florence, the moral discipline of Geneva, or the thriving commerce of Amsterdam, it was in great continental cities that styles of urban living were fostered and exported. Although there were many English towns, they were regarded as small, provincial, and dominated by other groups and interests – not least the crown, county gentry, and burgeoning metropolis. Moreover, the rich historiography attracted by these towns seemed to establish that, at precisely the moment Daye was writing, whatever urban culture or 'mentality' had existed in England was entering a phase of irreparable decline.[2] Exceptions only seemed to prove this more general rule. London by the mid-sixteenth century was a city of international proportions that continued to grow in size, significance, and stature thereafter. Not only was it increasingly populous. It was also socially diverse, culturally fecund, politically significant, and economically integrated into a national economy.[3] It was also, at least if the historiography is anything to go by, unrepresentative of other cities and towns – a place hardly comparable to a provincial capital like York, never mind

---

[1] Angel Daye, *The English secretorie* (1586), p. 38.

[2] Classic statements include Peter Clark and Paul Slack, 'Introduction', in Clark and Slack, eds., *Crisis and order in English towns, 1500–1700* (London, 1972), pp. 1–56; Peter Clark and Paul Slack, *English towns in transition, 1500–1700* (Oxford, 1976). For a useful overview see Jonathan Barry, 'Introduction', in Barry, ed., *The Tudor and Stuart town: a reader in urban history, 1530–1688* (Harlow, 1990), pp. 1–34.

[3] For recent discussions see Lawrence Manley, *Literature and culture in early modern London* (Cambridge, 1997), pp. 1–20; Mark S. R. Jenner and Paul Griffiths, 'Introduction', in Griffiths and Jenner, eds., *Londinopolis: essays in the cultural and social history of early modern London* (Manchester, 2000), pp. 1–23.

a market town like Ludlow.[4] The story goes that it was only during the 'long eighteenth century' that London's monopoly on English urbanity was broken, the last decades of the seventeenth century witnessing an 'urban renaissance' that transformed provincial towns into centres of status, culture, and civility for urban and rural elites.[5] This coincided with a growth in the size and number of provincial towns and cities that was as unprecedented as it was unrivalled – a process of urbanisation that, by the second half of the eighteenth century, had turned England (and latterly Scotland) into the second most urbanised country in Europe.[6] Here was, in effect, the emergence of an English (or British) urban tradition fit to rival its European predecessors. Apparent 200 years after Angel Daye's observation, it was a quintessentially modern urbanity rooted in commerce, industry, leisure, and empire.

This familiar narrative of English urban development condemns the 100 years after 1540 to what Patrick Collinson terms 'the narrow neck' of 'a metaphorical hour-glass' – a threadbare period connecting the 'rich, tumultuous, irrepressible animal' of medieval community with the 'civilisation, high society and social class' of the eighteenth-century town.[7] That neck becomes narrower still once the urban dimension of English political developments is considered. One of the legacies of historical 'revisionism' is the awareness that Tudor and Stuart politics was essentially local.[8] Beyond the 'summit' of Whitehall and Westminster, inhabitancy and place shaped (if not determined) political participation, attitudes, and identities.[9] As importantly, 'post-revisionist' interest in political thought, communication, and ideology has revealed a national political culture that became more integrated, and also contested, over time.[10] Yet despite these interpretative developments, the political place and importance of towns – either as particular types of locale or nodes of communication – has been strangely neglected. This was in part because revisionists and post-revisionists alike equated locality with the 'county community', resulting in a particular prism through which to view both local politics and its

---

[4] Barry, 'Introduction', pp. 32–4; Manley, *Literature and culture*, pp. 14–16.

[5] Peter Borsay, *The English urban renaissance: culture and society in the provincial town, 1660–1770* (Oxford, 1989).

[6] Jan De Vries, *European urbanisation, 1500–1800* (London, 1984), p. 39; Charles Phythian Adams, 'An agenda for English local history', in Phythian Adams, ed., *Societies, cultures, and kinship, 1580–1850* (London, 1996), p. 8.

[7] Patrick Collinson, *The birthpangs of protestant England: religious and cultural change in the sixteenth and seventeenth centuries* (Basingstoke, 1988), pp. 58–9.

[8] J. S. Morrill, *The revolt of the provinces: conservatives and radicals in the English Civil War* (Harlow, 1980). The approach has been restated by Andy Wood, 'Beyond post-revisionism? The civil war allegiances of the miners of the Derbyshire "Peak Country", *HJ*, 40, 1997, pp. 23–40.

[9] Patrick Collinson, 'The monarchical republic of Queen Elizabeth I', *Bulletin of the John Rylands Library*, 69, 1987, p. 397.

[10] Richard Cust and Ann Hughes, 'Introduction: continuities and discontinuities in the English Civil War', in Cust and Hughes, eds., *The English Civil War* (London, 1997), pp. 14–16.

interconnections with national processes and events.[11] As a consequence, the intense light focused on those gentry who dominated the county's political and social institutions obscured the position of other sorts of place and person, towns and their inhabitants included. Where urban localism was considered, it was found to be no different to county varieties.[12] The neglect of urban political culture also stemmed, however, from the fact that those social and economic historians who dominated urban historiography had, by and large, an alternative set of preoccupations. They examined the late medieval crisis of English towns; the recurring urban problems of population, poverty and plague; and 'local politics . . . at the expense of a proper discussion of the impact of ideological conflict'.[13] If the subsequent story of embattled and beleaguered communities made little room for urbanity, then neither did it suggest an especially urban dimension to English political culture.

In both respects the absence is perplexing. The later sixteenth and seventeenth centuries witnessed, after all, a dramatic increase in the national population, the creation of an integrated national market, the final establishment of agrarian capitalism, overseas expansion and colonialism, and the emphatic enlargement of public infrastructures – not least courts of law and the book trade.[14] It was networks of market towns, provincial capitals, county towns, ports and postal towns, corporate towns, and, of course, metropolis, that facilitated these processes, knitting England's 'mosaic of parochial diversity' into what has been styled 'cumulative social development'.[15] The relative size of England's urban population also rose steadily, if not spectacularly, in the 150 years before 1650. In England in 1500, an estimated 80,000 people (3.1 per cent) lived in towns of over 10,000 inhabitants or more. In Scotland the figure was 13,000 (1.6 per cent). By 1650, the proportion in England had grown to 495,000 (8.8 per cent);

[11] Alan Everitt, *The local community and the Great Rebellion* (London, 1969); Clive Holmes, 'The county community in Stuart historiography' in Cust and Hughes, eds., *The English Civil War*, pp. 212–33.

[12] Roger Howell, 'Neutralism, conservatism and political alignment in the English revolution: the case of the towns, 1642–9', in John Morrill, ed., *Reactions to the English civil war* (London, 1982), pp. 67–87.

[13] Ian W. Archer, 'Popular politics in the sixteenth and early seventeenth centuries', in Griffith and Jenner, *Londinopolis*, p. 27. Influential studies include Charles Phythian Adams, *Desolation of a city: Coventry and the urban crisis of the late middle ages* (Cambridge, 1979); Paul Slack, *The impact of plague in Tudor and Stuart England* (London, 1985); Paul Slack, *Poverty and policy in Tudor and Stuart England* (London, 1988).

[14] Keith Wrightson, *Earthly necessities: economic lives in early modern Britain* (Yale, 2000), chs. 5 and 7; Craig Muldrew, *The economy of obligation* (Basingstoke, 1998), chs. 1 and 2; David Harris Sacks, *The widening gate: Bristol and the Atlantic, 1450–1700* (Berkeley, 1991), 350–1; C. W. Brooks, *Pettyfoggers and vipers of the commonwealth: the 'lower branch' of the legal profession in early modern England* (Cambridge, 1986), chs. 4, 6.

[15] Keith Wrightson, 'The politics of the parish in early modern England', in Paul Griffiths, Adam Fox, and Steve Hindle, eds., *The experience of authority in early modern England* (Basingstoke, 1996), p. 36.

in Scotland it stood at 35,000 (3.5 per cent).[16] Moreover, recent investigations into various kinds of provincial 'urbanism' query the historical orthodoxy of urban crisis and disintegration. Robert Tittler has traced a contemporaneous and manufactured culture of urban oligarchy in the market towns and larger boroughs of post-Reformation England: a deliberate realignment of civic elites with national government that was legitimated through histories, buildings, and display.[17] Jonathan Barry has argued for an urban culture of association that, despite various mutations and pressures, nevertheless provided a shared repository of values and practices for different sorts of town inhabitant.[18] Paul Slack has shown that contemporaries regarded England's 'great and good towns' as cultural and political entities that evolved in terms of their institutions and powers over the period.[19] And Collinson has himself observed that the 'sand' of the Reformation 'fell finely but with considerable force' through the narrow neck of England's urban hourglass.[20]

These more recent studies suggest an approach to English urbanity that is neither fixated by modernity nor bound by demography. Urbanisation certainly involves the movement and concentration of people. However, it can also consist of what Jan de Vries terms 'behavioural' and 'structural' change.[21] For de Vries, 'behavioural urbanisation' 'involves people in "urban" behaviour, modes of thought and types of activities whether they live in cities or not': it is as much a qualitative as quantitative process. 'Structural urbanisation' relates, in turn, to 'that process of change in the organisation of society that fosters . . . the concentration of activities at central points': it refers, that is, to the definition of certain institutions as urban.[22] Conceived in these terms, urbanisation involves certain practices, values, and commodities (material and symbolic) becoming at once associated with towns and disseminated by them: the printing press, for example, or courts of law. It also marks a change in the way towns or networks of towns are institutionally linked to the wider world: this is as true for market towns or ports as it is for towns blessed with garrisons or cathedrals.

[16] R. A. Houston, *The population history of Britain and Ireland, 1550–1750* (Cambridge, 1992), p. 20.

[17] Robert Tittler, *The Reformation and the towns in England: politics and political culture, c.1540–1640* (Oxford, 1998).

[18] Jonathan Barry, 'Bourgeois collectivism? Urban association and the middling sort', in Jonathan Barry and Christopher Brooks, eds., *The middling sort of people: culture, society and politics in England, 1550–1800* (Basingstoke, 1994), pp. 84–113.

[19] Paul Slack, 'Great and good towns, 1540–1700', in Peter Clark, ed., *The Cambridge urban history of Britain, volume II, 1540–1840* (Cambridge, 2000), pp. 347–76.

[20] Collinson, *Birthpangs*, p. 59.

[21] De Vries, *European urbanization*, pp. 10–17. See also Peter Borsay, 'Introduction', in Borsay, ed., *The eighteenth century town: a reader in English urban history, 1688–1820* (Harlow, 1990), p. 4.

[22] De Vries, *European urbanization*, pp. 12–13.

As significantly, 'structural' and behavioural' urbanisation, while serving as general categories of analysis, also allow for historical and cultural specificity. They point to the ways in which urban values and behaviour – like different types of urban structure – can vary over space and time. The rituals, attitudes, and institutions defining early modern Venice were very different to those of contemporary Paris. Likewise, neither the urbane delights of eighteenth-century Bath nor the capital and industry of nineteenth-century Manchester need be taken as benchmarks for English urbanity. Viewed as a cultural and institutional as well as demographic process, urbanisation becomes a relative concept.

It is with this relativism in mind that we can return to Angel Daye in 1586. Although aware that urbanity was a word 'as never or very rarely used' in the vernacular, Daye was equally sure that the term encompassed a range of qualities familiar to his audience. It meant 'civil, courteous, gentle, modest, or well ruled, as men commonly are in cities and places of good government'.[23] Almost 100 years later, in 1695, Edward Phillips was still defining 'civil' as 'courteous, kind, well bred, honest, chaste; also political, belonging to the citizens, City, or State'.[24] The basic premise of this book is to take Daye and Phillips at their word. It charts, in effect, the propagation, institutionalisation, and practice of 'civility' and 'good government' within English cities and towns between the Reformation and the Glorious Revolution.[25] It argues that the sixteenth and seventeenth centuries witnessed not so much a diminution of urbanity as the opposite: sustained urbanisation. It outlines a process of cultural and institutional change that had profound implications for urban political culture, national politics, and the agency and identity of those people broadly defined as the 'middling sort' of English society. In so doing, the book also offers a re-evaluation of some of the historiographical assumptions outlined above. It contends that, in certain key respects, the metropolis and provincial towns should be regarded as similar and certainly comparable entities that were linked culturally and institutionally within an expanding urban system. It claims that the antecedents, nature, and chronology of modernity were much more complex than historians of the 'long eighteenth century' have allowed. And it suggests that, as a corollary of this, historians of both English politics and the English state have vastly underestimated the urban dimension of their subjects. This dimension was certainly apparent to contemporaries. Indeed, in all the chapters

---

[23] Daye, *Secretorie*, p. 38.   [24] Edward Phillips, *New world of words* (1658), 'civil'.

[25] See also Cathy Shrank, 'Civil tongues: language, law, and reformation', in Jennifer Richards, ed., *Early modern civil discourses* (Basingstoke, 2003), p. 23; Jonathan Barry, 'Civility and civic culture in early modern England: the meanings of urban freedom', in Peter Burke, Brian Harrison, and Paul Slack, eds., *Civil histories: essays presented to Sir Keith Thomas* (Oxford, 2000), p. 181.

that follow, the primary aim has been to recover and contextualise the language, concepts, and practices used by people at the time. If this is true of the principles of civility and governance upon which urbanity was ideally based, then it also applies to the cultural and institutional space in which those principles were embodied. It is to the mechanics of their embodiment that we must now briefly turn.

Incorporation and city commonwealths

The urbanity explored in this book was based on civic incorporation. This involved the successful acquisition by urban inhabitants of a royal charter of incorporation that either confirmed the material and constitutional resources situated in a settlement, or restyled those resources according to a legal formula that, by the seventeenth century, had become more or less standardised. The charter was invariably the product of often protracted negotiations between the clerks of the Lord-Attorney's office, the petitioning inhabitants, and the lawyers and courtiers who acted as brokers in the transaction. In its basic content it usually specified the five marks of corporatism that confirmed the city or borough as a legally constructed 'fictional person'. In this guise, the freemen, burgesses, and citizens who voluntarily participated in this person could act collectively as a single body, so transcending their individual lives and interests to form an entity that could sue in law and be represented in parliament. The financial corollary of this was possession of the fee farm: an annual and often nominal rent that the corporate body paid directly to the crown for possession of their territory and jurisdiction. As important were the economic rights and privileges confirmed by the charter – whether markets, fairs, common lands, tolls, rights of pontage, or craft guilds – and the legal and parliamentary privileges that were usually assimilated into the civic constitution. In particular, incorporation typically, though not invariably, conferred the right of burgesses and citizens to empanel and sit on their own juries; supply their own justices of the peace; choose their own parliamentary representatives; and convene their own borough courts for minor suits of debt and trespass. For those larger cities like York or Norwich that were able to incorporate as counties, these privileges could extend to marshalling their own militia and attending their own assizes. Standard practice by the seventeenth century was the creation of two legal positions that provided technical advice and support to citizens and burgesses – the recorder and town clerk – as well as a high steward who represented the incorporated body on the Privy Council. These supplemented the connections and expertise brought to cities and boroughs by their parliamentary representatives, who were, especially among the smaller boroughs, increasingly chosen from the ranks of gentry, lawyers, and magnates over the period. Before 1660, the election of recorder, town clerk, and high steward was a civic privilege.

Thereafter, any election of recorder and town clerk had to be certified by the crown.[26]

Incorporation endowed urban inhabitants with a remarkable range of powers and privileges. It was also an intensely political process resting on the agency of people in both locality and metropolis. Locally this might take the form of an organised and united populace, as was the case of Reading in the mid-sixteenth century, or a divided and factional body intent on using the charter as a political weapon, such as Beverley in the 1570s or Ludlow in the 1590s.[27] There might also be an ideological dynamic, whereby groups of citizens attempted to implement changes in, for example, the religious practices of freemen and other inhabitants.[28] Either way, incorporation usually precipitated external interventions – by local gentry, lawyers, ecclesiastics, courtiers, and patrons – at the request of townsmen. Like many boroughs, Windsor looked to the Earl of Nottingham and Sir Edward Coke after twenty-five years of lobbying for a charter. Huntingdon secured its charter through the influence of the Earl of Manchester in 1630. The Duchy of Cornwall and other sources of metropolitan influence were in large part responsible for the extraordinary success rate of Cornish boroughs after 1550.[29] A further political dimension involved disputes between citizens and other urban interests, in particular seigniorial power and authority. Enmity could focus on a manorial lord, as in the protracted struggles between the citizens of Aylesbury and the Packinghams.[30] It could involve an ecclesiastical institution: most obviously the influence of abbeys and monastic houses, but also post-Reformation bodies like universities, archbishoprics, and dean and chapters.[31] Other cities and boroughs could also provide a focus for civic discontent. Israel was never 'more burdened under the taskmasters of Egypt' than was Great Yarmouth by her urban rivals.[32] London encapsulated and

---

[26] The best accounts of the incorporating process are Tittler, *The Reformation and the towns*, ch. 5; Catherine F. Patterson, *Urban patronage in early modern England: corporate boroughs, the landed elite, and the crown, 1580–1640* (Stanford, 1999), pp. 164–80. See also Paul D. Halliday, *Dismembering the body politic: partisan politics in England's towns 1650–1730* (Cambridge, 1998).

[27] Jeanette Martin, 'Leadership and priorities in Reading during the Reformation', in Patrick Collinson and John Craig, eds., *The Reformation in English towns, 1500–1640* (Basingstoke, 1998), pp. 113–30; David Lamburn, 'Politics and religion in early modern Beverley', in Collinson and Craig, *Reformation in English towns*, pp. 63–79; Penry Williams, 'Government and politics in Ludlow, 1590–1642', *Transactions of the Shropshire Archaeological Society*, 56, 1957–60, pp. 282–94.

[28] David Underdown, *Fire from heaven: life in an English town in the seventeenth century* (London, 1993).

[29] *Annals of Windsor. Being a history of the castle and town*, I, ed. Robert Richard Tighe and James Edward Davis (London, 1858), pp. 647, 54–7; TNA SP16 176 34; John Chynoweth, 'Gentry of Tudor Cornwall' (unpublished Ph.D., University of Exeter, 1994), pp. 216–17.

[30] *VCH*, Berkshire, III, pp. 1–20.

[31] *VCH*, Hertfordshire, II, pp. 469–91.

[32] Henry Manship, *The history of Great Yarmouth*, ed. Charles John Palmer (1854), p. 167.

embodied these problems. Renowned and also feared nationally for their commercial imperialism, the citizens of London spent much time and energy protecting their own liberties and jurisdictions: against the burgeoning suburbs; Westminster; the Inns of Court; and the royal palaces.[33] That a city as powerful as London incorporated at all is illustrative of a third political dynamic: that incorporation legitimated as clearly as possible the control, by citizens, of property, territory, and institutional resources.

Whatever the politics surrounding incorporation, it was freemen, burgesses, and citizens who populated the community, or *communitas*, that resulted. The term 'freeman' denoted access to economic resources and privileges and was enjoyed by all enfranchised inhabitants. The labels 'burgess' (in boroughs) and 'citizen' (in cities) signified additional public powers and responsibilities within the body politic. Enfranchisement was formalised by oath-taking and other communal rituals and formally restricted to male heads of household. It could be secured either through patrimony, purchase, or, most usually, a seven-year apprenticeship under the authority of a freeman and the craft or guild to which he belonged. As such, enfranchisement was a conscious and deliberate act by which heads of household placed themselves and their household dependants under the authority of the community in return for the economic and political rights located there. Although only male heads of household could be elected to places of civic power, all household dependants were regarded as members of the community and enjoyed (in theory at least) mediated representation within the civic polity. Viewed in these terms, the basic structure of incorporated communities was threefold. First, it consisted of a core of civic structures – such as aldermanic benches, common councils, parishes, and guilds – through which and by which freemen were governed and represented. Second, it encompassed the jurisdictions and neighbourhoods in which members of enfranchised households lived. Third, households constituted it: those places in which the primary affective and economic relationships of a person were likely to be based. In these respects, incorporated communities resembled nothing less than the Aristotelian *polis*: a resemblance that, as is argued in the chapters that follow, was far from coincidental.

Historians have, by and large, approached incorporation as a restricted and restrictive process: as an arcane cul-de-sac of legal history; a tool of local oligarchs and aggressive statesmen; the political detritus of minor local elites. In contrast, early modern people had an expansive, ambitious, and essentially humanist conception of cities, boroughs, and corporate towns that was

---

[33] Paul Slack, 'Perceptions of the metropolis in seventeenth-century England', in Burke et al., *Civil histories*, pp. 161–80; Valerie Pearl, *London and the outbreak of the Puritan revolution: city government and national politics, 1625–1643* (Oxford, 1961), ch. 1; Paul Slack, *From Reformation to improvement: public welfare in early modern England* (Oxford, 1999), pp. 72–3.

encapsulated by the term 'small' or 'city commonwealth'. The civil lawyer Thomas Wilson observed in 1600 that the 'state of citizens . . . by reason of the great privileges they enjoy, every city being, as it were, a Common wealth among themselves, no other officer of the Queen nor other having authority to entermeddle amongst them, most needs be exceeding well to pass'.[34] For Henry Manship, town clerk of Great Yarmouth, incorporated cities were a reminder that:

as in the beginning of the World, the gathering together of society and men began not for one cause only, as for that they might be rich, or that they might be helpful one to another, which be to many reasons and motives; but also for that they might in all things live the more commodiously together and frame themselves a Commonwealth.[35]

City commonwealths represented:

a certain community or Society, both of life and goods, which makes a civil body, formed and made of divers members, to live under one power, as it were under one Head and Spirit, and more profitably to live together in this mortal life, that they may the more easily attain unto life eternal for ever.[36]

Less favourably, Thomas Hobbes lamented in 1651 'the great number of Corporations; which are as it were many lesser Common-wealths in the bowels of a greater, like worms in the entrails of a natural man'.[37] However, the tension between the city and larger commonwealth implied by Hobbes was not inevitable. Certainly the Elizabethan satirist Thomas Nashe noted that for a city commonwealth 'this common good within itself is nothing to the common good it communicates to the whole state'.[38] This was because city commonwealths, in addition to their civil and civic propensities, also enshrined what the cartographer John Speed termed 'commerce', and what others understood to be the communicative basis of community.[39] Indeed as late as 1695 Phillips' dictionary defined 'community' as 'the having things in common, partnership. Also a body of men united in civil society for their mutual advantage, as a corporation, inhabitants of a town, the companies of tradesmen.' The word 'society' denoted, in turn, 'company, conversation, civil intercourse, fellowship, friendship; company of several persons joined together for some common interest, or to assist one another in the management of any particular business'.[40]

---

[34] Thomas Wilson, *The State of England anno. dom. 1600*, ed. F. J. Fisher (Camden Misc. XVI, 1936), p. 20.
[35] Manship, *History*, p. 23.   [36] Ibid.
[37] Thomas Hobbes, *Leviathan*, ed. Richard Tuck (Cambridge, 1992), p. 230.
[38] Thomas Nashe, 'Nashe's Lenten Stuff', in *The unfortunate traveller and other works*, ed. J. B. Steane (Harmondsworth, 1985), p. 394.
[39] John Speed, *The theatre of the empire of Great Britain* (1616).
[40] Phillips, *New world of words*, 'community', 'society'.

This book is about the ideal and practice of 'city commonwealth' and the concepts of civility, governance, and commerce it embodied. In the words of F. W. Maitland, it examines the intersection of 'Italian thought' and 'English life' that lay at the heart of urban political culture during the sixteenth and seventeenth centuries.[41] It takes its cue from the fact that the 100 years after 1540 saw at once an astonishing proliferation of city commonwealths and their alignment into what can best be described as a metropolitan-based corporate system. Hobbes was not criticising a chimera. Even as humanists like Daye, Phillips, Wilson, Manship, and Nashe eulogised the English urbanity that the city commonwealth represented, its principles were being institutionalised and appropriated across the localities of England, Ireland, and the New World. Incorporation may have been a medieval invention; however, it was the early modern period that marked England's era of incorporation.

Citizens and freemen

That freemen, burgesses, and citizens should personify qualities of civility and governance might seem surprising given the contempt reserved for them by ostensible social and intellectual betters: a condescension that unerringly antic-ipates their subsequent historical neglect.[42] Certainly Hobbes was far from alone in his animosity. When Charles II accepted the freedom of the city of London in 1674, for example, the poet and courtier Rochester could only laugh that 'Monarchs rank themselves with Grocers'.[43] In 1663, the bureaucrat Samuel Pepys recorded his enjoyment of 'a true and allowable Tragedy' at the Duke's theatre but also noted that 'The house was full of Citizens and so the less pleasant'.[44] These were relatively subtle slights compared to the scorn that the gentleman and common lawyer Richard Carew poured on the Cornish citizenry at the end of the previous century. Carew regarded the 'large exemptions and jurisdictions' of burgesses in Elizabethan Cornwall as 'over-rich and wide for many of their withered and ill-disposed bodies', whereby 'an ignorant fellow of a cobbler becomes a magistrate, and takes upon him peremptory judgement in debts and controversies great and doubtful'. As far as Carew was concerned, Cornish burgesses lacked reason; were 'distrustful and injurious towards

---

[41] Susan Reynolds, *An introduction to the history of English medieval towns* (Oxford, 1977); F. W. Maitland, *Township and borough* (Cambridge, 1898), p. vi.

[42] For examples of neglect see Michael Walzer, 'Citizenship', in Terence Ball, James Farr, and Russell L. Hanson, eds., *Political innovation and conceptual change* (Cambridge, 1989), p. 216; Anna Bryson, *From courtesy to civility: changing codes of conduct in early modern England* (Oxford, 1998).

[43] Cited in *The poems and letters of Andrew Marvell*, vol. 1, ed. H. M. Margoliouth (Oxford, 1927), p. 304.

[44] *The diary of Samuel Pepys, vol. IV, 1663*, ed. R. C. Latham and W. Matthews (London, 1995), p. 2.

strangers' and unable to afford public responsibilities – 'for they cannot follow law, and work'; and were susceptible to alliances and 'friends' due to the impermanence and elective nature of their position. From 'these imperfect associates there spring pride amongst themselves, disdain at their neighbours, and monopolies against the commonwealth'.[45] He also noted that 'The ancients used to grace their cities with several titles, as *Numantia bellicosa*, *Thebe superbe* ... and the present Italians do the like touching theirs, as *Roma santa*, *Venetia ricca*.' It was amusing, therefore, that 'In an imitation whereof, some of the idle disposed Cornishmen nick their towns with by-words, as The *Good Fellowship of Padstow*, *Pride of Truro*, *Gallants of Fowey*.'[46]

In ridiculing the burgesses, Carew nevertheless hinted at their own sense of themselves. Certainly their appellations are the less incongruous if the civil and civic sensibilities they imply are taken seriously. As importantly, the social prejudices of one social group are no basis for understanding the culture of another. The following pages suggest that, no matter the conceits and snobberies of theorists, gentlemen, bureaucrats, and courtiers, it was clearly the case that, in Cornwall as in London, a freeman was also 'a citizen [in] a conscious and autonomous decision-making political community'.[47] Understood on these terms, the scope and significance for freedom and citizenship in early modern England were wide indeed. Citizens and freemen occupied a crucial place within the wider panoply of English politics. Moreover, the values and practices of city commonwealth were disseminated and appropriated far beyond the walls and boundary-marks of cities and boroughs. In both respects, what follows contributes to the burgeoning historiography on political culture beyond Whitehall, Westminster, and the 'county community'.[48]

The wider significance of city commonwealth is reflected in part by the civic and metropolitan connections of some familiar figures who appear on these pages – not least Sir Thomas Smith (Saffron Walden), William Shakespeare (Stratford-upon-Avon), Oliver Cromwell (Huntingdon and Cambridge), and John Lilburne (Newcastle-upon-Tyne). Particular attention is reserved for Andrew Marvell, a citizen who personified the long tradition of English urbanity as it had emerged by the later seventeenth century, and who serves as a crucial counterpoint to the lineage of the centralised state exemplified

---

[45] Richard Carew, *The survey of Cornwall*, ed. and introduced by F. E. Halliday (London, 1954), pp. 157–8.

[46] Ibid., p. 159.

[47] Jonathan Scott, *England's troubles: seventeenth-century English political instability in European context* (Cambridge, 2000), p. 292. See also J. G. A. Pocock, *The Machiavellian moment: Florentine political thought and the Atlantic republican tradition* (Princeton, 1975), p. 335; *Virtue, commerce, and history: essays in political thought, chiefly in the eighteenth century* (Cambridge, 1985), p. 40.

[48] See Phil Withington, 'Two renaissances: urban political culture in post-Reformation England reconsidered', *HJ*, 44, 1, 2001, pp. 241–6; Wood, 'Beyond post-revisionism', pp. 23–28.

by Hobbes. However, the majority of freemen and women who populated the corporate system were not famous at all. Archetypal in this respect might be James Wright. Born in March 1571 in the parish of St Martin's Micklegate in the city of York, James was the son of a York potter, Henry Wright.[49] Apprenticed as a baker, he took his freedom of the city in 1596 and married Isabel (Elizabeth) Carleton a year later, in 1597.[50] The young couple had their first child, Margaret, in 1602.[51] Clearly an industrious and successful baker, James served as churchwarden in the parish of St John's Micklegate in 1601 and became chamberlain of the city in 1614.[52] His daughter, Margaret, married a substantial freeholder in the neighbouring town of Tadcaster in 1629, and his son, Henry, followed the calling of baker, taking his freedom by patrimony in 1624.[53] By the time he drew up his will in February 1636, James Wright's household was an established feature of the parochial and civic community. He had accumulated some property in addition to his trade and credit; was an elected member the Common Council of seventy-two; and, despite the relatively humble nature of his trade, was a friend of mercantile neighbours like Mr Richard Baines and Alderman Edmund Cowper.[54]

There was, in short, nothing exceptional about James Wright and his household. He epitomised the Aristotelian 'middle class' around whom, as we shall see, city commonwealths should ideally be built. He was likewise reminiscent of the nameless burghers subsequently eulogised by Johann Fichte as the mainstays of European civilisation.[55] Nevertheless, it is the changing contexts of Wright's culture that this book is ultimately about.[56] As such, it is a fillip that the executors of James' modest estate wanted his memory to last longer than the next generation. An epitaph was commissioned announcing him 'one of the Commons of this City'. It reads:

> Look reader as thou passes by
> Underneath this stone does lie
> A citizen of great respect
> As free from vice and from defect.
> Civility and temperance,
> Frugality and governance,
> Were the epithets that spoke him blest

---

[49] BIHR, P Q 42.74 (printed), 16.

[50] Francis Collins, ed., *Register of the freemen of the city of York, II, 1559–1759* (Durham, 1900), p. 40.

[51] BIHR, PR Y/J 1.   [52] BIHR, PR Y/J 17, 2; Collins, *Register*, 63.   [53] Ibid., 74.

[54] BIHR, Will of James Wright, Prerogative Court December 1639, City of York.

[55] Aristotle, *The politics and the constitution of Athens*, ed. Stephen Everson (Cambridge, 1996), pp. 107–8; Johann Gottlieb Fichte, *Addresses to the German nation* (1808), ed. George Armstrong Kelly (London,1968) pp. 88–90.

[56] E. P. Thompson, *The making of the English working class* (New York, 1966), p. 12.

And gained him love among the best.
Religiously he lived and died
And now we hope in heaven does abide.[57]

The virtues that the epitaph celebrated, as well as the contexts in which they were practised, read like a checklist of the kind of urbanity excavated below. The next chapter establishes the geography and chronology of urbanisation as reflected through the process of incorporation. Chapters 3, 4, and 5 explore the ideological, spatial, and conversational resources of civic governance and civility. The final three chapters examine the intersection between citizenship and economic, patriarchal, and religious practice. A recurring theme is the inextricability of the personal and social qualities memorialised on James Wright's epitaph. In particular, the book draws out the interconnectedness of self and communal civility and governance that, for all its importance to contemporaries, is often ignored by historians or treated, somewhat anachronistically, as an organised programme of social and cultural repression.[58] If the chapters that follow demonstrate anything, it is that freemen and citizens, like any other social group, were very much present at their own making.

---

[57] J. B. Morrell, *The biography of the common man of the city of York as recorded in his epitaph* (London, 1948), p. 79.

[58] The classic statement, though confined to courtly elites, is Norbert Elias, *The civilizing process*, trans. Edmund Jephcott (Oxford, 2000). For reassessments of this relationship see Richard Tuck, *Philosophy and government, 1572–1651* (Cambridge, 1993), pp. xiii–xiv; Scott, *England's troubles*, pp. 318–20; Craig Muldrew, 'From a 'light cloak' to an 'iron cage': historical changes in the relation between community and individualism', in Alexandra Shepard and Phil Withington, eds., *Communities in early modern England: networks, place, rhetoric* (Manchester, 2000), pp. 156–79; Markku Peltonen, *Classical humanism and republicanism in English political thought, 1570–1640* (Cambridge, 1995), p. 57.

2   The formation of the English corporate system

'No little glory to the land'

In 1611 the cartographer and historian John Speed published *The theatre of the empire of Great Britain*, explaining that his 'principal motive of writing' was the 'zeal of my country's glory', the 'glory of our Nation being almost buried in the pit of obscurity'.[1] The importance of urbanity to this humanist agenda was reflected simply in the layout of the text. In the English section of the book, the centrepiece of each chapter was a detailed map or 'chart' of a county across two folios on which were marked rivers (but not roads), townships and towns, and great castles and houses. Around the county map were placed smaller maps and illustrations. Inset against thirty-five counties was a bird's-eye map of the leading county town: Norwich accompanied Norfolk; Ipswich Suffolk; Dorchester Dorset; Shrewsbury Shropshire; and so on. For a further five counties, two towns were represented in this way: while Kent was depicted with Canterbury and Rochester, Berwick-upon-Tweed and Newcastle-upon-Tyne adorned Northumberland. The same model of isolating 'great and good towns' within their local contexts was repeated for Ireland and Wales, reflecting at once their role as centres of commerce within particular localities and their status as distinct, autonomous places in their own right.[2]

The textual prominence of cities and boroughs reflected their cultural significance. In England they illustrated the wealth and commodity of the people: indeed, Speed's homeland was so commodious that there were 'more beautiful and richer Corporations' than could possibly be included. Nevertheless, it 'gives no little glory to the land in general, so to be replenished with store and choice, as hardly can be judged which can be omitted'.[3] The Scottish section was truncated because Timothy Pont was already constructing a similar kind of survey north of the border.[4] Nevertheless, Speed assured his royal patron and wider public that 'the Counties contained in this kingdom are many, and every where

---

[1] John Speed, *The theatre of the empire of Great Britain* (1611), pp. B2, C2.
[2] Slack, 'Great and good towns', pp. 347–8.   [3] Speed, *Theatre*, p. B2v.
[4] Patricia Dennison, 'Timothy Pont's portrayal of towns', in Ian C. Cunningham, ed., *The nation survey'd: Timothy Pont's maps of Scotland* (East Lothian, 2001), pp. 125–38.

bestrewed with Cities, Towns and Burghs, as is that of England'.[5] In Ireland and Wales, the meaning of towns was different, marking the forceful exportation of English and latterly Scottish civility, commerce, and authority rather than indigenous 'glory'. For Speed, Irish cities demarcated the limit of civil values and practices. Dublin was 'matchable too [sic] many other cities frequent for traffic and intercourse with merchants', and 'the people . . . do about the neighbouring parts of Dublin come nearest unto the civil conditions and orderly subjection of the English'.[6] The further away from the city, the more uncivil the people became. In Wales, cities were remarkable for their fortifications: intricate memorials to the 'industry both of Nature and Art' required for the previous conquest and settlement of the 'principality'.[7] Although certain settlements such as Cardiff were now prosperous centres, others like St David's acquired the status of ghost towns in Speed's description.

The *Theatre* presented, then, an historical landscape through a humanist- and imperial-tinted lens. The result was a kind of embedded antiquity: an immemorial landscape that brooked no alteration. In this Speed anticipated more recent local historiography. Whether talking of 'county communities' or 'cultural provinces', local historians have forcefully argued that until the eighteenth century there was little change in the basic fabric and borders of local society.[8] However, less obvious from Speed's compendium was the fact that the surplus of 'beautiful' and 'rich' corporations that contributed to this topography was the product of a recent and ongoing process. From the middle of the sixteenth century an increasing number of urban communities had been at once legally confirmed as semi-autonomous city commonwealths and incorporated into a metropolitan-based corporate system. Such places ranged from monastic or manorial boroughs like Wokingham upgrading their civic resources to 'ancient' cities and royal boroughs like Cambridge 'renewing' and 'amending and bettering' their customary freedoms, liberties, and political constitutions.[9] Three years before the publication of the *Theatre*, for example, the City of London, England's most ancient and powerful city commonwealth, purchased its first royal charter of incorporation. It did so along with Great Yarmouth in Norfolk, Newport on the Isle of Wight, Whitchurch in Hampshire, and Lostwithiel in Cornwall. Inhabitants of Cardiff, Cambridge, and Louth likewise renewed existing charters.[10] Such purchases had been happening year on year since the 1540s and continued until at least 1640. It was a process contemporaneous with a number of other developments which, taken together, suggest a major transformation in the relationship between nation and

---

[5] Speed, *Theatre*, p. 131.   [6] Ibid., pp. 139–40.   [7] Ibid., pp. 113–23.
[8] Phythian Adams, 'Agenda', pp. 9–18.
[9] BCRO, WO/01/1/1 and WO/AL; CCRO, City Shelf C, Book 7, f. 68v.
[10] Tittler, *Reformation and the towns*, p. 346.

locality – or metropolis and the towns – in the 100 years after 1540. It is with the chronology and geography of this process, as well as its political and economic contexts and implications, that this chapter is concerned.

The formation of the corporate system

There were thirty-eight incorporated cities and boroughs in England in 1500. By 1600, there were 130. As table 2.1 shows, the accession of the Stuarts to the throne encouraged rather than slowed their proliferation. Thirty-six cities and boroughs were incorporated in the first two decades of Jacobean government and a further fifteen between 1621 and 1640. By 1640 there were 181 incorporated cities and boroughs across England and a further fourteen in Wales. The figure rises to 267 if re-incorporations – a particular feature of Jacobean governance – are taken into consideration. As a result, in the 150 years after 1500 the number of city commonwealths in England completely outstripped their nearest Scottish equivalent, the royal burgh – places that, while not identical to English cities and boroughs, were predicated on similar assumptions of citizenship, civility, and commerce.[11] While the number of Scottish and English city commonwealths was more or less the same at the beginning of the sixteenth century, by the middle of the seventeenth there were 123 more city commonwealths south than north of the border. Even if only English incorporated cities and boroughs with parliamentary representation are counted, the gap remains seventy. A second point of comparison is the plantation of Ulster, where the incorporated city commonwealth was intrinsic to the Jacobean programme of colonisation.[12] During the sixteenth century incorporation in the Irish Pale marked the kind of reciprocity between metropolis and locality found in England. Under James, the expectations of the crown became more onerous: the citizens of Dublin and the other Irish staple towns only retained their customary rights, privileges, and extensive civic cultures in return for significant concessions regarding trade customs and, more problematically, Protestantism.[13] However, in Ulster incorporation was used as a straightforward tool of expropriation. That the majority of plantations subsequently failed as communities illuminates as well as anything the crucial point that urbanity reflected local conditions and relationships as much as the

---

[11] Ian A. Archer, 'Politics and government, 1540–1700', in Clark, ed., *Cambridge urban history*, pp. 23–8.

[12] R. J. Hunter, 'Towns in the Ulster plantation', in *Studia Hibernia*, 11, 1971, pp. 40–6; Philip Robinson, *The plantation of Ulster: British settlement in an Irish landscape, 1600–1670* (Dublin, 1984), esp. ch. 7; Raymond Gillespie, *Colonial Ulster: the settlement of East Ulster, 1600–1641* (Cork, 1985), ch. 7; Raymond Gillespie 'The origins and development of an Ulster urban network, 1600–41', *Irish Historical Studies*, 24, 1984, pp. 15–30.

[13] 'Letter of King James I for a new grant of charters to the ancient corporations of Ireland, March 1609', printed in Peter Gale, *An inquiry into the ancient corporate system of Ireland and suggestions for its immediate restoration and general extension* (London, 1834), p. 1.

Table 2.1 *Incorporated boroughs and royal burghs by 1640*

	Pre-1500	1501–20	1521–40	1541–60	1561–80	1581–1600	1601–20	1621–40	Total
England	38	2	4	42	20	24	36	15	181
Wales	3	1	0	2	2	2	3	1	14
Ulster	2	0	0	0	0	0	25	1	28
Anglo-Irish	5	1	0	3	8	1	36	4	58
Scotland	35	0	0	2	6	7	3	5	58

Sources: English and Anglo-Irish figures are taken from Robert Tittler, *The Reformation and the towns in England: politics and political culture, c.1540–1640* (Oxford, 1998); Martin Weinbaum, *British borough charters, 1307–1660* (Cambridge, 1943); Peter Gale, *An inquiry into the ancient corporate system of Ireland and suggestions for its immediate restoration and general extension* (London, 1834). Scottish figures are taken from George Smith Pryde, *The burghs of Scotland: a critical list* (Oxford, 1965), pp. 1–35. Ulster figures are from Philip Robinson, *The plantation of Ulster: British settlement in an Irish landscape, 1600–1670* (Dublin, 1984), p. 225. Scottish royal burghs have been first counted according to representation in parliament rather than participation in convention. Seventeen of the eighty-one royal burghs counted by Pryde have been ignored because they never achieved either privilege in practice, a further six because they achieved the privileges after 1660. The Anglo-Irish figures are preliminary and require much further investigation.

aggrandisement of the early modern state.[14] It could not be created willy-nilly. As the diverse settlements of North America also suggest, city commonwealths also depended on a culture of genuine citizenship, civility, and commerce on the part of freemen. In Massachusetts, this culture, exported from the cities, boroughs, and market towns of eastern England, was always evident. In Providence as in Ulster, aristocratic comptrollers back in London retained significant degrees of political and economic control, and never allowed a devolved sense of urbanity to develop.[15]

What is striking about England is not so much the unprecedented nature of a system of city commonwealths as the rate of its growth after 1540. In Scotland and Ireland, smaller numbers of towns had long maintained similar, if not greater, degrees of local civic autonomy and a national corporate presence. In Scotland, royal burghs possessed not only parliamentary representation but also an extra place of corporate identity in the form of the Convention, whereby burgh representatives would formulate a burghal position on various topics prior to sitting in parliament.[16] Indeed, this and the trading monopolies possessed by royal burghs, not to mention their close relationship with the crown and freedom from seigniorial lordship (which typified Scottish burghs of barony) defined the 'estate' of Scottish burgesses even more sharply than in England.[17] In Ireland, the staple towns provided a similar form of systemic citizenship, the cities and boroughs of Dublin, Cork, Drogheda, Galway, Kilkenny, Limerick, Sligo, Derry, Waterford, Wexford, and Youghal controlling commerce, credit, and debt across the country.[18] In England, the privileged and highly organised cinque ports in Kent and Sussex suggest a similar degree of systemic citizenship during the medieval period.[19] More generally, the provincial capitals and ancient royal boroughs of England were at once repositories of civic, civil, and commercial values, and templates for the civic development of smaller places. Coventry, York, Norwich, Oxford, Exeter, Bristol, and, of course, London all informed the urban development of their particular provinces. It was the extension and systematisation of English urbanity rather than its invention that characterised the early modern period.

These developments were, by and large, the result of a symbiotic relationship between locality and metropolis; or at least between certain sorts of people in each. Its chronology and geography can be mapped in England using Charles Phythian Adams' notion of the 'pre-modern cultural province'. These are

[14] Gillespie, 'Origins', pp. 26–8.
[15] Karen Kupperman, *Providence Island, 1630–1641: the other puritan colony* (Cambridge, 1993).
[16] Archer, 'Politics', p. 238.
[17] George Smith Pryde, *The burghs of Scotland: a critical list* (Oxford, 1965), pp. 1–35.
[18] Jane Ohlmeyer and Eammon O Ciardha, eds., *The Irish statute staple books, 1596–1687* (Dublin, 1998), p. 4.
[19] Graham Mayhew, *Tudor Rye* (Falmer, 1987).

geographical areas larger than individual counties but more compact and cul-turally coherent than regional blocks like 'the north' or the 'south-east'. They are demarcated by water systems – river-drainage basins, parallel or conver-gent rivers, estuaries, and coastlines – and divided by 'watersheds' of difficult terrain, such as the Pennines.[20] As figure 2.1 shows, the forty-two English counties surveyed by Speed and subsequently recorded by generations of anti-quarians are grouped into provinces that are meaningful in terms of a 'broad commonality of culture' and economic and social networks.[21] These provinces 'faced' in different directions: for example, while the province of Dutch Sea, containing Norfolk and Suffolk, was susceptible to cultural influences from the Low Countries and Northern Europe, the 'South British Sea' of Cornwall and Devon faced south and west. According to Phythian Adams' schema, provinces extended outwards, into 'wider, inter-provincial levels'; and divided internally into smaller *pays* and 'local societies'. Most importantly, cultural provinces enjoyed a shared past and present not because they formed definitive and singular entities but because they delimited spaces of recurring interaction, movement, and commerce that towns – either as provincial capitals like York or local centres of commerce like Ludlow – were vital in structuring.[22]

The national average of cities and boroughs per cultural province in England rose from three to ten between 1540 and 1640, and the chronology and geogra-phy of this process is shown in table 2.2. Incorporation was particularly intense in the 'Severn/Avon', 'South British' Sea, 'French' Channel, and Thames Val-ley. The Solway in the far north-west was the only province to really buck the trend. The table suggests that the process had a southern and western orientation that was all the more marked when incorporation in Wales, Ireland, Ulster, and the North Americas is also considered.

In this sense, urbanisation was intrinsic to the creation of new markets – in southern Europe and, eventually, the transatlantic seaboard – as well as symptomatic of the main military concerns of the monarchy. It was epitomised by the growth of Bristol, Exeter, and other south- and west-facing ports.[23] Equally telling was the extension of the hinterlands of London and Bristol along the Thames and Severn-and-Avon Valleys: clear evidence of the growth in domestic markets. As a result, by the middle of the seventeenth century the highest concentrations of city commonwealths were in a long and wide arc that began in Wales and the Shropshire end of the Severn/Avon. This arc swept south-west, through the Severn Estuary and the 'South British' Sea to Cornwall,

---

[20] Phythian Adams, 'Agenda', p. 10; see also Keith Wrightson, 'Northern identities', *Northern Review*, 2, 1995, pp. 29–32.

[21] Phythian Adams, 'Agenda', p. 13.   [22] Ibid., p. 17.

[23] For an excellent discussion of ports in general, and the western and southern economic drift in particular, see David Harris Sacks and Michael Lynch, 'Ports 1540–1700', in Clark, ed., *Cambridge urban history*, pp. 386–406. See also Harris Sacks, *The widening gate*, p. 332.

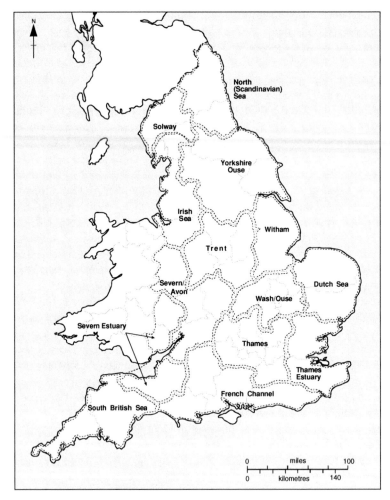

Figure 2.1 England's cultural provinces.
Source: Charles Phythian Adams, 'An agenda for English local history', in
Phythian Adams, ed., *Societies, cultures, and kinship, 1580–1850* (London,
1996).

and eastwards, through the 'French' Channel and the Thames, finishing at Kent
in the Thames Estuary and Suffolk in the 'Dutch' Sea. It was a process that, after
1540, was especially evident in the southern and western provinces; which was
steadily accumulative but also prone to phases of increased activity; and which,
by the Jacobean period, had produced a national corporate system that, through
regular renewals and re-incorporations, remained institutionally dynamic.

Table 2.2 *First charters of incorporation in England and Wales before 1640*

Cultural province	pre-1500	1501–20	1521–40	1541–60	1561–80	1581–1600	1601–20	1621–40	Total
Solway								1	1
'Irish' Sea	3	1				2		1	7
Wales		1		2	4	2	4		13
Severn/Avon	6			5	1	2	3	1	18
Severn Estuary	1			4	1	2	3	1	12
'South British' Sea	1	1	1	3	2	6	6	4	24
'French' Channel	4			3	3	5	8	1	24
Thames	4		1	9	2	2	5		23
Thames Estuary	4			6	2		1	1	14
'Dutch' Sea	4		1	3	2	1	3		14
Wash/Ouse	2			2	2		2		8
Trent	1		1	4		3	2	2	13
Witham	4			2				1	7
Yorkshire Ouse	6			1	2		1	1	11
North Sea	1				1	1	1	1	5
Total	*41*	*3*	*4*	*44*	*22*	*26*	*39*	*15*	*194*

Source: Charles Phythian Adams, 'An agenda for English local history', in Phythian Adams, ed., *Societies, cultures and Kinship, 1580–1850* (London, 1996); Martin Weinbaum, *British borough charters, 1307–1660* (Cambridge, 1943).

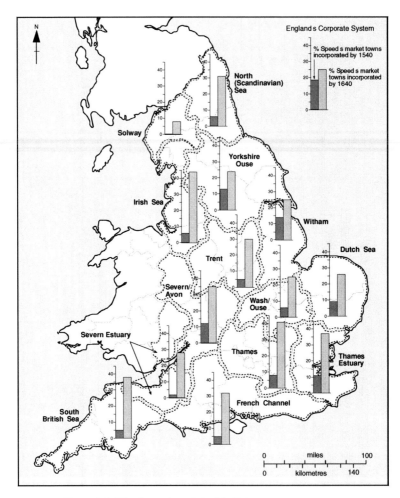

Figure 2.2 The formation of the English corporate system.
Source: John Speed, *The theatre of the empire of Great Britain* (1611) and
Table 2.2 above.

The impact of the process is shown in Figure 2.2, which compares the proportion of city commonwealths in 1540 and 1640 among the 'Market Towns fit for
buying and selling and other affairs of commerce' counted by Speed in 1611.
The institutional dynamism that Speed and subsequently Phythian Adams fail
to account for is self-evident: while 8 per cent of the market towns listed by
Speed were incorporated in 1540, the figure had risen to 32 per cent 100 years
later.

That said, there is strong evidence to suggest that not only did Speed underestimate the number of market towns in 1616, but that the number of market towns rose significantly between the sixteenth and eighteenth centuries. Using sources other than Speed, Alan Dyer has charted an increase of 590 market towns in 1588 to 657 in 1673 and 681 in 1720.[24] Table 2.3 shows the proportion of city commonwealths to market towns at these intervals. It suggests a process of dynamic reciprocity in the majority of provinces: the greater the number of markets, the even greater the number of cities and boroughs. This was especially so along the Thames, Severn, and Avon, where the number of markets and incorporations both rose, and also the 'French' Channel and 'South British' Sea, where there was a slight decline in the number of markets between 1588 and 1673.

Taken together, the cultural provinces of the south-west were not only served by a large number of markets; between a third and a half of them were incorporated by the second half of the seventeenth century. This compared to the corporate system accounting for a quarter of markets running up the eastern side of the country. The major exception to this national process of urbanisation was the Solway in the north-west, a highland area that had an unusually low number of markets and a disproportionately small number of boroughs. Elsewhere, markets and city commonwealths were closely connected. All of which is to suggest a correlation between commercialisation and incorporation that has gone relatively unnoticed in the historiography. It is to this relationship that we can now turn.

Urbanisation and *commonweal*

The genesis of the corporate system in the mid-sixteenth century coincided with a series of factors that made it for many the hardest of 'hard times'. These included a rapid increase in the national population, long-term inflation (and corresponding drop in real wages), the growth of vagrancy and poverty, and what has been termed the 'widespread reality of self-interested economic behaviour'.[25] The response of statesmen like Thomas Smith and William Cecil was a style of political economy initially outlined in Smith's *A discourse of the commonweal of this realm in England* (1549).[26] This was a dialogue that dissected contemporary economic and social relations within a humanist framework and suggested solutions that the corporate system was, in many ways,

---

[24] Alan Dyer, 'Small market towns, 1540–1700', in Clark, ed., *Cambridge urban history*, pp. 432–4.

[25] Keith Wrightson, *Earthly necessities*, p. 154.

[26] Thomas Smith, *A discourse of the commonweal of this realm in England*, ed. Mary Dewar (Charlottesville, 1969). For useful recent discussions of the text see Jennifer Richards, *Rhetoric and courtliness in early modern literature* (Cambridge, 2003), pp. 101–6; Wrightson, *Earthly necessities*, pp. 154–5.

Table 2.3 *The corporate system and urban markets, 1588–1720*

	Market towns in 1588 nos.	Proportion incorporated %	Market towns in 1673 nos.	Proportion incorporated %	Market towns in 1720 nos.	Proportion incorporated %
Solway	13	0	24	4	22	9
Irish Sea	29	14	42	19	38	21
Severn/Avon	60	21	70	38	69	39
Severn Estuary	39	19	39	49	38	48
South British Sea	57	15	53	33	67	35
French Channel	81	29	72	38	78	35
Thames	59	29	66	38	73	34
Thames Estuary	40	30	52	27	58	29
Dutch Sea	56	18	58	21	61	20
Wash/Ouse	31	19	36	22	36	25
Trent	39	15	50	26	46	28
Witham	31	19	33	18	27	26
Yorkshire Ouse	44	20	48	23	48	23
North Sea	11	18	14	21	20	20
Total	*590*	*19*	*657*	*29*	*681*	*28*

Source: Alan Dyer, 'Small market towns, 1540–1700', in Peter Clark, ed., *The Cambridge urban history of Britain*, volume II, *1540–1840* (Cambridge, 2000), p. 431; Robert Tittler, *The Reformation and the towns in England: politics and political culture, c.1540–1640* (Oxford, 1998); Charles Phythian Adams, 'An agenda for English local history', in Phythian Adams, ed., *Societies, cultures, and kinship, 1580–1850* (London, 1996).

intended to implement. The essential ethos of the *Discourse* was to propose 'ways of living with the imperatives of a more commercialised economy without giving free rein to the dynamics of the market and the elevation of self-interest in economic and social relationships'.[27] Whether in the formulation of parliamentary legislation like the 1563 'Statute of Artificers' or the Elizabethan poor laws, the extension of metropolitan supervision into the localities, or the discretionary implementation of statutes, orders, and proclamations within their jurisdictions, citizens and burgesses were in the vanguard of Tudor political economy.[28] However, along with England's towns more generally, cities and boroughs were also crucibles for the contemporaneous 'growth of the market'. While the thirty years after 1550 posed serious problems for many of England's householders, they also presented unprecedented economic opportunities, the formation of the corporate system coinciding with the 'most intensely concentrated period of economic growth before the later eighteenth century'.[29] Marked by significant increases in wholesale retailing, the expansion in internal trade, the growth in imports, and the increasing diversity and propensity of household consumption, the later Elizabethan period as a whole was one of sustained and intensified commerce.[30] By structuring intensified levels of dealing and traffic, the same city commonwealths responsible for market regulation were also tantamount to its expansion, marking the moment when 'we come to be as it were citizens of the *World*'. In this way 'the whole World become a common *Mart*, where each inhabitant thereof, though never so distant, may freely commute the Commodities of their own into the riches and treasures of another'.[31]

The tension between hardship and opportunity – and policy and profit – was never better demonstrated than by the availability of religious and communal property in the light of Henrician and Edwardian religious reforms. In the words of Ethan Shagan, 'the dissolution of the chantries was such a financially and politically adulterated event that even its explicitly evangelical character did not prevent it from cutting across ostensible lines of ideology and belief'. Indeed, with 'so much money at stake, the defensive strategies of all but the most preternaturally pious of subjects came to centre on the protection of scarce resources'.[32] Local strategies of survival ranged from surreptitious concealment or outright resistance to varying degrees of collusion. However, as Robert Tittler has demonstrated, the better equipped in terms of legal powers and abilities, the

---

[27] Wrightson, *Earthly necessities*, p. 157.

[28] Ibid., pp. 215–21; Paul Slack, *From Reformation to improvement*, pp. 26–8; Slack, 'Great and good towns', pp. 264–372.

[29] Muldrew, *Economy of obligation*, pp. 20–1; Joan Thirsk, *Economic policy and projects: the development of a consumer culture in early modern England* (Oxford, 1978).

[30] Wrightson, *Earthly necessities*, p. 171.

[31] Edmond Boulton, *The Cities Great Concern* (1674), Av–A2. This was a new edition of *The Cities Advocate* (1628).

[32] Ethan H. Shagan, *Popular politics and the English Reformation* (Cambridge, 2003), p. 237.

better able were communities – or at least particular factions within communities – to protect communal assets and place ex-religious lands and institutions within their common wealths.[33] Incorporation was the most elaborate of a number of alternatives available to townsmen: a mechanism that not only preserved or extended material resources but also provided educational and charitable institutions, sometimes generations after the initial shock of dissolution.[34] As Paul Slack puts it, corporate bodies multiplied because 'Crown and council had no alternative when they needed to fill the vacuum left by the dissolution of religious orders and fraternities.'[35] In the Shropshire borough of Ludlow, for example, the retention of the wealthy Palmers' Guild by the burgesses in 1551 was conditional on their maintaining the grammar school and instituting civil and godly reform.[36] Elsewhere, inhabitants of monastic and seigniorial boroughs extended their properties, liberties, and franchises and so, by extension, the symbolic spaces – charitable, educational – that the abbots and nuns vacated. It was on this basis that civic reformers of the later seventeenth century could look back to the Edwardian era as a golden age of social policy.[37]

Early modern urbanisation encased, then, the prospect of commerce and traffic within the imperatives of regulation and place. For the 100 years before 1650 urban historians have tended to focus on the latter rather than the former, interpreting the growth in political economy and social policy as a somewhat desperate reaction to 'a prolonged period of economic instability'.[38] As a result, the symbiotic relationship between civic and economic development has often gone unnoticed. This is especially so for corporate towns, where the rhetoric and practice of 'order' contrasted with the relatively unregulated productive vitality of rural industrialisation and 'agglomeration' in places like the Black Country, the Durham coalfields, and industrial Gloucestershire.[39] Of course, corporate towns could be characterised by large manufacturing bases: most obviously London, but also places like Norwich, Colchester, Newcastle, and Leeds. Others repeatedly sought to stimulate (usually unsuccessfully) new forms of manufacture within their jurisdictions. However, in terms of unprecedented economic intensification the corporate system was more associated with

---

[33] Tittler, *Reformation and the towns*, pp. 87–96 and 'The incorporation of the boroughs, 1540–1558', *History*, 62, 204, 1977, pp. 24–42.

[34] Wrightson, *Earthly necessities*, pp. 145–6.   [35] Slack, *Reformation to improvement*, p. 26.

[36] SA, SRRC Q63, p. 52; Michael Faraday, *Ludlow, 1085–1660: a social, economic, and political history* (Chichester, 1991), p. 91.

[37] Thomas De-Lanne, *The Present State of London* (1681), p. 81.

[38] Peter Clark, "'The Ramoth-Gilead of the good": urban change and popular radicalism at Glouces-ter, 1540–1640', in Jonathan Barry, ed., *The Tudor and Stuart town: a reader in English urban history, 1530–1688* (Harlow, 1990), p. 253.

[39] Ann Kussmaul, *A general view of the rural economy of England, 1538–1840* (Cambridge, 1990), pp. 138–9; Keith Wrightson and David Levine, eds., *The making of an industrial society: Wickham, 1560–1765* (Oxford, 1991); David Rollison, *The local origins of modern society: Gloucestershire, 1500–1800* (London, 1992).

the movement and exchange of goods, and also the provision of credit and capital, rather than wholesale transformations in manufacture and industry.[40] None of which is to say that the craft economies of master, apprentice, and journeymen could not respond to, and accommodate, increases in the demand for goods and services. As Christopher Brooks has demonstrated, levels of craft and guild apprenticeship actually outstripped the urban population growth for much of the later sixteenth and seventeenth centuries, many apprentices and future freemen entering a trade from households outwith civic communities.[41] However, apprenticeship was itself a prime example of the paradox of English urbanisation: the engine and point of access into civic economies, it was also a regulative institution that demarcated urban freedoms even as it replenished them.

The seven-year apprenticeship was not unique to incorporated bodies of free households; indeed, the 1563 statute explicitly made it a feature of rural as well as urban economic organisation. While not exclusive to city commonwealths, apprenticeship certainly remained a distinctive feature of urban freedom. It was assumed by the craft guilds of seventeenth-century Ludlow that 'any person so requiring to be made free with the said fellowship' who was 'a stranger' would 'hath been a prentice elsewhere in any other city or town corporate by the space of 7 years at the least'. As such, they would also be 'well skilled in the occupation and of good name and fame'.[42] Even for journeymen who had no intention of becoming enfranchised, proof of apprenticeship, in the form of an indenture, was usually a condition of skilled employment.[43] The uptake of apprenticeships indicated, in turn, the health or not of particular crafts and vocations within towns and so the more general prosperity of a community. In sixteenth-century London, for example, it has been estimated that 90 per cent of Londoners became citizens through apprenticeship.[44] It was also a means of exclusion and regulation. It enabled, for example, the control by freemen of both the size of household businesses and the number of future households competing for trade within a particular company. One of the primary concerns of craft companies in Restoration Newcastle was limiting the number of apprentices with whom a master contracted at any one time: this was as true for glasiers, plumbers, and goldsmiths as for barber surgeons and tallow chandlers.[45] Moreover, as well as training apprentices in the skills and 'mystery' of their calling, masters were also responsible for their governance and socialisation more generally. In this

---

[40] Muldrew, *Economy of obligation*, pp. 51–9; Wrightson, *Earthly necessities*, pp. 171–6.
[41] Christopher Brooks, 'Apprenticeship, social mobility and the middling sort, 1550–1800', in Barry and Brooks, *The middling sort of people*, p. 55.
[42] SA, LB 17/1.   [43] TWA, GU/GP/2/2, 8v.
[44] Steve Rappaport, *Worlds within worlds: structures of life in sixteenth-century London* (Cambridge, 1989), p. 47.
[45] TWA, GU/BS/2/1, 53v, 57v; GU/GP/2/2, 7v.

sense, the statutes of 1598 and 1601 which institutionalised the 'charity towards binding poor citizens children apprentices' extended the use of apprenticeship as a tool of social policy: a tool that increased rather than decreased in the later seventeenth century.[46]

The 100 years after 1550 saw urban apprenticeship keep pace with, and in some places outstrip, England's urban demographic, which rose from around 5 per cent to 14 per cent of the national population between 1520 and 1670.[47] In London, the extension of the urban franchise since the 1530s meant that by the middle of the sixteenth century three-quarters of Londoners were freemen and the freemen body was 'no longer the privileged minority it had been in the middle ages'. By 1600, new apprentices accounted for at least two-thirds of the 6,000 immigrants required to sustain the capital's overall rate of population growth.[48] In Bristol, apprentice registration rose from 193 in 1539 to 300 in 1629, while in Norwich between 1525 and 1570 apprenticeships in the retailing trades increased by 80 per cent within a population that remained stable at about 13,000.[49] The national replication of these trends has led Brooks to conclude that by 1640 'recruitment through apprenticeship in most towns had reached a peak which was never succeeded thereafter', guild and craft economies playing a more than significant role in the high levels of urban migration that characterised the period.[50] The mechanism of apprenticeship positioned a youth within household, company, and city commonwealth, reinforcing a sense of *communitas* and freedom within both province and metropolis. It was a sense of place that depended, however, on at least two kinds of mobility. The first of these was geographical. In London in the early 1550s, of the 1,055 men who became citizens and whose geographical origins are known, 83 per cent had migrated to the capital. The migration field of the metropolis encompassed the whole of England: indeed there were as many citizens from Yorkshire as there were from London.[51] Elsewhere, migration through apprenticeship reflected the provincial position of a settlement. In seventeenth-century York – where between two-thirds and four-fifths of households were free during the 1660s – one-third of apprentices were born in the city itself and almost two-thirds came from the city's provincial hinterland (though not the rival urban centres in the West Riding and East Riding). Of the remaining 10 per cent, over half came from the under-urbanised counties of Cumberland and Westmorland: patterns that at once reproduced and intensified migratory habits that had existed since

---

[46] Phil Withington, 'Citizens, community and political culture in Restoration England', in Shepard and Withington, *Communities in early modern England*, pp. 141–3.

[47] E. A. Wrigley, 'Urban growth and agricultural change: England and the continent in the early modern period', *Journal of Interdisciplinary History*, 15, 4, 1985, pp. 684–95.

[48] Brooks, 'Apprenticeship', p. 55; Rappaport, *Worlds within worlds*, p. 47.

[49] Muldrew, *Economy of obligation*, p. 51.   [50] Brooks, 'Apprenticeship', pp. 63, 69.

[51] Rappaport, *Worlds within worlds*, p. 78.

at least the early sixteenth century.[52] The second kind of mobility was social. Apprenticeships in different trades and crafts attracted sons from a range of backgrounds. Like the professions of law, university, and the church, trade and commerce increasingly attracted sons of the lesser gentry and upwardly mobile yeomen, the 'relative presence' of sons of 'gents' in the London retailing companies increasing threefold between 1550 and 1650.[53] Occupations and crafts requiring less of an initial outlay on the part of a young man's family attracted, in turn, apprentices from less wealthy backgrounds. At the bottom of the social scale, poorer freemen were paid by civic authorities to bind 'poor apprentices' in order to alleviate 'idleness' and 'dependence' within communities.[54]

Apprenticeship is one indicator of both the relationship between incorporation and commercialisation and the imperatives of commerce and place that this implied. Another is civil litigation. As Keith Wrightson has observed, records of law represent 'one of our best indicators of the sheer scale of the growth in commercial activity' in the later sixteenth and early seventeenth centuries if only because the majority of suits 'concerned failure to pay debts or to honour commercial agreements'.[55] At least one implication of increased litigation was that a greater number of commercial transactions were being undertaken *in toto*. The primary medium of exchange in a society relatively bereft of hard currency was credit, either in the form of oral agreements between persons or, increasingly, in transactions over distance, by written contracts like conditional bonds and bills obligatory.[56] Civil litigation in the central courts in Westminster by and large concerned the latter, and the increase in suits between 1560 and 1640 is remarkable. Brooks has shown that while 5,278 cases were in process in the King's Bench and Common Pleas in 1563, the figure had risen to 28,734 by 1640: increases that were comparable with other central courts.[57] As importantly, this business was more than supplemented by the work of local courts, prominent among which were borough courts of record. Litigation here was more likely to concern informal oral agreements that were part and parcel of a bargaining culture fuelled by unpaid sales credit. Moreover, the scale of local litigation was quite as impressive as the central courts. The borough court in Shrewsbury witnessed a tripling of business between 1540 and the 1580s, when an average of 1,516 suits were brought per annum, and in Great Yarmouth there was a threefold rise in the forty years after 1545. By the first years of the

---

[52] Chris Galley, *The demography of early modern towns: York in the sixteenth and seventeenth centuries* (Liverpool, 1998), pp. 133–6.
[53] Brooks, 'Apprenticeship', p. 61.   [54] Withington, 'Citizens', p. 142.
[55] Wrightson, *Earthly necessities*, p. 175.
[56] For a useful summary of credit techniques see Ceri Sullivan, *The rhetoric of credit: merchants in early modern writing* (London, 2002), pp. 23–6.
[57] Brooks, *Pettyfoggers and vipers*, p. 51.

seventeenth century Lynn in Norfolk averaged over 2,000 suits per annum and Bristol on the Severn over 6,000 per annum.[58]

Borough courts were closely associated with the corporate system. Of the 205 that had been created by 1640, 166 – 81 per cent – belonged to the liberty of an incorporated city commonwealth, 90 per cent of city commonwealths possessing a court of record.[59] While borough litigation was not exclusive to incorporated towns, it was certainly a prominent attribute. The correlation is unsurprising: courts depended for their business on a large and busy market and the largest markets also tended to be incorporated. Moreover, the distribution of courts outwith incorporated jurisdictions, such as Cirencester in Gloucestershire and Walsall in Staffordshire, followed the geographical orientation of the corporate system and the markets that sustained it. There was a concentration of courts along the valleys of the Thames, Severn, and Avon, and also in the coastal provinces of the south and south-west. The high correlation of markets, incorporations, and courts of record in the industrialised north-east only served to emphasise their relative absence in the north-west. The courts were an important source of employment for borough attorneys, providing another link between the corporate system and the growth of the legal profession. They also impacted on the place of city commonwealths in their local and provincial settings. Muldrew has shown that plaintiffs and defendants were drawn not simply from the towns and cities in which courts were located but also beyond their liberties, providing a medium of urban–rural interpenetration that mirrored the commercial networks through which goods were bought and sold. At Newcastle in 1659, for example, 26 per cent of plaintiffs and 39 per cent of defendants came from outside the town. While the majority of foreign defendants came from communities positioned along the Tyne, others originated in Northumbrian coastal towns or larger southern ports involved in the coal trade: King's Lynn, Boston, Great Yarmouth, Rye, Ipswich, and, in one instance, London. In a county like Cumberland that was, by and large, bereft of urban resources, the proportion was even higher: 50 per cent of both plaintiffs and defendants who attended the court in Carlisle in the first four years of the 1650s came from outlying rural areas. In contrast, foreign suitors in King's Lynn lived in either the immediate hinterland of the borough or along the water networks that connected the borough with Ely, St Ives, Cambridge, and Wisbech.[60]

As well as structuring local and provincial commerce, the corporate system was also a place of legal arbitration and resolution for the breakdown in credit and contract that a dramatic increase in commercial transactions and traffic induced. Equally suggestive of the relationship between incorporation,

---

[58] Muldrew, *Economy of obligation*, p. 204.
[59] Borough courts are listed in ibid., pp. 338–44.   [60] Ibid., pp. 212–13.

commerce, and economic regulation was the town hall. Robert Tittler has shown that the 100 years after 1540 were 'an especially concentrated period for the acquisition or rebuilding of town halls', witnessing 'the resurgence of the civic hall' that was no less impressive than the 'great rebuilding' of the Elizabethan countryside.[61] Both urban and rural building provided labour for urban-based artisans and craftsmen. Moreover, of the 133 halls built between 1500 and 1640 that can be precisely dated, 67 per cent were constructed in the fifty years after 1540 and 22 per cent in the first two decades of the seventeenth century. This compares with only fifteen new, renovated, or purchased structures between 1500 and 1540.[62] By 1640, at least 178 towns had invested in new civic build-ings (although this undoubtedly underestimates the scale of building, especially for badly recorded towns in Cornwall and Northumberland). While the chronol-ogy complements that of the corporate system, the geography of early modern building corroborates the distribution of city commonwealths, markets, and courts of records: there were, for example, particular concentrations along the valleys of the Thames, Severn, and Avon and on the south coast. That said, building programmes were also an attribute of market towns more generally: almost exactly half of new town halls counted by Tittler were located in city commonwealths. As with their relationship to urban markets, city common-wealths played a significant, though by no means exclusive, part in what was a much larger process of urban renovation. By 1640, eighty-nine cities and towns possessed a charter of incorporation, a court of record, and a new town hall.

As both the official 'doorway to the community' and, in many instances, the regulatory centre of the market place, town halls regulated 'the transfer of commodities and people' into and within boroughs and cities. Indeed, it was their role in controlling trade 'that mattered first and foremost, for the effec-tiveness with which commercial activity was conducted and regulated could determine the livelihood of the whole community'.[63] Moreover, as seats of civic governance they were also the epicentre of political economy. It was from the council chamber on Ouse Bridge that the civic governors of York co-ordinated poor relief, allocated charitable donations and loans, and responded to the demands of the city guilds, hospitals, and schools.[64] For all of these reasons, town halls were crucial in defining city commonwealths as politi-cal places: so much so that Tittler has argued that it was the 'peculiar polit-ical conditions' of the post-Reformation era, rather than economic change, that explains their proliferation.[65] This underplays, however, the economic

---

[61] Robert Tittler, *Architecture and power: the town hall and the English urban community c.1500–1640* (Oxford, 1991), p. 158.
[62] Ibid., appendix, pp. 161–8.   [63] Ibid., pp. 155–6.
[64] Phil Withington, 'Views from the bridge: revolution and restoration in seventeenth-century York', *P&P*, 170, 2001, pp. 126–33.
[65] Tittler, *Architecture and power*, p. 158.

conditions of their construction. For all their political functions and appropriations, buildings that tended to cost more than the annual income of a community
were only possible because of the peculiar dynamism of the post-Reformation
economy. In particular, they were built on credit. This was true of the hall in
Poole, where the mercantile elite initially raised loan money among themselves
at a high rate of interest. Once the funding collapsed, they resorted to secondary
loans to meet a £314 10s. 2d. debt. It was true of Blandford, in which a much
more communal enterprise nevertheless depended on credit as the single most
important way of meeting the final outlay of £255 17s. 2d. And it was true of
Plymouth, where an outlay of £165 19s. 8d. was met by 'credit from major
builders involved, and personal loans extended by townsmen'. In Plymouth,
the most important creditor, James Bagg, exemplified the inextricability of personal and communal profit: a privateer, merchant, and 'sometime desperado',
he was also a citizen, mayor, and eventually parliamentary representative of the
borough. Elsewhere, other creditors included not only burgesses, freemen, and
other urban inhabitants, but also local gentry, lawyers, and London merchants
and retailers.[66]

The increased presence of borough courts and towns halls suggests that urbanisation involved townsmen addressing, and also seeking to regulate and benefit
from, the intensifying economic demands of England's provinces, in the process
enmeshing communities within networks of commerce and credit that encompassed locality, province, and metropolis. While these interrelated processes
were by no means limited to the corporate system, they were certainly contexts
for its development – the more so given that city commonwealths still included
England's largest commercial centres. The point is important if only because
the communities that constituted the corporate system are generally regarded
as the last gasp of a static and traditional pre-modern urbanity: the remnants
of a dying society rather than the vehicle for early modern change.[67] In fact,
commercialisation occurred through rather than despite existing civic structures and practices, and in this respect city commonwealths were very much
present at their own refashioning.[68] It was only in the decades after 1650, when
the population of English provincial towns began for the first time to accel-
erate significantly beyond the national demographic trend, that apprenticeship
became less significant as a form of urban migration. As a result, the relative
size of enfranchised populations also decreased. In places like York, where the

[66] Ibid., pp. 57, 61, 67.
[67] Richard M. Smith, '"Modernisation" and the corporate medieval village community in England:
some sceptical reflections', in Alan R. H. Baker and Derek Gregory, eds., *Explorations in historical geography* (Cambridge, 1984); Phil Withington and Alexandra Shepard, 'Introduction',
in Shepard and Withington, *Communities*, pp. 1–18.
[68] Ian W. Archer, 'The nostalgia of John Stowe', in David L. Smith, Richard Strier, and David
Broughton, eds., *The theatrical city: culture, theatre, and politics in London, 1576–1649*
(Cambridge, 1995), p. 25.

population as a whole stabilised at around 12,000 persons, the balance between city commonwealth and the larger town was retained. In cities that grew or continued to grow at exponential rates – such as London, Bristol, Norwich, and Newcastle – bodies of freemen became less prominent features of the urban populace. And across the country as a whole, urban 'agglomerations' outwith the corporate system – most notably Birmingham and Manchester, but also the accentuated hinterland of London – became loci for the more recognisable era of urbanisation that was the hallmark of the eighteenth and nineteenth centuries.[69]

That said, England's second urban renaissance did not spring from nowhere. Industrial forms of manufacture, improvements in agricultural production, and the growth in imperial trade had all characterised commercialisation in the previous 100 years. Moreover, in many areas the corporate system remained pivotal to provincial, national, and increasingly international markets into the 'long eighteenth century' and beyond. The point is made in figure 2.3. The map shows, in the first instance, the percentage of urban overnight accommodation located in city commonwealths in 1686 (the sample is restricted to towns with fifty beds or over).[70] Provinces where the proportion was over 70 per cent include the Severn/Avon, Severn Valley, and South British Sea; the North Sea; and the Dutch Sea: places that had either undergone intensive incorporation over the previous 130 years or which were in the vanguard of agrarian capitalism. In contrast, in the Wash, Solway, Thames Estuary, Trent, and Witham the corporate system was much less important to provincial mobility. The map also shows the percentage of road traffic between metropolis and the provinces directed through city commonwealths in 1681.[71] Viewed in these terms, it suggests the continuing importance of the corporate system in England's most westerly and easterly provinces as well as their relative insignificance along the Thames, Thames Estuary, and in the Midlands. (What the map does not represent is the intense levels of coastal and river communication that linked London with the usually incorporated ports on the south and east coasts.) In the case of the Thames Valley and Thames Estuary, this was in large part due to the ease of access that the proximity of London allowed.[72] More interesting was the development of Lancashire townships like Manchester, Bolton, and Blackburn in the 'Irish Sea': unincorporated places that, like Birmingham in Warwickshire, were already closely integrated into the London markets. Different again was the apparent absence of metropolitan commerce with either the far north-east or

[69] Peter Borsay, 'Introduction', in Borsay, *The eighteenth century town*, pp. 7–12.
[70] TNA WO 30 48 'Survey of inns' 1686.
[71] Thomas De-Lanne, 'An alphabetical account of all the carriers, wagoners, and stage coaches, that comes to the several inns in London, Westminster, and Southwark, from all parts of England and Wales', in *The present state of London* (1681).
[72] Michael Reed, 'London and its hinterland 1600–1800: the view from the provinces', in Peter Clark and B. Lepetit, eds., *Capital cities and their hinterlands in early modern Europe* (Aldershot, 1996), pp. 51–83.

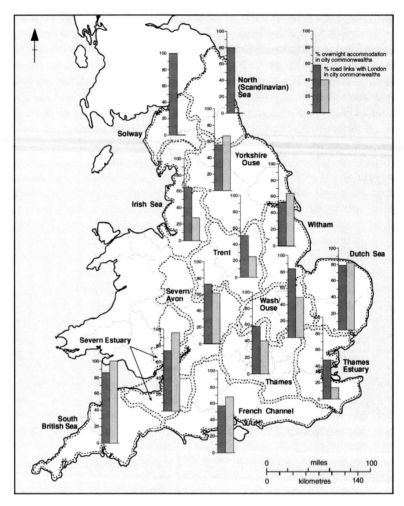

Figure 2.3 The corporate system and urban mobility by the later seventeenth century.
Sources: TNA WO 30 48 'Survey of Inns' 1686; Thomas De-Lanne, *The present state of London* (1681). The map shows the proportion of overnight accommodation and commercial road links located within city common-wealths in each of England's cultural provinces. For overnight accommo-dation, only towns with 50 beds per night have been counted.

north-west. In the case of the former, this reflected the intensive coastal traffic that still dominated relations between Newcastle and London. In the case of the latter, it demonstrated once again that the highland counties of Cumberland and Westmorland were also the least urbanised in England.

The corporate system and *De Republica Anglorum*

If economic opportunities and pressures provided one set of contexts for the formation of the corporate system, then the political difficulties inherited by Edwardian, Marian, and Elizabethan statesmen and townsmen were another. And, just as Thomas Smith's *Discourse of the commonweal* grappled with the former, so his *De Republica Anglorum* addressed the latter. This was a work of policy written in France and initially circulated in manuscript among fellow councillors at court, in particular William Cecil, the 'very Cato of the common-wealth', before its posthumous publication (and editorial alterations) in 1583.[73] The text obliquely addressed the recent history of England, which had witnessed a series of large and geographically dispersed rebellions by the English com-mons. The constitutional bed partner of Elizabethan political economy, it met head-on at least some of the commons' grievances that drove the mid-sixteenth-century troubles. These included the perceived absence of proper consultation or 'counsel' across the commonwealth; the dangers posed to communities by rapacious, greedy, and wilful gentry; and the need for closer and more equitable economic regulation.[74] If such demands were rooted in neighbourly concep-tions of common weal, hardened by a distrust of social superiors, and ignited by the fiery commonwealth rhetoric of Edwardian preachers, then for Smith the means to resolve them was clear.[75] Antiquity taught the universal lesson of political evolution: that, in terms of its government, 'the commonwealth must turn and alter as before from one to a few, so now from a few to many and the most part'.[76] England had reached such a juncture. The challenge for responsi-ble rulers was to ensure that the one, the few, and the many were each 'willing to

[73] Sir Thomas Smith, *De Republica Anglorum. The maner of governement or policie of the realme of England* (1583). The description of Cecil is from Archer, *The pursuit of stability*, p. 38.
[74] R. W. Hoyle, *The pilgrimage of grace and the politics of the 1530s* (Oxford, 2001), pp. 19–20, 97, 425–8, 433–9. Hoyle prints 'The Lincoln articles, 9 October 1536', 'Aske's proclamation to the City of York, 15–16 October 1536', and 'The Instructions for Sir Thomas Hilton and the Pontefract Articles, 4 December 1536', pp. 455–62. Diarmaid MacCulloch, 'Kett's rebellion in context', *P&P*, 84 (1979), pp. 58, 48 and Diarmaid MacCulloch, *Suffolk and the Tudors: politics and religion in an English county, 1500–1600* (Oxford, 1986). Anthony Fletcher, *Tudor rebellions* (London, 1968), p. 144 ('Kett's demands being in rebellion' (1549) especially article 27).
[75] For recent discussions of mid-century commonwealth ideology, see Andrew McRae, *God speed the plough: the representation of agrarian England, 1500–1600* (Cambridge, 1996); Shagan, *Popular politics*, ch. 8; Wrightson, *Earthly necessities*, pp. 149–53.
[76] Smith, *De Republica Anglorum*, p. 17.

save the politic body, to conserve the authority of their nation, to defend them-selves against all other, their strife being only for empire and rule'.[77] The way to ensure that they 'should do best for the commonwealth' was to 'have expe-rience made by bearing office and being magistrates': it was this that marked 'the first and natural beginning of the rule of the multitude which . . . the Latins [call] *Republica* by the general name'. If, however, the political body was not cut to match the 'manner of people, as when the shoe is too little or too great for the foot, it does hurt and encumber the convenient use thereof'. Indeed, if 'the free people of nature are tyrannised or ruled by one against their wills', then the result, as the risings in the north, the south-east, and south-west had demonstrated, could only be civil destruction.[78]

The proliferation of incorporated city commonwealths after 1540 was one means of negotiating the political difficulties facing England. Just as the rash of Thames Valley incorporations explicitly rewarded the political loyalties of townsmen in the 1550s, so the spate of Cornish and Devon city commonwealths in the Elizabethan era filled a representational and communicative void. The corporate system provided at least certain sections of the Commons with the requisite 'experience' of government; with appropriate national and local oppor-tunities for counsel and representation; and also legal protection from powerful persons and interests within localities. Moreover, it did so within the frame-work of the mixed monarchy. The estate of citizens and burgesses had long served *Republica Anglorum*, or the 'commonwealth of the English', in two particular arenas: 'in their cities and boroughs, or in corporate towns where they dwell'; and 'in the common assembly of the realm to make laws, which is called Parliament'.[79] What the corporate system did was extend and systematise the practice within the common councils associated with city commonwealth, providing citizens with a conciliar outlet for legislative energies that they were not slow to exploit.[80] The Elizabethan poor law was one, well-known conse-quence of this intensification of civic representation, and, as D. M. Dean has commented, 'even the great statute of artificers had its origins with the city of York and probably Exeter and other towns as well'.[81]

Table 2.4 demonstrates the significant increase in borough representation at the House of Commons between the 'puritan parliament' of 1584 and the 'long parliament' of 1641. It shows that in 1584, 168 boroughs sent repre-sentatives to London; by 1641, the figure had risen to 202. As importantly, it also shows the rise in the number of incorporated parliamentary boroughs with control of representative power. Here it is important to distinguish between

---

[77] Ibid.   [78] Ibid.   [79] Ibid., p. 29.

[80] Robert Tittler, 'Elizabethan towns and the "points of contact": Parliament', *Parliamentary His-tory*, 8, 1989, pp. 257–88.

[81] D. M. Dean, 'Parliament and locality', in D. M. Dean and N. L. Jones, eds., *The parliaments of Elizabethan England* (Oxford, 1990), p. 160.

Table 2.4 *Parliamentary representation and the boroughs, 1584 and 1641*

	1584				1641		
	Parliamentary boroughs	Parliamentary boroughs (later incorporated)	Incorporated parliamentary boroughs	TOTAL 1584	Parliamentary boroughs	Incorporated parliamentary brough	TOTAL 1641
Solway	1	1	0	2	2	1	3
'Irish' Sea	3	2	1	6	3	4	7
Severn/Avon	1	1	10	12	1	14	15
Severn Estuary	1	3	4	8	3	8	11
'South British' Sea	1	11	7	19	14	19	33
French Channel	26	13	8	47	26	23	49
Thames	7	2	10	19	11	13	24
Thames Estuary	3	1	6	10	3	8	11
'Dutch' Sea	1	1	9	11	1	11	12
Wash/Ouse	2	1	4	7	2	5	7
Trent	4		4	8		8	8
Witham	1		4	5	1	4	5
Yorkshire Ouse	4	1	6	11	6	8	14
North Sea	1	1	1	3	1	2	3
Total	56	38	74	168	74	128	202

Source: J. E. Neale, *The Elizabethan House of Commons* (London, 1949); Derek Hirst, *The representative of the people? Voters and voting in England under the early Stuarts* (Cambridge, 1975); Robert Tittler, *The Reformation and the towns in England: politics and political culture, c.1540–1640* (Oxford, 1998).

parliamentary boroughs, on the one hand, and *incorporated* parliamentary boroughs (city commonwealths with parliamentary representation), on the other. The former claimed the right to parliamentary representation but did not possess incorporated status or, in some instances, any civic culture to speak of. The latter enjoyed both. The distinction was relatively meaningless in the case of large cities and towns that had accrued freedoms and constitutions by custom and looked to incorporation primarily as confirmation of their privileges. In instances like London, Great Yarmouth, Salisbury, and Gloucester, parliamentary representation was already part of and protected by a well-developed civic culture long before the purchase of a royal charter. Conversely, it was by no means inevitable that incorporated boroughs should be represented in 'the common assembly of the realm': indeed fifty-two were without a parliamentary voice in 1641, Stratford-upon-Avon among them.[82] In the majority of instances, however, the difference between incorporated and mere parliamentary status was significant. Incorporation implied a set of constitutional resources through which freemen and citizens retained a degree of indigenous control over the process of representation. It allowed the civic body either to choose representatives from within the citizenry or, as Tittler and Patterson have both shown, to negotiate with interested parties on behalf of the city commonwealth from a position of institutional strength.[83] This did not necessarily make for more democratic elections. On the contrary, parliamentary selection was more likely to be reserved for common councils and civic elites. What it did do was embed the electoral process firmly within the city commonwealth, so making parliamentary representation an expression of the freemen's fictional personality and offering a degree of protection from – or at least grounds for negotiation with – external political interests. It enabled, in Mark Kishlansky's words, burgesses and citizens to select their representatives 'with a precise logic'.[84] It is no coincidence, for example, that in the elections of 1641, four-fifths of boroughs under some claim of lordship were parliamentary (rather than incorporated) in nature.[85]

Between 1584 and 1641 the proportion of Commons representation controlled by the boroughs rose from 79 per cent to 82 per cent. Over the same

[82] Alan Dyer, 'Crisis and revolution: government and society in Stratford 1540–1640', in Bearman, *History of an English borough*, pp. 83–5.

[83] Tittler, *Reformation and the towns*, pp. 234–5; Patterson, *Urban patronage in early modern England*, pp. 74–86.

[84] Mark Kishlansky, *Parliamentary selection: social and political choice in early modern England* (Cambridge, 1986), p. 48

[85] Mary F. Keeler, *The long parliament* (Philadelphia, 1954). This and what follows extends and to some extent qualifies observations about civic representation in Phil Withington, 'Two renaissances: urban political culture in post-Reformation England reconsidered', *HJ*, 44, 1, 2001, pp. 258–9.

period, the proportion of borough representation in incorporated city common-wealths rose from 37 per cent to 63 per cent. As a result, the proportion of all representation located in the corporate system rose from 35 per cent to 52 per cent: by 1641, citizens and burgesses held the key to parliamentary access in every cultural province except the 'French Channel'. Central to this shift was the incorporation of thirty-eight parliamentary boroughs over the same period: a third of all incorporated constituencies in 1641 had been parliamentary bor-oughs in 1584. Indeed, in the 'French Channel' and 'South British' Sea the proportion was over 50 per cent. That new parliamentary boroughs were cre-ated in their place meant that by 1641 England's most southerly and westerly provinces, together with the Thames Valley, were the three most incorporated and best represented provinces in England.

This excess of representation related to a number of factors, including the military threat from Spain, the rebellious pedigree of the Cornish commons, and the administrative reinvigoration of the Duchy of Cornwall. These political pressures complemented the gradual gravitation westward of English trade and shipping, the vibrancy of the Cornish tin industry, and (in the case of the Thames Valley) the integration of the 'home counties' as a suburban hinterland of London and its courts. As a result, alongside the large (and increasing) number of common councils, a diverse range of other political interests – including mil-itary governors, courtiers and magnates, Duchy officials, local gentlemen, and London lawyers – brokered parliamentary access in the south and south-west of England. In the south-east provinces of the 'Dutch Sea' and Thames Estuary, where a tradition of urbanity was better established, the city commonwealth was consolidated as the dominant form of borough constituency. The same was true along the Trent, Severn, and Avon, less so in the north-east and north-west.

Although patronage was clearly central to civic representation, a distinguish-ing feature of city commonwealths was the likelihood of electing from within their own body if required. Figure 2.4 shows that in the highly charged elections of 1641, this was one of the major distinctions between the electoral choices of parliamentary and incorporated boroughs: 43 per cent of city commonwealths elected their own compared to only 14 per cent of parliamentary boroughs.[86] The tendency was the more pronounced the older and better established the city commonwealth. Of the forty-five county towns mapped by Speed in his *Theatre*, 69 per cent elected one or more inhabitants as their representatives to the 'long parliament'. The 1641 elections revealed other differences between incorporated and parliamentary boroughs. Fewer city commonwealths were in the 'influence' of an external interest, a tendency which Speed's county towns once again accentuated: the proportion fell from 54 per cent for parliamentary boroughs to 40 per cent for city commonwealths to 29 per cent for county towns

---

[86] Keeler, *The long parliament*.

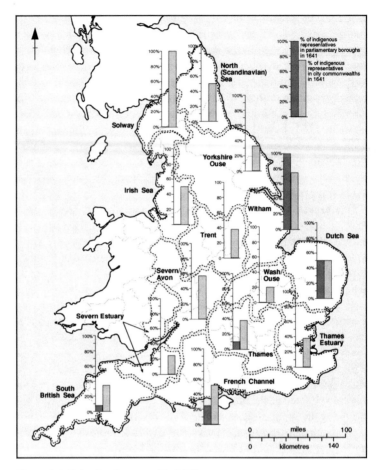

Figure 2.4 Selecting 'our own' in 1641.
Source: Mary F. Keeler, *The long parliament* (Philadelphia, 1954).

mapped by Speed. City commonwealths (though not county towns) were also more likely to divide allegiances between a 'parliamentarian' and 'royalist' representative.

However, in other respects boroughs were broadly similar – not least in terms of the proportion of contested elections and, as figure 2.5 shows, the nominal allegiance of representatives chosen by civic constituencies. Borough representatives were most likely to be parliamentarian or split between parliament and king: only a fifth of boroughs elected two royalists. Provincially, the trend was bucked in the provinces of the Severn and Avon and also the Yorkshire Ouse, where the royalism of parliamentary boroughs in particular was pronounced.

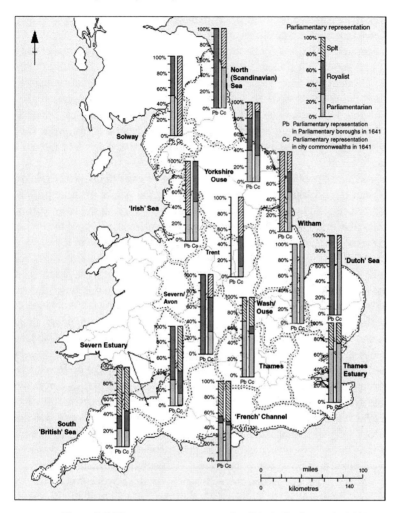

Figure 2.5 The corporate system and political allegiances in 1641.
Source: Derek Hirst, *The representative of the people? Voters and voting in England under the early Stuarts* (Cambridge, 1975); D. Brunton and D. H. Pennington, *Members of the long parliament* (London, 1968).

Parliamentarian support was accentuated, in contrast, in the easterly provinces of the Thames, the Cambridge Ouse, and the Dutch Sea (though not among parliamentary boroughs). Speed's county towns again form an interesting sub-set, proving more likely to be parliamentarian than other city commonwealths (47 per cent compared to 41 per cent) even in ostensibly royalist cultural provinces. This was true for York and Hull in Yorkshire as well as for Coventry and Warwick in the Severn and Avon.

That borough affiliations mapped so snugly on to what is known about more general patterns of allegiance is hardly surprising given the centrality of the corporate system to parliamentary processes by 1641.[87] This is not meant to imply that the affiliations of all freemen can be read from the political allegiance of their representatives or that city commonwealths somehow 'caused' the civil war. It is to argue that freemen, burgesses, and citizens were very much present and participatory in the political culture that spawned England's troubles.

A second kind of political context is less obvious than parliament as a feature of early modern urbanity but equally revealing of the nature of urbanisation. This was the geography of 'playing', or provincial theatre, in the latter part of the Elizabethan era: a practice at once 'poetic', commercial, and polemical that, like the equally urban-based book trade, was a foundation stone of the literary public sphere. The common assumption derived from a particular strand of 'puritanism' that the post-Reformation town and the theatre were antithetical has been exploded by recent scholarship. This has shown, among other things, the Calvinist convictions of playwrights like Thomas Middleton; the willingness of powerful magnates like the Dudleys to use theatre as a means of religious reform; and the commercial importance of travelling and playing to London-based playing companies until at least the Caroline period.[88] This coincided with increased licensing powers of civic officials, the removal of local performances indoors – usually into the new town halls that were also proliferating across the corporate system – and, by the Jacobean era, a certain ambivalence to 'playing' among civic elites.[89] Again, it is worth stressing that this ambivalence was not straightforwardly doctrinal. The 'idleness' and 'incivility' that companies were perceived to bring with them, as well as their dependence on royal or noble patronage rather than civic authority, were not especially 'puritan' concerns.[90] Neither did potential opposition from common councils prevent commercial success. The itinerary of the Queen's Men in the latter part of the sixteenth century suggests a thriving provincial business that in its movements outlined the skeletal shape of the public sphere and its close relationship to the corporate system. It did so not unlike the assize judges in their bi-annual circuits – events that also brought the locality to the town – and in a way that redefined in

[87] Mark Stoyle, *Loyalty and locality: popular allegiance in Devon during the English Civil War* (Exeter, 1994), pp. 229–55.

[88] Herbert Jack Heller, *Penitent brothers: grace, sexuality, and genre in Thomas Middleton's city comedies* (Newark, 2000), pp. 18–22, 27–40; Andrew Gurr, *The Shakespearian playing companies* (Oxford, 1996), ch. 3; Scott McMillin and Sally-Beth MacLean, *The Queen's Men and their plays* (Cambridge, 2000).

[89] Tittler, *Architecture and power*, pp. 139–50.   [90] Ibid., p. 148.

Table 2.5 *Types of playing location of the Queen's Men (excluding London playhouses) in the later Elizabethan era*

Types of playing location	1580s	1590s	1600–1603
Country house	11	7	2
Cathedral liberties	7	4	0
Royal court	12	2	0
Universities	4	8	0
Provincial cities and boroughs	150	205	24
Total	*184*	*226*	*26*

Source: Scott McMillin and Sally-Beth MacLean, *The Queen's Men and their plays* (Cambridge, 2000).

commercial and recorded terms the traditional venues of itinerant entertainers and travellers: acrobats, rope-dancers, musicians.[91]

Table 2.5 shows that, of the different venues played by the company between 1582 and 1603, between 82 and 92 per cent were city commonwealths, cities and boroughs vastly outnumbering alternative sites such as the country house, royal palaces, universities, or cathedral liberties. The circuits followed by the company confirm the main characteristics of urban development in the later sixteenth century, the division of the players into different groups, who would tour in different directions, facilitating greater geographical coverage. Figure 2.6 shows that the Thames Estuary was by far the most toured province. That the ports of the south-west, along with the cities and boroughs along the Severn and Avon Valleys, were also frequently visited is at one with the commercial, litigious, and political dynamism of the corporate system. More anomalous was the relative infrequency with which players visited the boroughs of the Thames Valley. Elsewhere, provincial capitals like Coventry, York, Norwich, Exeter, and Bristol were popular and lucrative locations, as were county towns like Bath, Gloucester, Shrewsbury, Leicester, and Nottingham. Newcastle and Carlisle in the far north and west were included in itineraries; so too were Dublin and Edinburgh in the 1580s. It is notable that the greater the distance from London, the more important provincial capitals were in facilitating performance. For example, Exeter and the Devon boroughs were the closest the company came to Cornwall, just as York, Newcastle, and Carlisle were the main venues in the north. In the Severn–Avon, in contrast, the players visited the full gamut of city commonwealth: a provincial capital like Bristol; county

---

[91] McMillan and MacLean, *Queen's Men*, p. 63.

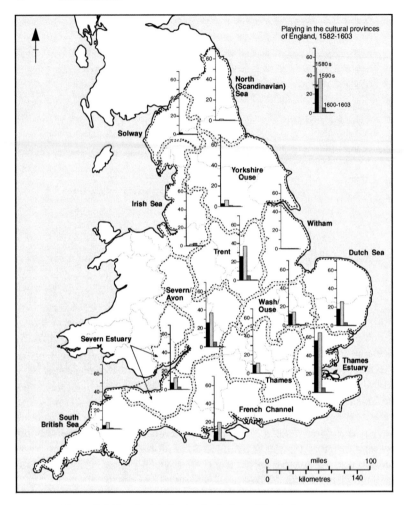

Figure 2.6 Provincial playing in the later Elizabethan era.
Source: Scott McMillin and Sally-Beth MacLean, *The Queen's Men, and their plays* (Cambridge, 2000), pp. 175–88, Appendix A.

centres like Gloucester, Worcester, Shrewsbury, Warwick, and Coventry; and smaller boroughs like Bridgnorth, Ludlow, and Stratford-upon-Avon.

Conclusion

A minor puzzle of literary history is why Shakespeare, the shrewdest of Renaissance impresarios, never wrote a city comedy, the most lucrative and 'popular' of dramatic forms. The answer is, of course, that he did. *The merry wives of Windsor* (1597) evoked precisely the kind of civic community around which city commonwealths were built, and upon which city comedies were based.[92] The defence (or not) of that community from the dangerous and uncivil encroachments of unenfranchised 'strangers' – in this instance, Falstaff and his crew – likewise replicated comedic conventions along the Thames, in Berkshire. That it was set in Windsor rather than London encapsulates the kind of process described by this chapter: the exportation of civic resources from the metropolis to the provinces on an unprecedented scale. Although clearly different to London in geography, scale, and complexity, Windsor, York, and Cambridge, or indeed Newcastle-upon-Tyne, Rye, and Ludlow, nevertheless shared with the capital a populace of enfranchised civic householders participating in an incorporated civic culture. This was not least because the 100 years after 1540 were a period of intense 'structural' and 'behavioural' urbanisation that was marked by the proliferation of city commonwealths into a corporate system. It says much about the nature of English urbanity in the sixteenth and seventeenth centuries that city comedies could have been set in any one of 181 English city commonwealths by 1640 – not least Stratford-upon-Avon, the civic politics of which Shakespeare knew first hand.

That *The Merry Wives* was most likely performed before Elizabeth, in Windsor, at the very moment the burgesses were petitioning (yet again) for a charter of incorporation, suggests an even closer relationship between play and process. This chapter has provided an historical geography of that process, outlining the westward orientation of the corporate system as well as the close relationship between coastal and river-trading areas: in particular the Severn, Avon, and Thames. It has also argued that incorporation was implicated in a number of practices and developments that can be understood as contexts for (rather than causes of) the formation of the English corporate system. One such context was the commercialisation of early modern society: a trend reflected by the increase in the number of market towns, town halls, and borough courts across the country. Others included the geographical enlargement of a parliamentary 'public' as well as the emergence of a profit-making – but also propagating – provincial theatre. Each served to reconstitute what Smith termed *De Republica Anglorum* in the light of the undoubted economic and political problems of the post-Henrician age. While characteristic of the corporate system, these processes were never unique to it: parliamentary representation was not the preserve of citizens and freemen just as many unincorporated towns had markets and town halls. Such attributes illuminate, in effect, the place of city commonwealths within a more extensive set of networks, relationships, and developments.

[92] Anne Barton, 'Falstaff and the comic community', in Barton, *Essays, mainly Shakespearean* (Cambridge, 1994), pp. 84, 80.

The developments that framed its formation suggest that the corporate system was paradoxical in at least two ways. In the first instance, there was a tension between the city commonwealth as an autonomous and demarcated place, and the city or town as a porous node of 'commerce' that was integrated into urban networks and local societies.[93] While notions of place implied fixity and distinction, commerce emanated from movement, traffic, and the collapse of distances. It was the intensification of commerce that in large part drove and funded sixteenth- and early seventeenth-century urbanisation: the invigoration of urban networks; the movement of goods, credit, and people; the integration of local, national, and international markets; the new kinds of conversation, or counsel, associated with parliament and playing. In this sense, the corporate system raised the possibility of greater dissemination and communication across space. However, city commonwealths also embodied liberties, boundaries, and a fundamental sense of separateness that, in theory at least, made communities of freemen and citizens distinct from their urban and local environments. Forces of integration effectively worked through and consolidated structures of segregation, producing an extended corporate system of enclosed city commonwealths. Second, as part of a set of processes that historians tend to associate with modernity, the ideologies upon which the city commonwealth drew were essentially retrospective. This was true for the 'ancient' cities that served as the primary template for incorporation, and which for Speed demonstrated 'no little glory to the land'. It was also true for the humanism and, indeed, custombased common law that provided the ideological energy for change. It is to these ideological contexts, and their implications for the meaning of citizen and subject, that we can now turn.

---

[93] The paradox is nicely put in Ann Hughes, 'Coventry and the English revolution', in R. C. Richardson, ed., *Town and countryside in the English revolution* (Manchester, 1992), p. 69 and Harris Sacks, *Widening gate*, pp. 9–10.

Part II

Cultural resources: ideology, place, company

3   Citizens and subjects

'Natural subjects'

Historians have long taken to heart the assertion of the anonymous 'apologist' of Elizabethan London that it was 'besides the purpose, to dispute, whether the estate of the government here be a *Democracy*, or *Aristocracy*'. Affixed by John Stow to the end of his *Survey of London*, the 'Apology' explained that in 'respect of the whole Realm, London is but a citizen and no city, a subject and no free estate'. Like any other city, London was 'no place endowed, with any distinct or absolute power'.[1] Lacking sovereignty, it was 'governed by the same law, that the Rest of the Realm is'; sent burgesses to Parliament 'as every poor Borough does'; and, 'in the persons of the Citizens', it was 'friendly interlaced, and knit in league with the rest of the realm'. As 'merchants, handicrafts men and labourers', citizens were 'by birth ... for the most part a mixture of all countries [counties]'. Moreover, at 'their ending of life and conversation' they more often than not returned whence they came. Far from being a distinct class or estate, citizens were 'a part of the commons', their city commonwealth 'a member of the commonalty': no matter their liberties and privileges, they remained 'natural subjects' like everyone else.[2] For all its defensiveness, however, the apology begs as many questions as it answers. Why was it that politics in London should be described as democratic or aristocratic in the first place? Was the apparent possibility of civic democracy and aristocracy an attribute of the corporate system more generally? If so, how did it inform the national political consciousness of citizens: 'subjects' occupying a central position among England's commons? And why were the commons 'natural subjects' in relation to parliament and law rather than the crown?

The previous chapter described the emergence of a corporate system of city commonwealths in England during the sixteenth and seventeenth centuries. Having outlined its geography and chronology, this chapter considers the

[1] 'A discourse of the names and first causes of the institution of cities' in John Stow, *A survey of London* (1603), pp. 557–8. The author is probably James Dalton. See Harris Sacks, *Widening gate*, p. 8.
[2] 'A discourse of the names', pp. 558–9.

ideologies that drove and legitimated its formation. As might be expected in a society undergoing the ferment of Renaissance, Reformation, and also a major expansion of its legal system, these ideas and interests were many, varied, and not always complementary. To this mix can be added the medieval legacies of corporatism and common weal; the pressures, from 1603, of an Anglo-Scottish monarchy; the complex relationship with Ireland; and colonial expansion across the Atlantic. This was a volatile melting pot by any standards, one that could only become hotter after 1642. The corporate system was central to these ideas and processes in a way that might appear surprising given its lack of historiographical recognition. Certainly when compared to the great traditions of European urbanity, English citizenship can appear unremarkable. Great Yarmouth, Stamford, Cambridge, Ludlow, or even provincial capitals like Newcastle-upon-Tyne or York hardly seem comparable to the Italian city-states, the great provincial capitals of France and Spain, the Swiss city-republics, or the free cities of the Holy Roman Empire. However, as the 'apologist' suggests, the defining feature of English urbanity was not the creation of discrete entities claiming sovereignty in their own right. Rather it was its systemic insinuation within both local and national culture: its presence in the politics of nation and empire and its role as a crucible in which these politics were experienced, and sometimes resisted, locally.[3]

Urban citizenship during the period has traditionally been described as 'oligarchic', amounting to 'the possession and exercise of power by a few individuals either directly, as a consequence of holding important political offices, or indirectly, as a consequence of controlling recruitment of officeholders and influencing their decisions'.[4] The formation of the corporate system has likewise been styled the 'rise of oligarchy': a process of political integration that was also central to the provincial ascendancy of the gentry, their 'invasion' of parliament, and the 'consolidating of the realm' by the crown.[5] More recently, social historians have regarded the same developments as integral to the formation of the early modern 'state'.[6] However, the paradigm of oligarchy has proved problematic in important respects. It elides the ideological conflicts that increasingly characterised the corporate system during the later sixteenth and seventeenth centuries; the practical extent of civic participation beyond the

---

[3] See Harris Sacks, *Widening gate*, pp. 9–11.

[4] John T. Evans, 'The decline of oligarchy in seventeenth-century Norwich', *JBS*, 14, 1974, p. 47. See also John T. Evans, *Seventeenth-century Norwich: politics, religion, and government, 1620–1690* (Oxford, 1979), ch. 2. In arguing for the decline of oligarchy in Norwich, Evans regards it as prevalent everywhere else.

[5] J. E. Neale, *The Elizabethan House of Commons* (London, 1949), ch. 7; G. R. Elton, *The Tudor constitution: documents and commentary*, 2nd edition (Cambridge, 1995), pp. 32–4, 248–9; Williams, *The later Tudors*, pp. 182–4.

[6] Michael J. Braddick, 'State formation and social change in early modern England: a problem stated and approaches suggested', *Social History*, 16, 1991, pp. 1–17 and *State formation in early modern England c.1550–1700* (Cambridge, 2000), pp. 17–20.

aldermanic bench; and claims of autonomous community made by civic elites and freemen alike.[7] It also denudes the morality that saturated the politics of the period: the sense that it was not so much the form of government as its ability to serve and defend 'the public good' of the city commonwealth that most concerned freemen and their households.[8] The conflation of civic and rural elites into a single class of 'gentry' – or what G. R. Elton terms 'the dominant section of the community' – likewise neglects the ways in which urban freemen distinguished themselves from unenfranchised inhabitants in general, and the pretensions and encroachments of local 'gentility' in particular.[9] Finally, an overtly sociological concept of the 'state' can also obscure more than it reveals. Functionally, the dependence of metropolitan authority on a range of semi-autonomous and local 'body politics' hardly reflects a remorseless centralisation of power: on the contrary, a process like incorporation 'reinforced local communities' even as it placed them within larger political contexts.[10] As importantly, the fact that metropolitan authority was itself a composite of institutional interests and ideological positions suggests a much more differentiated and potentially divisive political culture than an abstract concern with 'power' allows.[11] As Michael J. Braddick has argued, this need not necessarily preclude the existence of an early modern state so long as it is recognised that it was locally situated and appropriated for purposes not necessarily intended by its metropolitan custodians.[12] Even as subtle a formulation as this can elide, however, the contrasting ways in which political legitimacy was formulated and practised, not least by freemen, burgesses, and citizens themselves. It is with this ideological richness at the national and local level that this chapter is concerned. Just as urban citizenship was much more complex than the label 'oligarchy' suggests, so there was more than one way to act as a 'natural subject'.

Respublica, civitas, and state

A founding text of English humanism was Thomas More's *Utopia*, which he wrote in 1516 as a citizen and legal officer of London about to enter royal service. Its achievement was to imagine the existing civic institutions of late medieval England as a reformed and perfected commonwealth.[13] Conjoined

---

[7] Ann Hughes, 'Religion and society in Stratford-upon-Avon, 1619–1638', *Midland History*, 1994, p. 59; Archer, 'Politics and government', pp. 241–6; Barry, 'Bourgeois collectivism?', pp. 84–112.

[8] Tittler, *Reformation and the towns in England*, p. 183.

[9] Elton, *Tudor constitution*, p. 249.

[10] Patrick Collinson, *De Republica Anglorum; or history with the politics put back* (Cambridge, 1990), pp. 17–18.

[11] Braddick, *State formation*, p. 20.   [12] Ibid., pp. 26–7, 45–6.

[13] Thomas More, *Utopia*, ed. George M. Logan and Robert M. Adams (Cambridge, 1998), pp. xiv, 112–32; J. A. Guy, *The public career of Thomas More* (Brighton, 1980), pp. 6–7.

into an incredibly ordered corporate system, the cities of Utopia were 'all spacious and magnificent, identical in language, customs, institutions and laws'.[14] There was no prince of Utopia, no private property, and all inhabitants were city dwellers with public responsibility for both their cities and the kingdom. The citizens of each city elected their own civic head through a mediated system based, as in city commonwealths, on the household.[15] Elected citizens formed distinct and accountable representative bodies, their government guaranteeing the happy and pleasurable life: 'good and honest pleasure' that is best achieved by living virtuously, or 'according to nature'.[16] In accordance with these Aristotelian dictates, in Utopia the public service of private citizens is a fundamental virtue. Indeed, one of the only acts of conspicuous display was for Utopians to 'set up in the marketplace statues of distinguished men who have served their country well'. This was meant to 'spur on citizens to emulate the glory of their ancestors' and 'incite them to virtue by public honours'.[17]

It was this spirit of a reformed commonwealth that Francis Bacon definitively rejected in his own utopia, *New Atlantis*, written on his fall from power in 1621.[18] As Bacon described it, the key concept of social and political organisation was the monarchical state.[19] Governors were neither the products of household republicanism nor necessarily motivated by virtue. Rather they were salaried 'sufficient of the state for his service' and accepted no extra reward for their duties.[20] Patriarchs and king replaced citizens and elected representatives as the key protagonists of government.[21] Urban inhabitants were economic subjects rather than publicly minded citizens.[22] Finally, political activism and authority, the 'very eye of the kingdom', was based in 'an Order or Society which we call Salomon's House', dedicated to 'the knowledge of Causes, and secret motions of things; and the Enlarging of the bounds of Human Empire, to the effecting of all things possible'.[23] As governors of the 'lanthorn of this kingdom', its Fathers were treated with a reverence afforded monarchs by inhabitants and narrator alike, presiding over a fantastic conglomeration of 'natural' and 'artificial' resources available for the good of the populace.[24] Nature was no longer a code of behaviour so much as the most vital of human resources: one utilised by an intellectual elite, under the authority of the state, for the common good. It was successful inventors rather than virtuous citizens for whom 'we erect a statue' in Bensalem: a conception of science that also extended to government and law.[25]

---

[14] More, *Utopia*, p. 43.   [15] Ibid., pp. 48–9.   [16] Ibid., p. 69.   [17] Ibid., p. 84.
[18] *Francis Bacon: a critical edition of the major works*, ed. Brian Vickers (Oxford, 1996), pp. 457–91.
[19] Bacon, 'New Atlantis', in Vickers, ed., *Francis Bacon*, p. 785n.
[20] Ibid., pp. 459, 461.   [21] Ibid., p. 473.   [22] Ibid., pp. 475–8.
[23] Ibid., pp. 464, 471, 480.   [24] Ibid., pp. 480–7.
[25] Ibid., p. 487; Julian Martin, *Francis Bacon, the state, and the reform of natural philosophy* (Cambridge, 1992).

Thomas More's *Utopia* and Francis Bacon's *New Atlantis* sit at opposite ends of English humanism. While this is clearly true chronologically, it is also the case conceptually. While the former imagined a perfectly reformed commonwealth resting on the public virtue and energy of its citizens, the latter painted an equally reformed kingdom of subjects sustained by the ingenuity and wit of its governors. What More and Bacon shared was the humanist conviction that political authority should derive from the aptitudes, skills, and reason of the person rather than lineage: it was virtue and education rather than birth and blood that legitimated one man's power over another. However, in the utopias they sketch the social location of meritorious aristocracy is very different. Bacon invoked the restrictive assumptions of Henrician writers like Sir Richard Morison and Sir Thomas Eliot, who argued that it was 'most necessary in a common wealth [that] those that are the worse sort, to be content, that the wiser rule and govern them'.[26] Courtiers and gentry should earn rather inherit power because 'True nobility is never, but where virtue is'.[27] Authority rewarded 'good education'; 'senators' ruled because they were 'wisest'; and 'making laws . . . settling matters of religion . . . [and] discussing . . . what means a realm may best be kept in wealthiness [sic]' was out of bounds to any 'that utterly lack not discretion'.[28] As a result, the commonalty were effectively excluded from public life because, by definition, they lacked the requisite virtues and 'fitness' to govern.[29] In contrast, More anticipated the more encompassing vision of Elizabethan writers like Sir Thomas Smith and the educationalist Richard Mulcaster.[30] Master of the School of Merchant Taylors, Mulcaster argued that, given the right educational opportunities, any person with the requisite 'disposition', 'wit', and 'towardness' should and could participate in the public interest. He expected the educated to 'serve in public function' and 'turn their learning to public use'.[31] Below the *principal* magistrate of a commonwealth – 'Emperors, Kings, and whatsoever Prince of absolute sovereignty' – were the *subaltern* magistrates of England. These were men 'ruling other yet are subject to other, as in a Monarchy all the mean and inferior magistrates, and generally as in any estate those officers be, which be accountable for their doings'. Subalterns were crucial to the commonwealth: 'their places and functions concern every particular sinew, every particular vein, every particular artery, nay every small fillet, and finest string or strip in the whole body of any common weal'.[32] Moreover, it was the middle groups of society that were best placed to see the public places filled. As he explained, 'The middle sort of parents that neither welter in too much wealth, nor wrestle with too much want, seem fittest of all, if the children's

[26] Sir Richard Morison, *A remedy for sedition* (1536), A2v.   [27] Ibid., B4.   [28] Ibid., A3.
[29] Ibid., B2v–B3.
[30] Richards, *Rhetoric and courtliness*, pp. 83–6; Cathy Shrank, *Writing the nation in Reformation England* (Oxford, 2004), ch. 4.
[31] Richard Mulcaster, *The first part of the elementaries* (1582), p. 12.   [32] Ibid., pp. 13–14.

capacity be answerable to their parents state and quality ... to bring forth that student, which must serve his country best.'[33] Indeed, the public schooling of the relatively poor promised, in a way that the private tuition of the rich could not, to 'commend the common'. This was because 'the common education in the middle of common mediocrity brings up such wits to such excellence, as serve in all degrees, yea even next to the highest'.[34]

Distinctions within the English humanist tradition were replicated in the legal theory of Bacon and his great rival at the Jacobean court, the common lawyer Sir Edward Coke. As first statesman and latterly critic of the regime, Coke has been shown to be the formulator of what Alan Cromartie has described as common-law *res*publicanism, presenting common law as a 'universal science' by which the good of the commonwealth was reasoned, debated, and enacted.[35] One inference of this *res*publican position, that became increasingly popular from the 1620s, was that kingship was merely one aspect of, and ultimately subservient to, the practice of commonwealth as it was constituted by common law and parliament.[36] Another was that, no matter their privileged status, burgesses and citizens enjoyed magisterial and parliamentary authority only insofar as the common law and its practitioners, the common lawyers, allowed. In this way, common lawyers consolidated their position as arbitrators of the precedents, customs, and statutes that constituted the full edifice of legitimate social and political practice. They also demonstrated a reverence for 'custom' – and the possibility of reform through its adaptation rather than obliteration – that also characterised Mulcaster's educational doctrines. As Mulcaster put it, 'if there be any hope to procure liking in such a thing as custom is to rule, it must needs come by following, and not by forcing'.[37] The history of reform showed that 'enforcing to the contrary, or altering too far is almost desperate, if not altogether, because it hath always missed, with loss of labour where it offered service'.[38]

In contrast, Bacon outlined a process of wholesale reform indebted to Roman rather than customary law.[39] Rather than the organic assimilation of precedent and custom into artificial reason, he envisaged select and elite 'committees' of royally appointed lawyers sifting through the flotsam of parliamentary statutes,

[33] Richard Mulcaster, *Positions concerning the training up of children* (1581), p. 140.

[34] Ibid., p. 188.

[35] Alan Cromartie, 'The constitutionalist revolution: the transformation of political culture in early Stuart England', *P&P*, 163, May 1999, p. 88.

[36] Ibid., pp. 100, 107.

[37] Ibid. For alternative models see Cathy Shrank, 'Rhetorical constructions of a national community: the role of the King's English in mid-Tudor writing', in Shepard and Withington, *Communities in early modern England*, pp. 180–98.

[38] Mulcaster, *Elementarie*, p. 227; Richards, *Rhetoric and courtliness*, p. 86; Martin Elsky, *Authorising words: speech, writing and print in the English Renaissance* (Ithaca NY, 1989), p. 46.

[39] Martin, *Francis Bacon*, p. 124.

ancient royal records, and law reports that currently constituted 'the law' in order to create orderly, consistent, logical, and regulated 'digests'.[40] These digests, based on reason and 'wit', would form the basis of legal practice and judgement, making a 'code explicitly modelled on that of the Romans'.[41] The creation of a regular and written body of law by royally appointed experts was accompanied by the insistence that 'royal service would become independent of local status and interests', whereby all 'men who served the king would serve him alone'.[42] This was as true for constables and jurors as it was for justices of the peace and circuit judges, whom Bacon styled 'the Planets of the Kingdom' because of their revolving role within the geographical parameters of the state.[43] Public office was not intended to give 'persons ... countenance or reputation in the place where they live, but for the King's service sake only'.[44] Finally, Bacon called for the legal profession to be reformed into an elite vocation in which success would depend on the ability to invoke not Coke's *Reports* but the *Digests* that would form the official code of Bacon's *regulae juris*.

The intensification and bureaucratisation of Jacobean magistracy, well studied by social historians, was one manifestation of this attitude to governance.[45] The 1635 edition of Michael Dalton's *The country justice* likewise suggests the impact of Bacon's ideas. Designed primarily for justices of the peace, the text explained the mechanics of an increasingly complex administrative system. However, it began with a eulogy to the common law as 'ancient' and embodying 'the laws of God and Nature ... whereby this Realm was governed many hundred years before the Conquest'. Echoing Coke, Dalton explained that 'to that purpose, at the Common Law (long before Justices of the Peace were made) there were sundry persons to whose the maintenance of this Peace was recommended'. Such men 'with their other offices had (and still yet have) the conversation of the peace annexed to their charges, as a thing incident to and inseparable from the said offices'.[46] There was 'no humane law within the circuit of the whole world, by infinite degrees, so apt and profitable for the honourable, peaceable, and prosperous government of this kingdom'. Even so, 'at this day the conservators of the peace are held to be out of use; and that their authority for the keeping of the peace, is now only by virtue of the kings commission of the Peace, ordaining them to be Justices of the Peace'. This was a change that Dalton directly attributed to Bacon.[47] Excepted from it were, however, those Justices created by letters patent under the Great Seal of England: most notably 'Mayors, and chief Officers in divers corporate Towns'. As Dalton explained, 'if the king grants to a ... head Officer of a City or corporate Town, and to their

[40] Ibid., pp. 119–20.   [41] Ibid., p. 128.   [42] Ibid., p. 121.   [43] Ibid., p. 113.
[44] Ibid., pp. 122–3.
[45] Wrightson, 'The politics of the parish', p. 27; Steve Hindle, *The state and social change in early modern England, c.1540–1640* (Basingstoke, 2000).
[46] Michael Dalton, *The country justice*, 5th edition (1635), p. 1.   [47] Ibid., p. 2.

successors, to be Justices of Peace in their City or Town', then that power was 'not revocable at the Kings pleasure, as a Commission of the Peace is'.[48] As a Venetian visitor observed in 1557, 'In matters of justice' England was not 'like other kingdoms and Christian provinces, governed by civil and imperial laws, but by municipalities, almost like a republic'.[49] In particular, London was 'governed by about twenty-five aldermen, who have ultimate power, without the king nor his ministers being able to intervene'.[50]

It was from within this ideological tradition that Richard Butcher, town clerk of seventeenth-century Stamford, described 'Cities or Towns Corporate as . . . small County Palatinates within themselves'. No matter Baconian reformism, they enshrined the concept that 'for the better Government of such Places' it was best 'to have Magistrates of their own Members' who 'for their more ample authority, and Peculiar Rule to make Laws, Constitutions and Ordinances, to bind themselves and every member within their Jurisdiction'.[51] In this they at once embodied the concept of legal *res*publica and gave it a civic twist. As Butcher explained, burgesses had 'a Power within themselves in their Common Hall assembled, to make Laws as peculiar and proper Rules for their better Government, the said Assembly being a little court of Parliament'. Indeed, 'if it be lawful for me to compare small Things with great, or like a cosmographer, to frame a Model of the great world in one small skin of parchment, for in this small Model is a Representation of the highest and greatest Government'. As political 'microcosms', the courts and councils of England's corporate bodies replicated the mix of commons, lords, and monarch enshrined in parliament, serving as local embodiments of England's 'ancient constitution'. The mayor 'as the chief Magistrate represents the Person of the King' and the 'burgesses sitting round about him as so many Peers of the Upper House'. Moreover, the 'Capital Burgesses which we here call the Twenty Four being *senatores minorum gentium*, are the Representative Body of the whole Town'; the Recorder is the Speaker; and the town clerk 'the Register or Clerk of the same'.[52] Possessed with unusual powers of legal deliberation and representation, citizens were also the guardians and guarantors of local justice. The Dubliner Richard Stanihurst identified a similar sense of civic commonwealth within the Irish Pale. Citizens in Waterford were 'very heedy in all their public affairs, slow in determining of matters of weight, loving to look ere they leap. In choosing their magistrate, they respect not only his riches but also they weigh his experience.

---

[48] Ibid., pp. 10–11.
[49] Eugenio Alberi (ed.), 'Relazioni dInghilterra di Giovanni Micheli', in *Relazioni degli Amabasciatori Veneti al Senato*, series 1, vol. II (Firenze, 1840), pp. 291–380. Translated by Cathy Shrank.
[50] Ibid., p. 295.
[51] Richard Butcher, *The survey and antiquity of the town of Stamford in the county of Lincoln* (1717), pp. 19–21.
[52] Ibid., p. 23.

And therefore they elect for their mayor neither a rich man that is young nor an old man that is poor.' Citizens of Cork were entirely civil in their ordering of 'domestic and public affairs'.[53] Henry Manship, burgess of Great Yarmouth, likewise developed an intensely humanist portrayal of civic life. He argued that laws were 'the very mind, soul and council of the city' and stressed that 'neither can such laws benefit a commonwealth, except there be a magistrate to put life into them'. For Manship as for Cicero, 'a magistrate is a speaking law' and a city's elected 'senators' the subalterns 'of the State in general' and 'the town in particular'.[54] Indeed, the public capacities of burgesses in Great Yarmouth made them comparable to the generations of Spartan manhood in their 'courageous attempts for their country', their buildings and public works veritably Venetian in fostering 'the common good'.[55]

Common lawyers recognised the customary basis and public efficacy of citizenship while subordinating it to their authority and counsel. As Sir Thomas Widdrington put it, 'The justice, by which the people of this land is governed, is [vested] in the king, and other subordinates under him.' However, 'the king, as Sir John Fortesque observes, "sits not in judgement himself"'. Rather 'the streams of justice are carried to the people by the great courts of Westminster' and 'these, as to their several capacities, have an universal influence on all parts and people of the nation'. Cities and boroughs were, in turn, concentrations of 'some less rivulets of justice for smaller matters'.[56] In 1659 William Sheppard anticipated Widdrington by systematically reducing English *civitas* to the sovereign authority of common law, a move that was necessary if only because the civic twist that citizens gave their respublicanism could be sharp indeed.[57]

The idea of *civitas* was developed most spectacularly by the city 'comic-poets' of London from the 1580s, most obviously in their productions of the Lord Mayor's Pageant. An appropriation of the triumphs of the Roman Republic, these processions reached an aesthetic and ideological plateau in the 1610s, most notably in the work of Thomas Middleton.[58] The most popular of the London playwrights, Middleton was also a Calvinist, humanist, common lawyer, and, by the 1620s, not only the chief ideologue of the City but also its official and salaried chronicler.[59] In the greatest of his city comedies, *A chaste maid in Cheapside* (1613), he satirised the hypocrisies, errors, and vices

[53] Colm Lennon, *The life of Richard Stanihurst the Dubliner, 1547–1618* (Blackrock, 1981), p. 84.
[54] Manship, *History of Great Yarmouth*, pp. 191, 54.   [55] Ibid., pp. 16, 26.
[56] Sir Thomas Widdrington, *Analecta Eboracensia. Some remains of the ancient city of York collected by a citizen of York*, ed. C. Caine (London, 1897), p. 78.
[57] William Sheppard, *Of corporations, fraternities, and guilds* (1659).
[58] Manley, *Literature and culture*, pp. 276–93.
[59] Sarah Jane Steen, *Ambrosia in an earthen vessel: three centuries of audience and reader response to the works of Thomas Middleton* (New York, 1993), p. 38; Heller, *Penitent brothers*, p. 27.

that characterised the enfranchised households at the heart of the ancient city of London. In his Lord Mayor's Pageant for the Company of Grocers, written and performed the same year, he suggested the means of their reformation: namely the indigenous and autonomous practice of civic governance.[60] Culminating in the same Cheapside setting, the pageant outlined the role of civic governance amidst a civil society beset by the opportunities and problems of commerce and empire.[61] As represented by Middleton, citizenship reflected and embodied the virtue, industry, merit, civility, and obligations of its citizens: it made and depended upon them just as they made and depended upon it.[62] The role of civic governors was to ensure prosperity, eliminate the 'Error' that had seeped into neighbourhoods like Cheapside, institutionalise virtue, and propagate Protestantism, education, hospitals, and civility wherever trade and commerce were conducted.[63] Personal and public industry, like personal and public profit, went hand in hand. However, it did so not simply under the tutelage of common lawyers, or, indeed, the sovereignty of the monarch, but at the discretion and authority of citizens themselves.[64]

Ben Jonson, Middleton's contemporary and pre-eminent poet at the Jacobean court between 1612 and 1625, was less convinced. In 1614, the year after Middleton's combination of play and pageant, he remorselessly ridiculed the public conceits of the citizenry in *Bartholomew Fair*.[65] He did so as a poet who regarded Francis Bacon as the culmination of over a century of brilliant English humanists: the man 'who hath filled up all numbers, and performed that in our tongue which may be compared or preferred either to insolent Greece or haughty Rome'.[66] Operating within the genre of city satire, Jonson was equally effective as Bacon in circumventing the public conceits of citizens. *Bartholomew Fair* brought London to the stage through the microcosm of the Fair. Its Prologue welcomed 'Your Majesty' to 'Such a place, such men, such language, and such ware ... the petulant ways / Yourself have known, and have been vexed with long'. By these he meant not only the bawds and criminals inhabiting the Fair but also the series of ostensibly civil characters visiting it. These included Littlewit the Court Proctor and his wife; the Banbury baker

[60] Thomas Middleton, *A chaste maid in Cheapside*, ed. Alan Brissenden (London, 1968); Thomas Middleton, *The triumphs of truth* (1616).

[61] David M. Bergeron, 'Middleton's moral landscape: *A chaste maid in Cheapside* and *The triumphs of truth*', in *'Accompaninge the players': essays celebrating Thomas Middleton, 1580–1980* (New York, 1980), pp. 133–45.

[62] Middleton, *Triumphs of truth*, p. 2; see also Thomas Middleton, *Honourable entertainments, composed for the service of this noble city* (1621), p. 2.

[63] Middleton, *Triumphs of truth*, p. 6.   [64] Ibid., p. 9.

[65] The play was first published in 1631. Ben Jonson, *Bartholomew Fair*, ed. G. R. Hibberd (London, 1977).

[66] Ben Jonson, 'Discoveries', in Ian Donaldson, ed. *Ben Jonson: the Oxford authors* (Oxford, 1985) p. 54.

and preacher, Zeal-of-the-Land Busy; Coke, the country gentlemen infatuated with but also unsuited to the metropolis; and a gaggle of parasitic and predatory gallants. However, foremost among them was Adam Overdo, the Cicero-quoting citizen-magistrate who believes that 'a wise man, and who is ever so great a part of the commonwealth in himself, for no particular disaster ought to abandon a public good' (3.3.24). Overdo plans with 'my political brain' to disguise himself and walk the Fair 'as the careful magistrate ought, for the good of the republic of the Fair, and the weeding out of enormity'. In the process, he identifies and aims to rescue a 'proper young man from his debauched company', saving him for 'a State-course' and 'commonwealth's man' (3.5.1–9). In fact, his quarry already has a 'place and calling' as a hardened and accomplished criminal. The mistake is precipitous. For all his rhetoric, Overdo proves wholly incapable of administering justice, and in the face of the implacable Fair and his own incompetence undergoes a series of humiliating reversals that only serve to reveal his lack of wisdom and discretion. By the end of the play he has lost even his eloquence: rather than presiding, as comedic magistrates did, over the play's resolution, he is shamed to silence as Quarlous, the leading gallant and urbane wit of the ensemble, proves himself to be the real master of proceedings (5.6). The opportunistic, sceptical, and pragmatic Quarlous has none of the commonwealth platitudes or attachments of Overdo: however, it is the urbane gentility and wit of the former, rather than the empty rhetoric of the latter, that is best suited to the demands of a properly constituted monarchical state.

This was certainly the conclusion reached by Jonson's royal patron. Given James' status as 'the most writerly of British monarchs' it was no secret that James took the role of the Renaissance prince seriously, placing his public responsibilities and requisite virtues over and above the essentially private and economic estates of his subjects.[67] It was also apparent that, in the first decade of his imperial reign, this philosophy had received several slaps in the face. The new monarch was frustrated in his ambitions to unify Scotland and England as a legal and 'naturalised' entity; opposed in his subjugation and 'civilisation' of Ireland; and restricted in England in the use of a prerogative power of which he was publicly and painfully protective. In each instance, parliaments, common lawyers, and burgesses proved an impediment to royal policy. It is perhaps unsurprising, therefore, that two years after the first perform-ance of *Bartholomew Fair*, James expounded for the Court of Star Chamber a political sensibility that, while reflective of his humanistic upbringing under George Buchanan, also looked to the dominant legal and literary figures of his

---

[67] *King James VI and I: selected writings*, ed. Neil Rhodes, Jennifer Richards, and Joseph Marshall (Aldershot, 2003), p. 1; Roger Mason, *Kingship and the commonweal: political thought in Renaissance and Reformation Scotland* (East Linton, 1998), pp. 240–1.

court: Bacon and Jonson.[68] In what can be taken as a template for a reformed monarchical state, James contrasted the 'Sophistry or strains of wit' that characterised the 'interpretations' of common lawyers with 'my common sense and reason, and true Logic'.[69] He compared England to Denmark, the birthplace of his wife, in which 'the State is governed only by a written law'; where 'there is no Advocate or Proctor admitted to plead'; where questions and answers 'are plain' and 'the very Law-book itself is their only Judge'. He ruminated that 'happy were all Kingdoms if they could be so: But here, curious wits, various conceits, different actions, and varieties of examples breed questions in Law.' The problem was clear enough. 'For though the Common Law be a mystery and skill best known unto your selves, yet if your interpretation be such, as other men which have Logic and common sense understand not the reason, I will never trust such an Interpretation.'[70]

As tellingly, James explained that circuit judges were not only dispensers of justice but also the eyes and ears of the state. In particular, they were to make account of magistrates 'and report their service to me at your return'. As he put it, 'I esteem the service done me by a good justice of Peace, three hundred miles, yea six hundred miles out of my sight, as well as the service done me in my presence.'[71] Indeed, 'good Justices are careful to attend the service of the King and country, for thanks only of the king, and love of their country'.[72] In reality, however, a number of factors impeded the practice of this royal justice-in-absence, not least the quality of person upon which the monarch depended. 'Bad justices' included 'idle Slowbellies, that abide always at home . . . [more] like ladies than men' as well as the sort that 'go seldom to the Kings service, but when it is to help some of their kindred or alliance'. James described 'busybodies, that will have men dance after their pipe, and follow their greatness', who must be taught 'the country is ordained to obey and follow GOD and the King, and not them'. And he attested to 'Another sort of Gentlemen of great worth in their own conceit, and cannot be content with the present form of Government, but must have a kind of liberty in the people'. These magistrates 'in every cause that concerns Prerogative, give a snatch against Monarchy, through their Puritanical itching after Popularity'. Moreover, 'some of them have showed themselves too bold of late in the lower-house of Parliament'.[73] In an ideal state, the days of Adam Overdo were clearly numbered.

The final nail in the public coffin of citizens was that they were essentially private and economic subjects: estates amalgamated under the public and remedial gaze of their prince.[74] Writing before his succession to the English throne,

---

[68] James I, 'A speach in the Starre-Chamber', in *The workes of the most high and mightie Prince, James* (1616), pp. 549–69.
[69] Ibid., p. 556.   [70] Ibid.   [71] Ibid., p. 562–4.   [72] Ibid., p. 564.   [73] Ibid.
[74] James I, *A counter-blaste to tobacco* (1604), Preface.

James understood Scottish burgesses to be 'composed of two sorts of men; Merchants and Crafts-men'. He observed that 'the Merchants think the whole commonwealth ordained for making them up; and accounting it their lawful gain and trade, to enrich themselves upon the loss of all the rest of the people, they transport from us things necessary'. Similarly, 'the Crafts-men think, we should be content with their work, how bad and dear whatsoever it be'.[75] In England this self-interest was even more apparent, not least in their resistance to integration with Scotland. He was aware, for example, that 'some may think this Union [with Scotland] will bring prejudice to some Towns and Corporations within England' and conceded that, as a result, 'a Merchant or two of Bristol, or Yarmouth, may have an hundred pounds less in his pack'. However, 'if the Empire gain, and become greater, it is no matter: You see one Corporation is ever against another, and no private Company can be set up, but with some loss to another.'[76] Applying theories of 'civic greatness' and 'reason of state' to England's transformed monarchical circumstances, Bacon was not slow to corroborate citizens as essentially economic persons with no aptitude for or claim on the public business of running an empire.[77] He told the 1607 Parliament that 'this kingdom of England, having Scotland united, Ireland reduced, the sea provinces of the Low Countries contracted, and shipping maintained, is one of the greatest monarchies, in forces truly esteemed, that hath been in the world'.[78] While merchants were the '*vena porta*' of empire, ensuring fiscal nourishment for all its limbs, they had little to do with 'the true greatness of kingdoms and estates' or the 'sinews of state'.[79] On the contrary, with their lack of 'military disposition', resistance to the 'naturalisation of strangers', and concern only for 'present gain', it was not merchants but 'gentry and noblemen' that were 'fit for empire' both at home and in the running of plantations abroad.[80] That England had now mutated from the 'little model of a man's body [into] the great frame of kingdoms and commonwealths' made the division of commercial and public labour all the more necessary. Changed circumstances made it 'in the power of princes or estates to add amplitude and greatness to their kingdoms . . . for by introducing such ordinances, constitutions, and customs' – or indeed monopolies and patents – 'they may sow greatness to their posterity and succession'.[81] In *The Alchemist*, Jonson dramatised the same conclusions. If the shopkeeper Drugger and merchant Mammon demonstrated anything, it was that all citizens

---

[75] James I, 'Basilikon Doron', in *Works*, pp. 163–4.
[76] 'A speach to both the Houses of Parliament . . . 1607', in *Works*, p. 519.
[77] Markku Peltonen, 'Political philosophy', in Markku Peltonen, ed., *The Cambridge companion to Bacon* (Cambridge, 1996), p. 288; Peltonen, *Classical humanism*, pp. 194, 227–8.
[78] Cited in Martin, *Francis Bacon*, p. 133.
[79] Francis Bacon, 'Of empire', in Vickers, ed., *Francis Bacon*, p. 379.
[80] Ibid., pp. 400, 409.
[81] Francis Bacon, 'Of the true greatness of kingdoms and estates', in Vickers, ed., *Francis Bacon*, p. 403.

were really good for – or, indeed, really wanted – was the material profits of commerce and trade.[82]

It was precisely such principles that characterised the Jacobean incorporation of Ulster. Not only were its corporations envisaged as straightforward tools of imperial expansion and colonisation. The complicity of those, many of them Londoners, backing the project suggested an attitude more in keeping with 'the joint-stock company' rather than city commonwealth.[83] However, the Jacobean incorporation of Ireland was not limited to plantations. James also confronted the Anglo-Irish inhabitants of Ireland's 'ancient' cities and boroughs: participants in a corporate system that cherished respublican and civic traditions every bit as powerful as those in England. The incorporation of Dublin in 1549 had, for example, confirmed for the predominantly Catholic citizens their customary powers and privileges while establishing a contract of mutually beneficial trust with the Edwardian regime.[84] Across the 'staple towns' and beyond, Irish citizens and burgesses regarded themselves as the guardians of local and national public interest and bastions of precisely the kind of legal, 'civil', and commercial culture being planted in the north. Their wholesale incorporation by James was perceived, in contrast, as a discontinuity with the Elizabethan past: a form of constitutional ransom by which civic privileges were retained on the understanding that citizens and burgesses would accommodate royal policy over custom revenue. Failure to comply would lead to proceedings of *quo warranto* and the potential rescinding of all civic privileges: a threat that could easily be extended to other controversies, such as the implementation of penal laws against papists.[85] Against this context, the Ulster corporations were recognised as a crude strategy to pack the Irish parliament and prompted a powerful statement of civic and respublican sentiment. As a 1612 remonstrance against the 'new creation of Boroughs' put it, there was a 'fearful suspicion the project of erecting so many corporations, in places that can scantly pass the rank of the poorest villages in the poorest country in Christendom' aimed at only one thing. This was that, 'by the voices of a few, selected for the purpose under the name of burgess extreme penal laws should be imposed upon your subjects here contrary to the natures, customs, and dispositions of them all'. For Anglo-Irish citizens, it was clear that 'these new corporations (not being the thousand part of the kingdom, considering their quantity and quality) should

---

[82] Ben Jonson, *The alchemist* (1612). See below, ch. 6.

[83] BL, Add MSS 12497, f. 235, 'The Lord Treasurer to the Lord Mayor of London', 30 October 1609; T. W. Moody, *The Londonderry plantation, 1609–41: the City of London and the plantation in Ulster* (Belfast, 1939), p. 83.

[84] Colm Lennon, *The Lords of Dublin in the age of reformation* (Dublin, 1989), ch. 2.

[85] 'Letter of King James I for a new grant of charters to the ancient corporations of Ireland, March 1609', printed in Gale, *An inquiry*, p. l.

[not] make laws to bind the rest of the subjects against their own will and consent'.[86]

Religious differences aside, and as the musings of the Catholic Stanihurst also suggest, it was a *res*publican response entirely consistent with the values and expectations of burgesses and citizens across the Irish Sea. Manipulating the traditional distinction between 'public' and 'private' bills, James had long observed that parliament, as the 'Kings great council', was 'no place then for particular men to utter there their private conceits'. Neither was it 'a convenient place for private men under the colour of general Laws to propose nothing but their own particular gain, either to the hurt of their private neighbours, or to the hurt of the whole State in general'.[87] That parliament was a forum for the local or private needs of towns was an accepted facet of parliamentary process, which was nothing if not a concerted system of lobbying and clientage. This did not prevent private bills becoming public policy or parliament serving as a conduit for the public angst of English Protestants. The 'Instructions for the citizens in parliament', for example, devised in January 1621 by citizens of York, combined local economic concerns with a heightened *res*publican sensibility. The majority of instructions demanded co-operation with other corporations to procure legislation that would protect their interests against London wholesalers, customs and impositions, and merchants who 'live in clothing towns'. They also sought an act to 'have our River made navigable' and for the county to help foot the cost. At the same time, their representatives – a lawyer and a merchant – urged patience and co-operation, as they were busy with many concerns 'tending to the public and the good of the commonwealth'. Indeed 'the reason in the slow proceedings of private things' was that 'so many public grievances and Nuisances of the commonwealth are afoot'. They urged the citizens to provide subsidies if only because 'foreign Princes have insulted and grown insolent of this kingdom and State' and presume 'difference...betwixt the king and his subjects'. Money would 'take away these evil Rumours abroad and insolent humours at home', not least the 'ill opinion' of 'papists'. It would also allow 'us to inquire and search out the ferrets and maladies of the commonwealth'. The ferret-in-chief was Bacon; and the session saw Coke orchestrate the public destruction of James' leading statesman as a monopolist.[88]

By the second decade of the seventeenth century freemen, burgesses, and citizens operated in a national political culture that was triangular in nature. As participants of *res*publica, they were closely associated with law, parliament, and the authority of professional practitioners and representatives. As enfranchised

---

[86] 'Remonstrances of the ancient peers of Ireland to King James I against his new creation of boroughs, November 1612', in Gale, *An inquiry*, pp. ci–ciii.

[87] James I, 'A Speach in the Parliament House, as neere the very words as could be gathered at the instant', in *Works*, pp. 507–8.

[88] YCA B36, ff. 209, 207, 210–12; Withington, 'Two renaissances', p. 257.

inhabitants of 'civic palatinates', and practitioners of *civitas*, they could regard themselves as citizens with customary, extenuated and semi-autonomous powers of public deliberation and implementation. And as privileged functionaries of the crown, they were meant to ensure that the rational will of the sovereign was enacted locally. These contrasting positions were not necessarily contradictory, and historians have stressed the aptitude with which citizens, either as formal representatives of their communities or particular factions, could exploit all three in practice.[89] Nor were they unprecedented. Humanism had always had its more authoritarian practitioners; grants of charter traditionally functioned as acts of royal will; and William Cecil was by no means shy of bringing the full weight of sovereign authority to bear on civic office-holders when the need arose.[90] The very use of the word 'state' to describe sovereign power began, after all, in the final decade of Elizabeth's reign.[91] This should not obscure the sharper enunciation of the Jacobean monarchy or the equally strident – and not necessarily concordant – claims of common lawyers and citizens. Although articulated within the same humanist and reformatory language, by the seventeenth century these contrasting positions meant that the 'natural subject' was an unstable and sometimes contested identity. Nor did it allow for any simple dichotomy between governors and the governed. This complexity was only heightened by the local practice of city commonwealth: local political cultures that, in their crystallisation of Aristotelian categories and assumptions, formed yet another source of public agency and identity.

Aristocrats, democrats, and the public good

Aristotelian notions of democracy, aristocracy, and the public good were 'introduced decisively into England by mid-sixteenth-century humanists'.[92] Especially prominent in this respect was Sir Thomas Smith's account of *De Republica Anglorum*: a text that Michael Mendle describes as 'a gospel for all people'.[93] Smith simplified the complicated gradation of constitutional forms developed by Aristotle to a bare outline in which the 'good and just' governments of *monarchy* (king), *aristocracy* ('governing of the best men'), and *democracy* ('commonwealth by the general name') were juxtaposed against their 'evil and unjust' forms. These included government by tyrant (*tyranny*),

---

[89] David Harris Sacks, 'The corporate town and the English state: Bristol's "little businesses" 1625–1641', in Barry, *The Tudor and Stuart town*, pp. 297–333.

[90] BL, Add MSS 35, 831, f. 308, 'Lord Treasurer to the Mayor of Hull', 27 October 1583; Slack, *From reformation to improvement*, pp. 54–5.

[91] John Guy, *Tudor England* (Oxford, 1988), p. 352.

[92] Michael Mendle, *Dangerous positions. Mixed government, the Estates of the Realm, and the making of the answer to the XIX propositions* (Alabama, 1985), p. 3.

[93] Sir Thomas Smith, *De Republica Anglorum*; Mendle, *Dangerous positions*, p. 56.

by the 'usurping of a few gentlemen, or a few of the richer or stronger sort' (*oligarchy*), or the 'usurping of the popular or rascal and viler sort because they be more in number' (*popular*).[94] Smith also noted the unlikelihood of finding any commonwealth 'absolutely and sincerely made of any of them above named, but always mixed with another'.[95] Appropriated to describe the national polity, the categories of monarchy, aristocracy, and democracy could have nestled more or less snugly alongside the traditional language of 'estates' of bishops, lords, and commons. That they did not was, as Mendle has shown, in large part because of their appropriation by Scottish and English Presbyterians: under James, it became treasonous to imply that the Bishops were no longer an estate.[96] What Mendle fails to note is that, by linking the language of the One, the Few and the Many (and variations on that theme) so firmly with the concept of commonwealth, Smith also made those concepts pertinent for smaller corporate 'body politics'. As Henry Manship subsequently observed of Great Yarmouth, 'Every commonweal, as saith Aristotle (the prince of philosophers) is a company, and every company is ordained to some good, and most chiefly to obtain the most principal and most excellent good of others.'[97] Moreover, it was not simply Aristotelian notions of aristocracy and democracy but also the imperatives of public good and moral judgement that were disseminated across the corporate system. In this sense, the adoption of Aristotelian categories by urban freemen was an attribute of the fluid and localised ways in which 'commonwealth' was used in England, allowing freemen to act as aristocrats and democrats while simultaneously participating, as 'natural subjects' and 'part of the commons', in *res*publica and state.

It was not, of course, merely boroughs and cities but also universities, companies, hospitals, parishes, and households that conformed to Smith's definition of commonwealth as 'a society or common doing of a multitude of free men collected together and united by a common accord and covenants among themselves'.[98] What made incorporated cities and boroughs distinctive was the scale and scope of their civic resources; their relative autonomy; and, somewhat paradoxically, their 'interlacing' of locality, province, and nation. Indeed, because the corporate system was so constitutive of the polity – forming an increasing proportion of the parliamentary franchise and ensuring the public peace locally – it followed that civic politics had a direct bearing on the national public presence enjoyed by the commons. While civic aristocracy (or oligarchy) restricted this presence socially, so civic democracy (or populism) was likely to broaden participatory boundaries. From the mid-sixteenth century, a general feature of the incorporating process was the promulgation of aristocracy as the preferred form

---

[94] Smith, *De Republica Anglorum*, p. 3.   [95] Ibid., p. 5.
[96] Mendle, *Dangerous positions*, pp. 3–4.   [97] Manship, *History of Great Yarmouth*, p. 190.
[98] Smith, *De Republica Anglorum*, p. 10; Sheppard, *Of corporations*, pp. 2–7.

of civic governance. Whether as the middling-sort subalterns of Mulcaster, the state-bound functionaries of Bacon, or even the virtuous citizens of Middleton, those freemen entrusted with powers of governance and representation were ideally drawn from the 'better sort' of their communities. This preference was closely related to the appropriation and dissemination of Ciceronian notions of civility in the later sixteenth century – a process considered in more detail in subsequent chapters, and which exacerbated the perennial correlation between civic office-holding, wealth, and status.[99] As the London citizen and draper William Scott explained, 'Senators ought to be rich for these reasons.' 'Wealth is a pledge of their care of the Commonwealth: it is likely, he that hath done well for himself, will know how to do well for the public good.' It 'being gotten, their minds may with more diligence intend the public affairs'. And, finally, 'In Ruling, there must be power and command, which a poor man cannot have, all the world despises him . . . to have a poor governor is a great plague.'[100] The effect of Ciceronian humanism was to load, in turn, material differences with intellectual and moral freight: as Keith Wrightson has shown, for the 'better sort' in general, new learning was part and parcel of new wealth.[101] That is not to argue, however, that the virtues demanded of civic aristocracy were perceived as a simple function of economic virility. Governance came with duties and responsibilities that not only became more technical over the period, but were also framed in moral terms. The anonymous and democratically minded author of the play *Woodstock* presented ignorant and oligarchic bailiffs willingly and unquestioningly complying with the corrupt and ridiculous edicts of Richard II, signing and sealing blank taxation lists and arresting both residents and visitors to Dunstable for whistling treasonously. In this way, functionaries of a tyrannous monarch became local tyrants, so jeopardising the legitimate place and voice of the commons in the polity.[102] Ostensible proponents of civic aristocracy such as Thomas Middleton likewise questioned the ability of uneducated provincial burgesses to wield authority appropriately. In *The mayor of Queenborough*, London's chronicler satirised at once the petty factional squabbling that attended civic elections and the consequences of ignorant burgesses – in this instance, a journeyman tanner – wielding too much public power.[103]

[99] Richards, *Rhetoric and courtliness*, p. 2; Jenny Kermode, *Medieval merchants: York, Beverley and Hull in the later middle-ages* (Cambridge, 1998), ch. 2; Perry Gauci, *The politics of trade: the overseas merchant in state and society, 1660–1720* (Oxford, 2001), ch. 2; David Eastwood, *Government and community in the English provinces, 1700–1870* (Basingstoke, 1997), pp. 17–18, 119.

[100] William Scott, *An essay on drapery: or, the complete citizen* (1635), p. 116.

[101] Wrightson, *English society*, pp. 191–9.

[102] *Thomas of Woodstock, or, Richard the Second, part one/Anon*, ed., Peter Corbin and Douglas Sedge (Manchester, 2002).

[103] Thomas Middleton, *Hengist, King of Kent; or the Mayor of Queenborough* (Washington, 1938).

The introduction of common councils and aldermanic benches as the pre-dominant, and often more restrictive, form of civic governance was the most obvious manifestation of incorporated aristocracy. The problem facing its pro-ponents was that constitutional adaptation usually required both the rewrit-ing of civic constitutions and, in order to justify this, the reinterpretation of the customs, grants, and charters from which communities were held to derive their political legitimacy. The institution of self-selected conciliar bodies possessed of unprecedented and potentially unaccountable powers aggravated, in turn, democratic itches that by the end of the sixteenth century burgesses were only too willing to scratch. Certainly Nathaniel Bacon, in his mid-seventeenth-century annals of Ipswich, could 'not understand' how the common council sanctioned by the Elizabethan charter 'can consist with the charters formerly granted, which fix the legislative power upon the great court, nor with the ancient customs of the Town'.[104] Similar unease characterised the Shropshire borough of Ludlow at precisely the moment when London's apologist was deflecting charges of aristocratic and democratic conceits. Disputes over Ludlow's con-stitutional and material resources had simmered since at least the absorption, by the corporation, of the wealthy Palmers' Guild in 1551.[105] The Guild held extensive lands in both town and county, maintained a grammar school, and performed charitable works, all of which were jeopardised by the Dissolution. Its preservation by Edwardian patent was, therefore, a political success for the burgesses that significantly enhanced the common wealth of the borough as well as the public responsibilities of its governors. It also raised the prob-lem of how and by whom these additional public resources were to be used. By the 1590s, civic opinion had crystallised into contrasting aristocratic and democratic positions. These mapped fairly snugly onto the rift that had devel-oped between the town's common councillors and other burgesses: what the Recorder described as 'certain controversies between the Bailiffs, Twelve and Twenty Five councillors . . . on the one party and the burgesses . . . on the other party'.[106]

Thanks to an important essay by Penry Williams, Ludlow has long been regarded as a quintessential example of the 'rise of oligarchy'.[107] However, a full contextualisation of its politics demonstrates not so much the inexorable quality of oligarchy so much as the democratic and aristocratic tensions that characterised the corporate system as a whole.[108] Ludlow's 'aristocrats' were

---

[104] Nathaniel Bacon, *The annalls of Ipswich. The lawes, customes, and government of the same*, ed. William H. Richardson (1884), p. iv.

[105] SA, Q63, p. 52; Faraday, *Ludlow*, p. 91.

[106] SA, LB2/1/16, f. 40.

[107] Williams, 'Government and politics', pp. 282–94; Tittler, *Reformation and the towns*, pp. 189, 193, 195, 204.

[108] Williams, 'Government and politics', p. 291; Lamburn, 'Politics and religion', p. 71; Tittler, *Reformation and the towns*, ch. 9.

grouped around a network of 'kin and allies' descending from Walter Rogers and William Langford, the last two wardens of the Palmers' Guild. John Crowther led the democratic opposition from within the common council, co-ordinating with weaver John Bradford among the burgesses and Philip Bradford in the borough court.[109] The conflict reached a head when the ruling 'party' successfully purchased a new charter of incorporation in 1598 from Sir Edward Coke, so negating a pending *quo warranto* brought against their government by John Bradford.[110] John Crowther explained to the Court of Exchequer that 'there was never motion made to the Twelve and Twenty Five Persons called counsellors in any public assembly or upon any summons before the said charter was procured as usually they have done for matters of less importance'. This secrecy and misappropriation of the common seal merely reflected the fact that 'the new charter was procured for no other end [than] to maintain the covetous desires and greedy revenge of the defendants'.[111] As John Bradford put it, the 'last charter was fraudulently and in deceit of her Majesty's true intent and meaning procured' by 'plotters and devisers'.[112]

The aristocrats defended their position with a particular interpretation of borough history. It was claimed that the ancient government of the borough, long before the grants and charters of the fifteenth and sixteenth centuries, had been by the 'better, wiser, and worthier sort called the common council of the said town and representing all the rest of the burgesses'. Once incorporated, the commonalty by 'common decree and consent amongst themselves' had signalled this 'ancient usage' as their preferred form of government. As a result, the customary arrangement by which the 'Twelve and Twenty Five of the ablest wisest and worthiest of the burgesses should represent and supply the room of all the rest of the burgesses and commons of the said corporation' continued into the incorporated era. The thirty-seven 'best' burgesses had authority to elect annually the two bailiffs (equivalent of mayor); to elect other civic office-holders; to 'get and let' the town lands; and to 'determine all other affairs concerning the estate of the town'. The charter also confirmed their power to 'supply the room and place' of any member of the common council who, for whatever reason, vacated his office, so ensuring control over entry into civic governance. Finally, the aristocrats argued that 'the Twelve and Twenty Five, being of the most discreet and worthiest burgesses' were also 'the chief heads of the commonalty ... representing the estate and body of all the said burgesses'.[113] Alderman Richard Benson spelt out the implications of this to the Court of Exchequer in 1598. He had heard his fellow aldermen 'say that

---

[109] Faraday, *Ludlow*, p. 37; TNA Probate 91/99 (c.1600), will of Philip Bradford.
[110] Williams, 'Government and politics', p. 287; Faraday, *Ludlow*, pp. 35–7.
[111] TNA, E134/39 and 440 Elizabeth/Mich. 37, deposition of John Crowther.
[112] SA, LB7/768; TNA, E134/39 and 440 Elizabeth/Mich. 37, item 89.   [113] SA, LB7/773b.

their [legal] counsel had said down in writing' that, on the basis of ancient prescription, the 'charter granted by King Edward VI and Queen Elizabeth did give unto them [the common council] only And to none other'. It followed that 'all lands privileges and commodities of the said Town rested in them only'; that the 'residue of burgesses' were 'plebs'; and that 'martial law' was the best means of ending contention.[114]

Philip Bradford conceded that civic association had long been restricted 'for avoiding of troublesome assemblies'. Indeed, 'they might so have done still had not the [ruling faction] alleged to the XII and XXV and their successors all the lands liberties and privileges mentioned and granted in the charter of Edward IV given to the Burgesses'.[115] However, weaver John Bradford told a more democratic account of Ludlow's history and customs that contradicted the aristocratic narrative at almost every turn. Bradford described an era before civic record in which the lord of the town or his steward selected twelve of the chief burgesses to govern their neighbours. The grant of Richard, Duke of York, confirmed the rule of the Twelve and an additional Twenty Five but also specified they were not to meddle with the office of Lord Steward, the granting of lands and collecting rents, nor any of the powers 'belonging to the King's Constable'. These powers directly devolved to the 'burgesses of themselves and amongst themselves' with the charter of Edward IV, manorial lordship transmuting into burghal democracy without the insertion of conciliar mediation. For all the claims of the aristocrats, it was clear that the Twelve and Twenty Five were to have 'no more power than the rest of the burgesses' over elections or lands 'nor to exclude the rest of the burgesses from their free elections'. Thereafter there was no evidence of any general consent that the Twelve and Twenty Five 'should represent and supply the room of all the rest of the burgesses and commonalty of the said corporation'. There was no proof that burgesses had agreed that elections should not proceed 'in any large or ample manner as the whole body of the said town and corporation'. And 'the true meaning of the charter' was clearly not that the Twelve and Twenty Five should select their own replacements. These claims, including the aggrandising tag of 'common council', were recent innovations that the ruling faction was now seeking to legitimate with a new and secret charter of incorporation. As Bradford explained, previous governors 'had greater regard to their oaths And the benefit of the whole corporation than the now Twelve and Twenty-Five termed counsellors have'. As far as the democrats were concerned, the 'common soul' of the community could not be privately owned no matter how 'better' one neighbour was than another.[116]

[114] TNA, E134/39 and 440 Elizabeth/Mich. 37, depositions of Richard Benson.
[115] Ibid., deposition of Philip Bradford.   [116] SA, LB7/768.

The control of civic memory was one political tactic, the use of pejorative language to describe and undermine the civic credence of opponents another. Just as the democrats exposed the oligarchic propensities of the aristocrats, so the aristocrats emphasised the populist dangers of their opponents. Both sides worked their rhetoric with the help of legal counsel and attorney: not for each other, but for the benefit of Privy Council, Council of the Marches, the House of Commons, and the Court of Exchequer. The aristocrats argued that there was 'no contention' in Ludlow until certain burgesses and inhabitants, 'thirsting after more of the town lands', became 'aggrieved that they [were] not called to some place of government in the town'.[117] John Crowther was a person who 'do know how easy a matter it is to raise a multitude of the inferior sort against the head, when they shall be persuaded rather to be free men and rulers then to be ruled'.[118] John Bradford was likewise styled a 'common barrattor' who, at a common gaol delivery, 'most contemptuously and in derogation of the authority of the said Bailiffs did there publicly speak . . . and persuaded divers other burgesses to do the like disobedience'. Bradford and his 'confederates' were 'backward in matters of religion'; reluctant tax payers; 'men impatient of good rule and government as without any good cause of worthiness seek to intrude themselves in rule and authority'. Bradford was 'wholly given to faction . . . and bring all in common' through the agitation of 'the meaner sort'.[119] His allies were 'certain troublesome and mutinous young persons not fit to govern in any good commonwealth'; 'very light and disordered persons'; 'secret enemies to the poor town'; 'certain ignorant and simple people'.[120] The thought that people of this quality 'shall elect and choose of their governors' – parliamentary representatives included – was not only against the 'ancient government' of the town but also the public good of town and nation.

Nor were the democrats short of rhetorical punch. The reality of civic aristocracy was that 'some of their thirty seven burgesses greedily coveting to enrich themselves with the Lands and Revenues of the said town by drawing into their number their sons and kinsmen and such as they can procure to give voices with them'. As a result, they 'have gotten a great part of the best lands and commodities at small fines and rent and do misspend the Treasures and Revenue of the said town and neglect the public weal of the same'. The democrats belittled the appropriation of the very term 'common council' by the town's ruling 'company', referring to the 'late called common councillors', the 'persons terming themselves common counsellors', the 'supposed common councillors', and the town's 'supposed governors'.[121] They also demonstrated that the ideals and criteria of civic aristocracy were hardly reflected in the actions and intentions of the party that dominated government and representation in

---

[117] SA, LB7/773a.   [118] SA, LB7/736.   [119] SA, LB7/765.
[120] SA, LB7/741.   [121] TNA, E134/39 and 440 Elizabeth/Mich. 37, item 12, 17; SA, LB7/766.

the town. Ludlow's governors had infiltrated and monopolised the civic bodies
of the town to the extent that their 'private will' and the 'public good' had
become synonymous. Councillors had 'no grant or lawful election or calling
thereunto' and claimed 'an usurped custom and greedy desire of authority to
enrich themselves . . . preferring their own private gain before the common utility'. It was not aristocracy so much as oligarchy that was at work – oligarchy
in the morally corrupt and politically tyrannous sense of the term. Government
consisted of 'kindred and friends and such other person as are unfit for counsel
or service or to bear office but [are] rather chosen . . . to make the defendants
by most voices to carry any cause amongst them in question to effect their
own wills and purpose'.[122] It was on this basis that 'the Bailiff and common
council . . . do set and impose upon . . . the common burgesses and inhabitants
in all payment far greater sums then is due to the intent to free themselves'.
They 'also abridge . . . all privileges, liberties, and freedoms granted by the said
letters patent and divers other wrongs'.[123] As well as expropriating civic land
and liberty, the company was accused of fiscal mismanagement and corruption,
bribery, the persecution of burgesses through law, and the refusal to implement
previously agreed articles designed to 'restrain the insolent and bad practices
and wrongs done to the burgesses'.[124] This was not the 'better sort' of Ludlow
acting for the public good. It was a selfish and wilful faction that determined
'causes for their own profits and commodities' rather than 'for the good and
public wealth of the corporation'; that looked to 'their own private wealth and
the wealth of their friends before the common wealth'.[125]

Although the Court of Exchequer confirmed the new charter granted by
Lord-Attorney Coke, the Privy Council took the accusations of the democrats
seriously enough to place Ludlow's common councillors under close supervision.[126] Moreover, while the eventual departure of John Crowther from the
town might suggest the immediate 'triumph of oligarchy', there is every indication that civic dissension – and the principles upon which it rested – remained
endemic in the borough.[127] An informal campaign of insult, libel, and gossip against the personal capacities of 'so called common councillors' at once
severely damaged the 'good reputation and credit of this corporation' while
reiterating the corruption of commonwealth principles that had occurred.[128]
Likewise, the fact that, over the course of the later sixteenth and seventeenth
centuries, Ludlow underwent more re-incorporations than any other city commonwealth aside from Newcastle-upon-Tyne hardly suggests the remorseless

[122] TNA, E134/39 and 440 Elizabeth/Mich. 37, item 11.
[123] SA, LB7/767.
[124] TNA, E134/39 and 440 Elizabeth/Mich. 37, items, 30–52, 55, 56, 61–71, 83.
[125] TNA, E134/39 and 440 Elizabeth/Mich. 37, items 9, 10.   [126] SA, LB7/743; LB1/4.
[127] Williams, 'Politics and government', p. 288.   [128] SA, LB2/1/16, f. 42.

'rise of oligarchy' of historiographical orthodoxy.[129] On the contrary, it points to an intense civic politics in which the imperatives of commonwealth – and its historical antecedents – were routinely and authoritatively asserted and defended.

More intriguingly, the experience of Crowther anticipated that of Oliver Cromwell thirty years later. As in Ludlow, the incorporation of Cromwell's home borough of Huntingdon in 1630 demonstrated the complex networks of clientage and friendship that invariably accompanied a successful 'solicitation'. While tied into the network of the Merchant Taylors Company in London, the burgesses were also backed by the Earl of Manchester and his client Mr Bernard: the lawyer who negotiated the transaction and was rewarded with the place of Recorder in the new charter. Although Cromwell initially supported incorporation, he found his place in the town insupportable after 'disgraceful and unseemly speeches' against the new mayor and recorder.[130] These 'speeches' have been interpreted as 'personal' pique rather than 'political' principle: if there was any ideological motivation, it was religious in nature.[131] In fact, there is every indication that Cromwell struck the same democratic position as Crowther. Cromwell, like Crowther, expressed generally held fears from within the ranks of the civic elite that the new regime would tax the use of the common lands; 'dispose of the inheritance of their town lands . . . without the Burgesses'; and fine 'men that might be poor' for refusing civic office. For his pains he was accused, like Crowther, of seeking 'to gain many of the Burgesses against this new corporation' through 'indirect and unfit' methods. Just how 'causeless and ill-grounded' his complaints were is another matter. Although Manchester assured the Privy Council that 'three constitutions' had been drafted to prevent the 'fears of prejudice', it was noted fifty years later that 'most of the arable land [had] been enclosed' and 'the Burgesses cannot make good title for their common'.[132] Indeed, there is every indication that Cromwell recognised oligarchy when he saw it.[133]

Cromwell was out-manoeuvred politically, alienated religiously, and undermined personally by his 'uncivil' outburst against the new corporation. However, he also distinguished between a civic constitution that served 'all things for the public good and wealth' of the town – including the prevention of 'all oppression and extortion whatsoever touching to the impoverishment of the poorer sort of people' – from one that served merely 'private' interests.[134] Most importantly, by 1640 he had secured his freedom in the still democratic,

---

[129] Based on Tittler, *Reformation and the towns*, Appendix; Halliday, *Dismembering the body politic*, Appendix.

[130] TNA SP16 176, 34.

[131] John Morrill, 'The making of Oliver Cromwell', in J. S. A. Adamson and J. S. Morrill, eds., *Oliver Cromwell and the English Revolution* (Harlow, 1990), pp. 26–31, 33.

[132] HRO, HB28, f. 106.   [133] TNA SP16 176, 34.   [134] HRO HB28, f. 4.

if embattled and divisive, borough of Cambridge.[135] It was on this basis that Cromwell represented Cambridge's burgesses in parliament, at once personifying the ideological complexity and interpenetration of England's civic and national polities and raising important issues about the role played by citizens in the 'contestation between Regal and Parliamentary power' that ensued.[136]

'Consistent with the state or no?'

Civic politics in Elizabethan Ludlow and Caroline Huntingdon was replicated across the corporate system, suggesting that, in terms of both theory and practice, a functional concept of oligarchy needs serious qualification. The same is true of its interpretative bedfellows. Certainly the Aristotelian basis of city commonwealths raises questions about a model of 'localism' that reduces urban politics to a 'conservative and defensive' interaction with national events.[137] It also qualifies the imperative of communal 'unanimity', and the exclusion of 'ideology', that purportedly characterised civic decision-making before 1640.[138] While most citizens would have agreed on the importance of the 'public good', there was clearly much less agreement about how to structure it either locally or nationally. This is not to claim that citizens and freemen 'caused' the civil war or that all city commonwealths were inexorably allied to parliament. It is to suggest that the representational presence of city commonwealths in London between 1640 and 1642 meant that propagandists were required to speak their language. Freemen, burgesses, and citizens formed a crucial audience for the war of words between parliament and king, both as conciliar bodies exercising parliamentary representation and as 'middling sort' recipients of the sudden plethora in pamphlets and other printed texts.[139] In this sense, initial support for the 'parliamentary power' can be traced to, and at least partially explained by, the fact that parliamentary propagandists were more adept at talking in ways which citizens and their representatives could understand.[140] There was a degree of resonance between parliamentary and civic rhetoric that the king only achieved relatively (and fatefully) late in the day. Viewed in these terms, the national 'revival of the idiom of mixed government' in the early 1640s – not to mention the moral imperative of 'the public good' that accompanied

[135] Frederic William Maitland and Mary Bateson, eds., *The charters of the borough of Cambridge* (Cambridge, 1901), p. xi.
[136] Henry Parker, *Observations upon some of his Majesties late answers and expresses* (1642), p. 1.
[137] Howell, 'Neutralism', p. 87.   [138] Kishlansky, *Parliamentary selection*, pp. 16, 108.
[139] John Walter, *Understanding popular violence in the English revolution: the Colchester plunderers* (Cambridge, 1999), pp. 289–301; Keith Wrightson, '"Sorts of people" in Tudor and Stuart England', in Barry and Brooks, *Middling sort of people*, pp. 45–6.
[140] For suggestive comments see Ann Hughes, 'The king, parliament and the localities during the English civil war', in Cust and Hughes, *The English civil war*, p. 278.

it – was far from 'banal'.[141] On the contrary, it cut to the heart of civic culture as it had been prescribed, developed, and practised over the previous 100 years.

In conclusion, then, it is worth briefly considering the interplay of national and local ideology in the 1640s and 1650s. It is now well known that one point of linguistic convergence was the 'better sort' within particular communities identifying themselves as the 'middling sort' at the national level.[142] Another feature of parliamentary propaganda in the months preceding war was the appropriation of the 'public good' as an antidote to 'private will' and 'interest'. 'The humble petition of the Lords and Commons in Parliament', published in December 1641, noted that the 'Rights and Privileges of Parliament are the Birth-right and Inheritance not only of themselves, but of the whole kingdom'. Their 'preservation' was essential to 'the public peace and prosperity of your Majesty and all your people'.[143] As 'your greatest and most faithful Counsel', Parliament was crucial in 'procuring and confirming such a confidence and unity betwixt your Majesty and your People'.[144] In 'The remonstrance of the state of the kingdom' that followed, the petitioners reiterated how 'The *Commons* in this present Parliament assembled' had worked with a 'zeal to the public good of the Kingdom, and his Majesties Honour and Service': 'the public peace, safety, and happiness of this realm'.[145] They also explained that '*The Root of all this mischief, We find to be a malignant, and pernicious design, of subverting the Fundamental Laws and Principle of Government*'. These included Jesuits, Bishops, and '*such Counsellors and Courtiers as for private ends have engaged themselves to further the interests of some foreign Princes, or States, to the prejudice of his Majesty and the State at home*'.[146] Listing a catalogue of grievances running to over ten pages, the petitioners claimed to have consistently provided 'for the great necessities and other charges of the Commonwealth'.[147] They concluded with the plea that 'his Majesty may have cause to be in love with good counsel and good men' and acknowledge genuine 'endeavours of the public good' and 'common good of the Island'.[148] 'His Majesties answer', while refuting the accusations in the petition and reproving the petitioners for having their Declaration 'already abroad in Print', nevertheless responded in 'a Parliamentary way'. This merely involved reasserting 'the undoubted right of the Crown of

---

[141] Mendle, *Dangerous positions*, p. 138.   [142] Wrightson, '"Sorts of people"', pp. 44–51.

[143] 'The humble petition of the Lords and Commons in Parliament, concerning his Majesties speech of 14 December 1641', in *An exact collection of all remonstrances, declarations, votes, orders, ordinances, proclamations, petitions, messages, answers, and other remarkable passages between the King's most excellent Majesty and his High Court of Parliament* (1643), A.

[144] Ibid., p. 1.

[145] 'The remonstrance of the state of the kingdom' (1641), in *An exact collection*, p. 3.

[146] Ibid., p. 4.   [147] Ibid., p. 17.   [148] Ibid., p. 21.

England to call such person to Our Secret Counsels, to public employment, and Our particular service, as We shall think fit'.[149]

Henry Parker's *Observations upon some of his Majesties late answers and expresses*, published at the outbreak of armed hostilities in July 1642, further accentuated the role of parliament as the national embodiment of public good and in an idiom immediately recognisable to publicly minded citizens. Parker noted that political power, whether regal or aristocratic, was 'nothing else amongst Christians but the Factions and agreements of such and such politic corporations'. Far from '*any special ordinance sent from heaven*', power was 'originally inherent in the people, and it is nothing else but that might and vigour which such and such a society of men contains in it self'.[150] Within monarchies, 'that King is most great and glorious, which hath the most and strongest subjects, and not he which tramples upon the most contemptible vassals': rather than 'impoverishing' their people, they should 'magnify themselves by enfranchising their subjects'.[151] More pressingly, 'it were strange if the people in subjecting it self to command, should aim at anything else but its own good in the first and last place'. It followed that the king's 'dignity was erected to preserve the Commonalty, the Commonalty was not created for his service'.[152] The primacy of the 'public weal' was matched only by the primacy of parliaments in serving it: in 'public consultations, the many eyes of so many choice gentlemen out of all parts, see more than fewer'. This was especially so when 'a few shall act for many, the wise shall consult for the simple, the virtue of all shall redound to some, and the prudence of some shall redound to all'.[153] While this 'admirably composed court' encapsulated the public imperatives of civic aristocracy, monarchical courts were almost by definition private domains subject to unregulated will and interest. 'The wisest of our Kings following their own private advise, or being conducted by their own wills, have mistaken their best subjects, for their greatest enemies.' Charles more than any relied 'upon his own private reason, and counsel', defending his 'secret Court-Counsel', his 'own opinions . . . infused by obscure whisperers'. The Venetians well knew that there was no greater 'bondage' than 'that their Princes will dote upon their own wills, and despise public counsels and laws, in respect of their own private opinions'. It was this 'sting of Monarchy' that concerned Parker above all else. If 'Kings be so [inclined] to follow private advise rather than publique, and to prefer that which closes with their natural impotent ambition . . . then they may destroy their best subjects at pleasure, and all Charters and Laws of public safety are void'.[154] Encased in an overarching sense of *res*publica, this was the vision of Henry Manship writ large: the revenge of Adam Overdo indeed.

---

[149] 'His Majesties answer to the petition', in *An exact collection*, pp. 22, 24.
[150] Parker, *Observations*, p. 1.
[151] Ibid., p. 2.   [152] Ibid., p. 3.   [153] Ibid., pp. 11, 15.   [154] Ibid., p. 30.

By this time royalist propagandists Viscount Falkland and Sir John Culpepper were busy contesting the rhetorical high ground of the mixed Aristotelian polity.[155] For many royalist commentators the 'nineteen propositions', published by 'both Houses' on 2 June 1642, moved 'beyond making Charles their equal and had made him their inferior'.[156] It was ordered that 'such matters as concern the public, and are proper for the High Court of Parliament . . . may be debated, resolved and transacted only in Parliament, and not elsewhere'. Likewise 'such other matters of State, as are proper for your Majesty's Privy Council, shall be debated and concluded by such of the Nobility, and others, as shall be chosen for that place, by approbation of both Houses'. The person and household of the monarch was placed under public (parliamentary) control; likewise 'the Forts and Castles of this Kingdom'.[157] However, 'His Majesties answer' had lost the air of outraged bemusement that characterised previous ripostes. The propositions threatened rights 'that as for Our subjects sake . . . are vested in Us, so for their sakes, as well for Our own'. The king was 'resolved not to quit them, nor to subvert, (though in a Parliamentary way) the ancient, equal, happy, well-poised and well-enough commended Constitution of the Government of this Kingdom'. Nor would he 'make Our Self of a King of *England* a Duke of Venice, and this of a Kingdom a Republique'. It was not royal counsellors so much as a parliamentary 'cabal' that threatened the 'Balance' of the mixed polity to which the king was committed: a polity that combined the best of monarchy, aristocracy, and democracy. Sir Thomas Smith could have only concurred with the analysis offered. The 'good of Monarchy is the uniting a Nation under one Head to resist invasion from abroad and insurrection at home: The good of Aristocracy is the Conjunction of Counsel in the ablest persons of a State for the public benefit: The good of Democracy is Liberty, and the Courage and Industry which Liberty begets.'[158] It was this that parliament, not the king, now threatened: a mixed constitutionalism that proved attractive to citizens throughout the Revolution and beyond.

Viewed in these terms, it was local commonwealths – cities and boroughs prominent among them – which effectively linked the classical humanism of the mid-sixteenth century to the re-emergence of mixed constitutional rhetoric in the 1640s. However, this was not the only example of civic sensibilities inflecting and impacting upon national discourse. Equally striking was the close relationship between civic democracy and democratic appropriations of the 'ancient constitution'. From the mid-sixteenth century, civic historians had been prone to place the genesis of their towns – and the forms of association that ideally

---

[155] Mendle, *Dangerous positions*, p. 6.   [156] Ibid., p. 11.

[157] 'The humble petition and advice of both Houses of Parliament, with nineteen propositions, and the conclusion sent unto his Majesty 2 June 1642', in *An exact collection*, pp. 307–10.

[158] 'His Majesties answer to the nineteen propositions', in *An exact collection*, p. 320.

characterised them – long before the arrival of the Normans.[159] Nathaniel Bacon noted that in Ipswich as elsewhere 'it was the wisdom of our predecessors in those older times, having elected a place of habitation in this place commodious for traffic, to join together by mutual consent in a common pose'. They did so in order 'to maintain the common good and benefit of themselves as members of one body and to exclude such as refused to join with them from the common benefit of freedom'.[160] The same principles informed democratic agitation in Ludlow: weaver John Bradford was by no means unusual in using historical interpretation to justify his democratic outlook.[161] The civil war period enabled a radical convergence of local and national conceptions of the 'ancient constitution'.[162] From Ipswich, for example, Nathaniel Bacon extended his historical particularity into a more systematic formulation of England's democratic antecedents. In his *Historical discourse* of 1647 he outlined the 'beautiful composure' of the 'Saxon commonweal'.[163] This was an era of monarchy that resembled 'more of a democracy', a commonwealth 'mutually dependent in every part from the crown to the clown, the Magistrates being all choice men, and the king the choicest of chosen'. Elections based on 'esteem' and 'merit' 'bred love and mutual trust'; the bond of society was justice 'grounded on the wisdom of the Greeks, and Judicials of Moses'; office was sought only for 'honour and admiration'.[164] In this monarchical republic, the 'liberty of Township' was initially a 'liberty of market' derived from 'common right, and not as a corporation made by common charter; but as they are a multitude of people anciently gathered together and united'.[165] It was on this basis that other civic liberties followed, the 'place and people . . . being of such consequence in the public administration'. The last 600 years represented a prolonged jostling between the interests of commons, lords, and monarch in the light of the Norman Conquest. England was at the end of a period in which democratic antecedents had been appropriated but also assimilated and perpetuated by what Butcher termed the 'fencing and hedging' of 'Princes and Policy'.[166]

An alternative and less forgiving reading of the ancient constitution affirmed that original liberties could only be recovered once the 'Norman yoke' was

---

[159] Manship, *History of Great Yarmouth*, p. 23; Butcher, *Survey and antiquity*, p. 17.

[160] Bacon, *Annalls of Ipswich*, p. v.

[161] HCRO, HD4/2/17, 1611, Joyce Larkin c. William Sherwood; Andy Wood, 'The place of custom in plebeian political culture: England, 1550–1800', *Social History*, 22, 1, January 1997, pp. 47–8.

[162] Wood, 'The politics of custom', p. 47; J. G. A. Pocock, *The ancient constitution and the feudal law: a study of English historical thought in the seventeenth century* (Cambridge, 1987), pp. 42–3, 46–7.

[163] Nathaniel Bacon, *An historical discourse of the uniformity of the government of England* (1647), pp. 112, 111.

[164] Ibid., p. 112.   [165] Ibid., p. 82.

[166] Ibid., pp. 113–20, 135, 161–3; Butcher, *Survey and antiquity*, pp. 19–20.

undone. John Lilburne was quick to observe that the subsequent grants and charters of the corporate system constituted one particular manifestation of Norman
tyranny.[167] It was on the same grounds that the freemen of the city of London
challenged the exclusive privilege of Liverymen to elect annually the lord mayor
and sheriffs in 1650.[168] The 'several Companies and Societies of the City'
responded with an account of the evolution of electoral custom, through various acts, grants, and ordinances, since the reign of Edward III. They argued that,
while avoiding the 'continual altercations and often disturbances' of the past,
the present system had been 'course and custom' for 'near two hundred years
together' and constituted, in turn, an 'ancient right'.[169] However, Lilburne's
associate John Wildman, representing the freemen, characterised the same process as 'the imposition of the Governors upon a People without their voluntary
Election, importing the prevalence of mere Tyranny and Slavery'.[170] Freemen
now desired to have 'the Ancient Right of the Citizens of London restored to
them'.[171] The contest over rights was reduced to a forensic and laborious reading
of past orders and grants: a battle of interpretation, inference, and extrapolation
through which substantive differences over the current nature of civic power
were articulated. Such tactics served, however, a political ideology that was
very much directed at the present. Liverymen were 'Gentlemen' who, although
dispersed across the country, nevertheless 'may choose my Lord Mayor and the
Sheriffs . . . and yet live not under their power'. In contrast, 'Freemen of this
City pay Scot and Lot, and are bound to assist the chief officers of this city'.
As the 'aggregate body' of enfranchised households responsible for the daily
governance, profit, and perpetuation of their common wealth, representative
power was likewise their right, whether directly or through elected intermediaries. It was this that the democratic origins of city commonwealths proved. For
Wildman as for John Bradford before him, reclamation of the past was the only
guarantee of present and future freedom. And, like John Bradford, Wildman
was accused of 'popularity' for his pains.[172]

However, perhaps the most important and surprising development of the revolutionary era was also the most threatening to city commonwealths: the intellectual and, to some extent, functional realisation of an English 'state'. It was a
process encapsulated by the fact that the royalist Thomas Hobbes, Bacon's most
gifted protégé, published *Leviathan* to legitimate the parliamentary regime.[173]
Leviathan outlined in mechanistic terms the ideal of abstract, centralised, and
undivided sovereignty: an artificial man that was ideally embodied in the person

---

[167] John Lilburne, 'A remonstrance of many thousand citizens and other freeborn people of England
to their own House of Commons', in Andrew Sharp, ed., *The English Levellers* (Cambridge,
1998), pp. 34–5, 45, 46–7.

[168] *London's liberties* (1683), p. 3.   [169] Ibid., pp. 2, 6.   [170] Ibid., p. 3.

[171] Ibid., pp. 5, 7.   [172] Ibid., p. 30.   [173] Hobbes, *Leviathan*, p. ix.

of the monarch, but which was equally realisable in a governing assembly.[174] Within its orbit, corporations were 'body politics', or 'public' entities, purely because they were 'made by authority from the Sovereign Power of the Commonwealth'. Any other kind of association – including communities 'constituted by subjects among themselves' – were by definition 'private'.[175] Although a product of political contract rather than divine will, it was a conception of sovereignty that, in taking the insights of Bacon to their logical conclusion, left as little room for *civitas* as Carolinian notions of monarchy. Its contiguity with the remarkable preamble to the royal charter of incorporation that Archbishop William Laud procured for the burgesses of his home town of Reading in 1638 illustrates the point. Laud proclaimed that 'in every Monarchy the safety of the people depends upon the Crown and all authority is derived from the Prince'. 'Kings for that purpose are placed on the high throne of Majesty that as fathers of the Country they should protect the people committed to them by the King of Kings refresh with the Dew of their benignity.' Burgesses, 'being invested with our authority and animated with our favour will as is meet cause the Arts to be encouraged'. They will also ensure that 'our peace within the same Borough to be kept the depravity of morals to be corrected by the more severe sword of Justice and suitable rewards to be given to the well deserving'.[176] The formulation veered significantly from the assumption of previous charters that conciliar governance, ideally provided through common council, served the 'public utility and advantage of the said burgesses'. It also elided the principles of contract and trust that informed Thomas Cromwell's 'expediency' in 'empowering' the burgesses a century earlier, instead depicting citizenship as a straightforward extension of sovereign power.[177]

If *Leviathan* discounted the legitimating hand of the 'King of Kings', it nevertheless reflected the transformation of the parliamentary position from a *res*publican sense of public good into precisely the kind of state that had been initially resisted. The handmaiden of this transition was the New Model Army. The language of Captain Adam Baines, erstwhile attorney of Leeds, is a case in point. When the Parliamentary Ordinance of 24 November 1642 was 'enacted to engage the public faith of the kingdom', Baines personally raised a troop of seventy, costing £700, 'for which sum the public faith of this Nation is to be engaged'.[178] Seven years later, Baines and his company of soldiers were contemplating 'the gallant proceedings against Charles Stuart' as the final outcome of their 'public service'. Anticipating *Leviathan*, the military 'friends' and 'cousins' of Baines were emphatic that opinions conflicting with theirs were now no longer public but private, and that 'private opinions are more

---

[174] Quentin Skinner, 'The state', in Ball et al., *Political innovation*, pp. 90–1, 121.
[175] Hobbes, *Leviathan*, pp. 155–63.   [176] Fleetwood Pritchard, *Reading charters*, p. 55.
[177] Ibid., p. 10.   [178] BL, Add MS 21417, f. 3.

dangerous than public'. 'Malignants', 'cavaliers', and the 'disaffected' could 'plot privately': however, they were excluded from legitimate public debate.[179] The 'public' credentials of citizens likewise rested less on city commonwealth and more on their partisan affiliations. Thomas Dickenson, merchant and citizen of York, could remind Baines on 5 January 1649 that 'I have put forwards anything for the public good that was ever in my power and never looked upon as a hindrance to the public'. He 'hoped to make it appear at all times when occasion seems that I have laid of much, lost much for the public and got nothing'. Alderman Thoresby of Leeds likewise thanked his erstwhile neighbour for 'your good affection and special care as of the public so of your native country'. For both citizens, however, there was unease about the course 'the public' had taken in putting the sovereign to trial. Dickenson protested too much when he stressed that 'I desire to be looked upon a friend still and considered as others in my place of trust'. Thoresby warned that 'some with us' in the borough 'storm so exceedingly at your proceedings that they cannot confine their passions to private discourse' and that 'fit men' capable of civic governance 'will be something difficult to find'.[180]

Another friend and correspondent, Anthony Devereux, made the widening gap between civic polities and the revolutionary regime explicit. Raising 'some private queries of my own', he wondered 'whether a corporation be consistent with the state or no?' An advantage could be that it 'close all interests as Independents, Presbyterians or honest moderate persons . . . to the commonwealth for peace and unity sake'. Alternatively, it could 'be odious to Independents, Arms men and all honest men'. Government might be entrusted to 'three Justices at large'; but in a 'populous place', would 'equity' be achieved? Finally there was the problem of inhabitants disaffected to the current regime. Irreconcilable aldermen and legal officers could be removed and 'faction and division' ended through the state-sanctioned institution of religious oligarchy. As Devereux put it, 'choose so many for our Interest as burgesses and common councilmen who may out vote the rest upon a cause of necessity, to serve the state, or in election of the mayor'. That said, if the corporation served to have 'all interests joined' then 'they will be as guards one to another' and so 'less danger to the state'.[181] The Yorkshire gentleman and soldier Marmaduke Lord Langdale echoed the same sentiments two years later on his appointment as Lord Lieutenant of the West Riding. However, he did so from the opposite end of the complex spectrum of partisan allegiances that had proliferated over the last twenty years. Having fought against the 'parliamentary power' during the civil war, his conflation of the 'King's interest' with at once the state and his own party of returning Cavalier exiles replicated the position of the soldiers, saints, and republicans he replaced. The position of citizens remained no less

---

[179] Ibid., f. 24.   [180] Ibid., ff. 29, 252.   [181] BL, Add MSS 21427, f. 150.

vulnerable, Langdale complaining to his old royalist compatriot Sir Edward Nicholas, the new Secretary of State, that York like 'all corporations aim at the absolute government amongst themselves which is not for the Kings interest nor for any that serve under him'.[182] This was little different to Hobbes' contention that corporations were 'many lesser Common-wealths in the bowels of a greater'.

The implications of revolution for citizens and subjects were, therefore, extremely complex. Whether classically republican, radically Protestant, militaristic, or even nominally *res*publican, the regimes of the Interregnum were irresistibly drawn to the power and potential of the state. Moreover, in terms of its military and fiscal 'sinews', the organisation of centralised power was more efficient and successful than its Jacobean and Caroline predecessors could ever dream of. This need not have been detrimental to citizens either in terms of the imperial markets and military muscle that *Leviathan* could provide or the close and constructive relationship that the republic and the corporate system often enjoyed. More worrying was the appropriation of the state by religious partisans, and its implications for those notions of *res*publica and *civitas* that had developed over the previous 150 years. Whatever else revolution achieved, it had pushed the triangle of political identities completely out of shape. In this respect, the 'mixed constitution' – and the 'public good' it served – was eminently more palatable to citizens than Leveller democracy or a military state. The proof of the pudding was Restoration itself, citizens playing a full if wary role in the re-establishment of the 'mixed constitution' – an act that, more than anything, marked the triumph of constitutional royalism as outlined in the summer of 1642. However, a more lasting testimony to England's revolutionary legacy was presented by Nicholas Barbon in his *Apology for the builder*, a pamphlet first published in 1685, at the accession of James to the throne, and republished in 1689 after the Williamite invasion.[183] Barbon systematically disavowed the Aristotelian and Ciceronian assumptions upon which urban citizenship was based. Deploying instead the language of political economy, he justified the unregulated growth of the metropolis on the grounds of manufacture, trade, and progress on the one hand and government and empire on the other.[184] Citizenship implied not the morality and governance of place, person, and conversation so much as the liberty of the subject to trade, inhabit, and consume at will. Its benefits, based on the arithmetic of demography and economics, were scientifically demonstrable. Moreover, under the stewardship of 'such a Martial Prince as now reigns' its potential

[182] TNA SP29 36, 13.

[183] Nicholas Barbon, *An apology for the builder: or a discourse shewing the cause and effects of the increase in building* (1685).

[184] Ibid.; Paul Slack, 'Perceptions of the metropolis in seventeenth-century England', in Burke et al., *Civil histories*, pp. 175–8.

was to make London 'the Metropolis of the World': the centre of 'an Universal Monarchy over the Seas' that was at once more glorious, profitable, and extensive than 'either Caesar's or Alexander's'. Here was, in effect, *New Atlantis* and *Leviathan* writ large: a template of imperial, economic, and political expansion that, after 1688, was rapidly realised by the eighteenth-century 'fiscal military state'.[185]

---

[185] John Brewer, *The sinews of power: war, money and the English state 1688–1783* (London, 1989).

4   Placing the city commonwealth

'Fixed upon the surface of the Earth'

Robert Brady was no admirer of citizens and the 'Absurd Rights' they claimed. In 1690 he mocked 'the creation, and so many ready wrought, and framed, small commonwealths, lifted out of the chaos, and fixed upon the surface of the Earth, with their Walls, Gates, Town and Gild-Halls, Courts, Liberties, Customs, Privileges, Freedom, Jurisdictions, Magistrates and Officers, and Absolute Powers'. Deploying his considerable antiquarian skills, Brady demonstrated that cities and boroughs were not 'Eternal, appearing fully formed from heaven', but the product of grants and charters from 'our Ancient Kings, and their Successors' over time.[1] Self-consciously empirical, his treatise was nevertheless clearly weighted against both an expansive notion of *civitas* and a democratic conception of the 'ancient constitution'.[2] Coming so soon after the recent and wholesale assault on chartered privileges by 'Tory' gentlemen and the crown, it was a text both deeply partisan and strongly supportive of the monarchical state.[3] It nevertheless echoes some of the central contentions of the previous chapters. First, that Brady wrote his treatise at all was testimony to the fact that, as late as 1690, city or 'small commonwealths' remained a constitutive feature of early modern political culture. Second, the riddle that city commonwealths posed for the later Stuarts reflected at once the convergence of ideas and interests that had informed their creation, and the subsequent fragmentation of those ideas and interests after 1640. Third, Brady's mocking delineation of the incorporating process nevertheless captured the extraordinary corporate fecundity of the post-Reformation era and its impact on England's urban landscape.

Although Brady might seem an unlikely harbinger of modernity, his scepticism towards urban citizenship not only provided a framework for eighteenth-century historians but also anticipated more recent social historiography.[4] As

---

[1] Robert Brady, *An historical treatise of cities and burghs, or boroughs* (1690), p. A2.
[2] Rosemary Sweet, *The writing of urban histories in eighteenth-century England* (Oxford, 1997), pp. 66–7.
[3] Halliday, *Dismembering the body politic*, ch. 6; Joanne Innes and Nicholas Rogers, 'Politics and government, 1700–1840', in Clark, *Cambridge urban history*, p. 566.
[4] Sweet, *Writing of urban histories*, p. 67.

Keith Wrightson puts it, labels like citizen, burgess, and freeman 'remained to a very large extent a vocabulary of formal social description' that, by the later seventeenth century, was 'jerry-built' from 'the debris of the society of estates'. The 'informal language of sorts' was, in contrast, 'a more authentic product of the social dynamism of the later sixteenth and seventeenth centuries', providing 'an altogether more relevant everyday guide to the basic realities of social distance'.[5] It is a perspective echoed by urban historians, who have eschewed the technical vocabulary of citizen, burgess, and freemen for more general terms like the 'urban community'. Within this framework, the development of social distinctions is based on class rather than community. Robert Tittler associates the 'invention' of civic culture in the 100 years after 1540 with restrictive practices of corporate office-holding and 'the enhancement of oligarchic rule'.[6] The 'resurgence' of urban 'civility and sociability' in the 'long eighteenth century' is likewise regarded by Peter Borsay as 'social polarisation', the pressures of urban 'gentility' driving 'a cultural wedge between the upper and middling ranks of society on the one hand, and the populace on the other'.[7] Even Jonathan Barry's more communally orientated account of 'bourgeois collectivism' conflates freedom and citizenship with the 'merely urban', elucidating a culture of 'collective identity' in which the more particular place of city commonwealth is implied but never stated.[8]

The apparent invisibility of 'small' or city commonwealths is surprising given the tangibility, even at the end of the seventeenth century, of their presence. Even as harsh a critic of citizens as Brady could not disguise the extent and durability of their institutional and material resources: the buildings, offices, evidences, and territories that embodied civic rights and freedoms. Although Wrightson regards the language of citizenship as 'increasingly archaic', he likewise acknowledges that, as a 'mode of social description', it was 'remarkably resilient'.[9] However, while both Brady and Wrightson agree on the durability of civic nomenclature, their reasons for regarding it as incongruous are different. For Wrightson, civic appellations invoked the 'ghost of the Tudor regime, sitting enthroned upon the grave thereof'. As 'modes of social description', they 'perpetuated the characteristic status designations of the sixteenth century' and all its 'implications of oneness and order in a graduated ladder of dominance and subordination'.[10] For Brady, the opposite was true. Far from constituting a morgue, the material and institutional resources vested in citizens – their power and sense of place – made them a palpable threat to the

---

[5] Keith Wrightson, 'Estates, degrees, and sorts: changing perceptions of society in Tudor and Stuart England', in Penelope Corfield, ed., *Language, history and class* (Oxford, 1991), p. 51.

[6] Robert Tittler, *Reformation and the towns*, p. 339.

[7] Borsay, *The English urban renaissance*, pp. 37, 318.

[8] Barry, 'Bourgeois collectivism?', pp. 84–113.

[9] Wrightson, 'Estates, degrees, and sorts', p. 51.   [10] Ibid., p. 51.

monarchical state. The divergence points to a paradox that is encapsulated by the concept of place. For Wrightson and others, 'place' was central to the 'hierarchy of degrees described by Elizabethan and early Stuart writers' attempting 'to impose intellectual order on a changing social reality'. This involved combining a 'God-ordained social order' in which everyone had their place 'with an overriding emphasis on authority and subordination'.[11] Brady, in contrast, implies place to be a source of autonomy, identity, and communal agency in much the same way that Andy Wood has found the robust and assertive political culture of mining communities in the Derbyshire Peak to be founded on a sense and control of place.[12] City commonwealths were certainly one manifestation of humanist and Protestant attempts to control, reform, and civilise behaviour through the creation and prescription of place. However, they were also institutional and physical landscapes that, as late as 1690, provided a basis for early modern *civitas*.

This chapter considers, therefore, both the places of city commonwealth and their implications for civic agency and identity; or, more particularly, how early modern people made sense of that relationship. To this end, it focuses on early modern concepts of 'place' and 'person', arguing that, in terms of both theory and practice, they provide an historicised vocabulary for recovering city commonwealths as structural and experiential entities. The first two sections argue that place was both a fundamental aspect of early modern citizenship as well as a primary condition of the relative structure and position of particular city commonwealths in their local and larger environments. By examining spatial configurations in three incorporated communities it shows that, far from constituting a monolithic culture, places differed from one locale to another: indeed, a defining feature of the corporate system was its structural diversity. Even more contingent was the kind of spatial relationship considered in section three. Outlining a number of early modern theories of place and person particularly pertinent to city commonwealths, the chapter argues that early modern people did not need post-structural theory to know that the political was personal and the personal political. Nor would they have been surprised that the appropriation of place was often very different to its prescription.

Place and city commonwealth

The word 'place' had two connected meanings in early modern England. On the one hand, it denoted a specific and bounded location: places were positions

---

[11] Ibid., p. 43; Paul Griffiths, *Youth and authority: formative experiences in England, 1560–1640* (Oxford, 1996), pp. 63–71.

[12] Andy Wood, *The politics of social conflict: the Peak country, 1520–1770* (Cambridge, 1999), pp. 1–10, 169–78.

that people occupied and possessed, and which were characterised by a certain qualitative and functional unity. On the other hand, places were relational. Far from existing in a vacuum, they were located within – or in proximity to – other locations and positions. This relativity might involve similar kinds of place, in that they were characterised by the same qualities and functions, or different kinds of location entirely. Either way, bodies always existed in place. As Thomas Hobbes put it, 'we cannot but fancy it somewhere'. For Hobbes, place was 'the precise space within which the body is contained', the 'motion' of a body 'nothing but a change of place'. Motion was important because changes in place determined 'the Effect of a Body upon the Organs of our Senses': experience, perspective, and 'fancy' were at once relative to and dependent upon place.[13] This sense of the relativity of experience was matched by an equally generous sense of the kind of objective phenomena that could be described as places. A glance at the thirty-eight plays attributed to William Shakespeare between c.1590 and 1616 shows, for example, that among the 402 occasions a character used the word it referred to an institution eighty-nine times, an institutional role or office 127 times, and a geographical or physical site on 101 occasions. The institutions mentioned ranged from places of political authority and power, such as courts and prisons (twenty-eight times), to households and churches (both twenty-one times). Institutional roles and offices within institutions included places of public authority, such as monarch or magistrate (seventy-one times), soldiers and generals (nineteen times), and household positions, such as father, wife, brother, or servant (fifteen times). The 101 sites and locations included places demarcated for specific action, such as meeting places or gallows; objects and buildings; unspecified areas, like 'the country'; as well as named entities, such as the county of Kent or the city of Rome.[14]

These designations suggest that the term clearly resonated with what historians have styled 'local social systems', the 'framework of social relations', the 'built environment' or 'urban landscape', 'locality', and the 'embodied state'.[15] It implied, in effect, a broadly defined sense of structure – social, architectural, and geographical – that impinged in important ways upon the way in which a body experienced and perceived the world. While deployed unsystematically and, for the most part, descriptively, the ubiquity of the term nevertheless points to a prevailing and early modern sense of the structural basis of society. In this its use was not confined to Shakespeare who, like any playwright of the period,

---

[13] Thomas Hobbes, *Decameron physiologicum: or, ten dialogues of natural philosophy* (1678), pp. 16–17.

[14] The figures are based on a survey of the plays in Stanley Wells and Gary Taylor, eds., *The Oxford Shakespeare: the complete works* (Oxford, 1994).

[15] Keith Wrightson and David Levine, *Poverty and piety in an English village: Terling, 1525–1700* (Oxford, 1995), ch. 4; Archer, *The pursuit of stability*; Tittler, *Architecture and power*, p. 3; Borsay, *English urban renaissance*, pp. 41–6; Phythian Adams, 'Introduction', p. 7; Braddick, *State formation*, pp. 1–47.

was in the business of both reflecting and developing the English vernacular. On the contrary, the word appears in a range of texts and genres of the time: sermons and advice books, histories and surveys, linguistic and architectural treatises, as well as records of everyday correspondence and conversation.[16] It also permeates most kinds of civic record, serving as a recurring and almost unconscious signifier of civic authority. In a single set of entries of the city 'house book' in York made in August 1612 five of the six entries were concerned directly with institutional or physical place. It was noted, for example, that the Lady Elizabeth Players, the acting company of the king's daughter, had arrived at the city with licence 'to play as given such houses or place . . . as in all most halls schoolhouses town halls within any other cities or towns within his Majesties Dominions'. As such, it was 'thought good to put them to play within this city in such place as they shall procure or get so as they do not play on the Sabbath days or the night time'. On the same day, two letters were written under the common seal of the city, one to the Privy Council, and another to the Earl of Northumberland, the High Steward of York. These refuted the claims of a citizen that 'he was unfit to undergo the charge and duty of these places' – that is, civic office – 'in respect of the infirmity of his body the disability of his estate and his utter abandoning of trade and residency here amongst us'. According to the common council, none of these claims was true, and they now looked to the authority of external place – the Privy Council – to enforce communal obligations.[17]

Places formed the social and material fabric of cities and boroughs: the roles, institutions, buildings, and territories that constituted them. This comprehensive sense of structure was pivotal to both the theory and practice of city commonwealth. An urban 'liberty' was, first and foremost, a territorial jurisdiction in which peculiar rights, customs, properties, and privileges granted to or claimed by burgesses were legitimate. In related fashion, 'freedom' was predicated on urban 'occupation': either of burghal property possessed by a burgess, or the economic trade or 'mystery' in which a freeman was apprenticed – and free to practise – within a given liberty. Civic 'office' was, in turn, an obligation of 'liberty' and 'freedom' that enabled – or demanded – male heads of enfranchised households to govern and represent the parishes, wards, guilds, and commonwealths in which they and their households were positioned. Theoretically at least, the liberty, freedom, and citizenship derived from city commonwealths were not qualities innate to the person so much as interconnected and reciprocal attributes, functions, and requirements of place. Indeed, most boroughs owed their fiscal evolution to the communal occupation and control of one or more

---

[16] For a recent survey see Griffiths, *Youth and authority*, pp. 63–71; Garrett A. Sullivan, Jr., *The drama of landscape: land, property, and social relations on the early modern stage* (Stanford, 1998); Wood, *Politics of social conflict*, pp. 1–10, 169–78.

[17] YCA B33, f313v, 314.

kinds of urban place: the levying of tolls at markets and fairs; the rents from walls, bridges, and other burghal property; or the local monopolies and exemptions of a guild merchant.[18] The centrality of place was nicely illustrated in Cambridge, a 'small commonwealth' with which Robert Brady, as a fellow of Caius College, would certainly have been acquainted. In 1613 the Cambridge common council asserted that 'divers charters by divers kings and queens [and] confirmed by his Majesty that now is' made the free burgesses of the borough 'chief lords of that soil immediately under the king'.[19] By 1650, it was no longer felt necessary to mention higher authority: the burgesses were simply 'lords of the soil'.[20] With or without the sanction of prerogative, land and liberty were synonymous. Certainly it enabled them to combat encroachments 'upon the wastes of the said town' and the erection of 'large and many stalls [and] shops . . . contrary to any of the customs and ordinances of this town and to the great hindrance and decay of rents and revenues of this town'.[21] With the benefits of property, however, came the responsibilities of citizenship. The common council of Cambridge observed in September 1638 that 'divers foreigners have admittance to the freedom of this town whereby they do enjoy all the liberties and privileges belonging to the same freedom', in particular 'the several possessions which they hold by virtue of the said freedom'. Despite these economic benefits, they 'are not . . . charged with any office or . . . burden of the town affairs so that the Town does not receive any ease or benefit from them'. To ease a situation that was both 'unreasonable and repugnant to the orders of this town', it was agreed 'that henceforth all such foreign burgesses shall stand eligible and be yearly chosen at either of the elections into any offices of this town' or pay a fine of £10.[22]

The conglomeration of households, neighbourhoods, and civic structures that ideally constituted city commonwealths were positioned in larger local environments: far from being coterminous with a city or town, they shared and contested urban space with other inhabitants and visitors. The borough of Cambridge was unusual in that it was located in a town in which the colleges and university constituted rival communities at once wealthier and better equipped politically. Cambridge burgesses did not possess magisterial authority, which was situated instead with the university officers, and their attempts to control and regulate manufacture and trade were constantly undermined by the productive, purchasing, and regulative powers of the university population and its affiliates. As a result, the corporation lacked any control over economic 'occupations' and was without the usual constituency of manufacturers and tradesmen who made

[18] Faraday, *Ludlow*, pp. 20–31; Maitland, *Township and borough passim*; Sarah Rees Jones, 'Property, tenure and rents: some aspects of the topography and economy of medieval York' (unpublished D. Phil., University of York, 1987). Wrightson, *Earthly necessities*, p. 79.
[19] CCRO, City Shelf C, Book 7, f. 30.   [20] CCRO, City Shelf C, Book 8, f. 24v.
[21] Ibid., f. 51v.   [22] CCRO, City Shelf C, Book 7, ff. 289, 289v.

up bodies of freemen.[23] In addition, the parochial structure of the town was not integrated into and responsive to corporate government: whereas in places like York and Ludlow poor relief and the constabulary were co-ordinated by common councils, in Cambridge the civic business of parishes was much more autonomous. As such, free burgesses constantly struggled to protect and justify what places and attendant rights they possessed in an often hostile urban environment. This infra-structural weakness explains the ritual of conflict between 'town' and 'gown' – a rivalry that, for enfranchised burgesses, extended beyond the 'rhetoric' of contest described by Alexandra Shepard.[24] It was also a feature of daily social interaction among inhabitants. For example, in 1595 Francis Clarke, free burgess and bailiff for the year, approached Hugh Jones, a parish constable, in an inn. As bailiff, Clarke was responsible for policing the city markets. Jones, it seems, had been infringing his jurisdiction. Clarke now confronted him, saying 'what a busy fellow art thou to deal in those things which thou has nothing to do in, as to take upon thou to place and displace folks in the market, which does not belong to thy office'. Jones in return accused Clarke of being a poor inmate, or lodger, rather than householder, questioning not only his personal status but also the legitimacy of the city commonwealth he served.[25]

The structural exceptionality of Cambridge illuminates those spatial configurations that characterised the corporate system as a whole. In the first instance, the liberty and freedom of city commonwealths were usually placed in direct proximity to other, potentially antagonistic communities and interests within the same urban area. The burgesses and citizens of Cambridge and Oxford interacted and competed with the populations of colleges and universities. From the City of London outwards, common councils across the corporate system were in perpetual negotiation with the inhabitants and office-holders of cathedral precincts; royal precincts, garrisons and castles; autonomous 'liberties'; civil and common law courts; and the town mansions and lands of noble and gentry families.[26] Second, across a civic liberty the authority and influence of common councils was exercised in conjunction with, and depended upon, other, smaller civic bodies: parishes, trade companies and guilds, wardmoots and officers.[27]

---

[23] Ibid., f. 50.

[24] Alexandra Shepard, 'Contesting communities? 'Town' and 'gown' in Cambridge, c.1560–1640', in Shepard and Withington, *Communities in early modern England*, p. 231; CCRO, City Shelf C, Book 7, f. 348v.

[25] Cited in Alexandra Jane Shepard, 'Meanings of manhood in early modern England with specific reference to Cambridge, c.1560–1640' (unpublished Ph.D. thesis, University of Cambridge, 1998), p. 88.

[26] Pearl, *London and the outbreak of the puritan revolution*, ch. 1; Evans, *Seventeenth-century Norwich*, ch. 3; D. M. Palliser, *Tudor York* (Oxford, 1979), pp. 88–90; Walter, *Understanding popular violence*, ch. 3.

[27] Archer, *Pursuit of stability*; Nick Allridge, 'Loyalty and identity in Chester parishes 1540–1640', in Susan Wright, ed., *Parish, church and people: local studies in lay religion 1350–1750* (London, 1988), pp. 84–124.

Participants in one were often participants in another: James Wright, baker of York, was not only a 'citizen of great respect' and 'one of the Commons of this City' but also a parish, ward, and guild officer, and common councillor.[28] John Bradford, while intermittently excluded from the corporation in Ludlow for his democratic sensibilities, was nevertheless a conscientious churchwarden and also the first burgess to act as a searcher of the poor after the passing of the Elizabethan statute.[29] However, these smaller corporate bodies also encouraged degrees of autonomy and communal agency within the civic nexus. The very viability of guild economies depended on a close relationship between companies and councils in terms of representation, arbitration, and the protection of interests.[30] Incorporated trading and manufacturing companies were particularly well placed to establish their own boundaries, monopolies, and metropolitan connections, and transpose their interests on to conciliar government.[31] In London and the larger cities, the politics of lobbying and 'private bills' extended to parliament itself.[32] Such bodies could constitute, as John Wildman argued, places of power that contravened the representational rights of enfranchised inhabitants in parish and ward.[33] That said, parochial opinion and representation could also be marshalled into a corporate and coherent interest, especially when galvanised by religious activists: a process captured in satirical pamphlets like *The Reformado* of 1642.[34] Certainly the degree of representation enjoyed by the 'puritan' parishioners of St Martin's in Micklegate in York was far in excess of their number. Third, given the complex and potentially conflicting structural configurations within cities and boroughs, the relative power of any civic body – corporation or otherwise – depended not only on its local dimensions but also the quality of its connections with external, and especially metropolitan, institutions and interests.[35] Positioned within a corporate system, city commonwealths were, by and large, intrinsically privileged in this respect. As 'fictional persons', they possessed a legal personality that transcended the lives of their participatory members, constituting bodies designed to be represented at court, law, and, in the majority of instances, parliament. As conduits of magistracy, their local authority was compounded by direct link

[28] Morrell, *Biography of the common man*, p. 79; BIHI, MF 1718 (Will of James Wright); PR Y/J 17, f. 22.

[29] HCRO, HD4/2/17, 1611, Joyce Larkin c. William Sherwood; SA, LB2/1/1, f. 39.

[30] Donald Woodward, *Men at work: labourers and building craftsmen in the towns of northern England, 1450–1750* (Cambridge, 1995).

[31] Jenny Kermode, *Medieval merchants*, ch. 2.

[32] David Dean, 'London lobbies and parliament: the case of the brewers and coopers in the parliament of 1593', *Parliamentary History*, 8/2, 1989, pp. 341–65; Withington, 'Two renaissances', p. 257.

[33] See above, ch. 3.   [34] *The Reformado* (1642).

[35] Tittler, 'Elizabethan towns and the "points of contact"', pp. 287–8; Patterson, *Urban patronage passim.*,

to monarchical sovereignty, marking the convergence, in effect, of *res*publican and prerogative power. The common council in Cambridge was always careful to cultivate its legal and parliamentary presence, appointing state officials as high stewards and vigorously working the bonds of parliamentary clientage – a relationship that courtiers were likewise keen to cultivate.[36] Bacon, Coventry, and Finch formed an impressively well-placed series of patrons by any standards.[37] However, the free burgesses' lack of magisterial authority could not be ignored. On one occasion, for example, Toby Wood shoved the leading burgess Thomas Smart in the chest and called him a 'pillory knave millerly knave', reminding him 'thou art no Justice of the Peace, thou art but a shitten Alderman, go Goodman shit breech'.[38] Attempts by the burgesses to address this anomaly by renewing their charter were, in turn, repeatedly undermined by university officers possessing an even more effective metropolitan presence than their own.[39]

Finally, and perhaps most significantly, the precarious position of free burgesses in Cambridge reveals the tenet lying at the heart of an Aristotelian notion of commonwealth: that civic places, whether aristocratic or democratic, should be attuned to and symbiotic with the households and neighbourhoods they governed and represented. In Cambridge, household, neighbourhood, and citizenship were far from synonymous or mutually reinforcing. Reasons for this included the absence of an integrated craft-guild economy; an unusually high number of absent or 'foreign' freemen; a large and transient population of university students and tradesmen drawn to the markets and fairs; and the social and economic influence of the colleges. Although a residential and productive 'core' of free burgesses undoubtedly existed, alternative political, social, and economic networks were more significant than in urban centres where burgesses enjoyed a more integrated sense of place.[40] This disjunction was problematic, as ideally it was the household that constituted the primary institution of commonwealth. Just as the usual ways of achieving urban freedom – through apprenticeship, paternalism, or residence – were predicated on household occupation, so civic position ideally reflected the 'credit' of not simply the head of household but also the other household members he represented.[41] Commentators emphasised that a 'well-ordered commonwealth' ideally depended on the orderly constitution of households and the ability of household members to learn and act their places.[42] Outwith the household, familial roles and the relationships they

---

[36] Kishlansky, *Parliamentary selection*, pp. 37–48.
[37] CCRO, City Shelf C, Book 7, ff. 76, 131v, 145v, 146, 171, 310, 325.
[38] Shepard, 'Meanings of manhood', p. 145.   [39] CCRO, City Shelf C, Book 7, f. 68v.
[40] Shepard, 'Contesting communities?', pp. 228–9.
[41] Muldrew, *Economy of obligation*, pp. 159–72.
[42] Susan Dwyer Amussen, *An ordered society: gender and class in early modern England* (Oxford, 1988); Margot Todd, *Christian humanism and the puritan social order* (Cambridge, 1987).

structured extended through networks of kin, commerce, credit, friendship, and, within the propinquity of the city, neighbourliness.[43] A neighbour was someone 'that dwells near us or next unto us, or in the same street'; 'of one household of faith with us, in the love and possession of the same Gospel'; and 'whatsoever he be, with whom we have any dealings in our fellowship and trade of life'.[44] Along with the household, neighbourhood was the primary social context of civic authority; and while Cambridge contained many households and neighbours, relatively few were either positioned or participatory in the city commonwealth.

Structural dynamics in Cambridge were replicated – in different forms, arrangements, and relationships – across the corporate system. In any city commonwealth, they contributed to a cumulative sense of place that was at once particular to locale and generic in its constitutive elements. In Ludlow, burgesses were fully integrated into the city commonwealth, claiming membership by inhabitancy and scot and lot as well as economic occupation. By no means a premier centre of consumption and exchange like Cambridge, and bereft of its medieval woollen industry, the borough nevertheless had a significant place in the economy of the Marches.[45] The governing corporation was well endowed with commons, lands, and properties since the absorption of the Palmers Guild in 1551; it also administered educational, religious, and charitable institutions. In addition to its corporate personality, it possessed parliamentary and magisterial status. Its single parochial boundary was contiguous and responsive to corporate governance; its liberty divided into wards based on the four main streets of the town; and the borough economy was organised into two trading and manufacturing guilds that subdivided into particular companies.[46] The local challenges to civic authority were significant, however, consisting of the Council of the Marches, which occasionally assembled in the castle precinct, and neighbouring gentry, who intermarried with burgesses and allied with the 'parties' during the troubled 1590s.[47] Other positions of authority within the city commonwealth included the parish living; legal offices within the corporation, such as recorder and town clerk; and the borough court, from where attorney Philip Bradford criticised oligarchic malpractice. However, it was the essential synonymy of commonwealth and town, especially when compared to a place like Cambridge, which was striking in Ludlow. This extended to the parliamentary sphere. Cambridge burgesses preferred to exploit clientage

---

[43] Naomi Tadmor, *Family and friends in eighteenth-century England: household, kinship, and patronage* (Cambridge, 2001), chs. 4, 5; Wrightson, *English society*, pp. 51–7.

[44] Robert Horne, *The Christian governor in the common-wealth and private families* (1614), p. 192.

[45] Williams, 'Government and politics in Ludlow', p. 282; Faraday, *Ludlow*, ch. 6.

[46] SA, LB2/1/1; LB17/1; LB17/2; LB17/3.

[47] HCRO, HD4/2/17, Guardians of Ludlow c. Rowland Higgins, 1639; TNA STAC 8/269/27; E134/39 and 440 Elizabeth/Mich. 37, deposition of Richard Rascall; Faraday, *Ludlow*, p. 141.

networks, entrusting their representation to qualified 'foreigners' recommended by the high steward of the moment: in this respect, the election of Cromwell at the behest of the godly party within the borough marked a significant break with recent custom. In contrast, the common council of early Stuart Ludlow was one of many boroughs that retained at least one of its two parliamentary places for its own burgesses and legal officers.[48]

This is not to suggest that Ludlow enjoyed structural equilibrium. The very comprehensiveness of its city commonwealth made for faction and division. As the previous chapter suggested, this was due not to differences between the free burgesses and competing urban interests but rather to conflict within the city commonwealth itself. While freedom in Cambridge had a relatively marginal place within the urban community it was nevertheless organised democratically.[49] In Ludlow, conflict over the democratic or aristocratic nature of the constitution made for a tumultuous beginning to the seventeenth century. For all this political turmoil, just what was meant to constitute the 'public good' was suggested by a set of articles entered into the borough's 'Red Book' in February 1591 and supplemented in June 1594.[50] Brokered by the Recorder of the borough and marking a compromise between the borough's warring parties, the articles made for a 'mixed' civic polity that was referred to repeatedly by the burgesses and their attorneys over the course of the decade as a suitable pretext for civic government. Their sense of place was tangible. The articles delineated a city commonwealth supremely conscious of its boundaries, resources, privileges, and civic processes. The basis of freedom was, for example, clarified. To become a burgess any inhabitant had to be 'thought worthy' and pay 'scot and lot' (that is, local rates). Charges for entry for those 'born out of the town' were set (after the next feast day) at £3 6s. 4d.; apprentices were to pay 20s.; and freedom by paternalism or marriage to a freeman's widow or daughter remained as 'accustomed'.[51] Manufacture and trading within the borough were to remain the preserve of burgesses and conducted openly. Only burgesses were to brew or bake; the selling of linen cloth was to be based in the guildhall 'and not to be suffered to be sold in any private house'; and burgesses were to remain 'free at our fairs and markets' as accustomed.[52] Their 'liberties' were to be 'yearly walked and trodden by the masters [office holders] and common burgesses' and 'our charter be read over in English once every third year . . . in the hearing of all the burgesses that shall come thereunto by the Town Clock'.[53] Before every perambulation 'our' common lands were 'to be given to the burgesses beforehand' and 'surveyed by the said commons and masters' and 'recorded on a ledger immediately after harvest'. The same commons were to be 'maintained and cast open after sickle and scythe' and 'if any person or persons shall presume

[48] Williams, 'Politics and government', pp. 289–90.   [49] Maitland and Bateson, Charters, p. xi.
[50] LB2/1/16.   [51] Ibid., item 6.   [52] Ibid., items 4, 5, 11, 15.   [53] Ibid., items 17, 19.

to enclose any of the commons, which of right ought to lie open . . . he or they shall be prosecuted by law'.[54] In similar vein, the granting of all lands was to be equitable and transparent: no burgess was to have more than three parcels of land, public meetings would be informed who held what lands, and outstanding leases checked, confirmed, and limited to twenty-one years under the common seal. Opponents of the 'articles regarding land' were to be prosecuted at law and costs met from the common treasury.[55]

This pronounced sense of an integrated and participatory place extended to the civic constitution. It was anticipated that, for the election of burgesses into the common council, the bailiffs would select seventeen of the 'most ablest, wisest, and discreet common burgesses' to 'deliver' the names of three burgesses to be considered by the common council 'to supply the room'.[56] Bailiffs would select eight of the 'wisest and discreet' burgesses to audit accounts, and as many burgesses as masters would set and collect assessments. As a supplement, the seventeen common burgesses were to 'have access and liberty to peruse in the Town Clerk's office all accompts as well of the receipts . . . for that year'.[57] 'None but burgesses' were to serve on juries and inquests; 'decent places' should be provided for sessions; and the 'presentment of affrays and blood' were to be placed on a regular and procedural footing.[58] A house of correction was 'to be devised . . . according to the statute'. Moreover, admittance to the borough almshouses was to be limited to the 'aged and impotent' and those who 'spent their youth in the town'. While occasional searches would expel those 'thought not necessary by the company', the 'doors [were] to be locked every night at nine . . . and a key keeper appointed to shut and open the same'.[59] Finally, in the spirit of the Edwardian charter that had placed the Palmers' Guild under the liberty of the burgesses, a bailiff and ten 'discreet brethren of the company' were to inspect the material and intellectual fabric of the grammar school. Accompanied by 'the parson, preacher or some other learned man', they would check the state of the building and 'by convenient means try and examine how the free scholars of the said school do proceed and profit in their learning by the good industry of the schoolmaster'. It was also expected that 'from henceforth every morning and evening the scholars do sing among themselves to the glory of God some short psalm of David in metre verse as is used in the free school for the Town of Salop'.[60]

The burgesses envisaged, in short, the city commonwealth as a place that was judicious, reformed, discrete, and, for the freemen and burgesses enfranchised to it, accountable and participatory. Its boundaries were clear and protected; relations between household, neighbourhood, and the civic realm symbiotic; common and private interest appropriately balanced; and its constitution mixed

[54] Ibid., items 17, 18.   [55] Ibid., items 22, 23, 24, 25, 26.   [56] Ibid., item 1.
[57] Ibid., items 2, 3.   [58] Ibid., items 7, 10, 21.   [59] Ibid., 13, 14.   [60] Ibid., item 27.

between 'masters' and 'commons'. The rights, liberty, and property of the person were communal attributes rooted in active participation in the city commonwealth and the civic culture by which it was governed and represented. Variations on the mixed civic polity were found across the corporate system, participation in which defined the public identity of freemen. York, for example, was a different kind of place to either Ludlow or Cambridge. Endowed with a county jurisdiction, containing twenty-six administrative parishes as well as a functioning guild economy, serving as an ecclesiastical and provincial centre, the city was described by Postmaster General Whitley in 1673 as 'one of the greatest spheres in England'.[61] Whereas urban citizenship was marginal in Cambridge and contested in Ludlow, in York a properly 'mixed' civic polity that formally combined democratic and aristocratic elements remained a pivotal and relatively straightforward source of urban authority and identity throughout the period.[62] Corporate power was organised into the mayoral office and aldermanic bench; a 'privy-council' of ex-sheriffs; the shrieval office, with close connections to the borough court; and a common council of seventy-two drawn equally from the four wards of the city. The infrastructure was complemented by eight annually elected chamberlains – young citizens responsible for city finances – and the twenty-four jurors chosen four times a year to attend the quarter sessions. The city was also constituted by other powerful urban interests: as Whitley continued, 'besides the business of the city' there existed 'the Archbishopric, the Chancellors Court, and all their dependencies; the Garrison, and many other advantages' for a postmaster connecting these interests to London.[63] It was perceived encroachments by cathedral, gentry, crown, or army that were most likely to enflame a collective civic consciousness that derived from strong and effective connections between civic structures and the households and neighbourhoods they governed, forming a participatory culture reminiscent of England's other 'great' and 'ancient' cities.[64] Civic practice was based in parish, ward, guild, and quarter session as well as corporation, providing a plethora of public forums and offices for a large number of heads of enfranchised households. The councils of the corporation were positioned above these smaller civic groupings, providing representation, legislation, and arbitration for different interests and also linking the city to the larger corporate system. The result was a palimpsest of semi-autonomous civic bodies: a city commonwealth in which common councillors were also parishioners, jurymen,

[61] PORO, PO 94/12, Whitley to Rigden, 24 July 1673.
[62] For outlines see Palliser, *Tudor York*, ch. 3; B. M. Wilson, 'The corporation of York 1580–1660' (unpublished M.Phil., University of York, 1967); Withington, 'Urban political culture in later seventeenth-century England: York 1649–1689' (unpublished Ph.D., University of Cambridge, 1998), chs. 2, 3.
[63] PORO, PO 94/12, Whitley to Rigden, July 24 1673.
[64] Slack, 'Great and good towns', pp. 243–5.

and freemen, and in which a large proportion of corporate time was spent either responding to the petitions of guilds, parishes, and householders or intervening in local disputes and conflicts. This interpenetration was exemplified by the poor rate: administered and collected on a weekly basis by parishioners, but overseen and redistributed by the corporation from the council chamber on Ouse Bridge.[65] It was also reflected in the lexicography of status. The term 'elite', which today carries generalised connotations of wealth, status, and power, was derived specifically from the electoral procedures in parish, ward, and corporation. In York, urban 'elites' were those citizens, usually three, selected by the greater part of a civic body to be considered for office by the body's head.[66] Likewise the appellation of 'master', noted by Sir Thomas Smith as signifying England's new gentility 'made cheap', was also an attribute of civic participation. Much to the chagrin of local gentry, in York men only earned the right to be called 'master' after serving as city chamberlain, the most junior civic office: a custom that, as late as the 1730s, 'vulgar' citizens were energetic in enforcing.[67]

The very different city commonwealths of Cambridge, Ludlow, and York raise important questions about just how 'formal' and 'inauthentic' civic nomenclature was for those enfranchised householders who participated in, and contested and appropriated, the places that the language of citizenship signified. That is not to argue that city commonwealth formed the only, or even predominant, source of self-identification for freemen, burgesses, and citizens.[68] However, it was certainly part of the mix: one forged by the quite precise powers, rights, rituals, conflicts, and exclusions associated with this particular kind of community. The different places of civic participation provided the fullest possible context in which a personal and (as Hobbes would have stressed) relative sense of civic identity developed. The pinner John Fawcett and tailor William Smith, for example, were never in a position to hold corporate office. However, when stopped by soldiers in 1651 and asked 'what they were' both replied that 'they were citizens': 'lawful men' going 'about their occasions'.[69] The bakers, wine-coopers, carpenters, joiners, and tailors of York who in their wills described themselves as 'citizens of York' never dreamed of sitting on the aldermanic bench.[70] However, they were well acquainted with the more humble and interconnected sites of parish, ward, and guild governance. Across the neighbourhoods of the city there existed significant enclaves and networks of enfranchised householders who, while never considered the elites of the corporation, were elites of lesser civic bodies, performing and

---

[65] Withington, 'Views from the bridge', pp. 132–3.   [66] Ibid., p. 129.

[67] Smith, *De Republica Anglorum*, p. 27; Francis Drake, *Eboracum* (1736), p. 183.

[68] Allridge, 'Loyalty and identity', pp. 84–5.   [69] TNA ASSI 45 4/1.

[70] Withington, 'Urban political culture', p. 46.

acting in public positions that were only one or two mediated steps from the highest offices. Solidarity was further inured through networks of friendship, kinship, and neighbourliness.[71] James Wright, for example, called upon neighbours Richard Baines and Edward Cowper to be executors of his will. One was a merchant, the other an alderman; and both men were significantly wealthier than Wright.[72] This sense of place was apparent even for someone like William Smith. The son of a York citizen, Smith was a renowned petty criminal of the early 1660s who was eventually transported to Virginia while still an apprentice in order to protect him from appearing before the city magistrates. Assumed to have died in transit, Smith was nevertheless spotted by Catherine Lupton, a friend of his mother's, at Billingsgate almost twenty years later, in 1680. Lupton asked him 'what Smith he was and where he was born'. Smith answered 'I am William Smith, son of York and born in St Andrews Gate'.[73]

Household, neighbourhood, and citizenship

The different structural configurations of Cambridge, Ludlow, and York were reflected in the number and distribution of enfranchised households and neighbourhoods in each. An unusually detailed hearth tax return for Cambridge from 1664 highlights the somewhat precarious position of this particular body of freemen within the wider urban milieu.[74] Although the number of enfranchised Cambridge burgesses residing in the town is unknown, a conservative estimate, based simply on the number of free burgesses named in the corporate minutes in 1661 and 1662, suggests a figure of 120 (an underestimate dictated by the nature of the source).[75] Given that the 1664 hearth tax listed 1,667 households, then the freedom encompassed only 7 per cent of the urban population. Neither was this urban population stable. The 1664 hearth tax return included two surveys of the town, the latter coming six months after the former. A comparison of the two shows that, in the course of one year, 324 places of occupancy – 19 per cent – changed hands. While a third of new occupancies involved Cambridge inhabitants either moving to other places or acquiring additional property within the town, the remaining two-thirds were new inhabitants. This sense of flux was accentuated on the hearth tax return by the inclusion, in the second survey, of 456 entries that were not recorded at the beginning of the year. These 'new' entries, which mostly consisted of one or two hearth tenements, made up 27 per cent of the full list of entries. Half of them were noted as unable to contribute

[71] Shani D'Cruze, 'The middling sort in eighteenth-century Colchester: independence, social relations and the community broker', in Barry and Brooks, Middling sort of people, pp. 181–207; Tadmor, Family and friends, p. 165.
[72] BIHR MF1718, 'Will of James Wright'.
[73] BIHR CPH 3497, 1681, Jane Mabson c. William Richardson and Ann Saltmarsh.
[74] TNA E179/84/437.   [75] CCRO, City Shelf C, Book 8.

to the hearth tax, swelling the ranks of the town's 'poor' households to 326. At almost 20 per cent of the urban population, this represented a significantly larger proportion of locations than that occupied by the (conservatively) estimated number of free burgesses. That is not to say that there was a total absence of continuity. Of a parliamentary subscription list of 1641, which named 250 of Cambridge's wealthiest inhabitants, seventy-two heads of household still lived in the town twenty-four years later.[76] Discounting the Smiths, Coopers, Cooks, Greens, and Johnsons too numerous to trace, so did a further seventy local family names: the likely offspring and kin of the previous generation. Given the complexities of familial and kinship relations, this local genealogy was probably more significant than this estimated 30 per cent survival rate suggests. Even so, it was unlikely to have been much in excess of 10 per cent of the urban population, confirming Nigel Goose's impression of a town full of small households showing little sign of relationships of kin or the development of lineage over generations.[77] Moreover, free burgesses, or at least those listed in the civic records for 1661 and 1662, accounted for only just over a third of these 'core households', emphasising once again the disjunction between the city commonwealth and the larger urban economy.

The instability of place within Cambridge was all the greater because of the recent political troubles. As in other corporate towns, the Restoration brought a relatively rapid replacement of councillors and aldermen who had been energetic in supporting the parliamentary and Protectorate regimes. Authorised either by commission or by the threat of *quo warranto* proceedings, county gentlemen aided loyal townsmen in securing positions on the common council and aldermanic bench. Legal and parliamentary places were also targeted, as were seats on sessions' juries and other locations of civic authority. Struggles for civic place had long been a feature of the politics of commonwealth, and the 1640s and 1650s had seen similar state-sanctioned purges. However, manoeuvres at the Restoration were the more notable for their systematic nature, the retributive attitude of local gentry, the influence of partisan divisions inherited from the 1640s and 1650s, and the unprecedented use of parliamentary statute to co-ordinate policy.[78] With its Cromwellian associations, the corporation in Cambridge was particularly vulnerable, and the purge came in the summer of 1662. Alderman Samuel Spalding, who had opposed the corporation's support of 'the parliament power', exacted political revenge on his rival, Thomas French, by displacing him as mayor; seven additional aldermen were removed from office; and fourteen common councillors joined them. A further fifteen

[76] William Matlock Palmer, ed., *Cambridgeshire subsidy roles 1250–1695* (Norwich, 1912), pp. 70–3; Phythian Adams, 'An agenda', p. 19.

[77] Nigel Goose, 'Household size and structure in early Stuart Cambridge' in Barry, ed., *The Tudor and Stuart town*, p. 117.

[78] Halliday, *Dismembering the body politic*, chs. 3, 4.

Table 4.1 *Distribution of wealth in Cambridge in 1664*

Number of hearths	Distribution in town (1667 households) %	Distribution among free burgesses (121 households) %
1 to 2	59	36
3 to 6	32	39
7 to 10	5	18
Over 11	2	7
Total	98	100

Sources: CCRO, City Shelf C, Book 8; PRO E179/84/437.

burgesses subsequently surrendered corporate leases. Of the civic replacements, five aldermen and six common councillors had not previously been sworn members of the body of freemen, although a significant minority had lived in the town throughout the revolutionary era.[79]

It should be reiterated that the relative position of the city commonwealth in Cambridge meant that the number of persons involved in this politics represented only a fraction of the urban population. However, in terms of their material status they provide a useful insight into the wealth of free burgesses in relation to the rest of the town. Table 4.1 suggests that, across Cambridge, the majority of householders owned either 1-to-2 or 3-to-6 hearths respectively, with only 7 per cent of householders owning seven hearths or more. The generality of free burgesses – that is, enfranchised householders without civic office – more or less replicated this pattern, clustering in the lower two hearth brackets but also including a fair proportion of 7-to-10 hearth owners. In terms of wealth, therefore, free burgesses constituted a differentiated community within Cambridge rather than a particular class of tax-paying inhabitant. As Table 4.2 demonstrates, common councillors who preceded the Restoration reflected this constituency, being primarily drawn from the second hearth bracket. Aldermen were more often, though not exclusively, positioned in the third echelon. In contrast, a much higher proportion of inhabitants who became aldermen and common councillors at the Restoration were positioned in the upper two strands of urban society. This suggests that while civic authority had previously been dominated by middling inhabitants within the city, the Restoration witnessed an elevation in the status of civic office-holders. While a result of the immediate political situation, this was a shift that Caroline statesmen had pushed for – and which councillors in Cambridge had consistently resisted – throughout the 1630s.[80]

[79] CCRO, City Shelf C, Book 8, ff. 153–4.   [80] CCRO, City Shelf C, Book 7, f. 218.

Table 4.2 *Wealth and civic office-holding in Cambridge at the Restoration*

Number of hearths	Surviving aldermen	Excluded aldermen	New aldermen	Surviving common councillors	Excluded common councillors	New common councillors
	%	%	%	%	%	%
1 to 2	0	0	0	33	9	7
3 to 6	20	43	14	33	82	64
7 to 10	60	43	29	33	0	7
Over 11	20	14	57	0	9	21
Total	100	100	100	99	100	99

Sources: CCRO, City Shelf C, Book 8; PRO E179/84/437.

Households in seventeenth-century Cambridge formed a volatile topography in which the city commonwealth was as demographically marginal and unstable as it was functionally deficient. Comparison with Ludlow in the 1590s and 1660s is illuminating. While the topography of Elizabethan Ludlow was hardly stable, it was also different to Cambridge in important respects. Although it is impossible to be precise, an estimated 450 households lived in the Shropshire market town during the 1590s: a figure in line with Michael Faraday's estimate based on the parish register.[81] The figure is derived from a tax assessment of 1595; the number of burgesses registered as freemen between 1557 and 1600; and those inhabitants who either petitioned against oligarchy in the 1590s or were accused, alternatively, of oligarchic connections.[82] On this basis, it appears that 184 male heads of household were enfranchised to the corporation; 153 were inhabitants prosperous enough to be financially assessed; and 69 were both. Over the 1590s, 13 per cent of the population participated in civic office, either as aldermen and common councillors or as other, annually elected officers.[83] Those who were at once freemen and taxpaying inhabitants dominated this civic realm, making up half of the corporation's sixty office-holders. If this suggests that an authoritative place in the city commonwealth derived from the conjunction of economic and residential occupancy, then it is worth bearing in mind that a significant number of office-holders appear to have been either freemen or taxpayers, not both. Moreover, thirty-six persons who were neither one nor the other also participated in the frenetic politics that characterised the town. They did so not as common councillors but as affiliates of the aristocratic and democratic parties contesting civic resources. Four persons without an obvious place in the city commonwealth were listed among the thirty-eight kinsmen, friends,

[81] Faraday, *Ludlow*, p. 180.
[82] SA, LB7/2224; LB7/734; LB7/738; LB7/745; LB7/751, LB Fiche 1, 2–3.   [83] SA, LB2/1/1.

Table 4.3 *Wealth and civic allegiances in Elizabethan Ludlow*

Class of taxpayer in Ludlow	Aristocrat in Ludlow		Democrats in Ludlow		Aristocratic councillors		Democratic councillors		Neutral councillors	
	Nos.	%	Nos.	%	Nos.	%	Nos.	%	Nos.	%
2 to 8 pence			28	33			2	15	1	8
10 to 20 pence	8	33	51	61	5	24	7	54	7	58
Over 20 pence	16	67	4	5	16	76	4	31	4	33
Total	24	100	83	99	21	100	13	100	12	99

Sources: SA, LB2/1/1; LB7/2224; LB7/734; LB7/738; LB7/745; LB7/751.

and allies who constituted the oligarchic faction; thirty-two 'un-placed' persons joined the 141 petitioners or demonstrators against oligarchy between 1593 and 1600.[84] This wider politics of commonwealth embroiled, in effect, 40 per cent of the town's populace: over the course of the decade, 8 per cent of the town was involved in the local aristocratic network, 32 per cent were democrats, and the remaining two-thirds of households were apparently neutral. The problem for the popular party was that, while they were a major interest in the town, they controlled only 30 per cent of the common council. This was in comparison to the 47 per cent share enjoyed by the aristocrats and the further 23 per cent of councillors who remained uncommitted to either side.

In contrast to seventeenth-century Cambridge, therefore, city commonwealth in Elizabethan Ludlow was a central and defining aspect of urban culture: a presence with mutable and contested boundaries, the politics of which extended far beyond the formal civic realm. This politics was closely connected to economic and geographical place. As table 4.3 shows, among resident taxpayers the division between democrats and aristocrats was clearly related to differences in wealth: not between rich and poor, or even between common councillors and the larger body of inhabitants, but between the wealthiest and middling householders within the town.

Over two-thirds of Ludlow's aristocrats were in the highest class of taxpayer; in contrast, a third of democrats were in the lowest bracket and almost two-thirds in the middle bracket. These distinctions were replicated in the common council, although the fact that neutral councillors had almost an identical economic profile to democrats warns against regarding political differences as purely economic. They were also reflected geographically, though in slightly different ways. Table 4.4 shows the distribution of wealth across Ludlow's four wards. On each street the wealthier residents were a minority. In Broad Street and Old Street, the middle bracket predominated; in Corve Street and Castle

[84] SA, LB7/734; LB7/738; LB7/745; LB7/751; E134/39 and 440 Elizabeth/Mich. 37.

Table 4.4 *Topographies of wealth in Elizabethan Ludlow*

Class of taxpayer	Broad Street		Old Street		Corve Street		Castle Street	
	Nos.	%	Nos.	%	Nos.	%	Nos.	%
2 to 8 pence	14	27	24	35	24	44	18	40
10 to 20 pence	32	63	39	57	24	44	20	44
Over 20 pence	5	10	5	7	6	11	7	16
Total	51	100	68	99	54	99	45	100

Sources: SA, LB2/1/1; LB7/2224; LB7/734; LB7/738; LB7/745; LB7/751.

Table 4.5 *Neighbourhood and politics in Elizabethan Ludlow*

Class of taxpayer	Corve Street				Old Street			
	Democrats		Common councillors		Democrats		Common councillors	
	Nos.	%	Nos.	%	Nos.	%	Nos.	%
2 to 8 pence	6	30	0	0	8	35	1	14
10 to 20 pence	11	55	1	11	15	65	1	14
Over 20 pence	3	15	8	89	0	0	5	71
Total	20	100	9	100	23	100	7	99

Sources: SA, LB7/2224; LB2/1/1; LB7/734; LB7/738; LB7/745; LB7/751.

Street, there was an even distribution of first- and second-class taxpayers. Table 4.5 suggests that the structure of politics varied accordingly. In all the wards, common councillors were drawn predominantly from the upper tax bracket and democrats from the first and especially second class of taxpayer. However, while in Corve Street and Castle Street democrats also numbered among the wealthiest inhabitants, in Old Street and Broad Street they were excluded, the wealthiest inhabitants instead forming aristocratic neighbourhoods within the larger urban milieu.

By 1667, Ludlow was a different kind of place. This might be a chimera born of the evidence: without explicit statements of aristocratic or democratic sentiment, it is impossible to know what happened to political divisions in the intervening years. Available material instead includes a 1667 poll tax – which gives detailed information about the household wealth, structure, and occupations of inhabitants – and somewhat cursory borough and guild records: official documents hardly designed to reflect deep-seated political animosities.[85]

[85] M. A. Faraday, 'The Ludlow poll-tax return of 1667', *Transactions of the Shropshire Archaeological Society*, 59, 1971–72; LB2/1/1.

Table 4.6 *Household, wealth, and occupation in Ludlow in 1667*

Occupation/status	Heads of household nos.	Average paid per house shilling	Proportion of population %	Proportion of town wealth %
Female heads	42	2	7	4
Victuals	34	4	12	5
Services	15	13	6	8
Merchants	6	4	2	1
Artisan manufacturers	36	4	10	6
Artisan builders	22	3	6	2
Cloth (trade/manufacture)	60	3	18	8
Leather (trade/manufacture)	31	4	11	4
Gentlemen	22	20	6	18
Yeomen	20	3	5	2
Labourers	48	2	8	3
Titular	12	64	3	30
Unrecorded	70	3	7	9
TOTAL	418	6	101	100

Source: M. A. Faraday, 'The Ludlow poll-tax return of 1667', *Shropshire Archaeological Society* 59,1917–2.

What they do provide, however, is a fairly nuanced snapshot of a small urban community and the place of city commonwealth within it.

Table 4.6 divides the taxpaying population according to occupation and/or status. The labels 'gentlemen', 'labourer', and 'yeomen' were all used on the tax list; the remaining categories conflate occupational or other kinds of social description. The first column shows the number of households who paid tax. The second column shows the mean amount of tax paid by each household according to occupation or status. The third column shows the percentage of all town inhabitants belonging to each group (including spouses, children, kin, servants, apprentices, and journeymen). Column four demonstrates, finally, the percentage of town wealth (as suggested by the tax) in each group. Together they show that wealth in the town was concentrated in three groups that accounted for only a minority of the town's population: 'service' households (barbers, physicians, booksellers, scriveners, schoolmasters, clerics, carriers, and innkeepers); self-styled 'gentlemen'; and, in particular, titular households (esquire and above). Indeed, the latter accounted for almost a third of the tax and only 3 per cent of the population. At the other end of the spectrum were labouring and female households, although gradations between all the lower and more populous groups were much less pronounced.

The poll tax suggests, then, a fairly typical market town of the Restoration era: one dominated by a minority of magnates, gentry, and professionals; populated by a broad 'middling sort' of artisans, tradesmen, and yeomen; and containing a large bottom tier of labourers, spinsters, and widows. Although the city commonwealth had become more stratified, it had not disappeared. By the 1660s a clear distinction existed between the civic councillors and officers who formed its governing body; a larger number of burgesses enfranchised to the corporation; and the freemen who participated within – and were governed by – its craft guilds. In 1667, councillors and officers accounted for around 6 per cent of the town's heads of household and burgesses a further 15 per cent. Freemen – all those legitimately practising a trade within the town – accounted for a further 45 per cent of household-heads.[86] Most identifiable in this respect were the 'Hammermen', the guild controlling artisan crafts, and the 'Stitchers', the guild controlling those involved not only in the cloth and leather trades but also mercantile activity more generally. In both its political and economic roles, therefore, city commonwealth remained an important presence within the town. Moreover, as table 4.7 suggests, its key participants were drawn not from titular households so much as guild members: those involved in leather and cloth, as well as 'gentlemen' merchants and service 'professionals'. That the 'gentlemen' in question were two mercers, a haberdasher, a glover, and an ironmonger further suggests the close link between civic governance and economy – a link confirmed by the fact that the distribution of apprentices and journeymen remained closely linked to freedom and citizenship. The survival of the Hammermen in turn provided artisan manufacturers and builders with a civic forum, albeit one subjected to conciliar authority in a way that Newcastle guilds (for example) were not.[87] An estimated 75 per cent of 'Stitchers' and 59 per cent of Hammermen were involved in civic business in the 1660s. In contrast, women and labourers joined unenfranchised gentry, lawyers, and magnates by being firmly excluded from this civic terrain.

As in Cambridge, the Restoration had a significant impact on the social profile of civic office-holding. The commissioners of the 1662 Corporation Act displaced seventeen burgesses from office and placed fifteen new ones, including three of the gentry responsible for the purge. By 1667, nine displaced and nine placed burgesses were resident in the borough. A further twenty-seven burgesses survived the purge, twenty-two of whom were still participants in civic government at the time of the poll tax. The discrepancies in wealth between displaced, placed, and remaining burgesses likewise echoed the situation in Cambridge. Paying an average of only 4s. to the tax, those displaced from office were significantly less wealthy than either the incomers or, in particular, the civic survivors: the former paid an average of 9s., the latter 16s. Those

[86] SA, LB2/1/2; LB17/1–3.   [87] See below, ch. 6.

Table 4.7 *Economy and office-holding in Ludlow in 1667*

Occupation/status	Apprentices (nos. 44) %	Journeymen (nos. 15) %	Councillors resident (nos. 25) %	Officers resident (nos. 25) %	Burgesses resident (nos. 64) %
Female heads	0	0	0	0	0
Victuals	8	0	4	8	6
Services	0	0	16	16	11
Merchants	9	0	8	8	6
Artisan manufacturers	14	13	4	4	5
Artisan builders	9	0	0	0	3
Cloth (trade/ manufacture)	34	67	12	12	20
Leather	18	20	20	12	17
Gentlemen	9	0	20	24	14
Yeomen	0	0	4	0	5
Labourers	0	0	0	0	0
Titular	0	0	4	0	3
Unrecorded	0	0	8	16	9
TOTAL	101	100	100	100	99

Sources: M. A. Faraday, 'The Ludlow poll-tax return of 1667', *Shropshire Archaeological Society,* 59, 1971–2; SA, LB2/1/2.

displaced also came from occupational groups underrepresented in common council: they included a distiller, a maltster, and a weaver.[88] Although city commonwealth in Ludlow survived the Restoration, it seems the possibility of democracy did not.

In the mixed polity of York, in contrast, enfranchised householders remained socially distinct and demographically dominant throughout the seventeenth century. That said, there was undoubted differentiation in levels of corporate participation, some neighbourhoods containing more freemen – or freemen with better access to corporate authority – than other areas of the city. A snapshot of residential patterns in each of the city's four quarters illuminates this variability. It also provides a fairly precise sense of the place of citizens within the larger urban environment. It can be taken by combining surviving parochial tax lists with the names of contributors to the poor rate and its recipients. The result can be seen in table 4.8, which shows the household profiles of four York parishes during the 1660s: St Trinity Goodramgate in Monk Ward, Peter Little in Walmgate Ward, St Martin's and Gregories in Micklegate Ward, and

---

[88] Faraday, ed., 'The Ludlow poll-tax return of 1667'; SA, LB2/1/2.

Table 4.8 *Household distribution in four York parishes during the 1660s*

Parishioners	Belfrey Bootham 1665		Martin's Micklegate 1666		Peter Little Walmgate 1660		Trinity Goodramgate Monk 1663	
	Nos.	%	Nos.	%	Nos.	%	Nos.	%
All households	146		59		86		60	
Relieved poor	8	5	2	3	10	12	12	20
Ratepayers	88	60	38	64	24	28	17	28
Free households	117	80	37	63	54	63	34	57
Female households	18	12	12	20	19	22	13	22
Non-free households	11	8	10	17	13	15	12	20

Source: See fn. 89.

St Michael le Belfrey in Bootham Ward.[89] Each of the assessments was raised for different purposes, and so cannot be used to compare in any precise fashion the wealth of each parish. However, when combined with records of poor relief and freemen's records, they provide as comprehensive a framework as possible for comparing residential patterns in parishes located in the four quarters of the city.[90] Table 4.8 shows that, in each of the four parishes, enfranchised households predominated, constituting as much as 80 per cent of houses in the Michael le Belfrey in Bootham to just under 60 per cent in Trinity Goodramgate in Monk.

Female-headed households – usually the widows of citizens – were the second largest category; and tables 4.8 and 4.9 demonstrate that it was female householders who most usually received poor relief and least often paid assessments. This is not to argue that female-headed households were invariably impoverished: the two largest inns in St Martin's were owned by Mrs Key and Mrs Hey, for example, while across the city women could be prominent ratepayers. Nevertheless, male-headed houses without the freedom formed a slightly larger proportion of ratepaying households to women but a smaller number overall, emphasising the extent to which citizens and their dependants dominated each of these different areas of the city. The tables also show that those either receiving or contributing to poor relief, while by and large dominated by freemen and female householders, nevertheless formed only a proportion of the population of each parish. A majority of householders in Goodramgate and

[89] Trinity Goodramgate, Monk Ward: BIHI, Y/HTG 15 (assessment for constable 1665); Peter Little, Walmgate: BIHR, CPH 2542, Samuel Buck c. William Green (for wages for parish clerk); Martin's Micklegate: BIHR, PR.Y/MG 19 (parish subscription for 1666); Michael le Belfrey, Bootham: BIHR, Y/MB 34 (churchwardens' assessment for 1665).
[90] Collins, *Register*; YCA Series E (1653–78).

Table 4.9 *Poor households in four York parishes during the 1660s*

Parish	Relieved poor Nos.	Freemen Nos.	%	Women Nos.	%	Non-free Nos.	%
Belfrey 1665	8	2	25	5	63	1	13
Martin's 1666	2	1	50	1	50	0	0
Peter Little 1660	10	6	60	4	40	0	0
Trinity Goodramgate 1663	12	1	8	8	67	3	25

Sources: BIHI, Y/HTG 15; CPH 2542; PR.Y/MG 19; Y/MB 34; Francis Collins, ed., *Register of the freemen of the city of York, II, 1559–1759* (Durham, 1900); YCA Series E (1653–1678).

Table 4.10 *Occupations in four York parishes during the 1660s*

Occupation of households	Belfrey 1665 %	Martin's 1666 %	Peter Little 1661 %	Trinity Goodramgate 1663 %
Female heads of house	12	20	22	22
Victuals	8	2	10	5
Services	5	0	2	3
Merchants	12	32	6	5
Artisan manufactures	8	5	6	2
Artisan builders	1	5	7	7
Cloth trade and industry	24	7	20	15
Leather trade and industry	5	3	1	3
Free labourers	2	0	0	2
Unknown	16	8	10	15
Not free	8	17	15	22
Total	101	99	99	101

Sources: BIHI, Y/HTG 15; CPH 2542; PR.Y/MG 19; Y/MB 34; Francis Collins, ed., *Register of the freemen of the city of York* (Durham, 1900); YCA Series E (1653–1678).

Peter Little neither gave nor received money, while a third of occupants were exempt from the process in the wealthier parishes of Belfrey and Martin's.

The parishes can be regarded as fairly representative of the wards in which they were located. Records of poor relief and a more reliable hearth tax from 1671 suggests that Monk Ward, in the shadow of the Minster, contained by far the highest number of poor in the city as well as a higher number of unenfranchised households than other wards.[91] Bootham and Walmgate were at once the

[91] YCA, E80 (1671).

Table 4.11 *A snapshot of corporate participation in four York parishes in the 1660s*

Parish	Population nos.	Free nos.	Jurors nos.	Chamberlains nos.	Sheriffs nos.	Magistrates nos.
Martin's 1666	59	37	4	2	1	2
Belfrey 1665	146	117	6	0	0	1
Peter Little 1661	86	52	4	0	0	0
Trinity Goodramgate 1663	60	34	1	0	0	0

Sources: BIHI, Y/HTG 15; CPH 2542; PR.Y/MG 19; Y/MB 34; Francis Collins, ed., *Register of the freemen of the city of York* (Durham, 1900); Phil Withington, *Urban political culture*, ch. 3.

most populous and commercially active of the four wards, while Micklegate, separated from the rest of the city by the River Ouse, had the highest proportion of merchants, corporation land, and civic mansions. These patterns were reflected in the occupational profiles of the four parishes. The greatest concentration of occupational specialisation was among the merchants, mercers, and grocers of St Martin's in Micklegate. Moreover, of this mercantile network, three-quarters were merchants involved in long-distance trade. In Michael le Belfrey, a similar number of traders formed a much smaller proportion of the parish economy. In contrast to St Martin's, it was mercers and grocers rather than merchants who made up four-fifths of the mercantile community. As the most populous and urbane of the four parishes, Michael le Belfrey also had the most variegated of the four economies as well as the highest number and proportion of service, manufacturing, and clothworking households. The book trade was concentrated in Minster Yard, just as there were more apothecaries and barbers than elsewhere. In contrast, female household-heads were in the majority in Trinity Goodramgate along with householders not enfranchised to the city commonwealth.

Tables 4.11 and 4.12 illuminate, finally, the variations in corporate office-holding across the four parishes. Most apparent is the degree of participation in St Martin's compared to elsewhere. Although almost three times smaller than the Belfrey, and with a much smaller population of enfranchised households, more heads of household nevertheless served either as juror, chamberlain, sheriff, or magistrate. Almost a quarter of residents in St Martin's were involved in corporate governance in 1666 compared to only 6 per cent in the Belfrey a year earlier, 8 per cent in Peter Little in 1661, and only 3 per cent in Trinity Goodramgate in 1663. Table 4.12 suggests that this difference in participation was reflective of long-term patterns. While St Martin's was the best represented of any parish in the city, it is also indicative of four more general trends

Table 4.12 *An aggregate of corporate office-holding in four York parishes,*
1649 to 1689

Parish	Jurors 1649 to 1670	Chamberlains 1649 to 1673	Sheriffs 1649 to 1689	Privy Council 1649 to 1689	Magistrates 1649 to 1689
Martin's	55	23	13	19	9
Belfrey	100	33	16	8	4
Peter	20	3	1	1	0
Trinity	17	1	2	1	2

Sources: YCA, Series B (1649–1689), F7, F8; BIHI, Y/HTG 15; CPH 2542; PR.Y/MG 19; Y/MB
34; Withington, 'Urban Political Culture', ch. 3.

regarding corporate office-holding in York. First, corporate office-holders were
concentrated in the parishes adjacent to the Micklegate and Walmgate thor-
oughfares that converged on the council chamber on Ouse Bridge: All Saints
on the Pavement, St Michael in Spurriergate, St Johns on Ouse Bridge, and
St Martin's and Gregories itself. Second, merchants tended to dominate the
higher places of corporate governance: while the Belfrey and to a lesser extent
Peter Little had good representation among jurors and chamberlains, highest
office was monopolised not by craftsmen, artisans, and shopkeepers, or even
mercers and grocers, but by freemen involved in large-scale distribution. Third,
corporate office-holding was, by and large, related to levels of taxation: while
all office-holders, from jurymen up, tended to contribute to the poor rate, the
more senior the office the more significant the contribution. Finally, the physical separation of Micklegate Ward from the rest of the city by the River Ouse
was reflected institutionally in the fact that, until the amalgamation of 1668, it
also formed its own jury at the quarter sessions. This encouraged an intensity
of civic participation not matched by the much larger body of freemen living
in the west of the city. Instead, the wealthiest inhabitants of Bootham – in
St Martin's on Coney Street and Minster Yard – tended to form the heart of the
'town', consisting of lawyers, church officials, and other urbane gentry rather
than citizens (for discussion of the 'town' see below, chapter 5). Monk Ward,
the poorest and least incorporated of the four wards, also displayed the lowest
levels of office-holding.

The relative homogeneity of city commonwealth in York is suggested by
the fact that, unlike in Cambridge and Ludlow, the Restoration saw no major
shift in the sociology or topography of corporate office-holding. Faced with
vengeful and well-positioned gentry, as well as an influx of ecclesiastics and
soldiers, York's citizens fought a desperate rearguard action of lobbying, solic-
iting, and the cultivation of patronage to preserve their corporate integrity at the
Restoration. The result was that, although five aldermen lost their places,

citizens of almost identical wealth and background replaced them.[92] This continuity is neatly encapsulated by the vignette of Leonard Thomson, an excluded
alderman and wine merchant, entertaining Henry Brearey, his replacement,
friend, and neighbour in St Johns Micklegate, in front of his parlour-hearth
during Christmas 1661.[93] There was a much more dramatic shift relating to
jury membership, the number of non-ratepayers called to present at the quarter
sessions increasing from 4 per cent to 19 per cent between 1659 and 1663. Even
this change did not last, however, and by mid-decade participation was once
more the preserve of enfranchised ratepayers.[94]

Just as the place of city commonwealth varied across the country, so there
were significant variations of place within a complex city like York. Both types
of diversity pose empirical, descriptive, and comparative problems: for all their
structural similarities, no two city commonwealths were places – or indeed
placed – in the same way. While invaluable as a rule of thumb, ranking or
grouping types of city commonwealth according to sociological categories runs
the risk of removing them from precisely the contexts from which their spatial
character was derived and understood.[95] As significantly, it can also obscure the
fact that places – whether roles and offices, institutions, locations, territories, or
buildings – were nothing without the people who contested, occupied, and used
them. That any particular moment – whether the 1590s or 1660s – can only be
a keyhole into an ongoing historical process makes analysis and interpretation
all the more difficult. The differences between Cambridge, Ludlow, and York
are striking nevertheless: city commonwealths that were either marginal in their
urban context and separated from their household constituencies; institutionally
extensive but also contested and divided; or sufficiently extensive, 'mixed',
autonomous, and participatory. Of course, in such diverse and mutable urban
landscapes, the meaning of citizenship, and its implications for agency and
identity, was complex. It is to how contemporaries conceptualised that problem
that we can now, finally, turn.

Place and person

If the corporate system can be regarded as a kind of extended structural penum-
bra, then the problem of agency raises two related issues that only confuse
the picture further. These are social practice and cultural meaning. A danger
of purely empirical structuralism is that places are taken to be fixed, unitary,
and deterministic in terms of behaviour and attitudes: that people and communities were, to a very large extent, defined and constricted by the structure of their social relationships and physical environments. The value of

---

[92] YCA, B37, f. 177.   [93] BIHR, CPH 2560, Hester c. Hodgson.
[94] Withington, 'Views from the bridge', p. 145.   [95] Phythian Adams, 'An agenda', p. 17.

'post-structuralism' has been to bring what early modern people understood to be 'the person' back into the equation: not simply as a demographic quotient, but as a thinking, interpreting, and acting being.[96] It was on this basis that places and other shared resources were 'appropriated' in different ways and for different purposes; that they were prescribed with different and perhaps contradictory meanings; and that perspectives and identities varied according to the relative position of a person both synchronically and diachronically.[97] That city commonwealths were simultaneously regarded as embodiments of monarchical, *res*publican, and civic power demonstrates the difficulties in assuming a single 'language of place', even among England's ruling 'elites'. The possibilities of aristocratic, democratic, or mixed polities – and their corruption into oligarchic or populist regimes – similarly depended on how civic structures were conceived, occupied, and used. So, too, did their characterisation as 'public' or 'private' bodies within the national polity. Indeed, the only certainty about the places of city commonwealth is that they were contested and mutable terrain – something hardly surprising given the numerous and competing interests vested in them, and the ferment of Renaissance and Reformation ideology upon which early modern people could draw.

This was something of which even the most didactic of early modern moralists were aware. Certainly the amount of attention that early modern writers paid to the relationship between place and person rests uneasily with the recent assertion that place depersonalised 'its occupier, because the simple fact of authority was of far greater consequence than the character of whoever happened to possess it'.[98] On the contrary, in their concern for how and for what motives places were appropriated, as well as their acknowledgement of the vicissitudes of social practice, commentators displayed a profound interest in the dangers and possibilities of agency. Both civic aristocracy and civic democracy centred on the relationship between place and person: the one linking personal and public virtue to distinctions in wealth and learning, the other focusing on the symbiosis between household, neighbourhood, and civic position and participation. So, too, did another spatial theory close to the heart of city commonwealths: that of 'place and calling'. For that strand of humanist thinking exemplified by Thomas Wilson, callings were a form of social control designed to thwart

---

[96] Michel de Certeau, *The practice of everyday life*, trans. Steven F. Randall (California, 2002); Pierre Bourdieu, *Language and symbolic power*, edited and introduced by J. B. Thompson (Cambridge, 1991), pp. 1–29.

[97] Bob Scribner, 'Is a history of popular culture possible?', *History of European Ideas*, 10, 1989, pp. 175–91; Andy Wood, 'Custom, identity and resistance: English free miners and their law', in Griffiths et al., *Experience of authority*, pp. 250–1, 278–9; Martin Ingram, 'From reformation to toleration: popular religious cultures in England, 1540–1690', in Tim Harris, ed., *Popular culture in England, c.1500–1850* (Basingstoke, 1995), pp. 95–101; Walter, *Understanding popular violence*, p. 352; Shagan, *Popular politics*, p. 22.

[98] Griffiths, *Youth and authority*, p. 70.

personal ambition and social envy: his self-defined role as a rhetorician was to convince people that they were hierarchically fixed and subordinated by the vocation in which they were placed.[99] For Sir Thomas Smith, in contrast, callings structured not so much social hierarchy as civil society. All persons claimed some kind of social and participatory role – and also some degree of social worth – because all persons 'in their callings are taken wise'.[100] However, it was in the hands of Calvinist divines like William Perkins that callings were theorised most elaborately. According to Perkins, every man had both a general calling to God and a personal calling derived from 'the practice and execution of that particular office, wherein any man is placed'. The 'final cause or end' of each was *for the common good*.[101] Perkins directed his treatise at 'corporations', 'civil societies', and 'bodies or societies of men' – places where calling and vocation formed the traditional structure of governance and economy. He appropriated the concept by outlining a theory of social interaction in which every calling was endowed with communal and moral significance. In household, commonwealth, and church, each person worked, as the organs of the body of a man, 'not for it self [sic], but for the good of the whole body'.[102] Those unwilling to find their place in and contribute to the 'common-wealth', who 'are of no civil society or corporation', had the 'life of a beast'. This not only included 'rogues, beggars, vagabonds' – the 'rotten legs and arms that drop from the body' – but also the idle rich and men drawn to 'monkish living'.[103]

The adoption of place assumed, in turn, the recognition of both structural and personal distinctions. Persons were 'distinguished by order, whereby God hath appointed that in every society one person should be above or under another'. They were also separated by 'the inward gifts which God bestowed on every man'. It was 'by reason of the distinction of men, partly in respect of gifts, partly in respect of order, come personal callings'.[104] Central to this process of social calibration was the conviction that callings should be 'fitted to the man, and every man be fitted to his calling'. Choice depended on personal 'affection' and 'gifts': a reflective sense on the part of the man of 'what mind he hath to any calling' as well as 'for and to what calling they are fittest'.[105] Because men were 'partial in judging of their inclination and gifts', the advice of others should be sought, and Perkins recommended the Athenian custom of testing the inclinations and gifts of children by providing 'instruments of all

[99] Thomas Wilson, *The art of rhetorique* (1563), A3v.

[100] Smith, *A discourse of the commonweal*, p. 12.

[101] William Perkins, 'A treatise of the vocation or calling of men, with the sorts and kinds of them, and the right use thereof', in *The works of that famous and worthy minister of Christ in the University of Cambridge, Mr William Perkins*, vol. 1 (1626), pp. 749–51. The italics are Perkins'.

[102] Ibid., p. 751   [103] Ibid., p. 755.   [104] Ibid., p. 755.   [105] Ibid., p. 758.

sorts' in a 'public place' and seeing 'with what instrument they took delight'. A principal 'duty of parents' was, in turn, to establish for their child suitable callings 'before they apply them to any particular condition of life', assuring them that 'even in his first years' a child 'does affect some one particular calling'. Echoing Mulcaster, Perkins argued that 'parents cannot do greater wrong to their children, and the society of men, then to apply them into unfit callings . . . and set the members of the body out of their proper places'.[106] As Henry Manship told the burgesses of Great Yarmouth, there 'can no greater profit arise to the commonwealth than instruction of youth': 'truly that commonwealth is most miserable, wherein the tillage of infancy is neglected'.[107] One of the main criticisms advanced by democrats in Ludlow was likewise that the oligarchs had no 'fitness' or 'calling' for government.

Ideally at least, the fitness of person to place was based on the 'trial of gifts and free election, without particularity': an extension of moral and personal aptitude rather than privilege.[108] In this way, callings enabled not only the mobility of the 'active' and 'able' within the social body but also social reform and change, as the 'fittest' people were called to exercise and work their roles and affect the commonwealth accordingly. If this suggests the inextricability of theory and ideology, then the lawyer and writer Angel Daye provided a less idealistic account of agency. Ruminating in 1586 on the place of a 'secretary', Daye observed that the social position and actions of 'any one' were dependent on three, interrelated factors: their 'will, disposition or ability'. In this widely disseminated schema, the 'will' was 'the outward quality or condition of a man': the passions and humours discerned 'by his readiness, hate, affection, or dislike of a thing'. Dispositions were, in turn, 'the residue of his being'. Constructed from a person's life-positions and cycle, they constituted at once a person's 'whole manner of living' and 'his continual practices'. Daye regarded dispositions as shaped by, among other things, 'the country or soil wherein one is born'; 'off-spring', or how the person was 'born and bred'; and education: how the person was 'trained-up' and 'inured'. Finally, 'ability' depended on the social resources at someone's disposal: the social 'aids and supports' that could be 'measured by the credit, want, company, conceit, or instability of the person'.[109] It was this nexus of will, disposition, and ability that was seen to determine both the kinds of place a person occupied and the ways in which he or she appropriated them. The person, that is, was the product of place; but place was also the product and instrument of person. Daye was particularly concerned with 'the parts, place and office of secretary', and noted a series of characteristics 'of the person' that made for a suitable fit: 'good education';

---

[106] Ibid., p. 759.   [107] Manship, *History of Great Yarmouth*, p. 43.
[108] Perkins, 'A treatise of the vocation or calling of men', p. 761.
[109] Angel Daye, *The second part of the English secretorie* (1635), pp. 235–6.

'mind well-disposed'; 'sound conversation and order of living'; 'skill, knowledge and ability wherewith to discharge the place and calling'. He should also 'be of shape and countenance proportional to those required virtues', as it was 'by countenance we do further judge the qualities and disposition of men'.[110] For other places, the fit was less important. As the Presbyterian minister Edward Bowles said of episcopacy, 'If you suggest, Put better men in their Places, We answer, the places will make them worse by the office, the office never better by the person.'[111]

It was the contingency of place that at once fascinated and concerned seventeenth-century writers. City comedies were nothing if not commentaries on not only the failure of householders to meet the expectations of their respective callings, but also their flagrant exploitation and manipulation of social roles and relationships.[112] While Shakespeare made general use of the concept of place, in three of his major Jacobean plays the word figured much more often and notably than elsewhere, signifying in each instance a systematic exploration of the relationship between roles and offices and the person occupying, using, or coveting them. *Measure for Measure*, *All is True*, and *Othello* each scrutinised the disjunction between will, disposition, and ability on the one hand and the powers, platitudes, and necessity of place on the other. The hypocrisy and lusts of Angelo; the wolfish ambition of Wolsey; and the pathological scheming of Iago were constantly juxtaposed with the duties and appearances of office.[113] As Queen Katherine tells Wolsey: 'You're meek and humble-mouthed; / You sign your place and calling, in full seeming, / With meekness and humility – but your heart / Is crammed with arrogancy, spleen and pride'.[114] The very narrative of *Othello* rests on Iago's quest 'to get his [Othello's] place, and to plume up my will'.[115] The 1669 edition of *Flagellum*, the posthumous and vitriolic polemic against Oliver Cromwell, used precisely the same idiom to explain the civil war and 'tyranny' of the past twenty years.[116] Like Iago, Wolsey, and Angelo, Cromwell's public actions were characterised as a function of personality: he was 'a rebel in manners, long before he was a *Belial* in Policy'. Moreover, his delinquency was a direct result of the failure of the structural constraints of the city commonwealth in which he grew up. 'From his Infancy to his Childhood' in Huntingdon 'he was of a cross and peevish disposition', an 'obstinate and

[110] Ibid., p. 422.   [111] Edward Bowles, *Plaine English* (1643), p. 11.

[112] Swapen Chakravorty, *Society and politics in the plays of Thomas Middleton* (Oxford, 1996), p. 15.

[113] For example: *Measure for Measure*, 1.4.50–5; 2.4.12–15; 3.1.152–8; *All is True*, 1.1.161, 2.1.82, 5.2.74; 3.1.155, *Othello*, 1.1.11, 1.1.147, 3.3.251.

[114] *All is True*, 2.4.106.   [115] *Othello*, 1.3.385.

[116] James Heath, *Flagellum: or the life and death, birth and burial of O. Cromwell the late usurper* (1669).

perverse inclination', that was civilised neither by the free school or university. Indeed, it was only his father 'being in his own nature of a difficult disposition, and great Spirit . . . [that] . . . kept him in some awe and subjection'.[117] His father's death left 'him to the scope of his own inordinate and irregular will, swayed by the bent of very violent and strong passions'. Rejecting his mother's 'Employment and Calling of a Brewer', Cromwell, 'now in the room and place of his Father . . . his uncontrolled debaucheries did publicly declare; for Drinking, Whoring, and the like outrages of licentious youth'.[118] The only relief came when 'Lincoln's Inn was the place pitched upon' 'to remove the Scandal which had been cast upon the Family by his means . . . and thither Mr Cromwell in a suitable Garb to his fortunes was sent'. He did not remain there long, however. The 'nature of the place and the Students there, were so far regretful beyond all his tedious Apprenticeship to the more facile Academic Sciences . . . that he had a kind of antipathy to his Company and Converse there; and so spent his time in an inward spite'. Returning to Huntingdon he 'fell to his old trade' of tippling, fighting, whoring, and terrorising the burgesses. It was only with his trumpeted Reformation that his 'lustful wantonness' allayed, the 'heat of his blood' cooled, and his 'strange, wild, and dishonest actions' curtailed.[119] While his religious conversion was primarily to secure an inheritance, his 'scrupulous' and well-publicised 'conscience' allowed the 'cunning' cultivation of the godly friends, kin, and civility that eventually brought his return to parliament in 1640. Neither was his dispute with the new Recorder of Huntingdon in 1630 at all related to the defence of the commons. Rather it was because 'some difference about precedence of place happened betwixt them (Oliver's spirit being too high to yield to any person in that town, where his Family had continued of the best rank some years together)'. It was in order 'to avoid the Cession of his Honour to another' that 'he withdrew himself into the Isle of Ely'.[120]

While *Flagellum* was a profoundly biased, partisan, and unsubstantiated text, the presentation of Cromwell as an ill-mannered, disordered, uncivil, and dishonest person of problematic will, disposition, and conscience was rhetorically astute. As a character assassination it combined not simply the hypocritical, politic, and Machiavellian elements of Shakespeare's 'place plays' but also the dissolute gallants and gentry of city comedy. These were characters who, in their uncivil and wilful behaviour, suggested, crystallised, or exposed as bankrupt the values underpinning the place and places of city commonwealth: men like Whorehound in *A chaste maid in Cheapside* and Falstaff in *The merry wives of Windsor*.[121] As importantly, by exploiting what by the mid-seventeenth century

[117] Ibid., pp. 8, 9, 11.   [118] Ibid., pp. 11–12.   [119] Ibid., p. 13.   [120] Ibid., p. 21.
[121] Barton, 'Falstaff and the comic community', pp. 84, 80.

were established stereotypes, *Flagellum* cast Cromwell as the monster at the margins of what might be called a civic civility: those precepts and expectations that governed the practice of social roles and relationships in household, neighbourhood, and the civic realm. For social historians, such language was part and parcel of the perennial, ubiquitous, and multifaceted quest for 'order' in the face of social, economic, and cultural dislocation.[122] However, another dimension, less discussed in the historiography but perhaps more telling for city commonwealths, was the Ciceronian notion of *honestas*: those qualities of honesty, discretion, wisdom, fitness, and decorum designed to enable men and women to constructively engage in community without the dangers of wilfulness, passion, and violence.[123] As a template for social interaction, *honestas* expected a 'fitness' between place and behaviour; reason and self-control on the part of communicants; and the mediation, wherever possible, of will and power, especially between parties of unequal wealth and status. Such criteria had important implications for the kind of behaviour expected of freemen as well as the form that communicative processes took. It also suggested that only the social and self-regulation of the person, in conjunction with the enforcement of structural obligations, could secure the city and indeed national commonwealth from the dangers of wilful and dishonest persons.

Such assumptions had long underpinned participation in the households, neighbourhoods, and civic constitutions of England's 'ancient' cities and boroughs.[124] However, the humanist 'rediscovery' of Cicero, together with the expansion and incorporation of England's city commonwealths, at once revitalised and disseminated its principles as a basis for early modern urbanity. Civic bodies expended an enormous amount of time, money, and energy regulating the will and dispositions of both participatory members and their household dependants while promulgating the virtues of fitness, discretion, and honesty. The leading Jacobean burgess in Cambridge, fish merchant Thomas French, observed in 1615 that, if ancient history taught anything, it was that 'if everyone might live according to his own will without order or restraint there would be no peaceful government but desolation and confusion'. It was 'in all civilly governed commonwealths ... where people in uniformity live to good orders' that 'towns and cities flourish and increase'.[125] His rhetoric was aimed not at 'the vulgar' or 'poor' but at certain 'gentry' burgesses who were flaunting ceremonial codes of dress.[126] Seventy years earlier, ordinances of the Newcastle-upon-Tyne Goldsmiths, Plumbers, Pewtherers, and Painter-Glaisers were justified

---

[122] Wrightson, *English society*, ch. 6; Steve Hindle, 'The keeping of the public peace', in Griffiths et al., *The experience of authority*, pp. 213–48.

[123] Jennifer Richards, *Rhetoric and courtliness*, pp. 2–3.

[124] Barry, 'Civility and civic culture', pp. 181–96; Brooks, 'Apprenticeship', pp. 76–80; Slack, 'Great and good towns', p. 364.

[125] CCRO, City Shelf C, Book 7, f. 58.   [126] Ibid., f. 51v.

on the grounds that they mediated the 'wilful' and 'malicious' energies of its members.[127] Such concerns did not emanate merely from positions of authority. Rather, the discipline and mediation of will was equally sought by those socially and politically vulnerable as a stop to unrestrained power. Complaints against civic oligarchy invariably focused, for example, on the personal deficiencies of corrupt rulers and their appropriation of commonwealth for private gain. As we saw in the previous chapter, the democratic weaver John Bradford complained that councillors were not only unfit for office, but that they were using their places 'to effect their own wills and purpose'. By its very definition, oligarchy meant that they 'did and might use the common seal of the said corporation at their wills to the great oppression of the rest of the burgesses and commonalty of the said Town'.[128] It was not governance or authority that was the problem so much as its misappropriation. The epitaph of James Wright, baker of York, was written in a similar spirit.[129]

Rooted in the reciprocity of person and place, this conception of citizenship was very different to the unquestioning deference of hierarchy and degree associated with the language of estates and degrees. On the contrary, it reflected at the local level the more widespread conviction that persons needed to earn, deserve, and fit themselves to their place: that, ideally at least, office and calling were to be attained and achieved rather than simply given. There were at least two implications of this for seventeenth-century political culture. In the first instance, the fitness (or not) between person and place provided a critical perspective on how public positions were occupied and executed. While this was true within city commonwealths, where public personas of men, women, and youths were constantly and communally assessed, it also held for persons and places within the larger polity. This was the more so because James VI and I described monarchy in precisely these terms. Princes, like everyone else, 'are clothed with two callings'. Moreover, they discharged their worldly office through the just and equitable execution of place; and 'by your behaviour in your own person'.[130] Instructing Prince Henry 'in all the points of his calling', James prepared him for 'excelling all your people' not so much 'in rank and honour as in daily care and hazardous pains-taking, for the dutiful administration of that great office'.[131] By framing monarchy as 'the best of the best', he self-consciously drew attention to the suitability – or not – of the bodily person that filled it. Moreover, he did so in an idiom that the humblest civic office-holder could understand. This language of justification was also, as Charles discovered in the 1640s, a basis for criticism. As Samuel Pepys observed in 1660: 'I went . . . with a dog that the King loved (which shit in the boat, which made us laugh and me think that a King and all that belong to him are but just as

---

[127] TWA, GU/GP/1/2.   [128] TNA, E134/39 and 440 Elizabeth/Mich. 37, items 11, 18.
[129] See above, pp. 14–15.   [130] 'Basilikon Doron' in *Workes*, p. 155.   [131] Ibid., p. 138

others are).'[132] Second, as sources of power, status, and agency, the nature and relative position of places were taken very seriously indeed. The Stuarts had, for example, an extremely developed sense of their monarchical position, Charles pushing the Aristotelian definition of monarchy to its perfect and 'absolute', or 'thorough', conclusion. However, it was an equally pronounced right and sense of place that many citizens, as either the self-styled aristocrats or democratic representatives of their communities, claimed as theirs. That similar levels of spatial conceit also characterised the perspectives of lawyers, divines, bishops, landed elites, and, by the 1650s, the soldiers and grandees of the New Model Army points to both the spatial complexity and dissonance of the English polity. In a very real sense, England's seventeenth-century troubles stemmed not from the 'crisis of order' so much as the opposite: a plethora of places, powers, and authority, those of city commonwealth very much among them.

Placing 'true liberty'

'The whole social order in the church-state – imitated throughout the counties, towns, boroughs and hamlets, as at the political centre at Westminster – was buttressed by belief in a divinely ordained series of gradations between all things that existed: from God through the ranks of angels, humans, animate and inanimate creation.' So observes Andrew Sharp in his 1998 edition of Leveller writings – the corpus of petitions and pamphlets that, he claims, challenged for the first time 'the practical beliefs of all but a few pockets of dissidents'.[133] Central to this consensus was what the Westminster Assembly of Divines described in 1648 as the 'honour inferiors owe to superiors': in particular, 'the defence and maintenance of their persons and authority according to their several ranks and the nature of their places'.[134] It rested on a sense of divine order and right encapsulated by the famous and oft-quoted observation of Ulysses in Shakespeare's *Troilus and Cressida* that 'The heavens themselves, the planets, and this centre / Observe degree, priority, and place' (1.3.85–8). All of which is to suggest that what Paul Griffiths terms 'the early modern language of place' was fundamental to the kind of social 'order' and 'authority' that England's elites at once craved and instituted in the 100 years after 1550.[135]

This perspective rests uneasily with events in Ludlow 1598. Common councillors reported that John Crowther, confronted with a borough charter that consolidated the government of his civic opponents, had 'broken up the doors of the council chamber and chest of the said town wherein the common seal ordinances and Records of the said town were kept'. The chamber secured, they 'thence did take the said common seal and the two books of survey and

[132] Vol. 1, p. 158.
[133] Sharp, *English Levellers*, p. xx.   [134] Ibid.   [135] Griffiths, *Youth and authority*, p. 70.

particular of the lands of the said town'. The colonisation of the council chamber precipitated nothing less than the redistribution of common wealth. It was
recorded that, he 'being one of the Bailiffs of the said town did call a great
chamber of Burgesses together of his own Authority'. An assembly called,
'he the said Crowther And the same multitude of Burgesses did contrary to the
said ancient form of government displace four of the ancient councillors and the
Town Clerk of the said Town and elected and placed in their stead or places new
councillors and Town Clerk'. At the same time, they 'did replace and remove
divers of the ancient tenants of the said town their tenements and possessions
and placed others in their stead'.[136] In so doing, they demonstrated what the
democrat John Bradford later called the 'virtue of their office', acting with
the 'discretion', 'reason', and 'indifference' appropriate for a person executing
civic authority.[137] The physicality of the process was also tangible. The institutional and symbolic resources of the borough were embodied in halls, chests,
and common seals, and defined and exercised on the basis of personal presence
as much as political abstraction. Whereas previously they had structured civic
aristocracy, they now facilitated civic democracy: two different conceptions
of the meaning and practice of city commonwealth and the places that constituted it.

Neither did Ludlow's aristocrats exhibit a complacent or even God-given
attitude to power. Rather, their claim to the same buildings, offices, and lands
was based on the sustained politicking that culminated in the drafting of the
Elizabethan charter. The town clerk, Francis Jenks, described how he, the bailiff
Thomas Langford, and five other aldermen had been advised by legal counsel
to petition for the right to re-incorporate once they realised that a writ of *quo
warranto* had been taken against them. As soon as 'her Majesty had signified
her pleasure for the granting the said charter', the faction 'did repair unto
Edward Coke Esquire Her Majesty's Attorney General for the drawing of the
same'. Although secured under the authority of the common seal, no 'motion
[was] made to the so-called common council in any public assembly or upon
any summons . . . as usually they have done for matters of less importance,
whereby voices might be asked'. In London, Coke oversaw a first draft of the
charter 'which being drawn in paper' Jenks 'brought home to this Town and
delivered the same paper draft' for consultation by the six aldermen behind the
petition. Their alterations and additions made, the paper was returned to Coke
'who perused the same', engrossed it, and 'did subscribe his name'. Thomas
Langford then 'procured the same to be signed by her Majesty by means of one of
Dr [Julius] Caesar's men, and to be signed out under the great seal of England'.
Kin aided the faction in seeing through the transaction. A London goldsmith,
brother of one aristocrat, provided the credit for the purchase, while the son of

[136] SA, LB7/745   [137] HCRO, HD4/2/17, 1611, Joyce Larkin c. William Sherwood.

another, also London-based, liaised with the legal offices of Coke and Caesar.[138] Confronted with the newly minted charter, the Court of Exchequer ordered that 'seal and Evidences' be restored 'to the place where the same were formerly kept' and the 'four councillors and Town Clerk . . . placed again in their former places and use and exercise their places as formerly they were accustomed'. In the same way, 'all such Tenants and farmers as are also displaced are also restored to their former possessions'.[139] Anticipating Cromwell's dèbâcle in Huntingdon thirty years later, this political defeat undermined the position of Crowther in the town. Curtailed in his civic activities and deprived of a place in parliament, it was recorded in August 1600 that he had 'departed out of the town and does not bear scot and lot in the same therefore [he] be displaced and another chosen in his place'.[140]

Just as there was no single 'language of place' in early modern England, so in its various meanings and uses it was by no means limited to a singular and an integrated theory of subordination – whether divine right or oligarchy. Rather there was an early modern *concept* of place that positioned the person in a variety of structures – institutional, geographical, and architectural – and which was used within a number of political traditions. Shakespeare used the concept of place to dramatise political ideologies quite distinct from the 'great chain of being' – noble factionalism in *Macbeth*, civic republicanism in *Coriolanus*, and, indeed, city commonwealth in *The Merry Wives of Windsor*. So within the 'practical beliefs' of England's citizens and freemen, place was something to be contested, controlled, and used. It was also, as Robert Brady well knew, pivotal to civic ideology. The formation of the corporate system at once extended and invigorated civic conceptions and practices of place within national political culture. It is precisely this process that provided the context for events in Newcastle-upon-Tyne in 1651. The common council noted that the 'late King's Arms and the Portrait of King James were by Order of Parliament taken down from off the new building upon the Bridge and the Commonwealths Arms to be set in the same place instead thereof'. As part of this act of appropriation 'Latin words' were 'presented to the Common Council as a fit subscription to be ingraven under the same'. Read aloud, they were 'thought very fit and pertinent thereto', and it was 'Ordered therefore . . . that the same be forthwith Ingraven in these Latin words only the same being Englished as follows':'Princedome and liberty things unsociable in the year 1651'; 'True liberty takes away no man's right, or hinders no mans right'; 'That indeed (or at least) is true liberty that defends every man's right or property'. Moreover 'Licentiousness confounds all things' was considered but rejected.[141] It was at the grammar school in Newcastle, of course, that John Lilburne was educated: the place where, as

---

[138] TNA, E134/39 and 440 Elizabeth/Mich. 37, depositions of Francis Jenks, Richard Rascal.
[139] SA, LB7/745.   [140] SA, LB2/1/1, ff. 28v, 37v.   [141] TWA, MD/NC/2/2, f. 30.

Richard Tuck has shown, he would have learnt the same classical meanings of liberty, right, and property that councillors now engraved on their bridge.[142] However, those notions were not simply the stuff of an arcane curriculum or tiny elite. Used and contested on a daily basis, they were constitutive of city commonwealth itself.

---

[142] Richard Tuck, 'Civil conflict in school and town 1500–1700', in Brian Mains and Anthony Tuck, eds., *Royal Grammar School, Newcastle upon Tyne: a history of the school in its community* (London, 1986), pp. 1–138.

5   Civic conversations

'Publick matters and in hearing and telling news'

On 7 July 1684 John Farrington, 'a citizen and haberdasher of London', deposed to the court of Chancery how, fourteen years earlier, he had 'become partners' with three other citizens 'in the borrowing and taking of money at interest . . . which was to be employed in a common or joint bank'.[1] He was already familiar with the merchant Edmond Page, the two having dealt 'together in partnership in the trade of wholesale mercer in London and also as Merchants in diverse particular wares and merchandise in parts beyond the sea'. The new, 'unhappy acquaintance' was with merchant Edward Nelthorpe and confectioner Richard Thompson – two citizens who 'did also before that time deal together in partnership in wines and other commodities and merchandise'. According to Farrington, it was Thompson and Nelthorpe who claimed 'upon long and mature consideration' to have concocted a 'way of dealing in the world which would unquestionably turn to a great account of profit'. Based in Thompson's 'dwelling house' in Woollchurch Market, at the commercial heart of the City of London, 'in a short time the said joint bank and dealing grew into a very great credit and esteem'. Success was, however, short-lived. According to Farrington, Nelthorpe and Thompson were too ambitious, unskilled, and untrustworthy for commerce, committing themselves to designs that were 'expensive and fruitless' in the mistaken belief that 'by the ruin of others' they would be 'suddenly rich'. Worst of all, it quickly became apparent that Thompson was 'very negligent and altogether unfit and incapable of managing the joint affair', forcing Nelthorpe and Farrington to 'employ their whole time' in the bank's business to 'the neglect of the their own joint and particular trades and dealings'. This was primarily because instead of regarding 'his duty and engagement to mind the said office', Thompson 'was daily at the coffee houses and other publick places' where he 'spent his time in publick matters and in hearing and telling news'.[2]

---

[1] TNA, C7/581/73, petition of John Farrington.   [2] Ibid.

Farrington's travails nicely encapsulate a narrative central to urban, economic, and political historiography of the period: the emergence of a new generation of 'educated classes' and 'capitalists' who came to social, urban, and public prominence in the later seventeenth or 'long eighteenth century'. It is a story of new forms of commerce, association, sociability, civility, and politics that has been told from a variety of perspectives.[3] However, the most synthetic account remains Jürgen Habermas' description of the 'emerging public sphere of civil society'.[4] Engendered by 'structural transformations' within society, this 'public sphere' was dominated not by 'the genuine burghers, the old occupational orders of craftsmen and shopkeepers', so much as a new 'stratum of bourgeoisie'. While freemen and citizens 'suffered downward social mobility', losing 'their importance along with the very towns upon whose citizens' rights their status was based', the 'real carrier of the public' was an alliance of 'professionals', 'urbane' gentry, and a new class of 'entrepreneurs, manufacturers, and factory owners'.[5] They participated not in archaic entities like city commonwealths but in the 'town': a symbolic and physical space in which private individuals could socialise and discuss rationally and reasonably the public concerns of the day.[6] This 'town'-based (as opposed to 'civic') 'bourgeois public' was at once literary and associational: both the written word and new urban institutions like coffeehouses and clubs were loci for public discussion.[7] It was also a sphere qualitatively unprecedented in terms of the communication it structured, its private participants self-consciously acting as a critical and public check on the claims and policies of the state. According to this narrative, this bourgeois 'town' and 'public' effectively supplanted the pre-modern hegemony of crown and court over political and economic culture, contributing to a new kind of urbanity far removed from the older and decayed traditions of medieval *communitas*. As such, it was also part and parcel of what Peter Borsay has called the 'English urban renaissance', the 'town' providing a focus not only for public discourse but also new patterns of consumption, fashion, and status. It was, in effect, 'part of a wider movement, an English enlightenment, whose underlying mission was to rescue the nation from barbarity and ignorance; in a word, to civilise it'.[8]

With his entrepreneurial and public interests, Richard Thompson would seem to personify the 'town' and the new generation of men that made it – a link that is

---

[3] J. H. Plumb, *The growth of political stability in England 1675–1725* (London, 1967), ch. 1; Borsay, *English urban renaissance*, chs. 10, 11; Kathleen Wilson, *The sense of the people: politics, culture and imperialism, 1715–1785* (Cambridge, 1995), pp. 3–26; Peter Clark, *British clubs and societies 1580–1800: the origins of an associational world* (Oxford, 2000), chs. 2, 3.

[4] Jürgen Habermas, *The structural transformation of the public sphere*, translated by Thomas Burger and Frederick Lawson (Cambridge, 1992), pp. 23, 57.

[5] Ibid., p. 24.   [6] Ibid., p. 23.   [7] Ibid., chs. 2, 3.

[8] Borsay, *English urban renaissance*, p. 257.

all the stronger given his 'friends'. In December 1675 none other than Andrew Marvell wrote to Sir Henry Thompson in York with news in London. Assuring his correspondent that 'the daily contrary rumours concerning Parliament are not worth taking notice of', he also noted that despite the general crisis of credit in the metropolis 'our friends in Woollchurch Market ... proved cocksure'.[9] Moreover, it was to Marvell's house on Great Russell Street that Richard and Dorothy Thompson, along with Nelthorpe, absconded in 1677 to escape their creditors.[10] This was one year after Marvell had published the pamphlet that helped crystallise 'public' opposition to the policies of the Restoration court. He was also, as observed by Habermas, an early frequenter of the kind of public forum in which autonomous public opinion developed.[11] *An account of the growth of popery* was 'a naked Narrative of some of the most considerable passages in the meeting of *Parliament*' – a series of anonymous revelations meant to enable 'some stronger Pen and to such have more leisure and further opportunity to discover and communicate to the Public'.[12] If, however, both Thompson and Marvell can be regarded as harbingers of a self-consciously critical public domain, they were hardly detached from city commonwealth. Thompson was a freeman of the London Clothmakers, the same guild to which Lilburne apprenticed. Moreover, as London common councillors, both he and Nelthorpe were extremely active in civic politics throughout the 1670s.[13] Likewise, Marvell was a citizen and parliamentary representative of Hull, the town of his birth. From his election in 1658 he remained in constant communication with the citizens he represented until his unexpected death in 1678.[14] Marvell, Nelthorpe, and Thompson were connected through ties of kin and friendship to a wider community of merchants and citizens that, while certainly conscious of its public efficacy and role, was also firmly embedded in the corporate system.[15]

The corporate system poses significant problems for Habermas' distinction between 'the state' on the one hand and an emergent 'public' on the other. Previous chapters have shown that, far from experiencing terminal decline, the traditional urban *communitas* increased in size, number, and public confidence after 1540, marking a 'structural transformation' that diversified public authority, ideology, and civility outwith the monarchical state while retaining the legitimacy of sovereign authority. As importantly, the kind of reflexivity, civility, and discursive skill ideally expected of the bourgeois public sphere were more than reminiscent of the values already associated with city

---

[9] BJL, DDMM/28/1.   [10] TNA, C6/242/13, answer of Mary Marvell.

[11] Habermas, *Structural transformation*, p. 33.

[12] Andrew Marvell, *An account of the growth of popery* (1676), p. 17.

[13] TNA, C6/283/87, petition of Richard Thompson. See below, ch. 6.

[14] They form the bulk of correspondence in Margoliouth, *Poems and letters*, vol. II.

[15] Ibid., pp. 299–309, 313–21; TNA, SP29/401/232; SP29/402/166; SP29/402/232; SP29/404/215 and 228; BJL, DDMM/28/1.

commonwealths. Indeed, the corporate system was crucial in propagating certain kinds of conversational and associational practice: an important qualification to a narrative that pays so much attention to how and where people talked to each other. The prescriptive basis of civic conversation was the classical concept of *honestas*: that template of civility that, in its vernacular forms, was denoted by qualities of honesty, discretion, wisdom, and fitness. Such qualities were as requisite for public deliberations of common councils as they were for public correspondence in the form of letters and petitions. That the formation of the corporate system was in part a response to the perceived crisis in counsel that characterised the mid-sixteenth century only confirms the imperatives of communication that informed urbanisation: imperatives that were revealed once again by the struggle for counsel in 1641. All of which is to suggest that important sections of the English commons were well acquainted with, skilled in, and protective of forms of civil and public discourse long before the introduction of coffee to England in 1656.[16]

This is not to deny that change took place. Just as the revolutionary era saw the conceptual and institutional hardening of the 'state', so a 'public' that was independent of *res*publica and *civitas* consolidated itself as a vibrant dimension of national political culture. Likewise commerce and industry expanded apace, the possibilities of empire matched only by the emergence of new urban centres like Manchester and Birmingham.[17] At the very least, however, the freedom and citizenship embodied in city commonwealths formed a tangible presence in the changing dynamics of English society, providing a template for new political and economic practices and remaining an active element within changed and changing circumstances. This was never more so than for civil discourse and sociability – those aspects of early modern urbanity with which this chapter is concerned. It suggests that, given the precocity of England's civil society and public sphere 'is a problem not yet resolved', there is every possibility that the enlightenment 'town' occurred because of rather than despite the corporate system.[18] As a forum for conversation the coffeehouse was not so much a disjunction with the alehouse, as Steve Pincus has claimed, as contiguous with the council chamber.[19]

The politics of company

The ideal of community lay at the heart of city commonwealth; likewise, the ideal of communication lay at the heart of community. Community entailed

---

[16] Steve Pincus, '"Coffee politicians does create": coffeehouses and Restoration political culture', *Journal of Modern History*, 67, 1995, pp. 807–34.
[17] Wrigley, 'Urban growth and agricultural change', pp. 78–82.
[18] Habermas, *Structural transformation*, p. 57.
[19] Pincus, '"Coffee politicians does create"', pp. 823–5.

'participation, fellowship, or society: good correspondency, near familiarity one with another; a corporation or company incorporate'.[20] City common-wealths were a particular means of achieving what John Milton's nephew, Edward Phillips, described as 'common, or mutual participation': a body of 'fellowship' and 'brotherhood' that was particular to place and delineated by its civic powers.[21] As late as the eighteenth century community and incorpo-ration were conflated, community representing 'a body of men united in civil society for their mutual advantage – as a corporation, the inhabitants of a Town, the companies of Tradesmen'.[22] However, it encapsulated more general prin-ciples of association and commerce that were central to humanism. Thomas Hobbes was merely repeating an early modern commonplace when he noted that, without speech, 'there had been amongst men, neither Common-wealth, nor Society, nor contract, nor Peace, no more than Lions, Bears, and Wolves'.[23] Roger Williams noted that 'there is a savour of civility and courtesy even among these wild *Americans*, both amongst themselves and towards *strangers*', that smacked of a more general humanity.[24] When Timon of Athens removed him-self from the attachments of civil society it reflected a 'nature but infected,/ A poor unmanly melancholy' and 'slave-like habit' (4.3.205). The commu-nicative ideal was as true for civic bodies – such as corporations, parishes, and guilds – as the households and neighbourhoods they represented and governed. It structured 'the sociability of the nature of man' and the essential humanity of those who 'love society: families, cohabitation, and consociation of houses and towns together'.[25] Colonisation and new markets did not mitigate these princi-ples so much as extend them, citizens becoming the custodians of commerce on a world scale. Newcastle burgess William Grey eulogised how 'Our most Provident and Glorious Creator hath so furnished all Countries with several commodities, that amongst all Nations there might be a sociable conversation and mutual commerce.' Traffic and exchange in turn bred reciprocity, 'one Peo-ple standing in need of another' so that 'all might be combined in a common league, and exhibit mutual succours'.[26]

Even the most idealistic of commentators did not claim that 'mutual com-merce' was accessible to all. If city commonwealths were communicative, they were also exclusionary, depriving strangers of precisely those liber-ties that encapsulated freedom. They also divided internally, into places and roles that necessarily influenced who communicated what with whom. In this

[20] Thomas Blount, *Glossographia, or, a dictionary interpreting all such hard words* (1656). See also above, p. 11.
[21] Edward Phillips, *New world of words* (1658), 'community'.
[22] Edward Phillips, *New world of words* (1706), 'community'.   [23] Hobbes, *Leviathan*, p. 24.
[24] Roger Williams, *A key into the language of America* (1643), pp. 9–10.
[25] Williams, *A key into the language*, p. 47.
[26] William Grey, *Chorographia, or a survey of Newcastle-upon-Tyne* (1649), p. 26.

sense, communality of whatever kind was always inflected by relationships of power: topographies within which the person was placed, and which inevitably informed their experience of and participation in community. Social historians have done much to reveal these topographies, excavating the patriarchal, economic, and residential distinctions upon which community rested.[27] It has also been shown that communication was not simply reflective but also constitutive of distinctions. As Farrington and Thompson well knew, their economic efficacy was in large part dependent on the social construction and performance of 'credit': the circulation of reputation and knowledge by which a person's probity, trust, and honesty were constantly monitored and evaluated. It was by the sword of credit that their bank first lived and then died: a particularly dramatic example of what Craig Muldrew has shown to be a general feature of early modern economic practice.[28] Likewise, discursive constructions like 'reputation' and 'fame' were at the heart of patriarchal practice, the communal status of both men and women depending on what they did and said or, more tellingly, what was subsequently reported about them.[29] In this sense, conversations at once demarcated communal boundaries and determined communal distinctions. The credit of Thompson, Farrington, Nelthorpe, and Page extended far and wide, mapping their mercantile connections or what Philip Massinger in *The city madam* called 'the money men' (1.3.117). It also transformed over time, becoming so degraded that they were eventually forced to withdraw altogether from that community's penetrating scrutiny. However, the principles by which it functioned were no different to any other kind of community: whether in neighbourhood, parish, or common council, persons were constantly conscious of the credit and reputation of both themselves and others. All of which is to suggest the communal and, indeed, political significance of communicative practice.

Establishing the sociology of civic sociability – and the conversations that constituted it – is no easy business. Just as the records of organised association – such as the minutes of common council, guild, or indeed commercial partnerships – rarely record the minutiae of talk, so the vast majority of civic conversations were ephemeral, transitory, and unrecorded. Those that do survive, for example in depositions from the church courts, tend to emphasise exchanges that, in one way or another, subverted normal practice. That said, one term that described for freemen and women the nuts and bolts of social interaction was 'company'. The word had qualitative implications, in that

---

[27] Robert Scribner, 'Communities and the nature of power', in Robert Scribner, ed., *Germany: a new social and economic history* (London, 1996), p. 293; Withington and Shepard, 'Introduction', in Shepard and Withington, *Communities in early modern England*, p. 6.

[28] Muldrew, *Economy of obligation*, ch. 6.

[29] Laura Gowing, *Domestic dangers: women, words, and sex in early modern London* (Oxford, 1996), ch. 4.

company could imply an affective relationship between companions: for example, as friends, brethren, neighbours, kin, and soldiers. However, it was also a more general form of social description that captured the many and varied forms of urban sociability – from the most institutionalised of gatherings to the most fleeting and perfunctory of exchanges. Examples of company in seventeenth-century Cambridge were a case in point. In 1624, attempts to curb factionalism on the common council (the 'Twenty Four') led to an order 'about the electing of their own company.' This specified 'that upon every such election there shall be the number of twelve and if they shall put any out of their company there shall be the number of thirteen present'.[30] When all the free burgesses of the borough assembled for the common day in 1648, they did so as a company intent on feasts and oaths as well as civic business.[31] In 1643, the musician John Browne 'was chosen to be the Town Waits with his company'.[32] And in 1615 it was ordered that 'the several tradesmen of this town shall have authority under the town seal for the making up of them into several companies ... according to the laws of the realm of England and the customs and privileges of this town'.[33] However, company was equally ubiquitous beyond the civic realm. Gabriel Harvey, the son of a Saffron Walden ropemaker, noted that his university career at Cambridge was severely hindered by issues of company. He reported an occasion when Thomas Neville, a Fellow at Pembroke Hall, 'laid against me common behaviour, that I was not familiar like a fellow, and that I did disdain every man's company'. The accusation troubled Harvey, who regarded himself 'as fellowy [sic] as the best' and expostulated 'What they call sociable I know not: this I am sure, I never avoided company: I have been merry in company: I have been full hardly drawn out of company.'[34] Cambridge offered more than civic or scholarly fellowship, company forming and dissipating according to somewhat different expectations and rituals than those expected by Harvey. Young men were accustomed to 'drinking of wine in the company of divers young maids' or, as was the case of John Binns, regularly lying out of college with 'twenty one young men ... with whom he kept company.' One concerned father wrote that he hoped his son would 'avoid the company of Tobacco takers, Drinkers and Swaggerers ... as the young gentleman is by nature of a modest sober and civil conversation and no doubt will so continue if evil company draw him not from it'.[35]

It was in and through company that freemen and women conversed: just as city commonwealths were composites of places, so they were characterised by the recurring formation and dissipation of company. Robert Horne, the Jacobean

---

[30] CCRO, City Shelf C, Book 7, f. 126.   [31] CCRO, City Shelf C, Book 8, f. 9.
[32] CCRO, City Shelf C, Book 7, f. 368.   [33] Ibid., f. 50.
[34] Cited in Richards, *Rhetoric and courtliness*, p. 18.
[35] Shepard, 'Meanings of manhood', pp. 179, 181, 183.

minister of Ludlow, clearly identified himself with the aristocratic company of
the borough, participating in a set of friendships that encompassed the common
council of the borough; members of the county community; and lawyers and parliamentary representatives in London.[36] John Crowther, the leading democratic
burgess from the 1590s, was less successful in sustaining this kind of sociability.
The common council recorded in January 1599 that 'this company have thought
it good considering the said abuses and bad mind [of Crowther] to sequester
him from this company until the suit be ended and until he submit himself to
this company'.[37] This was in part because Crowther had joined the company
of John Bradford and others in opposing the town's common councillors. He
was responsible for the fact that 'many met together in your company' or 'went
in company ... within the said town [and] the fields, pastures [and meadows]
near unto the said town' in order 'to consult together touching the alteration
of the government of this town'.[38] Company in this instance structured civic
politics. What the term also offers is a comprehensive and historicised concept
of early modern sociability that is also attentive to the social politics implicit in
different kinds of interaction that characterise 'everyday social life'.[39] It does
so for those relatively well-defined and institutionalised forms of company that
filled the urban landscapes of early modern England: public civic bodies; the
licensed companies of soldiers, merchants, and actors; congregations, clubs,
and societies. It also encompasses the mostly unrecorded moments of face-to-
face interaction that have proved so conceptually and empirically elusive to
historians: doorstead gossip, alehouse tippling, and market banter.

Approached schematically, there was a threefold politics of company that
related to participation, function, and interaction, each of which can be illuminated with examples of company recorded in depositions to the Consistory
and Dean and Chapter Courts in York in the later seventeenth century. These
include the aftermath of a civic dinner in York 'for congratulating the happy
nuptials' of William of Nassau (subsequently Prince of Orange) and Mary
Stuart in 1677; the neighbourly company of midwife Bridget Hodgson of York
in 1663; and alehouse company in the Yorkshire village of Wistow in 1690.[40]
The politics of participation concerned who was included or excluded from
company; the criteria upon which participation was based; and the means by
which access was secured and boundaries maintained. The city's celebration of
the royal marriage was a ceremonial occasion that involved the civic companies

---

[36] David Colclough, '"The muses recreation": John Hoskyns and the manuscript culture of the
seventeenth century', *Huntingdon Library Quarterly*, 61, 3 & 4, pp. 386–7.

[37] SA, LB2/1/1, f. 28v.   [38] SA, LB7/759; LB7/736.

[39] Ann Branaman, 'Goffman's social theory', in Charles Lemert and Ann Branaman, eds., *The
Goffman reader* (Oxford, 1997), p. xlv.

[40] BIHR, CPH, 3314, Office c. John Warter; CPH 2560, 1662, Hester Browne c. Bridget Hodgson;
D/C 1691/11, Ann Wintringham c. Robert Shaw.

of the corporation: the lord mayor and thirteen aldermen; the 'Twenty Four'; the two sheriffs; the common council of seventy-two; and the eight chamberlains.[41] Participation was based, therefore, on the usual rules of office-holding. It was limited to male and enfranchised heads of household who were deemed to be of enough substance and *honestas* to hold office. Civic duty was extended in this instance to a public gesture of support for the Prince of Orange and the Protestant line of the Stuart dynasty. While like-minded friends of the citizens, such as the North Yorkshire cleric John Warter, were also invited, it was noted by the town clerk that 'the Military Officers to attend if they please': a grudging concession reflecting tensions between citizens and soldiers within the city.[42] The company experienced by the midwife Bridget Hodgson over Christmas 1663 involved some of the same citizens who feasted William and Mary fourteen years later. Hodgson was the wealthiest midwife in the city, and hers was the select company of friends, kin, and clients rather than civic affiliation. She joined the mercantile household of Leonard and Frances Thompson in their parlour to exchange news, where, along with Leonard and Frances she 'discoursed' with their daughter (and Hodgson's goddaughter) Mary; Mary's maidservant, Sapphire Stratford; and the merchant Henry Brearey, Leonard's neighbour, friend, and political ally.[43] Hodgson also attended the churching of Anne, the wife of another York merchant, where other guests included invited neighbours (including the daughter-in-law of the deceased James Wright) and the parish minister.[44] In both instances, the communality of neighbourliness was mixed with a degree of exclusivity that limited participation to 'better' neighbours. Different again was the company convened by Robert Shaw on his removal from the nearby village of Wistow in 1690. It consisted of male neighbours of his own status – all of whom went by the title of 'Mr' in the court records – and labourers he had hired to move his goods.[45] Access for the men of the village was based on neighbourliness and paternalism, and the resultant company was ring-fenced by patriarchy. This boundary was dramatically revealed when the wife of one of the labourers, Anne Wintringham, 'came into their company' at about midnight to 'desire her husband to go home'. Shaw told Alex Wintringham to 'turn his wife out of doors otherwise he would'. Anne replied that 'if there was room for her husband there was room for her'. The row escalated from verbal taunts to physical violence, Shaw eventually breaking Anne's head with a candlestick.[46]

[41] YCA B38, f. 133.   [42] Ibid.; BIHR, CPH 3314.
[43] BIHR, CPH 2560, depositions of Leonard Thomson, Frances Thomson, Mary Thompson, Henry Brearey, Sapphire Stratford.
[44] Ibid., depositions of Henry Proctor, Ann Ellecker, Ann Ramsden, Elizabeth Wright.
[45] BIHR, D/C 1691/11, depositions of John Cooper, Robert Bond, William Moore.
[46] Ibid., statement of Robert Shaw, deposition of Dorothy Wright.

A second set of politics related to the function, meaning, and appropriation of company. The ostensible reason for the procession and dinner in York
was a royal celebration sanctioned by civic authority. However, the reciprocity
between royal and civic interests that this implies is misleading. While assuming the paraphernalia of civic ceremony, the event was also a precocious display
of civic support for the Protestant succession. Organised on the eve of the so-
called 'Popish Plot', it was an implicit affront to the Catholic Duke of York
who was unpopular with the citizens for a number of reasons.[47] It was a company that anticipated, therefore, the support for the exclusion of James from
the crown by the citizens of York two years later, constituting a partisan as
well as civic act. This appropriation of civic ceremonial was all the more significant because it was the only celebration of its kind to be inscribed in the
city minutes during the period: the restoration of the monarchy in 1660, the
coronations of Charles II and James II, their respective marriages – all went
unrecorded. The company of Hodgson in turn demonstrated different practices
of neighbourliness: the 'telling of the news of the city' among friends, and
the churching of a female parishioner after labour. However, on both occasions Hodgson used her authority and knowledge as a midwife to gossip about
a local serving maid and, by extension, the serving maid's household. In the
house of Leonard Thomson, 'being in company with divers credible persons',
she announced that 'your neighbours waiting maid lies in at Micklegate Bar',
and when pushed to be more specific said 'as if you know not (or if you've
heard not) that Hester Browne lies in'.[48] At the churching of Anne Ramsden,
another guest recalled that 'some of the company being talking of a woman
that then lay in within that street said it was foolishly carried'. This prompted
Bridget Hodgson to observe 'that there was a business without Micklegate Bar
as sadly carried if it be true; and some of the company asking who it was
but the said Mrs Hodgson refused to tell'. Such reticence did not last long, as
Hodgson proceeded to tour the room telling each of the guests the name of the
culprit 'privately'.[49] In both instances, the company of neighbours transmuted
into a kind of committee of public morals standing in judgement of Hester
Browne and the household for which she worked. This could not be said of the
company of Robert Shaw, which intended the men of Wistow to 'make merry'
before his departure. Making merry was, however, hardly an undifferentiated
experience: as an association of freeholders and labourers, it conjoined neighbourliness, paternalism, and ultimately conflict in a heady and volatile mix that
exploded with the arrival of Anne Wintringham. Significantly enough, while
Shaw's social equals – the 'Mr's in the company – supported Shaw's version of
events, describing how Anne 'came into their company in a rude domineering

[47] Withington, 'Citizens', pp. 146–7.   [48] BIHR, CPH 2560, deposition of Mary Thompson.
[49] Ibid., depositions of Henry Proctor, Ann Ellecker, Ann Ramsden, Elizabeth Wright.

and huffing manner', the labourers described her behaviour as 'civil' and 'orderly' and Shaw's violence unprovoked.[50]

The interaction of participants was, in turn, political. It was a politics mediated on the one hand by the rituals and conventions associated with particular kinds of company: of behaviour, language, artefacts, and place. And, on the other, it was informed by the will, disposition, and ability that a person brought to the company in which they were involved. Unsurprisingly, civic celebrations were ostentatiously ritualised and symbolic. The company of citizens assembled 'at the council chamber on Ouse Bridge' and, attended by trumpets and music, went 'from thence to the High Cross on the Pavement', where they drank the 'Prince of Orange and his Princess' health in the golden bowl. The civic company then adjourned to the Guildhall, where toasts were repeated behind closed doors. In the meantime, it was ordered that 'the bells ring all day and bonfires made at night'. The structure of company was, in this instance, extremely precise. The hierarchy and material texture of the occasion were provided by civic office; the predominant rhetoric was oaths, toasts, and fellowship; and the day's topography traced the three primary sites of civic power: council chamber, market cross, and guildhall.[51] The experience of participants was less controlled. John Warter recalled that 'he went after dinner with other company along with the lord mayor to the Guildhall ... and there did amongst other company drink several sorts of wine in so much that when [he] came from the hall he found that the wine had got into his head'. He claimed that, although 'he staggered in the streets', he immediately made his lodging 'on purpose to prevent the exposing of himself to public view'. Unfortunately for Warter, the church authorities had received complaints from witnesses 'that the streets would scarce hold you' and that, on leaving the company, you 'exposed yourself to the view and censure of many good and grave gentlemen and citizens'. Even worse, 'at the coffee house in the Minster Yard ... in the public room there, with your arms and face upon the Table [you] fell asleep in the sight and presence of several gentlemen'. As a result, 'some whereof put tobacco pipes in your periwig, and another set the candlestick with the candle burning in it on your head, and thus you became the laughing stock to the whole company.' As such, the fraternity that characterised one company transformed into drunkenness and incivility in another. While clearly disposed to the toasting and partisan company of the guildhall, the disposition of a cleric who was, as he confessed, 'addicted to the drinking of strong beer and wine', was inappropriate for subsequently walking the 'public' streets of the city. That same disposition was disastrous among coffeehouse company situated in a quarter of the town that was at once outwith

---

[50] BIHR, D/C 1691/11. The reply of Robert Shaw tells a very different story to that of Anne Wintringham's deponents.
[51] YCA B38, f. 133.

the control of the corporation, an urbane haunt for the gentry and military, and firmly associated with support for the Duke of York. The result was not a mutuality of interest. It was ridicule.[52]

The company of Hodgson was no less ritualised than the public adventures of Warter, the midwife proving adept at using appropriate conversational techniques to spread her news about Hester Browne. In the parlour of Leonard Thomson, she instigated a series of questions and answers that involved both the two merchants talking by the fire and the three women sewing at the table. In this way, her prized nugget of information was slowly and effectively revealed. This talk was accompanied by gossipy and sly gestures: Henry Brearey remembered her 'waving her fan to her face [saying] "Do you not hear that one Hester Browne lies-in without Micklegate Bar"'?[53] At the churching of Anne Ramsden, Hodgson embarked on an exemplary performance of gossip. Having titillated the company in public she then informed the parish minister, Henry Proctor, that the culprit was Hester Browne 'privately so nobody else could hear' and 'whispered [Elizabeth Wright] in the ear that no body [would] hear them'. Through this chain of whispers the name of Hester Browne became publicly known, Wright 'afterwards [telling] the same to divers in the company'.[54] In this way, the strictures of civility were subtly undermined. Indeed, when Hester Browne brought a defamation suit against Hodgson, the midwife's defence was that she had never spoken maliciously or uncivilly. The experience of Anne Wintringham brought the politics of interaction into sharp relief. In defending his company, Shaw resorted to the usual tactic of sexual insult, bidding 'her be gone and guide her tongue and her tail'. Anne replied that if she 'had done that as well as him otherwise there would not have been such reports on him as there were'. It was in response to this affront of his own probity that Shaw then threw a candlestick at her and 'broke her head with it'.[55] As described by the labouring witnesses, the only response of a bloodied Anne was to grab his cravat. Shaw told a very different story in which Anne attacked not only him but also the artefacts of company and, indeed, the company itself, which he depicted as a kind of homogeneous presence. She took 'the flagon from the Table before them, and threw it into the chimney [and] abused Robert Shaw with very scandalous words'. She tore his cravat and got 'her hands into [his] hair and thereby pulled his head to the table till her hands were loosed by some in the company'. And she threw 'tobacco pipes and other things amongst the company without the least provocation or ill words given by any then in company'. The

---

[52] BIHR, CPH, 3314; *The memoirs of Sir John Reresby. The complete text and a selection from his letters*, ed. Andrew Browning, 2nd edition, preface and notes by Mary M. Geiter and W. A. Speck (London, 1991), pp. 579–80.

[53] BIHR, CPH 2560, deposition of Henry Brearey.

[54] Ibid., depositions of Henry Proctor and Elizabeth Wright.

[55] BIHR, D/C 1691/11, deposition of Simon Wright.

attack on patriarchal and paternal authority that Shaw so resented illuminated, in effect, the very politics upon which his alehouse company uneasily rested.[56]

Company and its politics provide, then, a comparative framework for understanding early modern sociability: a kind of historicised ethnography of social practice. It is a framework that extends synchronically, in that very different kinds of association were nevertheless regarded as types of company at a given moment in time. It also extends diachronically, in that the politics of company remained as much a determining feature of early modern sociability after 1650 as before. The nature of its politics varied, of course, from company to company. The explicit politics of patriarchy and paternalism that led to the conflagration between Shaw and Wintringham were different from the nuances of neighbourly civility exploited by Hodgson. Neither did they much resemble the ideological boundaries traversed by Warter on his epic journey from the Guildhall on Coney Street to the coffeehouse in Minster Yard. For all their differences, however, each instance of company displayed the same politics of participation, function, and interaction. Although early modern people did not conceptualise the term in precisely this fashion, they were certainly aware of its social implications. The company kept by John Crowther, Bridget Hodgson, John Warter, Robert Shaw, or Richard Thompson clearly communicated the sort of person they were. Likewise both the young Cromwell and Charles I were damned by hostile writers for the company they kept. This in turn reflected a more pressing concern of early modern writers: namely the relationship between company and the intellectual and moral qualities of the person. For example, when the London citizen and draper William Scott sketched his 'complete citizen' in the 1630s, he urged that he should 'not haunt Taverns too much which is the Epidemical fault of the City'. He elaborated that 'it is not company, but want of discretion in the choice and use of it, which overthrows a man; but besides needless expenses; how can a man be fit for business, who makes his body a continual quagmire?'[57] The Calvinist minister Robert Horne told the burgesses of Jacobean Ludlow that 'all the fault is not in the heart, when it becomes wicked and vicious': 'the heart is a spring that hath not only spouts to send out, as a Conduit, but pipes of sense wherewith it is fed'. As a result, corruption was a consequence of experience: the heart was inevitably moulded 'through seeing, hearing, talking, taste and handling'. However, 'they reason not sufficiently [who claim] If I had never known such company, I had never known such sin'. On the one hand, 'if their hearts had been good, the company could not have been evil'; on the other hand, 'ill company is not the whole, or principal cause of our error, but the heart'.[58] In these humanist and Protestant frameworks, company shaped the person, but

---

[56] Ibid., reply of Robert Shaw.   [57] Scott, *An essay on drapery*, p. 122.
[58] Horne, *The Christian governor*, p. 129.

it did not fully explain or define them: there was reciprocity but also distance between the two.

This points to a crucial difference between modern and early modern theories of sociability. Historians of early modern society have, by and large, focused on the structural differences and relationships of power that distinguished one person from another. In contrast, commentators at the time were as, if not more, concerned with the implications of discourse and association for the person: just as places required appropriate persons, so conversation was an activity imbued with moral significance. This was the more so because, like places, language and speech were known to be repositories of power, and so crucial to the person's agency, standing, and 'profit' in the world. Having suggested company as an idiom for approaching the ethnography of sociability, we can now turn to contemporary theories about its ideal nature: in particular, the kinds of conversation expected of civil citizens.

Conversations, civil and uncivil

A key into the language of America, written by Roger Williams in 1643, took as its starting point both the communicative basis of community and the instrumental power of language. The son of a London citizen, Williams was an archetypal 'subaltern' of the English Renaissance and fully inured in the linguistic theory that characterised it. Educated at Charterhouse Grammar School and Pembroke College, Cambridge, he was also a legal apprentice to Sir Edward Coke before becoming chaplain to the puritan household of Sir William Masham, in Essex, in 1629, and travelling with John Winthrop to Massachusetts in 1631.[59] His book was an ethnographic dictionary of the Narragansett that presented conversation as a cultural 'key' in at least three respects: as a tool of cultural dissemination; as a kind of discursive genre; and as a repository of the customs that constituted a culture. As he put it, talk was 'a *little Leaven* to season the *mighty Lump* of those *People* and *Territories*'. It enabled Europeans to 'converse with *thousands* of *Natives* over the *Country*: and by such converse it may please the *Father* of *Mercies* to spread *civility* (and in his own most holy season) *Christianity*'.[60] His book was, in turn, structured around two genres often used in the didactic literature of the period. These were the 'dialogue', by which the reader was enlightened through the scripted exchanges of others (in this case, between Williams and the Amerindians); and the sermon, by which the reader was connected, via the author, to the word of God. Through mastery of

---

[59] Edwin S. Gaustad, *Liberty of conscience: Roger Williams in America* (Michegan, 1991), pp. 5, 18, 23. For Williams' piety, see W. Clark Gilpin, *The millenarian piety of Roger Williams* (Chicago, 1979).

[60] Williams, *A key into the language*, A3.

these discursive strategies, Williams hoped to reveal not only the way to talk to the Narragansett, but also the fact that their ostensibly barbarous customs were more civil, natural, and godly than English equivalents. Finally, his book was *A key* that 'happily may unlock some Rarities concerning the *Natives* themselves'.[61] Only by learning and speaking the language could a stranger hope to fathom the customs that gave each culture its distinctiveness, as it was through language and communication that the customs and manners of a locale were reproduced, shared, and indeed altered by inhabitants.

Although developed in the context of the 'New World', these suppositions were wholly consistent with Williams' humanist and civic background. Since the sixteenth century a recurring concern of English reformers was that the ability to communicate persuasively and authoritatively was the key to any programme of cultural transformation. It was also well appreciated that any conversation – whether written or spoken – had its form, rules, and rhetoric. This was as true for treatises, ballads, and theatre as it was for gossip, counsel, or a petition. And, as the dictionaries, alphabets, and literacy campaigns of the period suggest, much time and energy were spent listing, reforming, and regulating the English vernacular and its dialects, as it was here that customs were enshrined and potentially adapted.[62] Texts directed at citizens shared this sense of the power of language. However, they also highlighted the relationship between conversation, personality, and social action in a way that Williams, with slightly different concerns, did not. Language was the God-given medium for expressing or disguising the self. It was also, as the primary resource of social exchange, an instrument for persuading or manipulating others. As Robert Horne put it: 'speech . . . should be the key to the mind to open it. For, the use of speech is to express the meaning of the heart, or to be the heart's interpreter.'[63] William Scott, citizen and draper of London, exclaimed 'O how excellent a thing is freedom! There is no better life than to live according to a man's nature, resolving always . . . to dip the pen of the Tongue in the Ink of the heart, speaking but what he thinks.'[64] However, Scott immediately qualified this by warning his 'complete citizen' that 'to utter all he thinks is eminent folly'. Indeed, 'because men are most taken with pleasing words, let them be discreetly chosen, and properly applied: For as speech makes a man more excellent than a Beast, so eloquence will make him more excellent than other men.'[65] Horne was even more circumspect, arguing that, 'As the tongue is governed well or ill, so wickedness breaks out, or is restrained in the body': 'the tongue well ordered, will comfort us, but set at large, shame us: who then will give such a member

[61] Williams, *A key into the language*, A2.
[62] Mulcaster, *The first part of the elementarie*, pp. 226–7, 154. Shrank, 'Rhetorical constructions of a national community', pp. 180–98.
[63] Horne, *The Christian governor*, p. 238.   [64] Scott, *An essay on drapery*, p. 29.
[65] Ibid., p. 90.

liberty?' Control of speech was, therefore, personally and socially essential, as 'a good tongue is the means by which our actions are well managed': it was with good reason that 'St James calls it the rudder of the man'.[66] It was a rudder both powerful and dangerous. Scott observed that 'my Citizen may deal pleasingly with all men; I would have him be a good Linguist, getting so many Languages, and those so well, that if it were possible, every man he deals with, should think him his countryman. These observations are necessary to his profit; for he shall hardly get by that man, whom he cannot please.'[67] There was, however, a thin line between pleasing and dissembling. The more godly Horne was quick to reiterate that 'the dissembler corrupts this use of speech and end of talk by a deceitful tongue; nay, overturns all humane society and dealings between man and man, by uttering with the tongue what was never conceived by the heart'.[68]

This awareness of both the social necessity and dangerous instrumentality of conversation clearly echoed the bittersweet conceptions of place and person outlined in the previous chapter. This was unsurprising given that the basic intellectual framework was derived from the same Ciceronian notion of *honestas* and the civility it structured. Within this framework, the personal characteristics that ideally accompanied the occupation and execution of place were equally relevant to communication between persons. One such attribute was honesty: the persons' ongoing and exacting quest for integrity in their relationships with others, with themselves, and with God. As Scott explained, the complete citizen was 'a good man ... opening his conscience, living as if he were always in public, rather fearing himself than others'.[69] Without honesty, society was vulnerable to the 'will' of men: as Scott put it, 'that deceit which is against justice towards others ... stands more in the wills, than wits of men'. The pursuit of will through lying was abhorrent for at least five reasons. It was 'cruel' and 'against nature'; it was against 'civil society; for the preservation whereof, it is necessary that men converse safely together, without fear one of another'; it jeopardised 'the common benefit'; and it was against Christianity'.[70] It was also, finally, against reason. 'The tongue is connected by veins to the brain and heart; by which nature teaches us, that it is to be governed by the intellect, whose feat is in the head, so that it may agree with the heart.' In 'a lie', in contrast, 'the speech always differs from the mind'.[71] Honesty was, however, only one dimension of *honestas*, or at least a quality the meaning of which was modified in the light of other, equally important virtues. These included wisdom, discretion, and decorum or fitness: qualities that, in terms of conversation, amounted to the ability of knowing what to say and how to say it according to time, place, and audience.

[66] Horne, *The Christian governor*, p. 249.   [67] Scott, *An essay on drapery*, p. 94.
[68] Horne, *The Christian governor*, p. 239.   [69] Scott, *An essay on drapery*, p. 3.
[70] Ibid., p. 18.   [71] Ibid., pp. 31–2.

Likewise intended to exclude the force of 'will' from social relationships, *honestas* provided a set of prescriptions that made heavy demands on a freeman or woman's 'disposition' and social 'abilities'. Its principles were directed at citizens through a variety of ideological agendas and through a range of literary genres. Robert Horne considered civil conversation an attribute of godliness. He took the Bible as the basis of his authority; preached and printed his views in the format of the sermon; and talked especially about conversation among neighbours. William Scott, who wrote his treatise for the Company of Drapers in London, drew on predominantly classical sources. He wrote in a tradition of civic aristocracy; chose the conduct book as his medium of expression; and focused primarily on conversation in relation to commerce and profit. Henry Manship, the town clerk of Great Yarmouth, used similar sources to develop the same notion of aristocratic civility as Scott; however, he did so in the form of a town history and with civic rather than commercial discourse in mind. William Fulwood was a Merchant Tailor and balladeer, Angel Daye a lawyer and secretary. Each used their literary and legal training to pen educational tracts on how to write effective and profitable letters and petitions for 'our equals, as to merchants, burgesses, citizens, &c'. Such letters were meant to enhance the civic, commercial, and neighbourly lives of freemen. Roger Williams was unusual in that ethnography was his primary source of intellectual authority. However, in his upbringing, education, and friendships with other civil-minded Londoners like John Milton – whom he taught Dutch in return for lessons in Latin – he was a veritable kaleidoscope of an English commonwealth tradition. It was more than symbolic, for example, that his primary reason for returning to London in 1643 was to purchase, on the advice of John Winthrop and with the help of his metropolitan friends, a 'Free Charter of Civil Incorporation' for the Providence plantations.[72]

The precise construction of *honestas* differed across these ideological traditions. For Horne, for example, 'wisdom' belonged to those that 'walk prudently in God's ways, following his word: for there is no sound direction for matter of religion, or manner of conversation, but from it'. 'People that know not God, that is, that know him not in his word, are called a foolish people' and 'have no wisdom in them'.[73] Indeed, 'to be wise, is not to have a politic head, but a sanctified heart; to be learned, is not to be able to discourse; but being able to discourse of points and matters in Religion ... and for a good conscience to perform obedience as we have believed'.[74] Scott was perfectly willing to concede that 'cunning is a crooked wisdom: let him shun that, and take that wisdom which is direct, which is not without honesty, nor ability'. However, his wisdom was classical rather than biblical and profitable rather than godly.

---

[72] Gaustad, *Liberty of conscience*, pp. 61–2.   [73] Horne, *The Christian governor*, pp. 70–1.
[74] Ibid., p. 73.

Scott noted that 'honesty without wisdom is unprofitable' because wisdom, as a combination of judgement and skill, allowed the citizen to express himself eloquently and effectively in social situations: it was 'the beautiful and noble composition of him in his words, his actions, and all his motions'.[75] In a similar fashion, discretion stood 'above Learning' as the key to civility because it 'does sufficiently enable a man to improve in all his affairs, whatever he is or hath, to the best advantage'. Discretion was 'neither Wit, Wisdom, Learning, Art, liberal or illiberal; but that which shows how to govern them all conveniently, and every other thing with them ... one who could rule and use all these'.[76] This was as true for personal governance, and the cultivation of the honest self, as it was for civic governance and the honest conduct of public affairs.

As this suggests, the communality that ideally characterised civic deliberations was neither unconditional nor opposed, in any simplistic fashion, to the interests of the person. While encouraging honest friendship and reciprocity, *honestas* nevertheless depended on persons who were self-reflective and socially astute. Scott warned that insofar as his 'speaking' was concerned, the citizen 'must take counsel with himself first and then speak'. He insisted that 'even the least circumstances be weighed; as you would choose what to eat, so choose what to speak: thou examines the meat that goes into thy mouth, so examine the word that comes out of it'. This was especially the case for citizens, who had constantly to 'deal with men of divers conditions'. In each instance, 'to speak according to the nature of him with whom he commerce is the best Rhetoric'.[77] As an instinctive rhetorician, the mind of a citizen 'must be stuffed with sufficiency to produce pleasing discourse' but also 'not ... so lavish as to hinder his observation, and become tedious to him he deals with'. The citizen required eloquence: 'his words should flow from the mouth [so that] it might be said of them, they are not so much words as Honey'.[78] As importantly, he must 'know how to be silent' as silence was 'more becoming, and instructing'. It also guarded against the very real difficulties in achieving meaningful commerce. As Scott explained, 'did all men think alike, secrecy were [sic] not necessary'. However, 'since the speaker and expositor utter and receive with different minds; speech cannot carry her meaning always just as a man would have her; therefore a man must defend her impotency by keeping her in'. Just as the 'tongue of a Wiseman is hidden in his heart', so 'my citizen may mingle profit with honesty, and enter into a composition with both'.[79] While 'he must never turn his back to honesty; yet sometimes go about and coast it, using an extraordinary skill, which may be better practised than expressed'.[80]

This 'extraordinary skill' was the essence of discretion and demanded psychological and social acuity on the part of the speaker. The wise citizen had 'a

[75] Scott, *An essay on drapery*, pp. 3–4.   [76] Ibid., p. 65.   [77] Ibid., p. 91.
[78] Ibid., p. 89.   [79] Ibid., p. 129.   [80] Ibid., p. 136.

true knowledge of the parties with whom a man deals'. Just as he 'must understand their nature, humour, inclination, designs, and proceedings' – their 'will' – 'so the nature of business in hand must be known too'. 'A superficial knowledge of it is not enough.' Instead, 'a man must penetrate into the inside, and see things in themselves, with the accidents and consequences that belong thereunto': 'knowing every man's nature and fashions, he may lead him; knowing his ends, he may persuade him; knowing his weakness or disadvantage, he may awe him'. Sensitive to 'the divers natures of the persons and affairs, he changes his style, and manner of proceeding'.[81] This required a clear sense of social distinctions. 'To his superior', the words of a citizen 'must carry much humility in them; to his equals, familiarity, which because he shall be sure of from them, must be mingled with a little state. To his inferiors familiarity too, but not too much of it, lest he breed contempt.'[82] It also demanded precise attention to self: the talk of a citizen 'must be assisted by behaviour: without this, his other qualities will not help him'.[83] As Scott noted, 'it cannot but be distasteful to any man, coming into a shop, when he sees a man stand as he were drowned in phlegm and puddle ... It is expected that the outward carriage should promise what's within a man.'[84] For citizens as for courtiers, it was the 'small ceremonious matters [that] win great commendations, because they are continually in use and note; whereas the occasion of great virtue comes but seldom ... they have in them a certain well-becoming majesty, if they be used without pride and affectation'.[85] Courtesy had to be balanced with 'a commendable close commodious carriage, which in matters of less importance must for a man's credit sake sometimes be laid aside; so with applause he may deal closely in matters of weight'.[86] In this way, 'it will be easy for him to profit'.[87]

The same principles extended to written communication. As William Fulwood observed in 1593, an epistle or 'letter is nothing else, but a declaration by writing of the minds of such as be absent, one of them to another, even as though they were present'.[88] Formed in part to connect province and metropolis, the corporate system was the institutional embodiment of 'presence in absence'. Handbooks on the art of petitioning and letter writing likewise stressed the value of *honestas*, and the instrumentality of communication, that honest profit within a society of complex gradations and overlapping hierarchies required. Himself a citizen, Fulwood intended written correspondence to provide 'profit' and 'pleasure' for a broad middle band of English society, observing that there were three 'principal sorts' of letters. As he put it, 'some are addressed to our Superiors as to Emperors, Kings, Princes, &c. Some to our equals, as

---

[81] Ibid., pp. 127–8.   [82] Ibid., p. 94.   [83] Ibid., p. 85.   [84] Ibid., p. 87.
[85] Ibid., p. 86.   [86] Ibid., p. 139.   [87] Ibid., p. 127.
[88] William Fulwood, *The enemie of idlenesse. Teaching a perfect platforme how to indite epistles and letters of divers sorts* (1593), p. 9.

to merchants, burgesses, citizens, &c. Some to our inferiors, as to servants, labourers, &c'.[89] Drawing heavily on Thomas Wilson and other rhetoricians, he outlined for his 'equals' both general principles of communication as well as ideal templates taken from the classical past that could be used for particular situations. Cicero exemplified different letters of friendship (to convey praise, lamentation, comfort, and dispraise) while Plato illustrated how citizens used the art of correspondence to negotiate their position with 'tyrants'.[90] Angel Daye, a lawyer and contemporary of Fulwood, acknowledged that 'every man naturally can speak and set down his own meaning'. However, 'Art prevailing in the cause, and by cunning skill marshalling every thing in his due order, proportion, and place, how much more the same is then beautified, adorned, and as it were in a new shape transmuted.' By learning conversational arts, 'learned' and 'unlearned' alike could 'advance the efficacy' of their conversation, be it 'to require, counsel, exhort, command, inform, commend, entreat, confirm, or whatsoever other intent, determination or purpose'.[91] Social distinctions were not to be negated through conversation, written or otherwise, so much as used in the process of persuasion. The emphasis was on enabling readers 'artificially or cunningly [to] handle an epistle' in a way appropriate to audience. Anticipating Scott, Fulwood advised readers to consider a recipient's estate, dignity, and quality; 'whether he be a public person, or a private'; 'whether he be rich or poor', a 'friend or enemy', a 'familiar acquaintance or a stranger', and even 'whether he likes reading letters or not'.[92] Daye likewise compared an unreflective correspondent to 'a foolish shoemaker, that making his shoes after one fashion, quantity and proportion, supposes the same forthwith of ability fit to serve every man's foot'.[93] Fulwood observed that it 'become not an inferior person, writing or addressing his words to his superior, or speak or write, by the imperative or commanding word, as if one should say this: "Sovereign king, behold such a one, who is a good Clarke, give him a benefice"'. Much more effective was a tone that was 'sufficiently obsequious' and demonstrated 'all humility'.[94] To this end, different modes of address and language were framed in standard rhetorical forms through which the 'benevolence' of a correspondent could be secured. It implied knowledge of distinctions in place and power, but also their negotiation.

The cultivation of benevolence was one tactic available to the discerning citizen. However, commentators were painfully aware that as equally artful and potentially empowering as civil conversation was its deliberate transgression: the strategic and subversive use of uncivil and illicit words. Writing from his place in the fractious borough of Ludlow, it is unsurprising that Robert Horne

---

[89] Ibid., pp. 11–12.   [90] Fulwood, *The enemie of idlenesse*, pp. 40, 70–90.
[91] Daye, *The English secretorie*, p. 2.   [92] Fulwood, *The enemie of idlenesse*, p. 15.
[93] Daye, *The English secretorie*, p. 4.   [94] Fulwood, *The enemie of idlenesse*, p. 13.

perceived 'neighbourliness' to be especially vulnerable to a range of conversational delinquents whom he placed under the broad category of 'slanderers'. Generically, 'A slanderer ... is a malicious informer ... an unauthorised relater' guilty of 'unmanly dealing with our Neighbour, by a whispering tongue'. As culpable were 'those who drink in with greater thirst of hearing and more eagerly, a false and uncharitable take against his neighbour'. There were inveterate slanderers: the 'walkers, and goers about with tales' who were nothing less than 'petty chapmen, or Peddlers, who carry wares about, selling in one place, and buying in another' within their communities. There were politic slanderers: 'the flatterers and sycophants, who insinuate themselves by the thrusting out of others'. And there were self-righteous slanderers, 'who proclaim their Neighbours secret faults to the wide world: and who, because their speech is true, though their end, in speaking, be evil and wicked, say they are far from slander'.[95] Horne decreed that, in the context of slander, the truth of a report was irrelevant: 'a wise man will be ashamed to speak the truth foolishly, when his words may do so much harm and no good: and, it is sin to speak slanderously (though truly) in a matter. Yea, a man may more sin by speaking some truth with an ill mind, then when (through infirmity) he shall speak an untruth, with a purpose to do good.'[96] It was on the basis of this civil conception of honesty that Horne decreed six rules of neighbourly conversation, each of which called for reflection, discretion, and goodwill on the part of neighbours. Most importantly, 'when we have a good calling, and just cause to speak, let us speak discreetly in time and place, that good may come of our speech, to the amending of him that is faulty, and to the bettering of him that hears'.[97]

In this sense, civility was a double-edged sword. Offering the possibility of structured discussion between unequal parties, it was also a tool of stigmatisation and exclusion. A petition from the corporation of York to Robert Cecil, Earl of Salisbury, in his capacity as Lord Treasurer and Privy Councillor, shows how citizens could work its rules to their own advantage.[98] Written in January 1612, it opposed attempts by a local landed interest, headed by the powerful Bellasis family, from purchasing ex-chantry lands in the city. Though currently leased by the corporation from the crown, the aldermen of the city had heard a sale was imminent. As befitted a letter written to a superior, the aldermen laced their prose with the 'honour, humility, and reverence' appropriate for the conversation. Concerned with an issue of what Fulwood styled 'gravity', it emphasised the 'matter as moral and civil', but also with 'respect to honour and profit' of the recipient. It argued the general point 'that this corporation might have habitations and places for the poorer sort of citizens and to keep others from having of them which might become chargeable to this city'. It did so

---

[95] Horne, *The Christian governor*, pp. 179–80.   [96] Ibid., p. 189.   [97] Ibid., pp. 190–1.
[98] YCA, B33, f. 281v.

according to the minor, major, and concluding phases of argument prescribed by the propagators of rhetoric. The minor section established the cause of the orators, or 'what moved us to write'. The major part explained their intent, or 'what our mind is'. The conclusion bore the final brunt of persuasion, offering either 'amplification' (inducing laughter and joy); 'commiseration' (phrased in sweet, pitiful and humble language); or an 'epilogue' (a brief rehearsal).[99] The aldermen at York (and perhaps their legal counsel) skilfully followed the rules, constructing a document that was as self-consciously obsequious as it was politically effective. The petition worked, and negotiation for the purchase of the lands by the citizens had begun by May 1612.[100] In contemporaneous Ludlow, in contrast, similar techniques were used not to repel the encroachments of local gentry so much as represent conflicting aristocratic and democratic positions within the city commonwealth to metropolitan authorities. Although petitioning was the main communicative resource available to democrats, it was the aristocrats who were especially astute in constructing their appeals. A draft letter to the Lord Chancellor, Sir Christopher Hatton, contained calculated slurs against the burgesses. Strategically arranged within the basic rhetorical framework of minor, major, and concluding sections, these emphasised the populist threat that the democrats represented. Two sentences in particular – 'many of them very light and disordered persons by the procurement of some secret enemy to the said poor town' and 'that such troublesome and busy persons may have condign punishment in accordance to their defects' – were emended to the final copy for added impact. It was the 'popularity' of the burgesses, rather than the justness of their grievances, which the authors wanted the Privy Councillors to remember.[101]

It was, however, counsel – the most symbolic and emblematic of civic conversations – which epitomised both the idealism and instrumentality of honest civility. Its ideal was encapsulated by Roger Williams' portrayal of ostensibly 'barbaric' Amerindian talk. He noted of the Narragansett that 'their manner is upon any tidings to sit round double or treble or more, as their numbers be; I have seen near a thousand in a round, where English could not well near half so many have sit'. Democratically assembled, 'Every man hath his pipe of . . . Tobacco, and a deep silence they make, and attention give to him that speaks'. On this basis, 'many of them will deliver themselves, either in a relation of news, or in a consultation with very emphatic speech and great action, commonly an hour, and sometimes two hours together'. For Williams, the broader implications of Amerindian practice were clear. Just as 'the wildest of the sons of Men have ever found a necessity (for preservation of themselves, their Families and Properties) to cast themselves into some Mould or form of Government', so 'The

---

[99] Fulwood, *The enemie of idlenesse*, pp. 31–6.   [100] YCA, B33, f. 297.
[101] SA, LB7/741.

whole race of mankind is generally infected with an itching desire of hearing News'. Indeed, the Narragansett's 'desire of, and delight in news, is great, as the *Athenians*, and all men, more or less; a stranger that can relate news in their own language, they will style him "Manittoe", a God'.[102] Williams noted that 'The Sachems [Narragansett Princes], although they have an absolute monarchy over the people; yet they will not conclude of ought that concerns all, either Laws, or Subsidies, or wars, unto which the people are averse, and by gentle persuasion cannot be brought.'[103] The lesson to be learnt in 1643 was that governors should welcome rather than distrust the discursive inclinations and practices over which they governed. However, the 1536 ordinary for a guild of 'Goldsmiths, Plumbers, Pewtherers, Glasiers and Painters' in Newcastle-upon-Tyne suggests that such principles had long been embedded in civic culture. One of its central concerns was the creation of a discursive environment in which members could 'meet together and counsel together, Of, or for, anything concerning the commonwealth and good ordinances of the said crafts'. Such counsel would achieve 'good order and manner for the common weal' as well as 'profit of the association and fellowship of the said five crafts'. Debate was to be 'after a loving manner and everyone to keep others counsel of or for anything that shall be uttered among them for their common weal'. Certainly brethren were expected to talk 'without any grudge or malicious words in the reproof of any of their honesties one to another'.[104]

The humanism of the later sixteenth century invigorated conciliar principles. As Henry Manship explained, 'counsel is, as says Socrates, a sacred thing; and, as Plato calls it, the anchor of the whole city ... and hath the same place in the commonwealth that the soul hath in living creatures'. Indeed, 'The commonwealth does chiefly depend on counsel and judgement, according to the disposition of which the affairs of the state are well or ill handled.' It was on 'this counsel [that] all the rest of the public government depends ... and it is by Cicero called the soul, reason and understanding of the commonwealth'.[105] As such, it was 'very meet that there should be in every great city and town, a competent number of senators elected (but not too many, for that is very dangerous) who are to have a place convenient appointed, where they may all assemble and meet together'. They did so 'either for service of the state in general, or for the benefit of the town in particular': indeed in Great Yarmouth as in other boroughs and cities 'the aforesaid guild hall was to that end ... first built and finished'. It was in this 'company ... ordained to some good, and most chiefly to attain the most principal and most excellent good of others' that 'sundry persons ... of divers different dispositions of mind inwardly ... [and] ... sundry professions, trades, and occupations, of body outwardly' are 'brought to union

[102] Williams, *A key into the language*, pp. 54–5.   [103] Ibid., p. 134.
[104] TWA, GU/GP/1/2.   [105] Manship, *History of Great Yarmouth*, p. 55.

and agreement'.[106] It was from the collective enterprise of counsel that citizens drew their individual strength. As Scott noted of his 'complete citizen', 'If he deal with superiors, let him make what use he can of them, but not trust in them; among all mortal things, there is nothing more fading then that power which hath not support from itself.' Indeed, 'it is common for that man to be unfortunate, which depends upon another'. Much more important than unequivocal patronage was 'to win speedily the opinion of all honest men, which much imports to the shortening that way, which guides to an eminent esteem'. Just as the rise of a citizen was 'assisted by many', so the '[diligent] quest of riches and credit' should not be 'over violent' or at the expense of virtue.[107] As such, it was the discreet friendship of equals rather than the naked patronage of betters that was the most valuable resource – indeed defining attribute – of citizenship. As Scott put it, 'to counsel is the best office of a friend; but let him be a friend with whom you counsel; deliberate of all things with thy friend; but first of him look that he want neither of his two proper qualities, honesty, sufficiency'.[108]

Conversely, astute citizens recognised that control of discursive practice was essential to political power. A primary concern for the reforming mayor of Jacobean Cambridge, fish merchant Thomas French, was conversational control. In what proved to be an extremely energetic civic career, the first recorded act of his mayoralty in 1608 was to initiate a survey of the borough's ancient customs in order to change debating procedures in the common council. Since 1581 a custom had prohibited the mayor of Cambridge from propounding 'any thing unto the house, unless he do acquaint the aldermen then present in the house with his purpose and that the more part of the aldermen then present do give their assent to the same'. On the grounds that 'many inconveniences have happened and fallen out to the prejudice of the good and quiet government of the said town', French now won 'a free and general assent' to abolish the restriction. Instead it was 'henceforth lawful to and for the new mayor of this town at his free will and pleasure to propound any thing to the said house at any common day or days hereafter ... without the assent of the aldermen first had or obtained'. 'An order for Decent speech and behaviour at common days', passed with 'full and absolute assent and consent' of the burgesses, likewise prescribed that after the mayor 'shall propound at any common day any matter ... touching the Town or the state thereof', responses were to be in order of office. When it came to the turn of the 'common burgesses', each 'should stand up to answer and speak in the same matter' and 'heard with quietness, and without disturbance of any other'. In the meantime, the mayor would act as a conversational referee, deciding who stood first (if more than one burgess wanted a voice) and whether a burgess should be allowed to reply at his 'discretion'.

---

[106] Ibid., pp. 55, 190–1.   [107] Scott, *An essay on drapery*, p. 143.   [108] Ibid., p. 135.

Any 'unseemly' or 'indecent' speeches out of turn warranted a 2s. fine.[109] Nine months later, the common council secured a writ from the Lord Chief Justice against alderman William Archer. French and other burgesses claimed that Archer, in opposing the reforms of French, had burst the bounds of civility. At the common day he had 'in very scornful, reproachful and contemptuous terms upbraided and reproved the said Thomas French most irreverently and unbeseeming to the great impeachment and disgrace of the place of mayoralty, discouragement of successors, and utter dislike of that grand assembly'. Archer was 'admonished' and agreed to publicly 'confess that he had wronged both the said mayor and his place ... and was therefore sorry'.[110]

In Ludlow in the 1590s, democrats countered the enclosure of legitimate counsel by aristocrats with alternative discursive strategies – slander and insult included. It was alleged, for example, that, during his tenure as bailiff, John Crowther had 'suffered base fellows both of life and living daily to abuse his fellow bailiff they calling him knave and other base terms'. Crowther 'himself ... does often call his fellow bailiff knave and likewise some of the ancient aldermen ... base and old companions'.[111] John Bradford was another discursive miscreant. At a 'gaol delivery' he 'most contemptuously ... did there publicly speak that the said Bailiffs were not the lawful bailiffs, and therefore did own no duty to appear before them, and he persuaded divers other burgesses to do the like disobedience'. The decade saw pamphlets, libels, letters, and writings 'cast abroad concerning the government of this town [and] defaming the governors'.[112] It was through his words that Bradford 'nourished a great faction in the town', intent on bringing 'all in common'; and it was likewise astute reportage that enabled the aristocrats to characterise the democratic grievances as 'a derogation of authority'.[113] Democratic opposition transmuted in the seventeenth century into neighbourly scandal and insult, so much so that in 1611 the common council noted 'the little respect and sometimes the contumelious behaviour of lewd and presumptuous persons towards our said governors'. Verbal licentiousness had 'not only greatly abused and disregarded the good credit of the corporation and greatly greened and discouraged many good persons so abused'. It had 'also ... ministered occasion of such savoury boldness and presumption in many inhabitants touching as lewd words and evil behaviour and at their pleasure'. As a result, any burgess 'who shall speak any lewd or savoury words ... or shall in vile scurrilous behaviour demean himself or herself towards any of the XII and XXV [to] the disgrace of their callings and place' would be fined 6s. 8d. A fine of 20s. was reserved for words and gestures against the two bailiffs. 'Lewd words' included 'knave, rascal, beggar,

---

[109] CCRO, City Box II, 9, f. 23.
[110] CCRO, City Shelf C, Book 7, ff. 1–1v, 8v.   [111] SA, LB7/736.   [112] SA, LB7/759.
[113] SA, LB7/765.

drunkard, or the like'. They were seen to damage 'the reverence and respect' burgesses should have for 'persons chosen for your government' as well as the 'good reputation and credit of this corporation'. As importantly, they prevented 'offices to undergo and perform with cheerfulness their said places of charge and troubles'.[114]

The problem of disputed counsel provided the context for Horne's plea to curtail slander: in Ludlow as elsewhere, the political uses of slander, rumour, and defamation were a powerful reminder that citizenship and neighbourliness were sides of the same discursive coin.[115] Just as talk between men and women about the personal and private lives of neighbours was a prominent feature of public company, so both forms of discourse had their tactics and arts. Circumstances in Ludlow suggest, in turn, that notions of civility could be deployed politically and strategically to marginalise threatening or dissenting voices. Just as civic democrats were most effectively presented as populists, so political criticism was best deflected or undermined on the grounds of its inappropriate and uncivil nature. Indeed, no one better demonstrated the contingency of civility than did Robert Horne. Even as he was castigating Ludlow's 'slanderers', the minister was collating an extensive set of manuscripts that displayed at once an historical interest in criticism against the crown and an 'intense interest in the most violently debated political issues of the early 1620s'. The collection, which served 'as a space where information was shared', dealt with matters 'ranging from freedom of speech to the impeachment of Bacon to the beginning of proceedings against Buckingham; from the debates on foreign policy to those on church government'. It did so as a 'mixture of learning, satire, obscenity, and wit', and in a manner that combined the personal and political as closely as any libel or slander circulated closer to home.[116] The manuscript was constructed with the help of Herbert Jenks, son of the Francis Jenks who, as town clerk of Ludlow, engineered the infamous incorporation of 1598. By the 1610s Herbert Jenks was one of several metropolitan-based 'friends' who kept Horne informed about national public news and affairs. Discursive gamekeeper in the borough, the clergyman played poacher abroad, engaging in conversations that, judged on his own terms, were nothing if not slanderous of the Jacobean court. In this instance, civility was as company did.

'The public stage and view of the world'

Just as structured conversations were a primary feature of city commonwealth, so freemen and citizens knew about language and its uses. Such reflexivity

---

[114] SA, LB2/1/16, f. 42.
[115] Hughes, 'Religion and society', pp. 58–84; Adam Fox, 'Religious satire in English towns, 1570–1640', in Collinson and Craig, *Reformation in English towns*, pp. 221–40.
[116] Colclough, '"The muses recreation"', pp. 387, 391.

inevitably qualifies the notion that the ideal of rational discourse only emerged with the 'transformation of the bourgeois public sphere' during the later seventeenth and eighteenth centuries. On the contrary, the very notion of civility brought with it rhetorical rules and 'arts' designed to achieve constructive, orderly, profitable, and reflective debate; or, conversely, illicit criticism and dissent. Such skills required, in turn, a sense of the reflective and knowing self that was at once placed in and detached from particular moments of company. Indeed, the very definition of citizenship stemmed from an acquaintance with the personal skills required of rational and effective discourse. Likewise, the topography of public discussion during the early modern period clearly extended beyond the palaces of sixteenth-century monarchs; the correspondence of more socially and intellectually elevated 'circles' or networks of correspondents; or the coffeehouses, newspapers, and clubs of Restoration and Georgian England. Instead we find the much earlier promulgation of civility in the counsels, letters and petitions, and commercial and neighbourly dealings that formed the communicative bread and butter of the corporate system. It was not simply a literary conceit that, when faced with the unwelcome attentions of the eloquent but distinctly uncivil Falstaff, the immediate response of the leading she-citizens of Windsor was to invoke the primary conversational resources at their disposal: 'counsel' and 'parliament' (2.1.26–7, 39–40). Londoners would, in turn, have appreciated the inference of Shakespeare that the dispute between Coriolanus and the Roman citizenry was essentially a breakdown in and about conversation. For all his military qualities, the general could neither comprehend nor exhibit the discretion, wisdom, and decorum demanded by the citizens.[117] Likewise the conceits of gallant sociability were given short shrift in plays like *The city madam*, which described how 'sitting at the table with / The braveries of the kingdom, you shall hear / Occurrents from all corners of the world, / The plots, the counsels, the designs of princes, / And freely censure 'em; the city wits/ Cried up, or decried, as their passions lead 'em, / Judgement having naught to do there' (2.1.86–92). In contrast, civility was essential to an English civic culture that valorised the public role and political potentials of conversation. The astrologer William Lilly recalled that the value of his citizen-master to the London Company of Salters was not his vocation. Rather it was the fact that, although he could neither read nor write, he was 'a Man of excellent Natural Parts, and would speak publicly upon any Occasion very rationally and to the Purpose'.[118]

That is not to say that a sense of 'the public' that was distinct from civic, *res*publican, and monarchical power did not emerge during the sixteenth and

[117] Cathy Shrank, 'Civility and the city in *Coriolanus*', *Shakespeare Quarterly*, 54 (2003), pp. 406–23.

[118] *The last of the astrologers. Mr William Lilly's history of his life and times from the year 1662 to 1681*, edited and introduced by Katharine M. Briggs (London, 1974), pp. 7–8.

seventeenth centuries, nor that its scale, scope, and political significance did not increase exponentially in the revolutionary era. The plethora of plays, pamphlets, newsbooks, treatises, sermons, and petitions clearly point to a printed public sphere that had enormous implications for the organisation of 'opinion', the dynamics of political participation, and the nature and location of public debate. The extent of printed public debate with the development of new or invigorated institutions like the coffeehouse and postal service during the 1650s consolidated its impact in the Restoration era.[119] Even then, though, the continuities and complexities of its 'emergence' are striking. Indeed, the concept of a printed public sphere was sketched as early as the mid-sixteenth century by the prefaces and preambles of printed texts to 'the reader' and 'the public'. These demarcated an audience that, no matter distances of place and time, could be appreciative of and communicate with the printed word. Constituted by the many genres of scribal, printed, and oral discourse that this implies – whether letters, printed or scribal 'books', ballads, theatre – this public combined, in theory, the 'openness' and presence of an audience with the sanction of political licence and patronage. Regarded as an important medium of reform and civility, the creation and control of a 'literary public sphere' was as much a priority for humanist reformers like Mulcaster as patrons of the Protestant theatre like Leicester.[120] James VI and I was similarly aware of its political efficacy, his willingness to publish his own 'works' – and publicly patronise those of his playwright, Jonson – standing in marked contrast to the suspicion with which both men viewed the public pretensions of corporations and parliaments. However, by its very nature this was a public of scribal and printed discourse impossible to control. John Donne noted in 1610 'that having observed, how much your Majesty had vouchsafed to descend to a conversation with your subjects, by way of your Books, I also conceived an ambition, of ascending to your presence, by the same way, and of participating, by this means, their happiness'.[121] Moreover, the possibilities of textual appropriation meant that even the most authorised and authoritative of pronouncements, such as John Speed's *Theatre of the empire of Great Britain* could be used in unexpected ways. The *Theatre* was commissioned at court and dedicated to 'so high an Imperial Majesty' and 'most potent monarch James'. It was then 'brought upon the public Stage and view of the world'.[122] Among the audience of this 'public Stage' was Henry Manship, town clerk of Great Yarmouth, who, on 'hearing of the great Theatre published by John Speed in the year 1611 … rode fourteen miles to see and read it'.[123] The *Theatre* in turn inspired Manship to compile a

[119] Mark Knights, *Politics and opinion in crisis, 1678–81* (Cambridge, 1994), chs. 6, 8; Withington, 'Urban political culture', ch. 7.
[120] McMillin and Maclean, *The Queen's Men*, ch. 2.
[121] John Donne, *Pseudo-martyr* (1610), Preface.
[122] Speed, *The theatre and empire*, B2, C2.   [123] Manship, *History of Great Yarmouth*, p. 6.

history of his own borough that celebrated precisely the *res*publican and civic authority so distrusted by James.

The reign of Charles can be viewed, in turn, as a concerted attempt to put the genie back in the bottle, be it through regulating the influential St Paul's sermon or restrictions on classical translations and other political texts. That in 1641 he was drawn into the conversation to end all conversations is evidence enough that he failed. *An exact collection of all remonstrances, declarations, orders, ordinances, proclamations, petitions, messages, answers, and other remarkable passages between the King's most excellent Majesty and his High Court of Parliament* (1643) is a compendium of the furious talk between parliamentary and royal 'power', all of it observed by 'the public'. Not only were exchanges between the two bodies made 'open'. The very nature and provenance of counsel was left to the discretion of the public. It was transformed, in effect, into a democratic idiom. Richard Overton and William Walwyn remonstrated for 'many thousand citizens' in 1646 that 'In the beginning ye [the parliament] seemed to know what freedom was, whether rich or poor. All were welcome to you and ye would mix yourselves with us in a loving familiar way, void of courtly observance or behaviour. Ye kept your committee doors open. All might hear and judge of your dealings.'[124] Such openness could not survive the war and the subsequent peace. By 1648 it was clear to London's democrats that the 'rackings and tortures the people in general have suffered' for the 'hopes of freedom and a well-settled commonwealth' were being undermined by 'secret, powerful influences, the more securely and unsuspectedly to attain an absolute domination over the commonwealth'. The petitions that had previously represented the diverse interests of commonwealth were now fobbed off with 'empty thanks', ignored, or threatened with burning by the common hangman.[125] Indeed, it was as a last bid to preserve 'the highest notions of freedom' known in the world that 'a company of honest men living in and about London ... rightly appropriate to themselves the title of the contrivers, promoters, presenters, and approvers of the late large London Petition'.[126] Warrants for their arrest meant that they had been unable to 'go our ordinary way to work to get subscriptions to it'. Moreover the Council of State '[reproached] them with such appellations as they know did most distaste the people, such as "Levellers", "Jesuits", "anarchists", "royalists"'. Just as oligarchs in Elizabethan Ludlow had labelled burgesses in ways that played on the Privy Council's fear of populism, so 'the Levellers' charged their opponents with using similar rhetoric to build 'upon the easiness and credulity of the people'. They nevertheless hoped that, 'in the sad apprehension of the dying condition of our liberties and freedoms',

---

[124] Richard Overton with William Walwyn's collaboration, 'A remonstrance of many thousand citizens' (1646), in Sharp, *The English Levellers*, p. 48.

[125] John Lilburne, 'England's new chains discovered' (1649), in ibid., pp. 146, 148.

[126] Ibid., p. 155.

their representatives would 'read these our serious apprehensions seriously and debate them deliberately' – as had been done, for example, at Putney.[127]

This enlarged and contested public sphere was firmly rooted in the corporate system both in terms of its participants and its logistics. Of the eight authors and printers that constituted the petitioning, printing, and counselling heart of the Levellers, six had held apprenticeships or were fully enfranchised citizens of London, and two had close connections with the citizenry.[128] Ian Gentles has likewise shown that 47 per cent of the 238 members of the New Model Army Officer Corps hailed from London or other large cities and towns. Their 'strongly urban character' was not only at odds with the subsequent myth of the russet-coated East Anglian farmer; it was recognised at the time. *Vox Militaris* explained that 'There are very few of us, but have most of this world's interest in the City of London, being chiefly and principally raised thence, and very many, especially of our officers, being citizens themselves, having their wives and children therein.'[129] Captain Adam Baines was an attorney from Leeds; based in London; and at the centre of an extensive web of kinship and friendship networks through which news was disseminated. Indeed, Baines' 'special care of the public' stemmed in large part from his position 'at the fountain's head of news' in London: he and the state he served enjoyed enormous discursive power through his accumulation and dissemination of 'intelligence' from and to his correspondents.[130] As one 'friend' in the 'northern parts' put it, 'we wait in expectation of news from your parts, which indeed is the fountain from whence it flows ... if you pipe it well ... we be so good artists as to dance'.[131] This merely reflected the prevailing institutional importance of the corporate system to the dissemination and exchange in news. The postal service was an urban institution that the soldiery both monopolised and extended in the 1650s. The book trade, in terms of the Stationers Company in London and the stationers, booksellers, and chapmen in the provinces, was always urban-based. The coffeehouse, like provincial playing companies before it, was also synonymous with the corporate system: in 1681 it could be claimed (somewhat hyperbolically) that 'most of the cities and boroughs of the nation' had one.[132] Their very proximity to and participation in such institutions made for discursively privileged citizens.

The 'coffee houses and other publick places' that Richard Thompson allegedly frequented in the early 1670s marked the extension rather than invention of places designated for civil debate and conversation. As such, they were part of a longer tradition of 'publick matters and in hearing and telling news' that citizens valued and contested both locally, in their city commonwealths,

---

[127] Ibid., pp. 151, 156. See below, ch. 6.   [128] Sharp, *The English Levellers*, pp. 202–13.
[129] Ian Gentles, 'The New Model Officer Corps in 1647: a collective portrait', *Social History*, 22, 1997, p. 133.
[130] BL Add MSS 21417, f. 12.   [131] BL Add MSS 21417, ff. 18, 34, 70.
[132] Cited in Pincus, '"Coffee politicians does create"', pp. 813–14.

and nationally, as a culturally defined public. Continuities were synchronic as well as diachronic. Both Thompson and Nelthorpe were central figures in the civic politics of the 1670s, playing a leading role in London's Common Council and its struggle with the Court of Aldermen over the balance of power within the civic polity.[133] In this way, the perennial struggle between London democrats and aristocrats was closely tied to the renewed tensions between Parliament and court; and it is no coincidence that Thompson's fondness for coffee coincided with a number of proclamations attempting to close down the coffeehouses as seminaries of subversion. Within the jurisdiction of civic authority, the coffeehouses survived.[134] However, it was Thompson's reflection on his private and public selves that most illuminates the way in which an earlier tradition of civility informed his participation in public life. Writing to his brother-in-law and old commonwealthsman Major Braman in June 1678, the citizen, confectioner, and erstwhile entrepreneur observed that 'the discipline of living well is the amplest of all other arts'. It was 'not only for an exterior show or ostentation that our soul must play her part but inwardly within ourselves where no eyes shine but ours'. He continued, 'everyone may play ... and represent well upon the stage, but that is not so much our nature as our art'. True virtue lay 'within ... where all things are lawful, because we think them concealed, to keep a due rule and decorum, that is the point'. In true humanist fashion, a well-ordered commonwealth demanded from its participants an 'exquisite life, which in its own privacy keeps itself in such awe and order'.[135]

The baker James Wright – that 'citizen of great respect / As free from vice as from defect' – would surely have concurred. So, too, would Thompson's friend Andrew Marvell. Noted for his virtuosity in a range of literary genres and idioms, Marvell's discursive slipperiness was testimony to his conversational art. In the official and supportive letters he regularly posted to his civic constituency in Hull; his civil correspondence with friends; his ideologically ambiguous poetry; his revelatory pamphlets; or his scathing libels and satires of the Restoration court, Marvell always wrote in a way appropriate to form and context. The diversity of his patrons, clients, and companions likewise demanded contrasting forms of talk. They included the Presbyterian household of Sir Thomas and Lady Fairfax, with whom he lived as tutor to their daughter during the early 1650s; their son-in-law, the libertine courtier Buckingham, whom he had befriended independently on a visit to Italy; and John Milton, his patron in the republican regime.[136] They also included the merchants and citizens with whom he socialised in London and communicated with in Yorkshire

---

133 See below, ch. 6.   134 CLRO, Microfilm MCFP/552, f. 189–192v.
135 TNA SP29 404 215.
136 David Norbrook, *Writing the English republic: poetry, rhetoric and politics, 1627–1660* (Cambridge, 1999), pp. 165–7.

and the continent. These were communities that required the classic attributes of *honestas* – a discreet and reflective self. John Aubrey observed that, 'in his conversation', Marvell was 'very modest, and of few words'. Though 'he loved wine he would never drink hard in company, and was wont to say that, he would not play the good-fellow in any man's company in whose hands he would not trust his life'. This did not stop him keeping 'bottles of wine in his lodgings' and drinking 'liberally by himself to refresh his spirits, and exalt his muse'.[137] This propensity for discretion has meant that even his marital status has long been doubted: by John Farrington; by his Whig hagiographers; and by literary historians who have taken Farrington's aspersions at face value.[138] Less controversially, it was certainly the case that 'for divers years before his death [Marvell] kept also lodgings in Maiden Lane in Covent Garden where he kept his moneys, bonds, books, writings and other goods and chattels'. It was 'in his study at that lodging' that 'he frequently lodged for his privacy and other conveniences'. It was also there that he kept 'many trunks and hampers wherein were great sums of money in gold and silver beside bonds, bills, books, jewels and other goods of value' that his wife assumed her husband had saved.[139] As Angel Daye explained in a passage written some 100 years earlier, but which might have been written by Marvell himself, 'secrecy, trust and regard' were the special requirements of a 'secretary' and man of public affairs. It was 'by this reason we do call the most secret place in the house appropriate unto our own private studies, and wherein we repose and deliberate by deep consideration of all our weightiest affairs, a closet'. This was 'a place where our readings of importance are shut up, a room proper and peculiar to ourselves'.[140] Just as Thompson valued his interior sense of 'rule and decorum', so Marvell's place of discursive and material production was also the most private of sanctums: the spatial embodiment, in effect, of the civil, civic, and public man.

---

[137] John Aubrey, *Brief lives: a selection based upon existing contemporary* portraits, ed. Richard Barber (Wallop, 1975), p. 202.

[138] Fred S. Tupper, 'Mary Palmer, alias Mrs Andrew Marvell', *Publications of the Modern Language Association*, 53, 2, 1938, pp. 367–92. For further discussion of the Marvell household see below, ch. 7.

[139] TNA, C7/587/95, deposition of Mary Marvell.   [140] Daye, *The English secretorie*, p. 391.

Part III

Honest Distinctions: Economy,
Patriarchy, Religion

6   The economy of freedom

'Our homogeneal and essential members'

In the early 1660s Sir Thomas Widdrington dedicated and presented his recently completed manuscript of the history of York to the citizens of the city whom he had served as recorder and parliamentary representative over the previous decade. In his various public capacities, Widdrington had proved a typical exponent of *res*publica and *civitas*, promoting the public ascendancy of common law while also working for the good of the body he represented – securing, for example, a 'private' bill to dredge the River Ouse in 1658.[1] With the political crisis of 1659 he supported, like his kinsman Sir Thomas Fairfax, the advance of Monk from Scotland and the subsequent return of monarchy in the name of the public and the public good.[2] The subsequent politicking that came with the king hastened his retirement from public life, and his civic history was intended as a lasting memorial of 'my affections to the city and citizens of York'.[3] It also reflected the values that shaped his political position: not least the ancient genealogy of the city, its importance as a conduit of common law, and his role as a lawyer in controlling its flow. However, the civic response to his gift took him by surprise – so much so that the manuscript remained unpublished until the nineteenth century. The aldermen and councillors who received it not only refused the dedication; they also took the opportunity to complain about the state in which Widdrington now left them. Their analysis was bleak and accusative. Moreover, it presented an economic imperative that had little in common with the constitutional sensibilities that characterised Widdrington's own position. The citizens found 'by experience that it is not a long series or beadroll of ancestors and predecessors but wealth and estate which set a value upon men and places. As for our wealth, it is reduced to a narrow scantling. If we look upon the fabric and materials of the city, we have lost the suburbs which were our skirts, our whole body is in weakness and distemper, our merchandise and trade, our nerves and sinews, are weakened and become very mean and

---

[1] YCA, B37, ff. 101v, 88–88v, 113v–114, f. 127.
[2] *The Monckton papers*, ed. E. Peacock, *Miscellanies of the Prohibition Society*, XVI (1884), p. 31.
[3] Widdrington, *Analecta Eboracensia*, p. 5.

inconsiderable.' In such circumstances 'a good purse is more useful to us than a long story'.

The 'Complaint' nicely captured the economic rationale of citizenship: the concern for both personal and communal profit that at once legitimated the perpetuation of city commonwealth and, in large part, drove the formation of England's corporate system. It also suggests the symbiotic relationship between economy, governance, and politics that was still felt to hold in the later seventeenth century. As the citizens explained, 'The body of York is so dismembered, that no person cares for the being the head of it.' Indeed, 'our present misery is, that we can hardly keep together our homogeneal and essential members . . . when our very government seems to hang by a weak, or upon some slender twig'. Problems were accentuated because the citizenry appeared to have backed the wrong political horse over the previous twenty years, trusting in allies like Widdrington who were now, 'as Absalom's mule did him, either leaving of us, or refusing to act as magistrates amongst us'.[4] Widdrington's withdrawal from civic office in January 1661 was the harder because the 'violence' of 'persons with honour and interest' against the city meant that, as the citizens told him, 'we have little hope [protecting] our rights'.[5] Not all of the city's problems were political, however. There was an awareness of York's geographical disadvantages as well as industrial and commercial developments that were undermining the city's provincial position. While 'Leeds is nearer the manufactures, and Hull more commodious for the vending of them; so York is in each respect furthest from the profit.' However, just as these challenges were associated with particular (and rival) city commonwealths, so any response to them was framed communally. Priorities included making 'our river' more navigable, re-edifying the decayed parts of the city, and setting up 'some manufacture in the city'. Most importantly, 'our poor' not only required relief but served as a constant reminder of the fate 'we may all of us fall if some timely course be not taken by which, through God's blessing, this tottering and wasted city may be upheld'.[6]

While the 'Complaint' may well have exaggerated, for political purposes, the immediate problems facing the city, the more general economic turbulence it described was no chimera. Keith Wrightson has recently confirmed that the previous 150 years had seen a series of related demographic, social, and economic developments that, in their cumulative impact, amounted to 'a process of commercialisation'.[7] Work on the 'long eighteenth century' likewise suggests that the 'Complaint' came on the cusp of even greater economic and social upheaval. This included the prospect of imperial expansion unprecedented in its scale and scope; the intensification of industrial and manufacturing practices; a new and vibrant corpus of political economy; the enlargement of ports and

---

[4] 'A sad complaint by the city of York to the author', in ibid., p. x.
[5] YCA, B37, ff. 165, 167v.   [6] 'A sad complaint', p. x.
[7] Wrightson, *Earthly necessities*, p. 331.

towns both within and outwith the corporate nexus; and further integration of, and diversification within, the market.[8] Although traditionally divided historiographically, these two epochs were clearly part of a longer continuum: a period of sustained transition that has long been associated with the rise of modernity.[9] Within this narrative, economic change was closely linked to those processes discussed in previous chapters – state-formation, the emergence of a 'bourgeois public sphere', and the replacement of *communitas* by 'the town'. The social implications were equally profound, not least in terms of the transformation of medieval degrees and estates into a national and three-tiered society of wage labourers, the middling sort, and the landed interest.[10] Viewed from this perspective, the citizens of York had every reason to be worried. They were among the 'debris' of a distinctly outdated past and on the brink of an even more uncertain future: custodians of antiquated privileges that were not only inequitable but also actively counter-productive to profit and success in an age of commerce.

Previous chapters have contextualised and historicised this narrative from a civic perspective, arguing that not only does citizenship complicate our understanding of oligarchy, the state, urban society, and public discourse, but that it was also a pervasive presence in their 'structural transformations'. This was equally true of economic culture. Corporate and craft governance was fundamental to the programme of economic and social renewal intended by the later Tudor regimes. Through their participation in the institutions of parliament, magistracy, common council and merchant- and craft-guilds, citizens and freemen were key proponents, implementers, and benefactors of economic and social policy. Likewise it was civic merchants, retailers, tradesmen, and artisans who were most active in the intensified commerce that characterised the age.[11] As was shown in chapter 2, the growth of the corporate system was in turn linked to a number of structural developments that firmly rooted city commonwealths in the wider worlds of province and nation: the growth in urban markets, borough courts, civic building programmes, and the institution of apprenticeship. This was as true for areas of new incorporation – such as the coastlines, valleys, and estuaries of the south and west – as it was for provinces with well-established civic cultures: for example, in Suffolk, Norfolk, and the Cambridge Ouse. Even a borough like Cambridge, which relied on lands and markets rather than urban manufacture for its common wealth, attempted to create a regulated craft economy in the Jacobean era.[12]

For all the commercial and regulative prominence of enfranchised artisans and merchants, a defining nexus of their work – the urban freedom – has received

[8] M. J. Daunton, *Progress and poverty: an economic and social history of Britain, 1700–1850* (Oxford, 1995), ch. 1.

[9] Wrightson, *Earthly necessities*, pp. 4–17.   [10] Ibid., pp. 269–72.

[11] Muldrew, *Economy of obligation*, pp. 51–9.   [12] CCRO, City Shelf C, Book 7, f. 50.

relatively little attention within recent economic history. While this is certainly true for the eighteenth century, when urban freedom is generally regarded to have withered on the vine, it is also true for the later sixteenth and seventeenth centuries.[13] Craig Muldrew's excellent study of England's 'economy of obligation' is a case in point. Although based on evidence drawn primarily from cities and boroughs, freedom and citizenship are hardly mentioned as a constitutive feature of economic relations – it is not noted, for example, that William Scott wrote his influential 'Essay on drapery' explicitly for 'the complete citizen'. [14] The burgeoning concern for civility, contract, and 'credit' that Muldrew traces are instead regarded as aspects of the centralising state on the one hand and the household on the other: the place of communal values and practices are left indeterminate.[15] This is despite the fact that, as Christopher Brooks has noted, apprenticeship and guilds were increasingly associated with the inculcation of *honestas*: the honesty of 'fair dealing, probity, and uprightness of character'; and honesty as 'a certain mode of behaviour and speaking, a certain dignity of deportment'.[16] Far from reproducing *Leviathan* locally, these institutions provided, and continued to provide, paradigms of civility that were central to *civitas*. Although intersecting with both the state and the household, they were not synonymous with either. Neither should they be conflated with those codes of honour and courtesy adopted by the gentry over the same period: there was, as Jonathan Barry has argued, a qualitative and self-conscious difference between the two.[17] Resting on structured commerce and traffic on the one hand, and property and possession on the other, freedom contributed to a sense and politics of place that was experienced communally – in the context of commonwealth and the 'companies' that constituted it – and personally, as an aspect of household profit.[18] Moreover, insofar as the values of urban freedom were propagated further afield, then its synchronic and diachronic implications were potentially immense, contributing to the wider culture of the 'middling sort' and providing templates for the imperial and manufacturing economies of the later period.

'Live a freeman without dependence'

It is perhaps ironic that the literary harbinger of 'modernity' that dominates early modern historiography should be Ben Jonson. Dramatist of the monarchical state and proponent of an informed and literary public sphere, Jonson

---

[13] Note its absence in Paul Langford, *A polite and commercial people: England 1727–1783* (Oxford, 1989).

[14] Muldrew, *Economy of obligation*, p. 428.   [15] Ibid., pp. 133, 149.

[16] Brooks, 'Apprenticeship', p. 77.   [17] Barry, 'Civility and civic culture', pp. 182, 195.

[18] Norah Carlin, 'Liberty and fraternities in the English Revolution: the politics of London artisans' protests, 1635–1659', *International Review of Social History*, 39, 1994, pp. 223–54.

was also supremely sceptical of the civil virtues that a Ciceronian conception of commonwealth entailed.[19] Beyond the rhetoric and platitudes of the public good, he perceived an acquisitive individualism driving the commercial energies of England's citizens, implying a cultural transformation held by Richard Tuck and Keith Wrightson to have occurred at the end of the sixteenth century. For Tuck, this shift was political in nature: one marked by the replacement of Cicero by the much more sceptical Tacitus on the bookshelves of England's reading classes.[20] For Wrightson, it was reflected in the much more explicit pursuit and display of individual and household profit at the expense of neighbourly and communal obligations: a new self-interest that was never better demonstrated than by the 'scorn' and 'resignation' of Jacobean satire.[21] It was a mentality encapsulated by the two citizens in *The Alchemist* – the young tradesman Drugger, who looks to 'necromancy' to maximise his household profits; and the great merchant Mammon, whose material ambitions transcend the boundaries of reason and language. A 'seller of tobacco' and 'free of the grocers', Drugger is 'a young beginner' intent on building 'a new shop'. A citizen who 'would be glad to thrive', he 'would know, by art' where to position his shop, doors, shelves, and pots. Face in turn assures him that 'This summer/He will be of the clothing of his company: And, next Spring, called to the scarlet' (I. 3. 7–15, 35). At the opposite end of the civic spectrum, Mammon intends to use the philosopher's stone to commodify everything. He explains 'I'll purchase Devonshire and Cornwall, / And make them perfect Indies' (II. 1. 35–6) and launches into rhapsodies about material accumulation that will make him more powerful than any monarch. When Subtle disingenuously reminds him that 'my labours' in the arts are meant to be put to 'the public good, / To pious uses, and dear charity', Mammon promises to create colleges, hospitals, and, 'now and then', a church (II. 3. 48–52). However, the spuriousness of these civic platitudes is revealed when he uses the power apparently within his grasp to seduce Dol Common. When she suggests he will have 'wealth unfit / For any private subject', he promises they will 'therefore go with all, my girl, and live / In a free state' (IV. I. 175).

While the materialism, self-interest, and dishonesty of the age were common tropes of city comedy, not all poets viewed their implications for citizenship in the same way. Jonson's comedies and masques were distinguished by the inference that the realities of commerce, empire, and human nature made the whole project of city commonwealth redundant. It was in men of untrammelled 'wit' on the one hand, and in the monarchical state on the other, that any possibility of social equilibrium and morality lay. While equally critical of urban pride and avarice, more 'popular' poets like Thomas Middleton nevertheless regarded

---

[19] See above, ch. 3.   [20] Tuck, *Philosophy and government*, pp. 45–64, 104–19.
[21] Wrightson, *Earthly necessities*, pp. 202–5.

thrift, industry, and honesty as virtues still central to citizenship and attainable by citizens – dispositions that made them eminently suitable for fulfilling a public role in city, nation, and empire. The Lord Mayor's Pageants of the 1610s and 1620s reiterated the insight dear to Sir Thomas Smith that commonwealth and commodity – and public good and personal profit – were not only reconcilable but actively reciprocal. Empire did not degrade citizenship so much as extend its potential, opening whole new communities ripe for commerce and reform. Indeed, it was not citizens so much as self-interested and wilful gallants, gentry, and courtiers positioned outwith city commonwealth that posed the gravest threat to urban and colonial society: uncivil figures like Middleton's Whorehound and Shakespeare's Falstaff who brought 'error' and degradation in their wake. Luke, the central character in Philip Massinger's *The city madam*, was another embodiment of the anti-citizen: a figure through which the principles of citizenship were at once expounded in words and subverted in practice. The antithesis he posed sheds important light on the key value that, even into the seventeenth century, defined urban freedom: the personal moderation and social mediation of 'will'.

Written in the 1630s and published as late as 1658, *The city madam* centres on the household of Sir John Frugal, a great London merchant and citizen who, with his enormous wealth and credit, personifies the acquisitive opportunities of the age.[22] A reworking of *Measure for Measure* within a city commonwealth, the narrative hinges on Frugal pretending to retire to a monastery and relinquishing control of his fortune to his profligate younger brother, Luke, who he has rescued from debt and now lives as a dependent in his household. Frugal then returns to the house disguised as an American Indian to expose the tyrannical nature of his brother. The stratagem has two purposes. It aims to test the widely held conviction that Luke is a reformed character capable of dealing more 'honestly' than Frugal himself. And it looks to curb the 'pride' of Frugal's wife and daughters who, on the back of Frugal's industry, have rescinded their civic roots and are intent on aping the worst excesses of the court. While a household dependent, Luke appears the archetypal citizen. He is eloquent, his conversational skills making listeners statuesque and act according to his wishes (3. 2. 176–7). He is also reflective and equitable. Luke explains of his brother that 'He is a citizen / And would increase his heap and will not lose / What the law gives him. Such as are worldly wise / Pursue that track, or they will never wear scarlet'(1. 2. 141–4). He then reminds his brother that civil sociability must temper the rigorous enforcement of bonds and contracts. Intervening on behalf of Frugal's debtors, he argues that 'Gentle in your abundance, good in plenty' is 'the distinction / And noble difference' between citizens and those 'born only for themselves' (1. 3. 50–8). Citizenship distinguishes and protects

---

[22] Philip Massinger, *The city madam*, ed. Cathy Shrank (London, 2004).

its practitioners from men who 'Though prosperous in worldly understandings /
Are but like beasts of rapine that, by odds / Of strength, usurp and tyrannize
over others/ Brought under their subjection' (1. 3. 69–73). Recognition of this is
the basis of honesty and Frugal grudgingly gives his debtors more time to fulfil
their bonds, though exacting the significant promise that they keep his leniency
secret: 'Should this arrive at Twelve on the Exchange / I shall be laughed at for
any foolish pity, / Which money-men hate deadly' (1. 3. 115–16).

It is because of Luke's intervention that Lord Lacey regards Luke as 'honest' and 'pious' and persuades Frugal to embark on their social experiment.
However, the results are unexpected. It becomes clear that, for all his apparent
eloquence and honesty, Luke is the antithesis of urban freedom and civil society.
The contracts, bonds, deals, and credit that he inherits from his brother become
the weapons of tyranny, the merchants' 'counting house' a veritable arms dump
(3. 3. 1–45). 'Sublimed' by the scale of his power, Luke vows to give over all
pretence at 'conscience' or 'honesty' (4. 2. 117–33). Lord Lacey finds the effect
of wealth on Luke difficult to grasp. He repeatedly reminds Luke that 'in your
poverty, you were a pious / And honest man'; that 'I once held you an upright, /
Honest man' (5. 2. 23–4). Luke's rebuttals are telling. While honesty and piety
are best 'interpreted, A slave and beggar', he boasts that 'I am honester now by /
A £100,000' and has 'other business than to talk / Of honesty and opinions'
(5. 2. 25–30). Eloquence for Luke was simply 'dissimulation and the shape /
I move of goodness': a technique for accruing profit without industry, piety,
or virtue (5. 3. 25). Once ensconced in the place of his brother, the reality of
his 'nature' – as opposed to the power of his words – becomes apparent. Luke
promptly arrests the debtors he had previously defended for breaking their
bonds and threatens Lord Lacey, whose estate, it transpires, is mortgaged to
Frugal, with financial and personal destruction. Most seriously, Frugal's wife
and daughters are promised as sacrificial slaves to the visiting 'Indians' in return
for a cash payment. It is with some relish that the previously maligned Frugal
finally reveals himself and asks Lord Lacey 'What think you now / Of this dear
soul, this honest pious man? Have I stripped him bare? . . . 'Tis not in a wolf
to change his nature'. And to Luke: 'My kind and honest brother / Looking
into yourself, have you seen the gorgon? . . . Monster in nature / Revengeful,
avaricious atheist / Transcending in example' (5. 3. 116, 130–5).

In fact, at the heart of Luke's transformation is an underlying consistency: his
preference for his 'will' and its gratification over civil sociability at each stage in
his life. As a dissolute youth he explicitly rejects city commonwealth for the life
of a gallant and debtor; reduced by profligacy to dependency he is a 'drudge' and
'slave' in Lady Frugal's household; and miraculously redeemed by his brother,
he becomes tyrannous. As he says on learning of his good fortune: 'My will
is still the same' (3. 2. 110). He corrupts Frugal's apprentices, Goldwire and
Tradewell, by mocking their reluctance to 'dare to serve our wills' and their

concern that any indiscretions 'our father's bonds, that lie in pawn / For our honesties, must pay for' (2. 1. 74–5). Once empowered with his brother's credit and bonds, however, such reasoning makes him equally free to use the powers at his disposal according to his own disposition and will. Two of his first acts are to arrest Goldwire and Tradewell for cheating and to seize their fathers' bonds. The 'monstrous nature' that saw him drink, gamble, and whore away his first inheritance also makes him a tyrant once he is empowered with the vast economic and social resources that his brother has earned through lawful credit, enterprise, and industry. The inevitable conclusion is that the freedom of the will is the inverse of freedom embedded in commonwealth: not only does it license idleness, insubordination, and the breakdown of communal profit; it also legitimates the potentially malicious acts of those with social, economic, and political power. Urban freedom, in contrast, protects poor and wealthy alike by at once enforcing legal, communal, and Christian obligations and cultivating from apprenticeship onwards the personal dispositions appropriate for civil society. In this way 'slavery' – the subjection of one person to the unmediated and unaccountable will of another – is avoided.

Similar concerns informed the debate of the General Council of the Army at Putney on 29th October 1647. Gathered to 'engage for our freedom', it brought Lieutenant-General Oliver Cromwell and his son-in-law, Commissary-General Henry Ireton, into 'company' with a collection of citizens and citizen-soldiers: most notably Colonel Thomas Rainborough, Maximilian Petty, John Wildman, and Captain Edward Sexby.[23] That it took the form of a common council was unsurprising given the civic backgrounds of most of the participants. Likewise, great emphasis was placed on controlling and accounting for 'will' – in terms of both the manner in which the conversation was conducted and the definition of freedom eventually reached. Cromwell's most telling interjection was that he 'was most dissatisfied with what I heard Mr Sexby speak, of any man here, because it did savour so much of *will*'.[24] He was referring to Sexby's earlier declaration that 'I am resolved to give my birthright to none. Whatsoever may come in the way, and whatsoever may be thought, I will give it to none.'[25] It was this refusal to talk and listen civilly – and so accommodate a compromise after reasoned debate – which prompted Cromwell's intervention. It had a sobering effect. Ireton, the most implacable and dominating of discussants, quickly agreed to moderate his position 'if I see but the generality of those whom I have reason to think honest men and conscientious men and godly men to carry themselves another way'.[26] The equally vociferous Rainborough likewise apologised 'for some passion and some reflections' and conceded important

---

[23] 'Extract from the debates at the General Council of the Army, Putney, 29 October 1647', in Sharp, *The English Levellers*, p. 116.

[24] Ibid., p. 123.   [25] Ibid., p. 120.   [26] Ibid., p. 122.

ground. As tellingly, the one issue that all could agree on was that will and freedom were antipathetic. Ireton reminded his companions that 'what the soldier of the kingdom has fought for' was the danger that 'one man's will must be a law'. Any future constitution must secure, in turn, 'a voice to those who are likely to be free men, men not given up to the wills of others, and thereby keeping to the latitude which is the equity of constitutions'.[27] That promised, he would 'go with you as far as I can'. Petty in turn acknowledged 'the reason why we would exclude apprentices, or servants, or those that take alms, is because they depend upon the will of other men and should be afraid to displease them. For servants and masters, they are included in their masters, and so for those that receive alms from door to door; but if there be any general way taken for those that are not so bound to the will of other men, it would be well.'[28] In this way, a quintessentially civil conversation took for its conclusion the civil basis of freedom.

The company could agree that the mediation of will was a prerequisite of freedom. However, its institution was more problematic. Wildman argued that their aim was 'not to constitute what is already established but to act according to the just rules of government'. To this end, 'Every person in England has as clear a right to elect his representative as the greatest person in England. I conceive that's the undeniable maxim of government: that all government is in the free consent of the people.'[29] As Rainborough famously put it, 'I do think that the poorest man in England is not at all bound in a strict sense to that government that he has not had a voice to put himself under.' Drawn from natural and divine law and the unequivocal fact of the Norman Yoke, their position was too abstract for Ireton, who thought that principles of 'birthright' were irrelevant to 'particulars'. As he put it, 'you must fly for refuge to an absolute natural right and you must deny all civil right; and I am sure it will come to that in the consequence'.[30] In practice, 'No person has a right to an interest or share in the disposing and determining of the affairs of the kingdom, and in choosing those that shall determine what laws we shall be ruled by here ... that has not a permanent fixed interest in this kingdom.' Freeholders and a 'freeman of a corporation' enjoyed just such 'a permanent and local interest'. A corporation was 'a place which has the privilege of a market and trading'. Likewise, the man that had 'his livelihood by trade and by his freedom of trading in such a corporation – which he cannot exercise in another – he is tied to that place, for his livelihood depends upon it'. As a result, 'that man has an interest – has a permanent interest there, upon which he may live, and live a freeman without dependence'. The mediation of will depended, therefore, not on personal rights so much as 'property': the 'interest' vested in 'the persons in whom all land lies and those in corporations in whom all trading lies'. It was on this basis that

---

[27] Ibid., p. 122.   [28] Ibid., p. 130.   [29] Ibid., p. 116.   [30] Ibid., p. 103.

borough representation, for all the inequities of its current distribution, was 'the most fundamental institution in this kingdom'.[31]

For defenders of citizenship, the 'interest' it constituted was more civil than most. Edmond Boulton wondered 'how much more worthy the whole is than the parts . . . to be marshalled as a man among societies of civil men, then to be distinguished by allusions to particular members'.[32] It was 'such of the Gentry, who live not in the city, and do . . . elevate themselves with contempt of others in respect of the Arts, and ways of maintenance' who were uncivil.[33] Not only were they men of 'vanity . . . causeless elation and arrogance' and reminiscent of the 'tyrannical appropriation of Gentry to some certain old families, as in Germany'; they were also responsible for 'the prodigious eating up of whole houses, towns, and people [and] the mystery of depopulation'.[34] He urged 'Fathers who are Gentlemen [to] put their children, who are not rather inclining to Arms, or letters, to Apprenticeship, that is to say, to the discipline and Art of honest gain, giving them a title of being somewhat in our country'. For justification one had only to look to 'the ancient wisdom' of the Romans, who 'did ever leave the gates of honour open to City-Arts, and to the mysteries of honest-gain, as fundamental in Common-weal'.[35] In the process, Boulton reconciled the imperatives of property and birthright. Apprenticeship was not 'a kind of bondage' so much as 'a mere civil contract, which as all the world knows, a bondsman is incapable of'. Indentures were 'a contract of permutation, or interchange [of] mutual obligation . . . a civil contract, occasioned, and caused by that prudent respect which the Contrahents mutually have to their lawful and honest commodity, and such only as are freeborn'. As a form of contract, citizenship was at once voluntary and open to all. Neither did it subsume other or prior identities: 'some Citizens may be a Citizen, and yet truly a Gentleman, as one and the same man may in several respects be both a Lord and Tenant'.[36]

Boulton's particular aim was to refute the assumption that citizenship and gentility were antithetical. However, the logic of his argument had wider implications. As a form of contract, freedom was the natural right and property of all freeborn Englishmen willing or able to participate in it. In practice, apprentice-ship brought sons of contrasting 'abilities' into different callings, so transposing wider social distinctions onto the occupational and civic structures that charac-terised city commonwealth. Gentlemen, for example, were synonymous with retailers, wholesalers, entrepreneurs, and great creditors: the self-styled civic aristocrats of the corporate system. Yeomen and wealthier husbandmen were, in turn, the skilled craftsmen, artificers, and mechanics. This was reflected in the self-description of freemen not only by trade but also by more general appellations of 'gent' and 'yeoman'. It was experienced materially in terms of

[31] Ibid., pp. 103, 108, 111.   [32] Boulton, *The cities advocate*, p. 59.   [33] Ibid., p. 54.
[34] Ibid., p. A2.   [35] Ibid., p. 51.   [36] Ibid., pp. 9–10.

the great differentials in wealth that freemen positioned in particular occupations were able to achieve. And it made for a civic gentility qualitatively distinct from the manners of 'Gentry who live not in the city'. Far from emulating the 'county community', civic 'gents' could perceive themselves as not only wealthier and more credit-worthy than their unenfranchised counterparts but also more civil: as exemplars, in fact, of the 'aristocracy' defined and propagated by humanist and religious reformers.[37] That yeomen and artisans also participated in the same civic and civil structures, and in certain instances were upwardly mobile within civic society, likewise made for a culture of freedom that was complicit with – but also, when necessary, critical of – the aristocratic claims of civic elites. The ever-increasing number of contracts, credit, and commerce linking town and country in turn meant that the values of urban freedom also percolated outwards, into province and locality. As a result, the gentry and commons able or willing to participate in city commonwealths enjoyed their freedom even as they retained other ties and identities. The precise structure of urban freedom varied, of course, from place to place: London, Ludlow, and Launceston were very different city commonwealths. However, that integrated networks of civic bodies should protect and regulate specific liberties and enshrine what Boulton termed 'the dignity of generous dispositions' was a basic principle of citizenship.[38]

'As free men do'

This was certainly the case in Newcastle-upon-Tyne, the citizens of which in 1651 inscribed on their bridge 'True liberty takes away no man's right, or hinders no mans right'.[39] The locus for what has been described as the 'first industrial society', and a place of national and international 'commerce', it was a borough that nevertheless emerged from the later middle ages with its guild economy not only intact but institutionally enhanced.[40] By the later seventeenth century it was a front-ranking provincial capital that encapsulated both *civitas* and 'town': a place with a clearly delineated city commonwealth that also saw its population increase from 12,000 to 16,000 between 1670 and 1700, and rise to 29,000 by 1750.[41] Studies that have focused on its precocious 'modernity' – whether in terms of an 'embryonic organised proletariat' created by the coal trade or the ferment of Newcastle's 'popular politics' – have nevertheless acknowledged the importance of a 'politically conscious citizenry' within the larger political

---

[37] See also Brooks, 'Apprenticeship', pp. 79–83.   [38] Ibid., p. 54.   [39] See above, ch. 4.

[40] Wrightson and Levine, *Making of an industrial society*, pp. 1–10, 76–81; Roger Howell, Jr, 'Newcastle and the nation: the seventeenth-century experience', in Barry, *The Tudor and Stuart town*, pp. 276–8.

[41] Wrigley, 'Urban growth and agricultural change', p. 42; Slack, 'Great and good towns', p. 370; Joyce Ellis, 'Regional and county centres 1700–1840, in Clark, *Cambridge urban history*, p. 675.

culture.[42] As such, Newcastle-upon-Tyne in the second half of the seventeenth century serves as an apposite context for examining the practice of urban freedom in what were transformed and transforming circumstances. Of particular concern is the freedom practised not by the city's mercantile elites but rather more modest artisans and tradesmen. Indeed, both the Company of Glasiers, Goldsmiths, Plumbers, Pewtherers, and Confectioners (the Glasiers) and the Company of Barber Surgeons and Tallow Chandlers (the Barbers) reveal a dynamic civic culture that was also a distinctive template for the more complex associational politics of the eighteenth century.

The Glasiers and Barbers were both democratic institutions in which the will of the company was decided communally and on the basis of the majority of voices. While two stewards were elected annually to perform administrative and executive roles, they were accountable to the whole of their brethren rather than a sub-committee of co-opted elites. In similar fashion, the borough charter enshrined company representation in the town's corporate structures, a representative being elected each year by his fellow brethren to attend the Spittle and elect the mayor of the town. Finally, while a number of different crafts constituted particular guilds, there is no evidence of occupational segregation or hierarchy until the end of the seventeenth century, when (for example) barber surgeons came to dominate tallow chandlers, and goldsmiths became somewhat estranged from their fellow glasiers, plumbers, pewtherers, and confectioners.[43] These democratic tendencies are especially apparent when compared to the organisation of freedom in the much smaller borough of Ludlow. Here the two main companies – the Hammermen and Stitchers – were organised along aristocratic lines, civic authority becoming enclosed within a co-opted body of 'Six Men' around the same time as the governing bodies of the borough were reconstituted into a common council.[44] In both the Hammermen and Stitchers, the Six Men were empowered by guild ordinaries to annually nominate the two stewards responsible for daily administration; exercise discretionary powers within the guild; represent their guild on the corporation; and select their successors after two years in office. Moreover, within each guild there was a hierarchy of occupations. Among the Stitchers, for example, retailing householders like the drapers, mercers, haberdashers, and merchant tailors had a degree of precedence over glovers, skinners, and cappers that was reflected in their preponderance among the Six Men. Stratification was to some extent

---

[42] Joyce Ellis, 'A dynamic society: social relations in Newcastle-upon-Tyne, 1660–1760', in Peter Clark, ed., *The transformation of English provincial towns 1600–1800* (London, 1984), p. 193; Wilson, *The sense of the people*, p. 315.

[43] For the Glasiers see TWA, GU/GP/1/2 and GU/GP/2/2; for the Barbers see TWA, GU/BS/2/1. Difficulties with foliation mean that subsequent citations will often give the year of the entry rather than the folio number.

[44] See SA, LB17/1, LB17/2, LB17/3.

Table 6.1 *Geographical origin of apprentices in the Newcastle Company of Glasiers, Goldsmiths, Plumbers, Pewtherers, and Confectioners*

		1640s	1650s	1660s	1670s	1680s	1690s
Within guild	(%)	39	24	32	32	24	4
Newcastle	(%)	11	24	21	19	33	25
Local province	(%)	39	33		38	32	65
Yorkshire	(%)	6	10	4	3		
Solway	(%)		5			2	2
Other*	(%)			4		2	
Unspecified	(%)	6	5	39	8	7	4
Total	(%)	101	101	100	100	100	100
TOTAL	(Nos)	18	21	28	37	42	51

*City of London and City of Edinburgh.
Source: TWA, GU / GP /2/2.

offset both by annual assemblies of freemen and the autonomy that individual crafts enjoyed over the nuts and bolts of their freedom: for example, apprentice-ships, journeymen, enfranchisement, and standards of workmanship remained the preserve of particular occupations. However, the authority that common council claimed over freemen was undeniably aristocratic in a way that the Newcastle guilds were not. Indeed, freedom in Newcastle-upon-Tyne bore a much closer resemblance to civic governance in Cambridge. This was despite the fact that it was constitutive of a very different kind of city commonwealth. In Cambridge, civic democracy was practised in a hostile urban environment; particular to the corporation rather than guild bodies (which did not exist); based on the control of fairs, markets, and land; and threatened on a recurring basis by external interventions in borough affairs. In Newcastle-upon-Tyne, in contrast, civic democracy characterised the culture of smaller bodies of freemen that were integrated politically into the larger city commonwealth – a social formation that dominated, in turn, the urban topography. It was, moreover, a civic and civil culture based around the practice of particular occupations, trades, and callings rather than the control of land and fairs: a culture that, unlike in Cambridge, prevailed throughout the seventeenth century. Indeed, for all the factionalism of their merchants – and their recurring and well-studied struggles to protect and control the trade in coal – it was through participation in the complex lattice of crafts, guilds, and companies that the citizenship of Newcastle freemen was forged.

Tables 6.1 and 6.2 show that, insofar as the Glasiers and Barbers were concerned, this lattice remained attractive throughout the later seventeenth century – not merely for sons of company brethren, but also for householders

Table 6.2 *Geographical origin of apprentices in the Newcastle Company of Barber Surgeons and Tallow Chandlers*

		1640s	1650s	1660s	1670s	1680s
Within guild	(%)	28	8	19	26	12
Newcastle	(%)				11	35
Local province	(%)	2	2		21	35
Yorkshire	(%)				5	2
Solway	(%)				3	5
Other*	(%)				2	2
Unspecified	(%)	70	90	81	32	9
Total	(%)	100	100	100	100	100
TOTAL	(Nos)	57	57	43	62	43

*Dorset and City of London. Registration procedures mean that the geographical origins of apprentices to the Company of Barbers, Surgeons and Tallow Chandlers only become apparent from the 1670s.
Source: TWA, GU/BS/2/1.

of Newcastle, the province, and beyond. Moreover, it did so at a rate that was not too removed from the pace of demographic change more generally. Recruitment to the Glasiers rose from eighteen apprentices during the 1640s, to twenty-one in the 1650s, twenty-eight in the 1660s, thirty-seven in the 1670s, forty-two in the 1680s, and to fifty-one by the 1690s. Whereas in the 1640s, 39 per cent of apprentices were sons of company brethren, by the 1690s the figure was only 4 per cent. In the meantime, the percentage of apprentices recruited provincially had risen from 39 per cent to 65 per cent: a nice indicator of the interpenetration of commonwealth and province that also contradicts the usual pattern of decline in extra-company recruitment.[45] Table 6.2 suggests that numbers for the Barbers were at once higher and more stable than the Glasiers: while fifty-seven apprentices registered indentures in both the 1640s and 1650s, the figure fluctuated between forty-three and sixty-two in the three decades thereafter. However, both companies enjoyed a similar geography of recruitment. By the 1680s, 12 per cent of Barber apprentices were sons of company brethren, 35 per cent came from Newcastle, and 35 per cent had provincial origins.

Tables 6.3 and 6.4 in turn demonstrate that, in the case of both companies, apprenticeship did not enclose freedom from external and unenfranchised householders. On the contrary, it was a mainspring of social mobility in much

---

[45] Brooks, 'Apprenticeship', p. 72.

Table 6.3 *Paternal status of apprentices in the Newcastle Company of Glasiers, Goldsmiths, Plumbers, Pewtherers, and Confectioners*

		1640s	1650s	1660s	1670s	1680s	1690s
Within guild	(%)	39	24	32	32	25	4
'Gentry'	(%)	4	5		11	5	26
'Yeomen'	(%)	28	29	4	14	21	31
Trade	(%)	23	32	18	16	32	26
Professional	(%)	6			5	3	2
Unspecified	(%)		10	46	22	14	12
Total	(%)	100	100	100	100	100	101
TOTAL	(Nos)	18	21	28	37	42	51

Source: TWA, GU/GP/2/2.

Table 6.4 *Paternal status of apprentices in the Newcastle Company of Barber Surgeons and Tallow Chandler*

		1640s	1650s	1660s	1670s	1680s
Company	(%)	28	7	19	26	12
'Gentry'	(%)				21	21
'Yeomen'	(%)				5	23
Tradesmen	(%)				6	28
Professional	(%)	2			2	2
Unspecified	(%)	70	93	81	40	14
Total	(%)	100	100	100	100	100
TOTAL	(Nos)	57	57	43	62	43

Source: TWA, GU/BS/2/1.

the same way that it encouraged urban immigration. Both companies attracted sons of company freemen; self-styled 'gentry' and 'yeomen'; 'professionals' such as ministers and lawyers; and other tradesmen and artisans until at least the end of the seventeenth century. It functioned, in effect, as Boulton's model suggests, bringing men from different social backgrounds into a single civic milieu. Indeed, in its sociology and geography apprenticeship bore more than a passing resemblance to the patterns of civil litigation discovered by Craig Muldrew in Newcastle-upon-Tyne for the same period. However, it did so not so much as an attribute of 'the state' as of *civitas*.

Closer consideration of the culture into which apprentices entered suggests that the idea of honest civility as a legally mediated, socially accountable and personally disciplined will was not simply a refrain of city satire or political debate. Rather it was a touchstone of urban freedom and bedrock against servility and slavery. One of the primary justifications for guilds and companies was that they facilitated 'honest' company: as arbitrators and custodians of economic honesty, guilds and companies were seen to connect the enfranchised householder with the *honestas* required of civil society more generally.[46] By placing themselves within these communal bodies, freemen – and, by extension, their households – insinuated their personal interests within the greater will of the company from which they drew their economic freedoms, privileges, and personal successes. On taking their freedom, for example, householders swore to be 'obedient to the orders and ordinances of this company . . . laws as shall hereafter be made by the stewards or major part of the company . . . and such orders as are at present kept by the said company'.[47] Such oaths represented a ritualised act of contract by which freemen were obligated to the will of the company, and were not taken lightly. In 1619 Lionel Featherstone and John Ord, two prominent members of the Barbers, 'refused to stand for the company's censure' over an order they had broken. As a result, it was decided that 'they shall not have voice' in the company until 'they have undergone the company's will'.[48] Seventeen years later, it was likewise noted that Edward Smith was 'content . . . to undergo the company's will for his fines that he is out of, and the company is content'.[49]

This practice of company was closely linked to notions of property and profit, or what Boulton significantly described as 'honest gain'. A 'Humble petition of the apprentices of . . . Tallow Chandlers and Barber Surgeons . . . to the common council of' Newcastle-upon-Tyne illustrates the point. Petitioning in 1619, the apprentices reminded their common councillors that 'by the laudable customs of the said town, it is not lawful for any persons to exercise any mystery or trade within the said Town except he be freeman of the said Town'. Moreover, before becoming 'a freeman of the said town he ought to serve as an apprentice for the said freedom diverse years'. It was on this basis that 'Masters who take prentices do receive with their apprentice great sums of money which the friends and parents of the said apprentices are willing to give in regard of the benefit that may arise to the said apprentice by the said freedom.' The apprentices' grievance was that Thomas Archibald and Leonard Featherstone, stewards of the company, 'out of a covetous and greedy disposition', were undermining this process. It was alleged that for 'a small some of money' the stewards 'have very lately made one Thomas Wittom foreigner, and one who never served as an apprentice in the town, free of the said company'. As a result, Wittom was now free 'to exercise the said trade and open shop within this Town for the sale

---

[46] See above, guild ordinances, ch. 5.
[47] TWA, GU/GP/2/2.   [48] TWA, GU/BS/2/1, f. 12.   [49] Ibid., 18 March 1635.

of his wares ... as free men do'. The apprentices argued that 'this inorderly course tends to the hurt of the said corporation and undoing of the apprentices and all other apprentices within the said Town who have given great sums of money and do endure (many times) extraordinary service diverse years for this freedom'. They requested that the common council call 'the stewards before you to show cause why they have broken custom' and 'also to take such order by your wisdom and prudence the like contempt may not be committed again'. In the short term, they wanted the council 'to prohibit Wittom to exercise the said trades or any of them within the said town'.[50] As a result, it was ordered that a committee of four councillors should hear the dispute and 'set down and certify our opinions of that abuse or abuses'.

A contractual arrangement on the part of the apprentices (and their 'friends and parents'), apprenticeship was also a rite of passage through which the profits of a calling were first earned and then enjoyed. Newcastle apprentices were fully sensible of not only the civic authority – and legitimate exclusions – upon which their investment depended, but also the discursive mechanisms through which their grievances could be represented. And, while the stewards had apparently compromised their immediate authority as wardens of the company, the committee of common councillors knew better and acted in favour of the petitioners. A new generation of apprentices demonstrated as great a communal sensibility – and also willingness to intervene in company politics – in 1648. The backdrop to their petition, directed at the company of Barbers rather than the common council of the town, was the concerted attempt by certain brethren to push forward plans to purchase a permanent place of civic residence. The project required concerted lobbying for permission from the common council; a substantial loan to purchase the property; regular assessments to pay back the debt; an increase in the cost of the freedom; and the creation of a committee to take care of the construction and running of the building.[51] It exemplified, that is, the impact of any major communal endeavour on the internal dynamics of a company, at once extending the range of financial commitments and imposing a new committee onto extant institutional structures. Twenty-one apprentices nevertheless declared 'our acknowledgement of the great care you had and leave to us and our successors in going about to provide a house and garden for the use of the Society which will not be only useful but also an honour to us and our successors'. They observed that while company finances might 'retard' the project, the company should not 'desist'. Indeed, they promised that 'when we shall be admitted to our respective freedoms', they would pay the fine of 13s. 4d. 'to be hereafter imposed and paid by everyone that after that should be made free by service (which we humbly conceive to be just and reasonable)'.[52] Of the petitioners, only three were sons of company brethren, the rest originating

---

[50] Ibid., ff. 1–1v.   [51] Ibid., ff. 139, 149, 160, 168, 171v, 173, 179.   [52] Ibid., f. 167v,

from elsewhere in Newcastle or beyond. While seven of the petitioners were apprenticed to four of the twelve masters who subsequently became lessees to the new property, two-thirds were apprenticed to masters who were not directly involved in the project. The petition was, in effect, an autonomous intervention based on a clear conception of the extenuated needs of the company: needs that served, in turn, the personal profit of current and future members.

The kind of fines levied on company brethren suggests that profit and place went hand in hand with civility. Encompassing all those potential misdemeanours outlined by guild ordinaries (and subsequently added thereafter), these ranged from the number of apprentices contracted to a master, to the illicit employment of foreigners and journeymen, to the stealing of work from another master, to working on the Sabbath. However, most striking is that in companies like the Barbers and Glasiers, fines were most frequently imposed for uncivil conversation amongst freemen: in particular, what brethren said – and how they said it – to and about each other both as individuals and as a collective body. In both companies the average wealth of freemen (as indicated by the hearth tax) was three hearths: these were, for the most part, men of lower middling rank positioned some social distance from the rarefied heights of Newcastle's mercantile elites.[53] One recurring conversational crime was 'giving the lie': accusing a person or the company of dishonesty in an angry and 'provocative' manner. It was a crime to which David Shevill was particularly susceptible: he gave the lie to a steward in 1646, to Charles Clarke three times in one meeting in 1656, and to Peter Bates twice in 1671.[54] In 1669 Peter Bates had himself given 'unbrotherly speeches in saying Robert Frazer junior and one of the stewards swore falsely', while in 1662 Robert Archibald gave the lie to the company as a whole.[55] Another recurring trope was the accusation, by brethren, of incivility or indecency towards them. Richard Todd complained in 1671 that William Green, servant to Thomas Barley, 'came into his shop without liberty and gave him uncivil language'.[56] Robert Lampton and Henry Mattison gave each other 'unbrotherly speeches according to the tenor of the ordinary' in 1663, and a year later Arthur Newham used 'indecent language unto Charles Clarke . . . provoking him and calling him a base fellow'.[57] Brethren also accused the company of incivility. Peter Bates was fined in 1669 'for abusing the company and saying they acted uncivilly in the last meeting and abusing the stewards'.[58] Two years later, Thomas Brierly 'used these uncivil words' against steward George Wood: that he 'acted out of envy and that he gathers the company together to catch them and set them by the ears'.[59] As this suggests, freemen were not averse to

[53] TNA, E179/158/101.
[54] TWA, GU/BS/2/1, 5 May 1646, 24 July 1657, 21 September 1671.
[55] Ibid., 7 September 1669; 11 December 1662.   [56] Ibid., 2 January 1671.
[57] Ibid., 18 March 1663; 21 July 1664.   [58] Ibid., 4 January 1669.
[59] Ibid., 26 October 1671.

commenting on the civility (or not) of the company as a discursive and regulative institution. Thomas Young was fined in 1653 for saying 'he wondered the company was so sottish and called them Lords of Misrule'.[60] Henry Watson was fined in 1670 for 'going away and saying we were turbulent fellows'.[61] George Durham swore in 1642 that 'by God he would drink tobacco' at the meeting.[62] In 1656 John Hall declared 'before the company that what Charles Clarke [a steward] spoke was precious and tended to the mutiny of the company'. He was then fined some more for 'not obeying the stewards being commanded silence several times and to withdraw from the company which he refused until he thought his own time'.[63] And in 1663 twelve freemen were fined for saying the steward – George Wood again – 'kept prattling and kept the company to no purpose and absenting themselves out of the meeting house'.[64]

Democratic companies made for combative arenas in which the communal will was constantly negotiated through public conversations. In the process, notions of honesty were at once reified and subverted as freemen argued and jostled through the language of civility. The Barbers valued truthfulness and the reputation for truth, decorum in speech and behaviour, and the exclusion of violence (verbal or physical) from social interactions. These were all attributes of the classical concept of *honestas*, and were likewise valorised in other trades. The Glasiers fined George Coward in 1677 'for giving his brother Joseph Goften the lie'.[65] In 1681 the plumber Percival Soulsby was fined first for 'abusive words and striking at Christopher Lodge in anger' and, second, for 'gross abuse to the company in getting upon the table with his foot and striking violently with his cane', threatening to 'beat [the] brains out' of a brother.[66] And ten years earlier William Husband had been fined for 'abusing the whole company with very bad language' and '[telling] them they draw in all Hugger Mugger'.[67] However, the pattern in fining and accusations reveals a fourth sense of honesty that related specifically to work and the skill of a person in their calling. Robert Lampton was fined in 1664 for 'giving Richard Potts unbrotherly speeches saying he was not worthy to trim any man because where he took one hair off he left three hairs on'. He then developed his theme, claiming 'that he hath set razors of eight pence a piece for a woman that trim better than many brethren of the company'.[68] Thomas Osborne had been similarly aggressive in 1646. He called 'John Hall a fool a knave a dissembler and hath no art in his trade and was a left-handed man'. Worse still, 'Robert Frazer, William Bednal, [and] Robert Ogle were all alike and had no judgement in their trades and a great many more in the company'.[69] Such accusations had implications for the reputation,

---

[60] Ibid., 28 July 1653.   [61] Ibid., 3 October 1670.
[62] Ibid., 29 April 1642.   [63] Ibid., 25 July 1656.   [64] Ibid., 23 July 1663.
[65] TWA, GU/GP/2/2, 18 July 1677.   [66] Ibid., 6 September 1681.
[67] Ibid., 10 January 1672.   [68] TWA, GU/BS/2/1, 18 March 1664.
[69] Ibid., 28 April 1646.

worth, and profit of individual freemen: the glasier John Goddard was outraged
when John Moore 'told Mr. Anderson that [Goddard] could not cut no glass but
that he cut all his glass for him'.[70] However, in economies based on the exclusion of unenfranchised inhabitants, the 'art' of those who were free – and their
skill in the mystery they had apprenticed to practise – was fundamental to the
legitimacy of their collective occupation. Without it, honest company became
dishonest monopoly. It was on similar grounds that disclosure, or the 'revealing secrets of company', was also discouraged. Hence Arthur Newham's fine
of 20s. in 1675 'by a general consent for disclosing the secrets of the company and persuading the foreigners not to pay their fine of £13 for selling their
candles'.[71]

Insofar as freemen of Newcastle-upon-Tyne were concerned, authority did
not impose the *honestas* by which their company was regulated. Nor was the will
of the company simply a euphemism for the decisions made by the wealthiest
and more powerful brethren. On the contrary, the pattern of fining suggests that
freemen most likely to incur the displeasure of the company – and repeatedly
pit their personal will against the will of the whole – were the 'better sort' of
brethren within the trade. In this sense, company worked as *honestas* ought in
protecting the weaker members of particular societies from their more powerful
and potentially wilful participants. When pewterer William Husband described
his company as 'hugger mugger', he did so as the second wealthiest freeman
in his society: while the average number of hearths owned by his brethren was
three, he was listed in 1667 as paying for five.[72] The barber surgeon David
Shevill, who, like Husband, was repeatedly at odds with his company, was also
the owner of five hearths and also (on that basis) the second wealthiest company
member.[73] While Charles Clarke senior and junior formed the most powerful
dynasty of barber surgeons in the town, they were also constantly restrained
by their society. Not only did freemen like Shevill and John Hall object to
Clarke's 'precious' words at company meetings; any sign of aggressive trading
practices – whether contracting with more apprentices than allowed, or 'taking
cures out the hands' of other brethren – was scrutinised and regulated by company. Conversely George Wood, a barber surgeon repeatedly elected steward of
the company, was neither the wealthiest of his peers (he owned three hearths)
nor spared criticism when his stewardship appeared 'prattling' and 'to no purpose'. Indeed, in either company the only example of a freeman outgrowing
their society was the goldsmith William Ramsay. Paying for seven hearths in
1667, Ramsay was ominously absent from company meetings throughout the
period, carving out a career in city politics instead. His rise through the common
council to sheriff and alderman coincided with his manipulation of company

---

[70] TWA, GU/GP/2/2, 14 October 1682.   [71] TWA, GU/BS/2/1, 26 May 1675.
[72] TNA, E179/158/101.   [73] Ibid.

restrictions concerning the size of individual businesses, and by the 1680s he was regularly poaching apprentices already indentured to other masters in order to extend his commercial interests.[74]

No other freeman enjoyed what was, by 1690, officially recognised as the 'liberty' of William Ramsay. On the contrary, the experiences of the plumber Joseph Goften and the barber surgeon Arthur Newham point to the ongoing importance of *honestas* in the second half of the seventeenth century. Both men were recidivists in terms of contravening company, Goften being fined at least eleven times between 1675 and 1683 and Newham eighteen times between 1664 and 1681. Moreover, for both men the main bone of contention was the employment of workers – whether freemen, journeymen, or apprentices – within their household businesses. Goften's problems began in 1675 when he told the company that 'Thomas Milburne the Latin man should work with him whether the company will or not'.[75] While Newham already had a reputation for 'taking patients out of hands', company hostility crystallised over his 'keeping two journeymen at work that did not serve by indentures to the trade'.[76] Fined for every month he kept them working, he retorted that 'the devil a penny less be paid to the company for his journeymen than twenty shillings'.[77] Related issues continued to rear their heads thereafter: although in 1669 Newham promised his 'journeymen shall go away to London immediately after this year be out', the next decade was marked by repeated disputes over apprenticeship numbers. Although Goften compounded for his fines in 1677, by the early 1680s he was again refusing to register his journeymen and apprentices, one apprentice lodging his own complaint in 1682.[78] In both instances, these disputes were articulated through the language of civility. Newham was repeatedly fined for 'departing [meetings] without leave and license'; 'disobeying the steward and saying he would not be liable to command'; and 'not going down the stairs when he was commanded by the steward'.[79] Moreover, his antagonism was a household affair: in 1670 the much-maligned George Wood complained that 'John Simpson, Arthur Newham's man, did both in language and mimic posture abuse the said steward'.[80] Goften likewise said 'he scorned the company and would never come amongst them nor obey their orders' and 'for going away without leave of the company according to order'. This despite being steward at the time.[81] As this suggests, one strategy of reconciliation was the election of these erstwhile alienated freemen to positions of authority. While Goften served as steward on several occasions – once with William Husband, then in the midst of his own feud with the company – Newham was an important member

---

[74] TWA, GU/GP/2/2, 29 September 1690.   [75] Ibid., 29 September 1675.
[76] TWA, GU/BS/2/1, 4 December 1668.   [77] Ibid., 17 November 1669.
[78] TWA, GU/GP/2/2, July 1682.
[79] TWA, GU/BS/2/1, 2 January 1671, 22 August 1671, 6 July 1680.
[80] Ibid., August 1670.   [81] TWA, GU/GP/2/2, 25 March 1676.

of committees charged with 'suppressing unfreemen for selling candles and other abuses ... prejudicial to the company'.[82] Another tactic was, as expected, recourse to higher civic authority. Goften appeared before the mayor at a 'private guild' in 1677 and Newham was 'bound by order of sessions' in May 1674 to pay the three pounds in fines that he had accumulated for indenturing more than two apprentices at one time.[83] While Goften was ultimately reconciled to his company, Newham had departed from Newcastle by 1681.

'The poor of this city'

The company of guilds was one civic context in which the values of *honestas* were nurtured and subverted in the course of daily interaction. However, as democrats like John Bradford and John Wildman were quick to point out, civil society extended beyond the particular interests of a trade and calling, common councils also ensuring that economic resources more generally were maintained, defended, and distributed 'honestly'. Given the territorial basis of many city commonwealths, the integrity of common lands and corporate leases were an especial concern of freemen that was periodically expressed by walking the practical and symbolic bounds. Bodies of freemen spent much time and energy protecting such resources in law – either through direct intervention by common councils, as in Cambridge, or council-backed litigation by pasture-masters (ward offices) as in York.[84] A point of tension within towns was the enclosure and subsequent leasing of 'void' and common ground to freemen and other parties for rent – a process that characterised democratic Cambridge as much as aristocratic Ludlow, where burgesses either side of the political divide nevertheless petitioned for leases.[85] The leasing of enclosed lands transformed and 'improved' the assets of a borough into regular cash payments that could then be redistributed as part of a city's 'stock of the poor' – a policy that, after the legislation of 1601, also characterised the use of manorial commons.[86] As the 'common day' in Cambridge decided in 1627, 'Jesus Green shall be let out for the space of seven years ... towards the setting of the poor of this town on work and for raising up the stock of their maintenance'.[87] It was a process that was usually accompanied by the more rigorously enforced exclusion of unenfranchised or undeserving inhabitants from use of the commons, as well as

[82] TWA, GU/BS/2/1, 4 January 1669.
[83] TWA, GU/GP/2/2, 26 July 1677; GU/BS/2/1, 11 June 1674.
[84] YCA, B37, f. 96–96v, 99b–100, 101v, 112–13v; BIHR, CPH 2439; CCRO, City Shelf C, Book 7, ff. 51v, 350v.
[85] See for example, CCRO, City Shelf C, Book 7, ff. 11, 13v, 18v, 25v; SA, LB4/3.
[86] Sara Birtles, 'Common land, poor relief and enclosure: the use of manorial resources in fulfilling parish obligations 1601–1834', *P&P*, 165, November 1999, p. 86.
[87] CCRO, City Shelf C, Book 7, f. 170.

stricter rules relating to which freemen were allowed to do what with particular parcels of land.[88] The potential cost was resentment at the enlargement of particular households – the more so when, as in Ludlow during the 1590s, leases and enclosures were awarded to 'friends' and 'kin' rather than enfranchised freemen. However, as John Walter's account of relations between Colchester and Sir John Lucas has shown, such resentments were nothing compared to those generated by perceived encroachments by neighbouring gentry landlords into civic jurisdictions.[89] Lucas was the seventeenth-century head of an Essex family that owed its recent rise in status to acquisitions at the Dissolution (John's great-grandfather exploiting his place as town clerk of Colchester). The result was a mansion built on monastic properties close to Colchester, withdrawal from civic society, and the invention of a noble genealogy based on 'Blood' and 'Honour'.[90] Moreover, from the later sixteenth century repeated attacks on the borough's communal resources were instigated at the 'pleasure', 'will', and 'command' of their ennobled neighbour – in particular its charter and common lands.[91] Such incursions threatened the very basis of freedom, uniting an otherwise divisive and stratified urban populace against the local menace and engendering a widespread hostility that culminated in the attack on the Lucas estate in the summer of 1642.

Even in a borough as socially and religiously divided as Colchester, therefore, ideals of commonwealth were crystallised by the management and protection of local 'charity'. Often marginal in terms of their physical place within a community, the relief and reform of 'our poor' was nevertheless a central aspect of *civitas* throughout the period. Increasingly after 1540, it was through common councils and their various sub-committees that charities and bequests were established; civic loans and gifts allocated; schools, hospitals, and houses of correction governed; and manufacturing projects initiated. Most spectacularly, city commonwealths were not only the primary initiators of national legislation during the later Elizabethan era but also responsible for implementation across the corporate system.[92] It was the parish that provided the institutional context for assessment, collection, and distribution of the dole: ratepayers and recipients were ostensibly 'neighbours'; the key offices were parochial; and wealth was assessed on the 'common estimation' of parishioners. However, in city commonwealths elected magistrates played a supervisory role that was not apparent in rural parishes. The mechanics varied, of course, from place to place. In Ludlow, where civic and parochial boundaries were coterminous, parish officers such as churchwarden and overseer worked as *de facto* representatives of

---

[88] CCRO, City Box II, 9, 'Orders 1608 – 1611', 27–28v; City Shelf C, Book 7, f. 182; City Shelf C, Book 8, f.13v. HCRO, HB28, f. 106.
[89] Walter, *Understanding popular violence*, ch. 3.   [90] Ibid., p. 91.   [91] Ibid., p. 89.
[92] Slack, *From Reformation to improvement*, pp. 36–46.

the corporation.[93] In a more complex jurisdiction like York, with its numerous parishes, aldermen and common council took a magisterial 'view of the poor', sanctioning petitioners for parochial charity, regulating the poor rate, and over-seeing the redistribution of money from wealthier to poorer neighbourhoods from the council chamber on Ouse Bridge.[94] By the Restoration period, poor relief was fully co-ordinated with other forms of civic intervention, such as civic apprenticeships, placements in the orphans' school, referral to the workhouse, house of correction, or widows' hospitals, the provision of 'stock' and, for younger freemen starting out in business, civic loans and credit.[95] It was only in places like Cambridge, where burgesses were without magisterial author-ity, or in London, where the scale of the process necessitated more devolved decision-making – as well as the establishment of corporate institutions like Bridewell – that the provision of relief remained outwith the ken of council-lors and aldermen. Even in Cambridge, however, free burgesses had access to Sir Thomas White's charity.[96] White was a citizen of the London Merchant Taylors – and Marian Lord Mayor – who made his enormous fortune from the cloth trade in the middle of the sixteenth century. His charity, which provided £25 loans to five journeymen clothiers for five years, was based in the city of Bristol and administered by twenty-four different common councils across the corporate system.[97] Still functioning in the Restoration era, it epitomised at once the national reach and public efficacy of citizenship: what the puritan minister Robert Jenison described as the 'impartial uprightness in executing justice and regarding the cause of the poor'.[98]

Such undertakings institutionalised the requisites of *honestas* as a basis for both the decision-making of those administering charity and the deportment of those petitioning for and benefiting from it. The introduction of William Lamb's charity into Ludlow was a case in point. The charity was established by an indenture between the master and four wardens of the Guild of Cloth-workers in London and the 'bailiff burgesses and commonalty' of Ludlow in 1580. Negotiated by the Shropshire lawyer, Henry Townsend of Lincoln's Inn, the indenture provided £100 'towards the further and better maintenance and setting up of certain young occupiers and craftsmen within the said town'.[99] To this was added a further clause explaining '[whereby the poor inhabiting within the said town] may be set at work and kept from idleness and thereby their wives children and families the better maintained and relieved'. The charity took the form of loans that selected beneficiaries would return without interest

---

[93] SA, LB2/1/1, ff. 39–40.   [94] YCA, Series E (1632, 1642, 1648, 1653–78).
[95] YCA, E68; Withington, 'Citizens', pp. 141–6.
[96] CCRO, City Shelf C, Book 7, ff. 74, 162, 203v, 222, 229; Book 8, ff. 160, 264v.
[97] Robert Tittler, *Townspeople and nation: English urban experiences 1540–1640* (Stanford, 2001), ch. 4.
[98] Cited in Slack, *From Reformation to improvement*, p. 30.   [99] SA, LB7/1425.

after three years. As well as providing credit, however, the indenture also specified a process of allocation that would prevent 'all fraud guile and evil conscience . . . touching the employing and bestowing of the said £100'. While this made the provision of credit a power of common council, it also required personal honesty on the part of common councillors. None of the Twelve and Twenty-Five empowered to choose which craftsmen should receive the loan could have 'fallen into poverty and decay' themselves, as this might compromise their judgement. As such, any councillors unable to select 'without favour affection corruption or fraud' were to 'be dismembered from the said society or company of Twelve and Twenty-Five by his or their own request and special desire'. The method of selection also imposed civil conversation onto the council: 'The common sergeant of the said town for the time being so silence to be made and immediately thereupon those present indentures and all things therein contained to be then and there publiquely and distinctly returned to the said assembly.' The previous loans returned, new recipients would be chosen by the 'most voices assent and consent of those so there'.[100]

Commitment to a system of poor relief that required regularised and mediated charity rather than personal 'hospitality' was likewise symptomatic of citizenship as it emerged after 1540. The poor rate was saturated with *honestas*: a process that was at once 'calculating and discriminating' and distinct from the hospitality and neighbourliness of equals.[101] Although the transition has been well studied in rural parishes, it is well to remember that in its legislative impulses and practical antecedents this was an urban process: its parochial adaptation marked the wider dissemination of civil society.[102] The principles informing its practice – such as discretionary decision-making, the rhetoric of petitioning, and the requisites of moral, honest, and 'deserving' behaviour – made for communities that were self-consciously civil. Moreover, the conflation of charity with civic authority inevitably accentuated the communal efficacy of governance and its ability to define a community's boundaries. Jury presentments, the distribution of poor relief, the provision of corporate apprentices and credit, the allocation of leases and loans, tax assessments, the distribution of charity, the defence of common lands: these defined the inclusions and exclusions of *civitas* both sociologically and symbolically. This sense of place was certainly felt by the enfranchised better sort of city commonwealths. Fifty years after the institution of Lamb's charity, for example, an assessment for repairs to Ludlow's parish church prompted Rowland Higgins, the King's Messenger in the Council of the Marches, to allege that 'persons of great estate and great account within the parish of Ludlow are not taxed at all'. Other burgesses

---

[100] Ibid.

[101] Hindle, 'The keeping of the public peace', p. 216; Felicity Heal, *Hospitality in early modern England* (Oxford, 1990), p. 402.

[102] Wrightson and Levine, *Poverty and piety*, pp. 178–79; Wrightson, *English society*, pp. 181–2.

(the assessors among them) – the 'guardians of Ludlow' – were 'remitted and forgiven their whole lewne [assessment], or a part thereof received and accepted for their whole assessment'.[103] In the meantime, genteel but unenfranchised inhabitants like Higgins were assessed too high. The burgesses argued in their defence that the tax was 'indifferent', 'proportional', and 'paid by the parishioners according to their several estates and abilities'.[104] This knowledge was arrived at discursively – the sum allotted Higgins was 'guessed' according to 'common estimation' of his 'place' (office) and 'the worth of [his estate]'. Moreover, it was set by 'some of the best and sufficientist in the knowledge of the state of the said parish'; 'some of the better rank and sort of the parish of Ludlow (who had interest therein)'; the 'better sort of the parish'.[105] They claimed, in effect, the moral and local authority afforded by civic governance. For all his ostensible gentility, Higgins was denied this civil company, complaining 'there was nor any notice public or private given before unto [him] of the time and place when and where nor by whom the lewne was to be made, nor for what use or purpose'.[106] No doubt the Cornish gentleman and common lawyer Richard Carew, so scathing about Cornish citizens, would have been sympathetic.[107]

However, this sense of community was not simply the preserve of the better sort. Directed at 'the poor inhabiting within the said town', the very provision of loans, apprentices, credit, and relief reified civil and communal boundaries. Like the economic and civic privileges of freedom, charity reflected residency and permanency: it was not, after all, the absence of hospital facilities that Ludlow's 'democrats' objected to in 1594 so much as the indiscriminate apportionment of places to persons outwith the commonwealth. In civic as in rural parishes the convergence of charity and place entailed localised discretion and a powerful discourse of exclusion, citizens seeking to control, however ineffectually, the settlement of strangers and so prevent additional claims on communal resources.[108] The flip side of this was that inhabitants identified as 'our' poor were the embodiment of community both rhetorically and sociologically. The point is made in Table 6.5. Derived from a series of poor rate records in York spanning the period 1653 to 1678, it divides the 405 recipients of parochial poor relief in 1665 according to gender and shows the number of years either or both sides of 1665 that they collected relief. The table is striking for both the

[103] HCRO, HD4/2/17, 1639, Guardians of Ludlow c. Rowland Higgins, complaint of Higgins.
[104] Ibid., deposition of Samuel Weaver.
[105] Ibid., depositions of Samuel Weaver, Adam Acton, Edward Jones, Richard Baker.
[106] Ibid., deposition of Rowland Higgins.   [107] See above, Introduction.
[108] Cynthia Herrup, *The common peace: participation and the criminal law in seventeenth-century England* (Cambridge, 1987); Steve Hindle, 'A sense of place? Becoming and belonging in the rural parish, 1550–1650', in Shepard and Withington, *Communities in early modern England*, pp. 98–102.

Table 6.5 *The number of years that poor recipients in York in 1665 received relief*

| | 1–5 years | | 6–10 years | | 11–15 years | | 16–20 years | | 20 + years | | TOTAL |
	male	female	male	female	male	female	male	female	male	female	
City ward											
Micklegate	9	14	6	13	4	12	2	17	0	3	80
Bootham	3	7	4	10	5	6	2	6	0	2	45
Walmgate	13	24	17	35	13	23	3	16	3	3	150
Monk	12	15	9	28	9	27	5	14	1	10	130
TOTAL	37	60	36	86	31	68	12	53	4	18	405

Source: YCA E70. The table is based on a series of records running from 1653 to 1678. Recipients for 1665 were listed and the number of years they received the dole both before and after that date counted. In some instances longevity has been underestimated because of the parameters of the series.

high proportions of women receiving dole and the longevity with which they (and their male counterparts) did so.

The table shows that 46 per cent of all recipients (186 persons) received the dole in the same parish for eleven years or more; of those, 74 per cent (139) were women. Just under half of recipients were caring for their own or others' children and certain of 'the poor', such as the Gyles household, were clearly involved in fostering on a recurring basis. Other recipients qualified through age or infirmity – parochial relief was by and large unavailable to that large and vulnerable section of society dependent on the labour market for their daily subsistence. They instead depended on occasional petitions to various civic institutions and, perhaps, charity from their craft or guild. After the Settlement Act of 1662 itinerants – or 'passengers', as they were styled in constables' accounts – received one-off payments.[109] The point remains that if, as Phythian Adams has argued, it is only in 'the longest established local families' that ' "society" and "community" . . . meet at fixed points', then 'the poor' as recognised by the poor rate personified that convergence.[110] It is likewise difficult to find a better example of Ireton's 'permanent', 'fixed', and 'local interest' than someone like Anne Buckton of Bishophill in Micklegate, who received monies for herself and children (whether hers or others' is unclear) from at least 1647 until her death in 1678. In a very real sense, therefore, poverty was pivotal to civic homogeneity, social amelioration working as a badge of communal belonging – and form of communal recognition – for poor and better householders alike.

The poor rate was the rightful and communal property of one set of persons: the young, aged, and infirm. Its avoidance reflected another set of qualities relating to industry, labour, and thrift: the social hallmarks of the 'honest' labouring poor. Distinctions drawn by Sarah Jones in Ludlow in 1639 were a case in point, her sense of material worth merging easily with an equally strong moral probity. Both were measured in relation to others. She described herself as 'aged 46 years and upward and that she was born in the parish of Churchstoke and maintained herself by her labour [and] lives in Ludlow and so hath done for the space of these 30 years last past'. Other women of the same material condition were nevertheless different in fundamental ways. Anne Griffiths 'was a very poor woman and relieved by the alms of the parish' and Anne Hewes 'was a very poor wench and of no credit or estimation and that she is famed to have lived incontinently with Edward Roberts, John Lewes, and one Jonas Taylor'. Both women were of 'no good name or fame and of a vicious life and conversation'.[111] Richard Llewelyn deposed in turn that Ann Griffiths 'was a very poor woman and not worth anything more than her rags or clothes

[109] BIHR, Y/HTG 15.   [110] Phythian Adams, 'An Agenda', p. 19.
[111] HCRO, HD4/2/17, 1640, Catherine Price c. Richard Llewelyn, deposition of Sarah Jones.

that she did usually did wear and lodge in and therefore she was relieved and suckered by the alms of her parish and partly by Catherine Price'. Moreover, her husband, Howell, was 'a mere wanderer and of no certain dwelling' who had 'a former wife yet living'.[112] As confirmation of their dishonesty, William Hackluck, a Ludlow husbandman, testified that 'the said Anne and Howell are stolen away and privately gone out of the country no man knows whither': they had rescinded, that is, their place in the town.[113]

Nor were these distinctions dissipated over time. In 1685 Daniel Awtry, a labourer in York, acknowledged that he was not 'worth in goods lands or tenements of his own the sum of one single farthing'. It was nevertheless the case that he 'works and labours daily with his hands to get necessaries for the support and maintenance of himself and family'.[114] The same year John and Elizabeth Stevenson found themselves the central witnesses in a suit for defamation brought by Elizabeth Ballard against Thomas Penrose. As was usual in such cases, the reputation of all parties came under severe scrutiny, and the Stevensons were no exception. While all deponents agreed that Elizabeth and John were 'poor', poverty was by no means the summation of their status. Elizabeth Ballard described the couple as 'very honest laborious and industrious people of good fame and repute': while they 'sell and retail ale' in the neighbouring village of Heslington, Elizabeth Stevenson supplemented their household income with a weekly allowance 'to nurse and bring up' Ballard's child.[115] Three husbandmen who had known them in the village of Morton described them as 'very honest and peaceable neighbours'; 'due frequenters of the church'; 'neighbours' whom husbandman Thomas Straker 'intrusted', and who never 'found them or either of them dishonest to him'.[116] Penrose, in contrast, presented them as 'very indigent, necessitous and poor, of bad fame and repute'. He argued that 'little or no credit is to be given' to their status as public persons because they 'share a dependence upon' the Ballard household and because John Stevenson in particular was 'a man of ill repute and of knavish practices' wherever 'they live and have lived'. Penrose assembled a series of witnesses to prove his point. Richard Straker testified that he had caught Stevenson secretly grazing a horse in his close at night. Butcher Richard Harrison described how Stevenson 'cheated' him over some labour the previous summer. Weaver Martin Woodcock claimed that seven years ago Stevenson stole two pounds of bacon and also 'wronged him for his wages' when the two of them 'were working together at Peter Pearsons'. And labourer William Holderness remembered how Stevenson would surreptitiously milk Thomas

---

[112] Ibid., deposition of Richard Llewelyn.   [113] Ibid., deposition of William Hackluck.
[114] BIHR, D/C 1685/8, Elizabeth Awtrey c. Daniel Awtry, response of Daniel Awtry.
[115] BIHR, CPH 3692, 1686, Elizabeth Ballard c. Thomas Penrose, deposition of Elizabeth Ballard.
[116] Ibid., depositions of Thomas Straker, Gabriel Jillson, Tobias Bevill.

Potter's cow and how, two years ago, he stole a 'book of arithmetic' from the house of Roger Rayes in order 'to learn something out of it'.[117] The relative poverty of these deponents did not prevent them differentiating between Stevenson as either an 'honest' and 'industrious' neighbour or a 'dishonest' and 'cheating' 'knave'.

Such values merged seamlessly with the honesty required for trade and commerce. In 1673 John Salmon, a twenty-five-year-old tallow chandler, described Mark Knaggs as 'a man of no reputation credit or esteem among his neighbours' and 'of a vicious and lewd and loose life and conversation'. Salmon 'had heard [Knagg's] master Anthony Harland say he dare not trust him when he was his apprentice for he had wronged him and he was afraid and suspected that if he should trust him with any of his goods he would sell or otherwise embezzle them'.[118] Harland confirmed that, during the four years Knagg lived in his household, he 'often took [him] in untruths and found that he was so much given to lying that he dared not trust him about his business'. Indeed, by 'his swearing lying and cheating he had almost set away all his customers who threatened to send their work to some other person rather than have him come about their houses'.[119] Similar concerns drove the bookseller Christopher Welburne to prosecute his neighbour, William Beeforth, for defamation in 1690. It was recorded by a number of tradesmen along Petergate in York that Beeforth came into Welburne's shop 'to pay what he ought him and laid down some moneys'. Having 'counted it', Welburne told Beeforth 'he was indebted to him above that sum, whereupon Beeforth in a malicious mischievous manner called Welburne "A Rogue, A knave and a Rascal"'.[120] The neighbourhood of freemen was not slow to explain the significance of such 'scandalous and opprobrious words' in the 'city of York'. Rogue 'denotes and signifies a man to be a Rascal . . . one that will stick not aft the commission of no villainy and injustice'; 'a man to be a knave or an unjust man'; 'a wicked and unjust man and one that uses no conscience in his dealings'. Welburne, in contrast, had always been found 'to deal justly and honestly'. He was 'a man of sober life and conversation', 'a person as could not be prevailed with to do an unjust thing' who 'lived quietly amongst his neighbours and gained the love of them by such his honest and fair dealings': a 'neighbour . . . never found or reputed to be dishonest'.[121] For all that, goldsmith Mark Gill confessed that 'by reason of the speaking of the words' he no longer held Welburne 'in such esteem and

---

[117] Ibid., depositions of Thomas Penrose, Richard Straker, Richard Harrison, Martin Woodcock, William Holderness.

[118] BIHR, CPH 3023, 1673, Martha Coates c. Elizabeth Ashton, deposition of John Salmon.

[119] Ibid., deposition of Anthony Harland.

[120] BIHR, D/C 1690/5, Christopher Welburne c. William Beeforth.

[121] Ibid., depositions of George Pickering, William Pickering, Thomas Thomlinson, Roger Wynne.

repute as he did before . . . nor would he deal with him willingly until he be acquitted from the said aspersion'.[122]

Such language certainly suggests that, over the course of the period, householders increasingly stressed their moral virtues 'because a reputation for these factors generated their wealth and the communal security needed to maintain this wealth'. Less clear is why this represented the replacement of 'localised faithfulness' by 'service to the monarchical state'.[123] The 'civil legal institutions' that mediated interpersonal relations were not part of a single and centralised monolith so much as a composite of local conversations, companies, and places: civil societies in which householders went about their daily lives, and which in city commonwealths were demarcated by the practice of freedom. Beyond the need for equitable commerce, the ongoing practice of honest company and charity consolidated rather than diminished communal identities. Likewise civic appropriations of *honestas* consolidated citizenship, providing justification for the very practice of *civitas*. Certainly the focus on 'our poor' by York's governors in their *Complaint* to Widdrington was not unprecedented. Just as the 'poorer sort of citizen' had justified the civic (as opposed to gentry) purchase of chancery lands in 1610, so 'the poor of this city' justified civic opposition to the Duke of York in the 1670s.[124] Likewise the refusal of local gentry to commit themselves to the obligations of civic governance at the Restoration provided the citizens of York with their most effective argument for retaining civic autonomy. Of particular concern for York citizens were the landed inhabitants of the Ainsty, a city liberty that stretched fourteen miles into the West Riding – especially the Slingsby family, which had a relationship with the citizens quite as volatile as the Lucas family with Colchester. The citizens explained in 1662 that, 'unless those gentlemen would be freemen of the city and so by consequences to bear such other offices of charge and trouble as we undergo', then 'the Gentlemen of the Ainsty' had no right to be Justices of the Peace in the city.[125]

This suggests, finally, a mode of civic civility – or gentility – which, even into the later seventeenth century, contrasted with concepts of lordship, honour, and paternalism held by those 'Gentry who do not live in the city': gentlemen like Luke Frugal, Sir John Lucas, Rowland Higgins, and the gentry of the York Ainsty. The bequests of two of the dominant 'gentlemen' in York after the Restoration are a case in point. On the face of it, the courtier and governor Sir John Reresby and the merchant and alderman Sir Henry Thompson were indistinguishable. Both men had amassed considerable fortunes and, on most objective criteria, were members of the same social class. Both men had noble

---

[122] Ibid., deposition of Mark Gill.   [123] Muldrew, *Economy of obligation*, p. 151.
[124] Withington, 'Citizens', p. 149.
[125] LS, NH 2443, February 1662, York aldermen to their parliamentary representatives.

patrons; both had invested in land; both were active in civic and parliamentary politics; and both retained powerful partisan affiliations structured by the crisis over the 'exclusion' of James from the throne (Reresby was a Tory 'trimmer' and Thompson a 'factious' Whig). In his will of 1689, Reresby divided £5,500 between his three daughters, the contents of houses in Thirbridge, London, and York to his wife, and the profits of a number of manors and estates to his sons. To his patron, 'my dear' Marquis of Halifax, he gave 'the best horse in my stable, my best case of pistols and my best sword', and 'all my tenants that have lived in my family as servants 20s per annum during their natural lives'.[126] The wine trade provided Thompson with an array of manors and estates of his own. However, in his will of 1683 he conceived of them not in terms of tenants, servants, patron, and household hospitality so much as socially differentiated towns. The 'overseers' and 'most substantial inhabitants' in the 'towns' of Escrick, Marston, and Settington were granted sums of £10 and £15. His main obligation, however, was to the city that had made him rich. Following the practice of many of his predecessors on the aldermanic bench, he gave the 'lord mayor and aldermen of the City of York £100 ... to use [of] the poor': money that was to 'be let out upon good security secure with profits to bind poor decayed freemen's children apprentice'.[127] If this smacks as paternalism by other means, then it was nevertheless a perspective that united civic society. If John Bradford was a vociferous and 'democratic' opponent of Ludlow's oligarchy during the 1590s, he was also notable as one of the first burgesses to hold the place of searcher of the poor after the legislation of 1601. Likewise, although the baker James Wright was accredited with many classical virtues, 'hospitality' was not one of them. As 'one of the best' of York's citizens he was, however, fully involved in contributing to and administrating poor relief within his civic neighbourhood.

Freedom and civil society

The provision of charity, like manufacture and trade, at once proliferated and diversified in the last decades of the seventeenth century. And, just as England's urban landscape expanded and transformed, so the institutions that structured urban freedom entered a long process of atrophy and decline.[128] Whereas the lawyer Sir John Hewley worked his nonconformist agenda through York's civic structures, his like-minded widow, Lady Sarah, was instrumental in establishing the kind of autonomous charitable trust typical of the 'voluntary associations' of the 'long eighteenth century'.[129] The 'common or joint Bank or stock' formed

[126] BIHR, Wills, York, August 1689, Sir John Reresby.
[127] BIHR, Wills, York, July 1683, Sir Henry Thompson.
[128] Brooks, 'Apprenticeship', pp. 71–2.   [129] Slack, *From reformation to improvement*, p. 163.

by Farrington, Nelthorpe, Page, and Thompson in 1670 suggests, in turn, the kind of imperial and deregulated enterprise that made freedom obsolete. The joint bank was innovative in theory and entrepreneurial in practice, the partners 'setting up woolen and silk manufactures in the most uncultivated parts of Ireland ... factories in Moscow ... and many other remote parts beyond the seas'.[130] Business encompassed the 'import of one hundred and fifty nine hogsheads of Virgin tobacco' in December 1676, plus numerous 'bills of exchange' from factors in cities in Turkey, India, Spain, Italy, Portugal, and France.[131] In terms of the scale of its geography, not to mention its potential for profit margins, this was a company quite removed from the localised trading practices and mysteries of barber surgeons or glasiers in Newcastle-upon-Tyne. It was a project anticipating the wealth of nations of Adam Smith rather than the regulated commonweal of his namesake, Sir Thomas.

Such discontinuities can be misleading, however. Lady Hewley's famous charity marked not so much a break from city commonwealth as its continuation by other means. Just as its trustees took the form of a common council, so relief was distributed according to 'such Rules as she had appointed'.[132] Moral and material sustenance went hand in hand. Cultural continuities between 'common or joint Bank' and companies of freemen were likewise numerous. For 'the better management and carrying on' of their 'joint and equal advantage' the partners drew up 'Articles' on 2 January 1670 to be 'mutually executed by and between' them. What was, in effect, their company 'ordinary' divided all profits and losses 'in four fourths' and designated Thompson's 'dwelling house' and shop in Woollchurch Market as the place where 'the Common Bank of moneys books and accounts were to be kept'. The partners were not to access money 'but by the consent of the rest'; nor were 'their own particular and different dealings' to 'effect or change the ... joint bank'. Finally, while 'a general cashier or Bookkeeper [was] mutually chosen', each partner was 'to have free access to or take copies of the books and accounts touching the same'. The 'articles ... covenants and agreements' were nothing, however, without a degree of honesty, skill, and civility between the partners.[133] Farrington blamed the eventual collapse of the bank on the profound deficiency of Thompson and Nelthorpe in all of these respects. Both were 'ambitious and thinking by the ruin of others to be suddenly rich did engage in diverse chargeable and hazardous undertakings privately': that is, by 'treachery and connivance' they withdrew 'far greater sums from the said joint stock' than the articles allowed for 'their own private and sinister ends'. As well as lacking honesty and discretion, Thompson 'was altogether unskillful in the way of merchandize'. When in March 1675 'diverse of the creditors of the said Bank having notice of the said

---

[130] TNA, C7/581/73. See above, ch. 5.   [131] TNA, C10/48/71; C6/526/178.
[132] NYCRO, ZTP 1 2098.   [133] TNA, C7/581/73.

improvident way of dealing of the said Nelthorpe and Thompson and pressing for their moneys at one and the same time', the bank was 'exhausted and drained of moneys'. Money had either been frittered on private projects or 'lent out and owing to the said Bank upon securities': it was committed, in effect, to labyrinthine networks of credit that would take years to unravel. In the meantime (and according to Farrington) Thompson and Nelthorpe 'privately . . . departed from their habitations', they 'and the said Thompson's wife' taking with them 'all the cash with all the books papers accounts writings securities and pawns for money then belonging to the said bank'. With Edmond Page dead, Farrington was 'arrested by many of the said creditors . . . in several actions amounting to £50,000 and upward'. Not only was the public reputation and credit of the company and its members ruined: the loss of credit among Massinger's 'money-men' was the cause of ruination. The scale of credit and public reputation involved was exceptional: it was not many freemen and citizens who, facing a bill in the House of Commons calling for their execution, felt compelled to publish a pamphlet defending their honesty. However, the epistemologies at work were those of urban freedom.

Neither were the links between trade and *civitas* broken. The Woollchurch Market bank was a partnership of citizens and Farrington, Thompson, and Nelthorpe took their citizenship seriously. Throughout the first half of the 1670s, all three were representatives of their respective wards in the Court of Common Council, serving on committees ranging from the leasing of property left by Sir Thomas Gresham to debating the merits of enfranchising James Duke of York to the city.[134] Thompson and Nelthorpe in particular were energetic proponents of civic democracy as articulated through the power struggle between Common Council and the Court of Aldermen. Both men were selected, for example, onto a committee called to consider a bill presented by the Common Council in November 1674 'for compelling aldermen to dwell and inhabit in the city'.[135] The bill was a direct continuation of the constitutional position extrapolated by John Wildman in 1651: one that sought to keep political power within the city and among the citizens and prevent the expropriation of urban freedoms by otherwise disinterested gentry. The Court of Aldermen responded by publicly declaring 'their protest and dissent'. Thompson and Nelthorpe were also at the centre of a series of disputes concerning the respective powers of the two courts. The most important of these was the 'negative voice' claimed by the lord mayor and aldermen within the Court of Common Council – a power which theoretically granted the upper court the final say over the appointment of officers and civic legislation. The issue, which was perceived as pivotal to determining the aristocratic or democratic nature of civic government, was reviewed, debated, and arbitrated throughout the 1670s.

[134] CLRO, Rep 80, ff. 138, 143v, 129.   [135] Ibid., 122.

The crown was particularly interested in seeing the negative voice confirmed. It was, therefore, with some relish that Sir John Robinson reported to Secretary of State Williamson that 'Thompson, Nelthorpe, Farrington, Page the bankers in partnership have lost their reputation they have summoned their creditors to meet to tomorrow'.[136] Enemies were also quick to highlight that the Corporation Act of 1662 stipulated that 'no person' could be elected to common council that 'through inability to pay his debts in due time has summoned his creditors together'. Indeed, such persons could only be 'looked upon as very unfit for those places and would bring a disreputation and scandal to the authority of the city'.[137] The implications were spelt out for Thompson and Nelthorpe, who were 'the principal cause of the slander and insufficient execution of these places [of common councillor] they being grown thereof into contempt or slight regard (as becoming only the meaner sort of people)'.[138] On 22 February 1677 the Court of Common Council had no option but to issue new writs for the election of members unable to subscribe to the 'declaration mentioned in the Act of Parliament for Regulating Corporations'.[139] This followed the decision by King's Council in December 1676 that the lord mayor and aldermen did indeed 'have a negative voice' within the civic constitution.[140]

For all the breadth of their trading horizons, therefore, Thompson and Nelthorpe remained fully committed to the reciprocal nature of freedom and governance. This commitment extended far beyond the City of London. Their kin and 'friends' included Sir Henry Thompson and his brothers, Edward and Stephen, in York; the old Leveller, Major Braman in Chichester; Andrew Marvell, parliamentary representative of Hull; and Marvell's nephew William Popple, a wine merchant in Bordeaux who traded with both the York and London merchants. They participated, in effect, in a civic and mercantile community of national proportions, and one closely associated with 'Whig' opposition to the succession of James Duke of York to the crown.[141] More generally, the cultural premises central to freedom and commonwealth were at once perpetuated and appropriated in the period of urbanisation after 1650. Such mutability has been implied by Jonathan Barry's notion of the long chronology of English 'associational culture', the city commonwealth marking a crucial but ultimately transitional phase in the story of urban development between the sixteenth and eighteenth centuries.[142] It is also suggested by work on the later period. As John Smail and others have shown, wealthier inhabitants in eighteenth- and nineteenth-century Halifax, Manchester or Birmingham were more than

---

[136] TNA, SP29 376, 169.   [137] TNA, SP29 387 122.   [138] TNA, SP29 387 123.
[139] CLRO, CC Rep 82, f. 95.   [140] Ibid., ff. 28–33v.
[141] Gary S. De Krey, 'The London Whigs and the exclusion crisis reconsidered', in A. L. Beier, David Cannadinen and James M. Rosenheim, eds., *The first modern society: essays in English history in honour of Lawrence Stone* (Cambridge, 1989), pp. 457–82. See below, ch. 9.
[142] Barry, 'Bourgeois collectivism?', pp. 108–11.

willing to promote civic building programmes – and perceive themselves as the 'best' within their communities – with or without the sanction of a royal charter of incorporation.[143] The civility that Margaret Hunt argues was characteristic of the 'middling sort' of eighteenth-century England bears more than a passing resemblance to the values of urban freedom practised during the previous 150 years.[144] Likewise the 'three kinds of capital' that Keith Wrightson has argued structured economic success in the eighteenth-century market – skills, networks, and background – are not too far removed from the requisites of successful citizenship.[145] The same could be said for notions of honest and dishonest labour, and also the formation of artisan collectives, by the early eighteenth century: certainly, Kathleen Wilson has demonstrated the central role that Newcastle freemen took in radical politics of the eighteenth century.[146] Viewed on these terms, urban freedom was neither implicit nor incidental to the emergence of eighteenth-century civil society. Rather it was constitutive.

[143] John Smail, *Origins of middle-class culture: Halifax, Yorkshire, 1660–1780* (Ithaca, 1994).
[144] Margaret R. Hunt, *The middling sort: commerce, gender, and the family in England, 1680–1780* (Berkeley, 1996).
[145] Wrightson, *Earthly necessities*, p. 290.
[146] Ibid., p. 327; Wilson, *The sense of the people*, ch. 7.

7   The patriarchal commonwealth

'She did know and could tell all that was done in Mr Mayor's house'

In 1607 Anne Taylor and Susan Swapper were accused of witchcraft by civic magistrates in Rye, a cinque port on the border of Sussex and Kent. Anne had recently married a minor Kent gentleman but continued to live in the town with her mother, Anne Bennett, who was a renowned local healer and also widow of a wealthy butcher and freeman. Susan was the wife of a poor sawyer, as well as a neighbour and tenant of Bennett.[1] The accusations came at a particularly telling moment in the endemic civic politics that characterised the port. Against the backdrop of a silting estuary and shrinking local economy, this politics centred on two rival factions: the brewers and the butchers. The brewers represented the entrepreneurial and aristocratic spirit of the town: an alliance of families that, until very recently, had at once prospered materially despite difficult circumstances and, in the process, secured an effective monopoly on civic office. The butchers, in contrast, were demonstrably poorer and also representative of the artisans and smaller tradesmen in the borough. Although the brewers had enjoyed a relatively long period of civic supremacy in the town, by 1607 their authority was precarious – not least because three of their leading burgesses had died in quick succession. It was in these circumstances that Anne Taylor became a focus for factional hostility. Heiress to an old civic dynasty with close connections with the butchers, her husband was also pushing for enfranchisement as a resident householder.[2] It was in this context that Anne Taylor was accused of using *maleficium* against her enemies: in particular, Martha Higgins, the recent widow of two ex-mayors, accused her of bewitching to death her first husband, Thomas Hamon.[3] This was in addition to initial charges that Anne and Susan had sought the counsel of fairies in order to obtain treasure. However, when the case finally came to trial in 1609 the local jury acquitted Anne; Susan was released by a

---

[1] Annabel Gregory, 'Witchcraft, politics, and good neighbourhood in early seventeenth-century Rye', *P&P*, 133, 1991, pp. 35–6.
[2] Ibid., pp. 38–50.   [3] Ibid., pp. 37, 62.

general pardon two years later; and, in the meantime, Anne's husband, George Taylor, secured his freedom and became an active member of the civic elite.[4]

Anne Taylor's public presence was palpable. A central figure in the town's political allegiances and conflicts, the power she wielded was rooted in those reproductive aspects of personal and communal relations that early modern people regarded as feminine: the rituals, practices, and morality surrounding sex, birth, sickness, and death.[5] Like the masculine spheres of civic decision-making and participation, this feminine realm had its places, conversations, and social codes and knowledge: forms of female company that Anne Taylor prowled, and which provided a forum for political criticism quite as telling as any common council. This was because, as historians have increasingly realised, the bodily, moral, and 'domestic' concerns that constituted the realm of gossip, slander, and reputation were not only gendered but also politically charged, making 'women the brokers of oral reputation'.[6] Anne Taylor's talk, made the more authoritative by her status as a 'cunning' woman, was a case in point. It was deposed 'that Mrs Taylor did then tell her that she the said Mrs Taylor heard that Mr Mayor was taken sick and that he should die of the said sickness for she knew it well'. As described by Susan Swapper, Taylor was the quintessential gossip whom 'did know and could tell all that was done in Mr Mayor's house and in every house in Rye if that she Mrs Taylor would trouble herself above it'.[7] The power of a woman who made all acts public could only be enhanced by her knowledge of spirits and bodies. Anne allegedly told Swapper 'that everybody would see that after Mr Mayor was dead what an ugly corpse he should be to look upon and that one side of him should die before the other'. Moreover, 'one of the spirits before his death should give him A gripe upon his members and that they should look very black after his death'. Most worryingly for her civic enemies, Anne's knowledge and skills facilitated a scathing moral critique of Higgins' suitability to govern that was informed by her own millenarian sensibilities.[8] Swapper continued: 'And after Mr Mayor's death Mrs Taylor further said that it were no matter if the devil did fetch away his body for ever to be an example to others for.' Indeed, 'she doubted not that the devil had his soul already for that he was an evil liver for he had misused his other wife greatly which she knew very well'. In particular, 'this woman which he married last should sit at meat with him and his old wife should sit in the kitchen and pick the bones that this woman left and be glad of them if she could get them'. As far as Anne was

---

[4] Ibid., pp. 38, 49.
[5] Sara Mendelson and Patricia Crawford, *Women in early modern England* (Oxford, 1998), p. 204.
[6] Gowing, *Domestic dangers*, pp. 121, 123.
[7] ESRO, Accession N 2936, third examination of Susan Swapper.
[8] Gregory, 'Witchcraft, politics, and good neighbourhood', p. 45.

concerned, 'his lewd life would bring him to his end and that he did never any man good but such as was of his Religion'.[9]

A pressing question for historians of early modern gender is the extent to which women could act and think politically in a society that was patriarchal in theory as well as practice.[10] It has been shown that, in terms of their offices and responsibilities, women were perfectly capable of behaving as *de facto* citizens; that they appropriated the legal discourses and institutions that defined the English subject; and that they could achieve direct (and indirect) representation within local and national civic realms.[11] Well-placed women – be they queens and courtiers or educated gentry like Lucy Hutchinson – could exercise significant degrees of political and discursive power.[12] Beyond these elevated ranks, women filled places and roles ostensibly enclosed by men: as members of guilds, for example, or as civic functionaries exercising authority within their communities.[13] Likewise, as members of godly congregations, 'societies', and reading communities, or as petitioners and remonstrators within local and national politics, women clearly impacted on early modern political culture.[14] None of these participatory practices was exclusively feminine, and most depended on mitigating factors for their efficacy: social position and wealth; kinship networks and marital status; a certain level of education or religiosity. However, as Patricia Crawford has recently reiterated, the absence of women in a setting like the Putney Debates need not imply their exclusion from politics more generally. While not always visible, they were certainly present.[15]

Although these accounts reveal women appropriating ostensibly masculine places and roles, what they largely fail to address is the kind of public activism regarded by contemporaries as specifically, if not exclusively, female. The contention of this chapter is that feminine political agency – symbolic, sociological – was rooted in precisely the places and conversations that Anne Taylor patrolled: company that historians have traditionally described as 'private'. It argues that the division between public and private – and its conflation with civic and domestic – is not only anachronistic but also elides the very real powers of

[9] ESRO, Accession N 2936, third examination of Susan Swapper.
[10] Crawford and Mendelson, *Women in early modern England*, ch. 7.
[11] Ibid., pp. 49–58; Patricia Crawford, '"The poorest she": women and citizenship in early modern England', in Michael Mendle, ed., *The Putney debates of 1647: the army, the Levellers and the English state* (Cambridge, 2001), pp. 197–218.
[12] Ibid., pp. 365–80; David Norbrook, '"Words more than civil": republican civility in Lucy Hutchinson's "The life of John Hutchinson"', in Jennifer Richards, ed., *Early modern civil discourses* (Basingstoke, 2003), pp. 68–84.
[13] Crawford and Mendelson, *Women in early modern England*, pp. 52, 56.
[14] Crawford and Mendelson, *Women in early modern England*, pp. 387–94; Crawford, '"The poorest she"', pp. 206–7, 214–16; Ann Hughes, 'Gender and politics in Leveller literature', in Susan Amussen and Mark Kishlansky, eds., *Political culture and cultural politics in England: Essays presented to David Underdown* (Manchester, 1995), pp. 162–88.
[15] Crawford, '"The poorest she"', pp. 197, 216–18.

public criticism and intervention possessed by women both locally and, when circumstances allowed, nationally. Focusing on the phenomenon of 'common fame', the first sections examine how conceptions of *honestas* – and the possibilities of their subversion – served as a framework for talk and association within feminine public spheres. The second half of the chapter considers the patriarchal household. It suggests that, far from encapsulating absolute notions of hierarchy and subordination, it, too, was a place of *honestas* in which masculine authority was perceived in terms of sociability and reciprocity and structured, like other kinds of association, by the everyday contingencies of company. As with the practice of urban freedom, an ungoverned will within the house was regarded by commentators, householders, and servants alike as uncivil and illegitimate: a mode of 'slavery' every bit as dangerous as unmediated economic or civic power. In this way, the household commonwealth was at once a political entity in its own right and analogous to political practices more generally. The chapter concludes with the household of Andrew and Mary Marvell: an arrangement that in its very particularity encapsulated the diversity and complexity of urban domesticity by the later seventeenth century.

Publicness and the conceit of privacy

The public efficacy of female agency has been obscured by the assumption that it was private. Sir Thomas Smith was not unusual when he noted that it was for male heads of household to 'consult in common' as the 'politic body'. Women, 'whom nature hath made to keep home and nourish their family', were not to meddle with matters abroad, nor to bear an office in a city or commonwealth no more than children and infants'.[16] A tradition of interpretation within gender and social historiography has tended to recycle this 'fantastical' division as a framework for historical analysis, presenting 'female culture' as 'private', 'separate', and segregated from the 'male and public' settings of communal life.[17] The most authoritative survey of women in early modern England focuses on the creation of distinct 'female cultures' that were 'organically linked' across a range of 'private' spaces, associations, rituals, and conversations. It argues that this culture was, by and large, exclusive of men and engendered a 'shared . . . female consciousness': even 'the dominant [patriarchal] discourse acknowledged (however reluctantly) that women had created private spaces and distinctive rhetorical genres'.[18] Steve Hindle has argued that the 'political

---

[16] Smith, *De Republica Anglorum*, p. 20; John Dod and Robert Cleaver, *A Godlie forme of house-holde government: for the ordering of private families, according to the direction of God's word* (1612), pp. 167–8.

[17] Alexandra Shepard, 'Manhood, credit and patriarchy in early modern England, c.1580–1640', *P&P*, 167, 2000, p. 76.

[18] Crawford and Mendelson, *Women in early modern England*, pp. 204–5, 218.

charge' that women's words possessed in the seventeenth century stemmed from their 'clandestine' nature. He claims that 'the world of private speech was regarded by women themselves as an arena of social autonomy [and] the repository of a specifically female "social memory"', offering 'an important refuge from patriarchy'.[19] However, the characterisation of female place and words as private hardly fits with the 'sociability, neighbourliness, and mutual interdependence' that characterised them. Households were 'fluid and open expanses' and the 'flexibility and liminal ambiguity of feminised household boundaries were embodied in women's habit of posting themselves at their doorsteps'.[20] Laura Gowing has observed that 'throughout the seventeenth century, the nature of the female body was necessarily both a private matter and public business: the politics of sex and reproduction were at the juncture of household and state'.[21] This was a nexus of surveillance that, as the talk of Anne Taylor suggests, also had male bodies in its sights. That women's words had civic currency is further suggested by Crawford's consideration of women and citizenship in the seventeenth century and Ann Hughes' examination of the gendered rhetoric deployed by Levellers and their wives in political pamphlets of the 1640s. Both point to the empowering and public nature of household rhetoric, and the links that were repeatedly made by both men and women between domestic exigencies and civic decision-making.[22] Likewise, the importance of female talk to the 'development of public opinion' was by no means limited to Rye, but rather occurred across the corporate system and beyond.[23] In this sense, the words of women were not distinct from civil society; they were civil society.

Neither is the conflation of public/masculine and private/feminine consistent with the language 'of historical actors themselves'.[24] By the seventeenth century, the most general and usual meaning of 'public' was simply all that was 'common, open, abroad'.[25] The term was certainly tethered to the idea of legitimate political power, and, as we saw in chapter 3, a rhetorical strategy of any political interest or party was to style opponents as acting 'privately'.

---

[19] Steve Hindle, 'The shaming of Margaret Knowsley: gossip, gender, and the experience of authority in early modern England', *Continuity and change*, 9 (3), 1994, pp. 393, 408.

[20] Crawford and Mendelson, *Women in early modern England*, pp. 207–8.

[21] Laura Gowing, *Common bodies: Women, touch, and power in seventeenth-century England* (New Haven, 2003), p. 208.

[22] Crawford, '"The poorest she"', pp. 214–16; Hughes, 'Gender and politics in Leveller literature', pp. 170–2.

[23] Hindle, 'The shaming of Margaret Knowsley', pp. 393, 403–6; Bernard Capp, *When gossips meet: women, family and neighbourhood in early modern England* (Oxford, 2003), pp. 272–81; Adam Fox, *Oral and literate culture in England 1500–1700* (Oxford, 2000), p. 362; Ulinka Rublack, *The crimes of women in early modern Germany* (Oxford, 1999), ch. 1.

[24] Amanda Vickery, 'Golden age to separate spheres? A review of the categories and chronology of English women's history', *HJ*, 1993, 36, p. 412.

[25] John Bulloker, *An English expositer. Teaching the interpretation of the hardest words used in our language* (1616).

However, the term also conveyed a sense of audience, spectacle, and observation within any context of sociability or 'company'.[26] Understood in these terms, certain places were, by their very nature, public on a recurring basis: markets, streets, neighbourhoods, playhouses, taverns, common councils, or, indeed, coffeehouses. For example, the annulment of the marriage between Frances Welburne and the husband of her deceased sister, Robert Harpham, entailed that they 'shall not privately meet or talk together, but openly in the market, church, or public place'.[27] However, it was the possibility of observation, display, and subsequent dissemination – of the fact of company itself – rather than the inherent nature of a location that defined the publicness of speech and action. Welburne and Harper were also warned, for example, from meeting anywhere 'except it be in the presence of two or more honest and sufficient witnesses'. It was this sense of an observatory 'presence' that formed the public basis of neighbourly and, increasingly into the seventeenth century, national relations. When midwife Bridget Hodgson gossiped about Hester Browne in first the parlour of Leonard Thomson and then the churching ceremony of Anne Ramsden it was a public act not because of the domestic setting so much as because she did so 'in company'.[28] Likewise, Elizabeth Ballard accused the York hearth-tax collector, Henry Penrose, of treating her publicly 'in a haughty and uncivil manner'; 'crushing her against a table'; and calling her as 'A whore, A bitch ... London whore, Newgate whore and Billingsgate whore' despite the incident occurring in the Ballard's parlour.[29] It was nevertheless a public moment, involving public defamation, because three witnesses observed it. As was shown in the previous chapter the defence of Penrose centred on proving them not only poor but also dishonest, so discrediting their testimony and their status as creditably public persons.

Three points follow from this. First, England's cities and boroughs contained local and often female-dominated public spheres in which, as Jacobean minister Robert Horne stressed, civility was closely tied to 'honest' conversation and reputation, and in which news and opinion was constructed, contested, and circulated through what contemporaries termed 'company' and 'discourse'.[30] Second, distinctions between public and private were not synonymous with the boundaries between civic power and the households and neighbourhoods they governed. On the contrary, the civil sociability and opinion of 'honest' and 'substantial' persons – be they male or female – was common to both: the cultivation of *honestas* was required both within and outwith the council chamber. Third, because publicness in whatever context was based around acts and words that were spoken and witnessed honestly, those that were 'secret'

[26] Shagan, *Popular politics*, p. 19.   [27] BIHR, CPH 2626.
[28] BIHR, CPH 2560, 1662, Hester Browne c. Bridget Hodgson.
[29] BIHR, CPH 3692, 1686, Elizabeth Ballard c. Thomas Penrose.   [30] See above, chapter 5.

were implicitly uncivil and anti-social. Although historians have stressed the pejorative connotations of the 'common' woman, the badge of secrecy was no less dangerous – especially when conflated with sexual immorality.[31] It was alleged in 1663 that Ann Whitely of Halifax 'kept with other wives' husbands secretly' and 'was not fit to live in the town'.[32] Sarah Hudson of York was discredited as a servant of 'light and unhandsome carriage' who 'much frequented the company of soldiers in very unbefitting and secret places'.[33] However, such distinctions were not spatially fixed as it was quite possible to act secretly in public locations, Margaret Green noting that 'going to the market' in the postal town of Tadcaster she saw Thomas Pinder and Ann Stower 'privately in company together'.[34] In fact, it was men rather than women who were, by and large, capable of public privacy, if only because public in the sense of civic activity was regarded by contemporaries as peculiarly masculine. It was Andrew Marvell, not Mary, who kept a private closet in which to compose his political writings and thoughts. Likewise, when the Leeds landowner William Pickering was accused in 'public' of fathering a bastard child, the 'Justices not wishing to hear the business in open court' transferred the meeting to the privacy of the mayor's house.[35] Indeed, while the many publics of honest, substantial, and civil neighbours that constituted England's city commonwealths were distinctly feminine in nature, the possibility of legitimate privacy existed for the most part as a masculine privilege. This was especially the case for the common councils and other civic bodies: companies that, no matter their aristocratic or democratic structures, were at once male, discrete, and enclosed by oaths and conventions of secrecy.[36]

Viewed in these terms, it was masculine places that were exclusive and private, feminine places that were inclusive and public. This was certainly the inference of Jacobean literature. City poets used either the idealised or pejorative forms of the female body – the nurturing mother on the one hand, the incontinent and 'common' whore on the other – to characterise the civil (or uncivil) basis of city commonwealths. Either way, it was the female city that shaped its male protagonists, her body imprinting itself on her progeny. In Thomas Middleton's *The triumphs of truth*, London took the form of 'a grave feminine shape . . . attired like a reverend mother, a long white hair naturally flowing on either side of her'. Having nurtured her citizens to be free of 'all pollution, / Sin, and uncleanness', she now watches over them and keeps them

---

[31] Lyndal Roper, '"The common man", "the common good", "common women": gender and meaning in the German Reformation commune', *Social History*, 12, 1987, pp. 1–22.
[32] BIHR, CPH 2429, 1663, Anne Nichols c. Anne Whitely.
[33] BIHR, CPH 3023, 1673, Martha Coates c. Elizabeth Ashton, deposition of John Salmon.
[34] BIHR, CPH 2690, 1666, George Haxby c. Thomas Pinder, deposition of Margaret Green.
[35] BIHR, CPH 2951, 1671, Martha Thornton c. William Pickering, deposition of Abraham Horne.
[36] Paul Griffiths, 'Secrecy and authority in late sixteenth- and seventeenth-century London', *HJ*, 40, 4, 1997, pp. 925–51.

honest.[37] For Ben Jonson, in contrast, London predictably crawled with 'comically misshapen civic functionaries who highlight the city's insistent sexual and excretory energies'.[38] In his *Famous voyage*, Jonson evoked the 'grotesque exposition of female excess': a city that is 'mother' only to 'famine, wants, and sorrows many a dozen, / The least of which was to the plague a cousin'.[39] Likewise in city comedies a usual narrative was the sexual threat presented to enfranchised households by gallants and others, and the resourcefulness, or not, of 'she-citizens' in resisting or negotiating those encroachments. Plots excavated and tested female dispositions, developing situations that exposed feminine avarice, incontinence, vanity, and other kinds of dishonesty, or else revealed conscience, discretion, modesty, and an appreciation of the conversational and associational resources at their disposal. In the course of events, the moral boundaries of city commonwealths were examined and redrawn, the wives and daughters acting and speaking not only for themselves but also for their husbands, households, and communities. In two exemplary versions of the 'Old' and New' comedic form – Shakespeare's *The merry wives of Windsor* and Middleton's *A chaste maid of Cheapside* – female characters form the moral centre of the play, acting as custodians of civil society. Conversely, in *Bartholomew Fair* Jonson personifies urban degeneration in the form of Ursula and her pig-booth: a woman who stands as 'the seedy metropolis in microcosm'.[40] The final breakdown of civility and citizenship occurs when the prominent 'she-citizen' of the play, Mistress Overdo, accompanied by Win, wife of a young attorney, are seduced by Whit and Knockem into relinquishing their honest status, become whores, and cuckold their husbands. The transformation begins in the pig booth, where Ursula is told to 'take 'em in, and fit 'em to their calling. Green gowns, crimson petticoats, green women' (4.5.88). The process is complete when Adam Overdo – the Ciceronian magistrate who acts only 'for the good of the republic in the Fair' – is not only revealed as foolish, but also robbed of his eloquence by the sight of his wife vomiting and attired as a whore (5.6.65). The collapse of female civility precipitated, in effect, the collapse of civic authority: an inevitable causality when, as dramatist after dramatist reiterated, the one was inextricable from the other.

Common or public fames – also known as 'reputes' and 'voices' – marked the quintessence of this inextricability. Indeed, it was in the politics of opinion and reputation that the full extent of female public agency – and also the femininity of early modern political culture – is to be found. Fames were characterised by two, related dynamics. First, they were about someone or something. They

---

[37] Middleton, *The triumph of truth*, pp. 2–3.
[38] Andrew McRae, '"On the famous voyage": Ben Jonson and civic space', in Andrew Gordon and Bernhard Klein, eds., *Literature, mapping and the politics of space in early modern Britain* (Cambridge, 2001), p. 192.
[39] Ibid., p. 190.   [40] Neil Rhodes, *Elizabethan grotesque* (London, 1980), p. 159.

denoted publicly what someone or something actually had done, said, or was, and so arbitrated issues of reputation, credit, honesty, custom, and other forms of socially constructed fact. Second, they were the sets of practices through which such facts were constructed: a complex and 'collective process of gathering and exchanging information' about issues of common concern within communities.[41] Fames that achieved the status of truth were an important and sometimes binding feature of legal process, and authorities constantly sought to evaluate their social provenance, motives, and reliability. In so doing, distinctions were drawn between honest discussion, such as public fame and its synonyms, and types of dishonest talk: secret gossip and malicious rumour, scandal, and libel.[42] The innumerable instances of defamation, gossip, slander, and insults that made up the business of the church courts reflected at once the social power of these fames and the uncivil ways in which they were constructed.[43] Less recorded, but also much more usual in the parochial neighbourhoods of early modern England, was the civil construction of public opinion through legitimate modes of conversation and what contemporaries described as 'discourse'. The distinction was drawn when Francis Taylor, a well-placed apothecary and citizen of Restoration York, was accused of fathering the illegitimate child of his mother's maidservant, Mary Stanley. The court demanded whether the fame against him was civil or uncivil. It asked, 'of what persons as [the witness] heard the said pretended public fame? And where did it originally arise?' It wondered 'was it from any lewd or dishonest behaviour or carriage of the said Francis Taylor or was it from any secret suspicious meeting or communication with infamous persons in suspected places'. In particular, did it emanate 'from the bare and sole accusation of the said Mary Stanley or from the secret whisperings of the greatest enemies and ill-wishers of the said Francis Taylor'?[44]

It was, therefore, quite possible to have a common fame constructed in a civil and legitimate fashion. It was equally possible to engender defamation 'secretly', and for malicious and uncivil purposes. Women were central to the construction of both. The power of fame lay in the apparent objectification of subjective opinion. Its considerable dangers lay in the prospect of counter-fames, legal retribution, and the stigmatisation of its formulators as 'dishonest': a fate that threatened Anne Taylor and overwhelmed the more socially vulnerable Margaret Knowsley in contemporaneous Nantwich.[45] One feature of post-Reformation cities and towns was the way in which ecclesiastical courts increasingly acted as public sites in which opinions that had already been constructed publicly could be expressed and contested, encouraging a constant

---

[41] Rublack, *The crimes of women*, p. 26.   [42] See above, chapter 5.
[43] Gowing, *Domestic dangers*, chs. 3, 4; J. A. Sharpe, *Defamation and sexual slander in early modern England: the church courts in York* (York, 1980).
[44] BIHR, CPH 2828, 1667, Office c. Francis Taylor, response of Taylor.
[45] Hindle, 'The shaming of Margaret Knowsley', pp. 404–6.

interplay between the civil and social spheres.[46] They also brought an additional set of concerns and procedures to bear on the business of opinion that varied according to subject matter. In cases of defamation, the plaintiff had to prove that their public reputation had been seriously, maliciously, and falsely damaged by the words of the defendant. In cases of marital separation and adultery, public fames were relied upon as indicators of the 'truth' – for example, whether Francis Taylor was indeed the father of Mary Stanley's child. However, public fames were concerned not only with the sexual proclivities, moral reputations, and material responsibilities of neighbours and acquaintances, but also arbitrated local issues traditionally regarded as public in the civic sense, such as disputes over parochial taxation, local elections, responsibilities of public office, and the provision of education. In both respects, they were the means by which people digested and regurgitated rumour and news of national significance, in the process demarcating and regulating their communities.

To be participant in or the subject of fame was to join in a shared conversation. It was also to be susceptible to the conventions and expectations on which conversation and company drew. This was as true for men as it was for women. Certainly causes of defamation in Restoration York suggest that, no matter the 'double standard' that characterised early modern attitudes to male and female sexuality, men – and in particular married men – had much to lose from sexual scandal, especially if it was implicated in an abuse of place.[47] This was clearly the case for religious ministers, who were especially vulnerable to charges of immorality and the undermining of their place and calling.[48] It was also true for politically active citizens. In Restoration York, apothecary Francis Taylor was excluded from his mother's will in the light of his seduction of Mary Stanley, her maidservant; his name became synonymous with sexual double-dealing in York and the surrounding area; and his career in civic politics was notably curtailed. Thomas Pinder, for example, blamed the pregnancy of Anne Stower on her 'going to Doctor Tailor to take some physick off him'.[49] In the later 1670s the soap-maker John Mould, a renowned Tory in a Whig city, was suspended from the common council while rumours of his attempted rape of Margaret Richardson – euphemistically styled 'several misdemeanours and breaches of law tending to the Dishonour of this City' – were investigated.[50] So damaging was Margaret's assertion 'that Mr. John Mould was uncivil to her and that he

---

[46] Gowing, *Domestic dangers*, ch. 2.

[47] Gowing, *Domestic dangers*, pp. 114–15; Shepard, 'Manhood, credit and patriarchy', pp. 76–7.

[48] For some Yorkshire examples see BIHR, CPH 2419, 1663, Office (churchwardens) c. John Legard; CPH 2739, 1666, Office c. Richard White; CPH 2786, 1669, Office (John Baines) c. Gerrard Desborough; CPH 2999, 1672, Office (John Hardy) c. Christopher Smedley; D/C 1673/5 Office (Sir Philip Monckton) c. Reginald Hopwood; D/D 1681/1 Office (Richard Coulson c. Robert Sharpe; D/C 1690/1 Office (Francis Jeffries) c. Charles Howlett.

[49] BIHR, CPH 2690, 1666, George Haxby c. Thomas Pinder, deposition of Robert Morley.

[50] YCA, B38, f. 189v.

rent the smock from her shoulder [. . .] and took her by the crocky' that he eventually accused her of defamation in the church courts.[51] The causes of defamation launched by Susan Hartness in 1662 and Hester Browne in 1663 not only defended their own reputations but also the reputation of eminent male citizens. Elizabeth Addison accused Hartness of whoring with George Lamplough, an alderman of the city: she told anyone who would listen that 'Mr George Lamplough had had the use of her for five years together both above stairs and below or any where he pleased and he had her at command'. The implication was that the husband of Hartness was a cuckold, their tavern a bawdyhouse, and Lamplough a wilful and dishonest rogue.[52] Similarly Hester Browne was in all probability a serving maid in the household of Christopher Topham, another alderman of the city and one politically aligned against the company in which Bridget Hodgson, as we saw in chapter 5, disseminated her rumours. Certainly it would have taken household support for someone of Hester Browne's standing to meet the potential costs in money and reputation that a defamation suit against Hodgson – the most powerful midwife in the city – required.[53] If this is a reminder that the behaviour of householders reflected on the household as well as themselves, it also corroborates the boast of Martha Thornton of Leeds after warnings from Elizabeth Bowes and Alice Sykes against fathering her bastard falsely on Mr William Pickering, 'a person much above her'. Martha replied 'If I lay it on his back let him get it of as he can I'll lay such scandal upon him as he shall never claw of whilst his name is Pickering'.[54]

Fames did not materialise out of thin air. Rather, certain people were instrumental in both disseminating a rumour and convincing of its veracity. To do so, they drew on different forms of social authority, association, and conversational technique. Grace Johnson, wife of Thomas, a humble cordwainer who also ran a licensed alehouse off Thursday Market in the centre of York, was the architect of the successful fame against the much better-placed Francis Taylor, who lived a few streets away on the boundary of the parish. In court, Johnson carefully based her opinion that Taylor was the father of Mary Stanley's child on the existence of the public fame. When pressed by the court as to the genesis of the fame, all the deponents – even those supportive of Taylor – had testified that it 'did originally arise from Mary Stanley'. Johnson alone merely reiterated that she 'cannot particularise any single person of whom she heard it, the report being so general, yet for her part believes in her conscience the said common voice and fame to be true'. This obfuscated her role as mistress of the alehouse where Mary Stanley 'lay-in' and the fact that she not only cared for Mary during

[51] BIHR, CPH, 1680, Margaret Richardson c. John Mould.
[52] BIHR, D/C 1661/2, Susan Hartness c. Elizabeth Addison, deposition of Isabel Slater.
[53] BIHR, CPH 2560, 1662, Hester Browne c. Bridget Hodgson.
[54] BIHR, CPH 2950, 1671, William Pickering c. Martha Thornton, deposition of Alice Sykes.

her pregnancy but also stage-managed the birth.[55] She gathered the women, or gossips, to witness Stanley in labour and persuaded Jane Smith, a sixty-year-old midwife from the other side of the river, of 'the necessity and occasion of her going' to Mary Stanley's side. Smith in turn established herself as an authoritative and neutral witness, assuring the court that she was a stranger to Mary, Taylor, and all the women gathered for the birth. The interrogative technique of midwives in establishing the identity of the father was tried and tested: at the point when Mary was 'in strong labour and peril' the midwife 'desired her declare before the good women then present who got her with child'. Mary answered 'Mr Francis Taylor her Mistress son and none other' and described the 'sundry times he had solicited her to act with him'. The gossips were then able to tell their husbands – some of who were involved in parish government – of 'the many oaths she has taken thereupon and with weeping tears affirmed none but him ever had any thing to doe with her'. Jane Smith could draw on the authority of her skill and experience to inform the court that she 'verily believes in her conscience Mr Taylor to be the true and only father' of the 'bastard child'.[56] This ritualised and semi-official form of objectification was supplemented by the robust doorstead culture of which Johnson was also a part – a setting captured, albeit fleetingly, in a series of depositions describing a long-term feud between two of Johnson's neighbours, Elizabeth Ashton and Martha Coates, during the 1670s. One Sunday afternoon in 1673 Grace Johnson was already 'standing at her husbands door' when hostilities commenced, Coates telling Ashton 'go thou brazen-faced whore I had better have no children then have them ill-begotten as thine are [. . .] go thou pocky whore you have a fireship in your Arse'. It does not take too much imagination to see how, on another occasion, the condition of Mary Stanley would have been the topic of conversation.[57]

By utilising the discursive settings of bedside and doorstead, Johnson ensured Taylor's guilt despite wealthier parishioners like Mr Robert Hunter testifying that he believed 'in his conscience Mr. Taylor to be innocent'. As Mrs Rachel Hunter also put it, she believed Taylor 'not at all guilty of committing this Crime for that he behaves himself civilly amongst his neighbours and was never before nor since suspected of any such crime'. However, even the Hunters had to acknowledge that the common fame was against their friend, suggesting that it was possible for humble householders like Johnson to use conversational strategies in order to curb and militate against the will and opinion of ostensibly

---

[55] BIHR, CPH 2828, 1667, Office c. Francis Taylor, response of Taylor, deposition of Grace Johnson.
[56] Ibid., deposition of Jane Smith.
[57] BIHR, CPH 2923, 1674, Martha Coates c. Thomas Ashton; CPH 3145, 1674, Martha Coates c. Elizabeth Ashton.

more powerful neighbours.[58] That said, the quite different experience of Martha Thornton in Leeds revealed the politics of reputation as extremely hazardous. This was despite the fact that her previous employer, Mr William Pickering, had begrudgingly agreed to maintain her child at the quarter sessions in Leeds in 1670, observing that while 'he did take up Martha Thornton's coats he would not get her with child with his finger'.[59] Despite this acknowledgement of guilt, Martha lost control of the fame upon which her maintenance depended. Instead, a counter-fame was disseminated in Leeds, Bradford, and surrounding townships that had Martha, under direction from her father, maliciously and falsely fathering the child onto Pickering. According to the fame her motive was to revenge her dismissal for 'taking money out of his pocket' and to cover the desertion of the real father, Robert Calsey, whom Martha loved.[60] As a further twist, it was rumoured that Robert Thornton clearly relished the predicament in which the much-wealthier Pickering now found himself. Entering alehouses he would ask if anyone had 'seen his son Pickering' and, when challenged, explain 'he got my daughter with child and he would call him son whenever he met him'.[61] This inversion of status was too much for Pickering; and it was women who were central to reclaiming his reputation by establishing the Thorntons' dishonesty. Ellen Locke, wife of the constable, encouraged Martha to confess that 'Robert Calsey and she was long in love together' and that they would have married 'but that her friends would not consent to it'.[62] Midwife Isabel Walker reported that, at the birth, neighbours had been excluded and Martha in any case named Calsey as the father.[63] Alice Sykes described how Martha admitted in an alehouse in Bradford that Pickering was accused 'undeservedly' and laughed when warned on the dangers of compromising a 'person much above her'. Sykes also deposed that, during the York assizes, she 'drank a glass of ale' with Robert Thornton and agreed 'to prevail with [Pickering] that . . . Martha might come and ask him forgiveness' and 'endeavour a reconciliation betwixt them'.[64] By these means, Alice Sykes brokered Pickering's fame in much the same way that Grace Johnson decided Francis Taylor's.

The significance of fame and defamation for civic politics is clear enough. Whether in Rye, York, or Leeds, men as well as women – and governors as well as governed – had to protect their honesty in order to vindicate their communal place and social position. Certainly for household-heads this honesty was less gendered than historians have sometimes suggested. Just as women

[58] BIHR, CPH 2828, 1667, Office c. Francis Taylor, response of Taylor, depositions of Robert Hunter, Rachel Hunter.
[59] BIHR, CPH 2951, 1671, Martha Thornton c. William Pickering, deposition of Abraham Horne.
[60] BIHR, CPH 2950, 1671, William Pickering c. Martha Thornton, deposition of Margaret Ward.
[61] BIHR, CPH, 2954, 1671, William Pickering c. Martha Thornton, deposition of John Comyn.
[62] BIHR, CPH 2950, 1671, William Pickering c. Martha Thornton, deposition of Ellen Locke.
[63] Ibid., deposition of Isabel Walker.   [64] Ibid., deposition of Alice Sykes.

were fully implicated in the credit of their household economy, so men were susceptible to accusations of immorality levelled against themselves and their household-dependants. Moreover, the fact that women were so important in constructing opinion inevitably imbued them with degrees of authority not necessarily reflected in the minutes of civic meetings: this was especially the case for midwives, healers, and those with skill in, and power over, bodily and reproductive processes. However, the efficacy of opinion was also closely connected to the company in which it was generated and the techniques used to disseminate it. The company of midwife Bridget Hodgson was impeccable, her authority as York's premier midwife unimpeachable. What she could not account for was that Hester Browne had not, in fact, given birth to a child. Margaret Richardson, in contrast, had no friends of substance and no ritualised setting with which to substantiate her claims of incivility against Mould – claims that were themselves tainted as dishonest by the fact that her husband owed Mould money. Similar problems faced Elizabeth Addison. Her claim that Susan Hartness was 'an arrant whore and Mr George Lamplough's whore five years together and he had the use of her seventeen times where he pleased' was contested on three counts. It was shown that among her neighbours 'Susan Hartness was accompted an honest woman'; that the rumour against her was the product of malicious assertion rather than civil and inclusive 'discourse'; that it was motivated by economic jealousy on the part of Addison.[65] While similar doubts, cleverly assimilated by Alice Sykes, dogged the fame of Martha Thornton, Grace Johnson used every discursive trick in the book to pit the word of Mary Stanley against the civility and class of Francis Taylor. Sixty years earlier, Anne Taylor likewise emerged triumphant from her protracted and vicious struggle against oligarchs in Rye.

It is worth noting, finally, that the political power of fame and defamation – and also the gendered associations of this kind of power – had repercussions far beyond particular locales. Just as common fames formed an interface by which news and information outwith communities were disseminated and interpreted within them, so they were one dimension of the formation of early modern 'public opinion'. The development of scribal networks; the trade in print and politicisation of traditional literary products like almanacs and ballads; and the intermingling of 'oral' and 'literate' cultures provided new technologies and genres for common fames to be disseminated as 'rumours' among discursive communities that transcended the propinquity of place.[66] Pamphlets by the

[65] BIHR, D/C 1661/2, Susan Hartness c. Elizabeth Addison, depositions of Isabel Sanderson, Ralph Lane, Jane Fernwell; D/C 1662/4, Susan Hartness c. Deborah Young, deposition of Isabel Slater.
[66] Fox, *Oral and literate culture*, ch. 7 and 'Rumour, news and popular political opinion in Elizabethan and early Stuart England', *HJ*, 50, 1997, pp. 597–620; Ethan H. Shagan, 'Rumours and popular politics in the reign of Henry VIII', in Tim Harris, ed., *The politics of the excluded, c.1500–1850* (Basingstoke, 2001), pp. 30–66.

Presbyterian propagandist Edward Bowles were a case in point. In 1643 Bowles explained that 'Common fame, none of the worst witnesses, hath brought to every man's ears the noise of the King favouring the Irish Massacre' and his plan to use the Irish against the 'English Parliament and Puritans, as the King's enemies and theirs'. His own, printed contribution was, in turn, an attempt to persuade 'honest men' to 'withdraw their thoughts from their perplexed reflections . . . and apply themselves to a diligent observation of the contexture and comprehension of affairs, as they have been these latter years managed by our Adversaries'. For Bowles, this involved showing the 'common fame' to be true – not 'as if a judicial proceeding were undertaken' but in the sense that 'a rational judgement may be passed'. His evidence, which hinged on a reported conversation between two strangers in a Dublin tavern, was hardly more convincing than reported conversations in York and Leeds alehouses. However, he assured his 'honest reader' that 'I have not written any willing or negligent falsehoods, nor (to my best understanding) any unseasonable or unnecessary truth'. Indeed, if 'other men do their share as I have done mine, and the world will certainly be either honester or wiser'.[67] The same year he acknowledged that 'a judicial proof could not be produced to satisfy the world' about the 'work of darkness' threatening the realm. What did exist was 'the common fame which runs abroad': a fame which his 'bare opinion', printed for the judgement of 'indifferent men', could only corroborate.[68]

Although the community was enlarged, the same rules that characterised the construction of local fames applied: insofar as he justified it, Bowles was propagating an honest opinion for the attention of an honest audience. Although the subject, genre, rhetorical strategies, and audience were very different, as a broker of opinion he was little different to Grace Johnson or Alice Sykes. The power of common fames nationally likewise corresponded to their influence locally – an efficacy best measured by attempts to prevent them. Richard Atkins explained to Charles II in 1664 that 'the Liberty of the Press was the principal furthering cause of the confinement of your most Royal Father's Person'. It ensured that 'every Malcontent vented his passion in Print: some against his Person, some against his Government, some against his Religion, and some against his Parts'. It was by virtue of this pronounced incivility that 'the Common People became not only Statists, but [also] Parties in the Parliament's Cause, hearing but one side'.[69] Just as common fames in towns were often the product of libels, malice, and 'secret whisperings', so for Sergeant Morton 'the dispersing of seditious books is of great danger to the kingdom': an act 'very near akin to raising of Tumults'. Indeed, 'they are as like as Brother and Sister; Raising of Tumults

---

[67] Edward Bowles, *The mystery of iniquitie* (1643), p. 33.
[68] Edward Bowles, *Plaine English* (1643), p. 8.
[69] Richard Atkins, *Original and growth of printing collected out of history and the records of the kingdom* (1664), A.

is the more Masculine, and Printing and Dispersing Seditious books, is the Feminine part of every Rebellion'.[70] There was nothing especially 'royalist' about this position. By 1646, Bowles, like many Presbyterians, had changed his perspective on the legitimacy of discourse outwith authorised places and company. With his 'party' now a dominant grouping in the post-war parliament, he noted that 'Men in trust and Authority should take care that the People may rather have the advantage, then the knowledge of their proceedings. Things that are done by them are necessarily to be made known to them, and to satisfy them in their obedience, the ground of the command, or something showing the Equity and necessity of it, is usually permitted, as is done in the preamble of Acts, Ordinances, and Declarations.' However, 'to make known the debates, and those humane passions incident thereunto, it were sometimes to discover nakedness where it ought not, to minister strifes, to make the people Judge of them whom they have made so'. He had heard 'that the custom in Scotland is otherwise, where there is a diligent eye had on the Press . . . and a reverend reserve kept upon their Counsels and actions'. In this way, the link between personal and public civility was retained, the Scots showing that 'those that are reserved at home, will not judge it meet to be very open elsewhere'. In England, in contrast, 'one of our faults' is that the 'Press' was 'prostitute to the lust of every Pamphlet'.[71]

Bowles' language was telling. Unauthorised printing was 'feminine'. The press was a 'prostitute' to lustful and passionate opinion. Its revelations were as intrusive and titillating as 'secret whisperings' and doorstead 'conferences', leaving statesmen as 'naked' as the mayors of Rye after Anne Taylor had finished with them. Intended to stigmatise the trade in seventeenth-century opinion, such language also confirmed that common fames and public opinion were analogous both in terms of their political efficacy and their gendered associations. Just as 'gossip, whether simply informative or, more especially judgmental, was overwhelmingly regarded by contemporaries as a female activity', so 'public opinion' fomented outwith civic authority was characterised in the same pejorative and gendered way.[72] Whether they liked it or not, male commentators were faced with the fact that an increasingly important dimension of seventeenth-century public life was feminised in terms of their own patriarchal categories. It was just such a realisation that informed *The parliament of women*, a complicated and ongoing satire on parliamentary practice that described women forming an

---

[70] 'An exact narrative of the tryal and condemnation of John Twyn for printing and dispersing of a treasonable book' (1664), in *Freedom of the press: four tracts with the diary of Edmund Bohun* (London, 1975), 50.

[71] Edward Bowles, *Manifest truths* (1646), p. 18.

[72] Hindle, 'The shaming of Margaret Knowsley', p. 393; Gowing, *Domestic dangers*, p. 121; Dagmar Freist, *Governed by opinion: politics, religion and the dynamics of communication in Stuart London, 1637–1645* (London, 1997), pp. 290–1, 298.

assembly 'to the Dignity and Profit of the Female Common-weal'. By 1684, its central conceit was that various kinds of pejorative female behaviour could be used to ridicule the nation's male representatives, who were accused, in effect, of behaving like uncivil women. The problem of female conversation was a recurring theme. Early on in the pamphlet the Speaker explains that Bishops 'have their Convocations, Soldiers their Council of Wars, even Emmets have their assemblies upon *Ant-Hills*; only Women of all Creatures are debarred from all Society'. The reason is not difficult to fathom. Verbally incontinent women constantly interrupt the Speaker, who also warns the 'membresses' that, now they have been called 'to the great work in hand, not to be tumultuous in your disputes, but to show yourselves moderate and discreet'.[73] In order to 'out-do our Oppressors Men as well in Fact as in Talk . . . prudence and good Management' were required. A particular concern was the feminine tendency towards immoderate disclosure. Given that 'Women are not ignorant that Women do those things in secret which they would not have all the world know; therefore if any Gentlewoman or Lady be privy to any secret of her Friend, let her by no means divulge it in Heat and Passion.'[74] Another was the effeminate desire for talk to be open and unregulated rather than 'private' and 'reasonable'. Lady *Twittle-cum-Twattle*'s opposition to committees was:

that some must be packed one way into one Room others another way into a Room and there forsooth they must have all the Talk by themselves, and we must sit hear by ourselves, and not hear a word what they say – No, no, by my Faith, that's not the way; I say let's all talk together. I am for that Court ye call *Dover Court*, all Speakers and no Hearers.

Committees proved unavoidable. However, the 'tyranny' of Reason was not; and the women vowed that the educational institutions that enabled men to 'beat us down with our own Weapons, Long Talk and Words' to be spoilt 'with a Vengeance'.[75]

According to *The parliament of women*, the feminisation of political culture was based on verbal incontinence, public disclosure, and discursive cacophony – charges that were also levelled at coffeehouse culture.[76] Feminisation was also linked to the sexualisation of the representative body and the commonwealth it served: for female representatives, cuckoldry, bigamy, adultery, and pornography were to be sanctioned by statute. This, too, was consistent with more general perceptions regarding the uses and abuses of political power. Bodily corruption was a recurring idiom of political criticism throughout the seventeenth century, marking another point of equivalence between common fames

---

[73] *The parliament of women* (1684), pp. 5–6.   [74] Ibid., pp. 7–8.   [75] Ibid., p. 17.
[76] Pincus, '"Coffee politicians does create"', p. 824.

and public opinion. The point was made by Milton: 'Court ladies, not the best of Women . . . when they grow to that insolence as to appear active in State affairs, are the certain sign of a dissolute, degenerate, and pusillanimous Commonwealth.'[77] Be it in the letter books of Robert Horne, the scandalous newsbooks of Marchamont Nedham, or the Restoration satires of Andrew Marvell, the personal deficiencies and degradations of courtiers and courtesans were as vicariously exposed as those of any civic dignitary.[78] The paradox was that, just as the presence of women sexualised politics, so the public disclosure of sexual transgression was implicitly effeminate. Either way, public knowledge of courtly corruption increased rather than decreased over the course of the century. This was in part because of technological and commercial developments. The proliferation of cheap print during the civil war brought the Jacobean commerce in libel and scandal among scribal communities and urbane 'wits' to new audiences. It was also due to the conflation of 'defiant royalism, cuckoldry and immodesty' as part of the 'same cause' during the 1650s.[79] The stereotype harked back to Jacobean city-comedies: the sexual vulnerability of city commonwealths and the custodial role of she-citizens in protecting them. It could only be confirmed by the priapism of the Restored Stuarts. The well-documented insinuation of sexual and political power by Charles and James; their 'arbitrary mix of hedonism and repression'; and the sheer incompetence of the monarchical state after the relative successes of the 1650s dictated the form that political criticism should take. Certainly the 'fundamental distinction between the serious public sphere and private realm of pleasure' did not obtain in England in the decades after 1660.[80]

This was as true for a 'model subject' like Samuel Pepys – a royal administrator fully committed and loyal to the 'king's service' after 1661 – as it was for an archetypal citizen like Andrew Marvell. Both could not help but link the inadequacies of the restored monarchical state with its libertinism. It was what they did with their knowledge that distinguished them. On one day in July 1667, for example, Pepys had a number of conversations with fellow administrators and servants of the 'king's service'. He talked about how diplomacy was made 'only to preserve the King for a time in his lusts and ease, and to sacrifice trade and his kingdoms only to his own pleasures; so that the hearts of merchants are quite down'. He heard 'the King and Court were never in the world so bad as

---

[77] Cited in Norbrook, *Writing the English republic*, p. 116.

[78] Marchamont Nedham, *Mercurius Britanicus*, 92, 28 July–4 August 1645; Colclough, 'The muses recreation', pp. 386–7; Steven N. Zwicker, 'Virgins and whores: the politics of sexual misconduct in the 1660s', in Conal Condren and A. D. Cousins, eds., *The political identity of Andrew Marvell* (Aldershot, 1990), pp. 85–110.

[79] Gowing, *Common bodies*, pp. 38–9.

[80] James Grantham Turner, 'Pepys and the private parts of monarchy', in Gerald MacLean, ed., *Culture and society in the Stuart Restoration: literature, drama, history* (Cambridge, 1995), pp. 106–9.

they are now for gaming, swearing, whoring, and drinking . . . so that all must come to naught'. He learnt that 'the Court is in a way to ruin all for their pleasures' and that the 'Duke of York is suspected to be the great man that is for raising of this army and bringing things to be commanded by an army'. He was told that the King must at least make 'a show of religion in the government, and sobriety; and that it was that that did set up and keep up Oliver, though he was the greatest rogue in the world'. After all, 'it is so fixed in the nature of the common Englishman, that it will not out of him'. It emerged that 'the King adheres to no man' but vacillates between factions 'to the ruin of himself and business'. And it was 'discoursed', finally, that the King 'is at the command of any woman like a slave': he lacked control of both his personal and corporate bodies.[81] Pepys kept his conversations to himself and his diary. Marvell did not. In his *Last instructions to a painter*, the 'scratching courtiers' who 'undermine a *Realm*' were exposed to the eye through a series of pictorial vignettes that moved ever closer, and finally fully implicated, the 'lust and infidelity' of the king's own body.[82] His 'naked Narrative' of England's drift towards 'Absolute Tyranny' and 'downright Popery' was equally clear about its revelatory duty to 'the public' – an obligation fulfilled anonymously and by the printed equivalent of 'secret whisperings'.[83] Marvell played, then, a game every bit as dangerous as Anne Taylor, Grace Johnson, Martha Thornton, and countless other women across the corporate system: that of naming and shaming in order to shape opinion. That one Widow Brewster was accused of publishing his 'late libels' is a reminder, finally, of the unusually large number of women involved in licensed and unlicensed printing in the years after 1660.[84] Like common fames, the trade in public opinion was feminine, uncivil, and a crucial dynamic of political culture.

Civility and slavery

Whether they liked it or not, the conversations and places that early modern people styled (and stigmatised) as feminine were fully insinuated within the political cultures of both city and national commonwealth. *Vice versa*, the civic household was a public construction perforated by, and permeated with, the functions and language of the body politic. This immediately runs the risk, of course, of joining the unusually large number of 'dubious statements' and 'contradictory claims' that have been made by historians of 'the early modern family' over the previous forty years.[85] Given the nebulous nature of the subject,

---

[81] *The diary of Samuel Pepys, Vol. VIII, 1667*, pp. 354–6.
[82] Zwicker, 'Virgins and whores', pp. 101–5.
[83] Marvell, *An account of the growth of popery*, p. 17.   [84] TNA SP29 406, 37.
[85] Collinson, *The birthpangs of Protestant England*, p. 81.

it is worth clarifying what 'household' means in this instance.[86] A starting point is Sir Thomas Smith's notion of the kind of 'house' upon which commonwealths were ideally built. This he defined as 'the man, the woman, their children, their servants bond and free, their cattle, their household stuff, and all other things, which are reckoned in their possession, so long as all these remain together in one'.[87] This framing of the household as a place of co-residence under the authority of a head or heads has been shown by Naomi Tadmor to remain predominant well into the eighteenth century.[88] However, while Smith and other commentators placed conjugality at the household's authoritative centre, Tadmor has demonstrated that, within the parameters of the house, a variety of relationships and hierarchies could pertain. It was the fact of co-residence – rather than specific ties of blood and marriage – that mattered. Her extrapolations from the 'household-family' mark, in effect, a decisive break with the sociological categories that have traditionally dominated the historiography. Rather than looking for 'pre-modern' and 'modern' families, 'extended' and 'nuclear' families, or, indeed, 'Open Lineage', 'Restricted Patriarchal Nuclear', and 'Closed Domesticated Nuclear' families, Tadmor has elucidated a 'descriptive concept' similar to that of cultural urbanisation – an interpretative tool that identifies, without determining, a key component of early modern society.[89]

The proximity of house and *polis* was accentuated by the Ciceronian-invigorated Aristotelianism of the sixteenth and seventeenth centuries. Smith felt that in any 'society that consists only of free men', the 'natural and first conjunction of two toward the making of a further society of continuance is of the husband and of the wife after a divers sort each having care of the family'.[90] Educationalists like Mulcaster and Perkins accentuated this interdependency by encouraging parents to educate their children in ways at once consistent to their 'calling' and beneficial to 'the public'. More controversially, John Milton justified divorce on the grounds that it could only be 'unprofitable and dangerous to the commonwealth, when the household estate, out of which must flourish forth the spirit and vigour of all public enterprises, is so ill-contented and procured at home, and cannot be supported'.[91] In each of these perspectives the household served as a base from which men served their commonwealth

---

[86] Keith Wrightson, 'The family in early modern England: continuity and change', in Stephen Taylor, Richard Conners, and Clyve Jones, eds., *Hanoverian Britain and empire: essays in memory of Philip Lawson* (Woodbridge, 1998), pp. 1–22.

[87] Smith, *De Republica Anglorum*, p. 13.

[88] Naomi Tadmor, 'The concept of the household-family in eighteenth-century England', *P&P*, 151, 1996, pp. 111–40.

[89] Wrightson, 'The family in early modern England', p. 17.

[90] Smith, *De Republica Anglorum*, p. 12.

[91] John Milton, 'The doctrine and discipline of divorce restored to the good of both sexes', in Stephen Orgel and Jonathan Goldberg, eds., *John Milton: a critical edition of the major works* (Oxford, 1991), p. 187.

'abroad', women taking the complementary role of 'nurturer' or 'help meet'. However, the fact that, over the course of the period, households also came to be conceived as commonwealths in their own right meant that their internal structures were also configured politically. Although the conflation of monarchical and patriarchal sovereignty by Jean Bodin and subsequently Robert Filmer are the most familiar of these representations, they by no means reflected the full gamut of commonwealth ideology.[92] For Smith, household government was ideally aristocratic, whereby 'a few and the best do govern, and where not one always: but sometime and in something one, and sometime in some thing another doth bear the rule'. Endowed with complementary skills and abilities, husband and wife 'each obey and command other and they two together rule the house'.[93] Milton in turn regarded 'conjugal society' as an opportunity for discursive reciprocity: 'in God's intention a meet and happy conversation is the chiefest and the noblest end of marriage', allowing the man to become 'copartner of a sweet and gladsome society'.[94] In Ben Jonson's *The alchemist*, Dol somewhat naively conceives her house with Subtle and Face as democratic: a place of 'common work', a 'republic' and 'venture tripartite' that was 'begun out of equality' to bring 'all things in common . . . without priority' (1. 1. 110, 133–5, 155). More pragmatic was the contractual arrangement negotiated by Millament and Millecent in William Congreve's *The way of the world* – a legal agreement that apportioned roles and rights on an equal, if gendered, basis (4. 1).

The use of such language was widespread. However, its relevance either to political discourse or social practice is less clear: Smith himself acknowledged that 'this cannot be called Aristocracy, but Metaphor, for it is but an house, and a little spark resembling as it were that government'.[95] That said, there are good reasons to take the 'little spark' more literally. Well into the seventeenth century, citizens assumed that the imperatives of communal- and self-governance naturally extended from *polis* to house. In the early 1660s, for example, William Smith exasperated not only his parents but also a series of masters with his roguish and petty-criminal behaviour. When magistrates warned that, if he could not be taught self-discipline, he would be brought before quarter sessions, William's father paid for his own son's transportation to America.[96] When the Dean and Chapter in York complained about Shrove Tuesday riots in the cathedral precinct in 1673, the civic response was twofold. A delegation of prominent citizens was sent to London 'to vindicate this city and

---

[92] Tuck, *Philosophy and government*, p. 26; J. P. Sommerville, *Politics and ideology in England 1603–1640* (Harlow, 1986), pp. 27–34.
[93] Smith, *De Republica Anglorum*, pp. 12–13.
[94] Milton, 'The doctrine and discipline of divorce', pp. 186, 191.
[95] Smith, *De Republica Anglorum*, p. 13.
[96] BIHR CHP 3497, 1681, Jane Mabson c. William Richardson and Ann Saltmarsh.

the Magistrates thereof from the scandal cast upon them'. And parish constables were ordered to 'give notice to the several masters of family within their several precincts that they take all care of and admonish their children and servants not to give any trouble or disturbance by walking or otherwise upon any Sabbath Day in the cathedral church'.[97] Likewise, it was as household representatives that freemen and citizens held office – be they deliberative places like common councillor, or more onerous positions like the city watch that continued to be delegated by 'houserow', or lottery, well into the later seventeenth century. Nor was the *polis* spatially excluded from the sanctum of domesticity. Common councils, committees, and courts could be held in domestic locations: in York in 1654, even the mayoral swearing was held in the parlour of the incoming mayor.[98] Assessments were collected in the house – it was, after all, in the Ballard's parlour that Henry Penrose had his eyes scratched and his periwig dislodged while collecting the hearth tax in 1685. Likewise, subscriptions for petitions and local elections were collected in the street, at the doorstead, in the alehouse, or in the house itself. Householders in the York parish of St Michael le Belfrey testified in 1666 that it was customary for persons seeking the post of parish clerk to 'go along . . . from house to house through the parish and [get] the subscriptions of the Inhabitants thereof'.[99] The custom, asserted as a plea for parochial democracy rather than the closed elections run by the Dean and Chapter, became a template for contested parliamentary elections soon after.[100]

These overlaps in political space and function were matched by the interpenetration of civic and domestic morality. At the outbreak of civil war, for example, parliamentary propagandist Henry Parker compared a husband leaving his wife to a king leaving his parliament. He argued that there were certain circumstances in which the behaviour of a wife or parliament justified desertion: adultery by the former, tyranny by the latter. In other circumstances, however, desertion was unjustifiable: 'if the husband will causelessly reject [his wife]' or 'if ill Counsaile have withdrawn [the king], for this wicked end merely, that they might defeat this Parliament, and derogate from the fundamental rights of all Parliaments'.[101] Framed in these terms, the judgement that Parker invited from the public rested on social conventions rather than constitutional niceties. He invoked, in effect, the household morality of the *polis*. Conversely, Daniel Awtry's account of his separation from his wife, Elizabeth, in 1682 was laced with the language of commonwealth: a sad narrative of conjugal betrayal that was punctuated with notions of 'will', 'duty', 'trust', 'submission', and 'common fame'. Things came to a head when, 'contrary to [his] express will and prohibition', Elizabeth spent 'two nights at a reputed bawdyhouse'. There she

---

[97] YCA, B38, f. 84.   [98] YCA, B37, f. 53.
[99] BIHR, CPH 2811, 1666, Robert Hutchinson c. Peter Wright, deposition of James Shorswood.
[100] BL Add MSS 28051, f. 26.   [101] Parker, *Observations*, p. 10.

'notoriously committed the crime of fornication or Adultery' despite his 'fair and civil attempts to bring her to sense . . . of her duty'. With Elizabeth showing no signs of penitence, he 'gave her a box on the ear and a kick on the britch and turned her out of doors'. For 'his own security and to prevent her running him into debt' he also 'caused the Bellman of the City of York to give Notice publicly that he disowned her and that none should trust her for anything whatsoever but at their own peril'. Excluded from the 'conjugal society' that materially and morally sustained her, but still refusing to make 'any submission . . . for her former faults', Elizabeth was 'now publicly reputed a drunken arrant whore'.[102] Unfortunately, Elizabeth's own account of the separation does not survive. However, the fact it was she who brought the case against her husband – witnesses describing her 'a person of good life and conversation' who 'behaved herself obediently [and] respectfully . . . as a good wife ought to do' – suggests a more complicated narrative than that described by the husband. Awtry's desertion, like the king's, was indubitable. The legitimacy of either was not.

Even as Elizabeth Awtry was attempting to salvage her household place and public reputation, John Locke and the editors of Robert Filmer were engaged in their own famous 'discourse' concerning both the nature of house and *polis*, and the relationship between them. It is an argument that suggests that, even as late as the 1680s, the household was not simply analogous to the *polis* but also, in important respects, equivalent: an equivalence that was conceived by the authors in sharply divergent ways. As is well known, Filmer's *Patriarcha* collapsed the boundaries between family and state in order to construct an absolute system of obedience and subjugation around the figures of the kingly father and fatherly king.[103] Locke echoed Smith and the whole Aristotelian tradition in his rebuttal of the model. Although 'a *Master of a Family* with all these subordinate Relations of *Wife, Children, Servants and Slaves* united under the Domestic Rule of a Family' might resemble 'in its Order, Offices, and Number too . . . a little Common-wealth, yet it is very far from it'.[104] Unknotting the threads connecting household and state with one hand, Locke nevertheless retied them with the other. He replaced the conceit that the family was 'a Monarchy, and the *Paterfamilias* the absolute Monarch in it' with the assumption that '*Conjugal Society*' was predicated on 'Community of Goods, and the Power over them, mutual Assistance, and Maintenance' – a community that was 'varied and regulated' by contract. As such, the '*Power of the Husband*' was the very antithesis of 'an absolute Monarch'. Wives had 'in many cases, a Liberty to separate from him; where natural Right, or their Contract allows it, whether that Contract be made by themselves in the state of Nature, or by the Customs or Laws of the Country

---

[102] BIHR, D/C 1685/8, Elizabeth Awtry c. Daniel Awtry, response of Daniel Awtry.
[103] Robert Filmer, *Patriarcha: or the natural power of kings* (1680).
[104] John Locke, *Two treatises of government*, ed. Peter Laslett (Cambridge, 1988), p. 323.

they live in'. Likewise, the *'Father's Power* of commanding extends no farther than the Minority of his Children, and to a degree only fit for the Discipline and Government of that Age'.[105] Although the family was 'far different from a Politick Society' in terms of its 'ends' and powers, both were constituted by right, custom, and contract rather than unmediated and absolute will.

The household envisaged by Locke was hardly a blueprint for female equality or emancipation. There was nothing to suggest, for example, that Awtry was acting illegitimately if, as he claimed, Elizabeth posed a genuine threat to the 'common concern' of their household. Moreover if (as inevitably they did) the 'different wills' of husband and wife clashed, 'the last Determination, *i.e.* the Rule . . . naturally falls to the man's share, as the abler and the stronger'.[106] What Locke did idealise was a household that, in its opposition to absolute monarchy, had its genealogy within commonwealth discourse and practice. Although the husband's will ultimately ruled, it was a will that was nevertheless mediated – not least by daily and civil participation in the household's 'community of goods'. Locke's position reflected, at least for certain households, the realities of social practice. In the forty years after 1640, for example, twenty-five apprentices to the Barber Surgeons in Newcastle-upon-Tyne had their calling interrupted by the death of their master. Of these, five elected to finish their apprenticeship with their 'Dame' or 'Mistress' rather than move to another household. Although none of these dames ever attended a civic meeting, they were clearly fully involved in the shops and partnerships on which urban freedom rested as well as the sociable events, such as feasts and dinners, which punctuated the civic calendar.[107] The last will and testament of York citizen John Brice, written in 1671, suggests the affective implications of this. He bequeathed to his 'Dear and loving wife Jane who hath been my fellow worker' not only the customary 'third part of all my estate' but also his house and rented watermill 'to the end that my said dear wife may be enabled to educate my said children'.[108] The Brices' neighbour Rebecca Harland likewise regarded the 'house', 'shop', and 'business' of her husband, cordwainer Anthony Harland, as the materials of 'their trade'.[109] The Bristol merchant Thomas White likewise asked in his last will and testament 'to lie by my wife who was to me a most comfortable yoke fellow'.[110] Adopting a more discursive idiom – but also one that was naturally implied by the emphasis on community – Locke's patron Shaftesbury echoed Milton when he remembered his wife Margaret as 'in discourse and counsel far beyond any woman'.[111]

---

[105] Ibid., pp. 322, 321, 316.   [106] Ibid., p. 321.   [107] TWA, GU/BS/2/1, list of apprentices.
[108] BIHR, York Wills, January 1671/2, James Brice.
[109] BIHR, CPH 3023, 1673, deposition of Rebecca Harland.
[110] TNA Probate 91/99, 1600, Thomas White.
[111] Ralph Houlbrooke, ed., *English Family Life 1576–1716: an anthology from diaries* (Oxford, 1989), p. 111.

This is not to suggest that householders achieved or necessarily wanted Milton's 'sweet and gladsome society'. What the household did constitute, however, was a place of daily negotiation in which, as in any commonwealth, the clash of 'wills' and 'dispositions' was determined as much by contingency and personality as patriarchal platitudes.[112] This politics, and the strategies and factions that characterised them, was as variegated as households themselves. Pepys appropriated the stratagems of political economy to prevent his wife 'running on in her liberty before I have brought her to the right temper again'.[113] Elizabeth could remonstrate, in turn, about 'her want of money and liberty' and threaten to 'not live with me but would shame me all over the City and Court'.[114] Remembering his time as an apprentice to a large and productive household in Salisbury, the astrologer Simon Foreman evoked a veritable state of nature: mistress fighting against master; apprentices, servants, and journeymen dividing into male and female factions; authority residing as much in physical strength as rightful position.[115] Relations reached a crisis for Foreman when he pinned his mistress behind a door after she tried to blame him for a mistake she had made in the workplace and she called on her husband, 'Master Comins', to beat the apprentice as punishment. According to Foreman, his master knew the request to be inequitable, as it was obvious who had spoilt the cloth; moreover, while master and apprentice had an affectionate relationship, that of husband and wife was (as described by Foreman) spiteful. Foreman was beaten nonetheless, prompting him to cancel his indenture and return to 'school'.[116] The astrologer William Lilly recalled joining a citizen-household in London that, while similarly fractious, was not a place of economic production and consisted only of husband and wife.[117] Unlike Foreman, Lilly successfully squared the expectations of his master with those of his dame, exploiting to his own profit the conjugal unhappiness of both.[118] York alderman Sir Henry Thompson, friend of Marvell and probable associate of Locke, implied similar levels of conflict in his will of 1683. Making his 'dear wife' and 'their most dear and loving mother' guardian of his children, he ordered them 'to pay unto her all filial and faithful duty and obedience'. His two elder sons in particular were 'to pay and exact obedience to their mother my dear and affectionate wife and be assisting and helpful to her in all their services she requires'. Their 'love and respect' were also to extend to sisters, brothers, and wider kin: obligations that clearly needed reiterating.[119]

---

[112] Wrightson, *English society*, pp. 95–7.   [113] *The diary of Samuel Pepys, Vol. III*, p. 150
[114] *The diary of Samuel Pepys, Vol. IX*, pp. 20–1.
[115] *The autobiography and personal diary of Dr Simon Foreman the celebrated astrologer 1552–1602*, ed. James Orchard Halliwell (London, 1849), pp. 6–8.
[116] Ibid., pp. 9–10.   [117] Lilly, *Last of the astrologers*, p. 8.   [118] Ibid., pp. 11–12.
[119] BIHR, York wills, July 1683, Sir Henry Thompson.

The daily round of household politics need not imply a 'crisis' in gender relations during the seventeenth century. Locke appreciated, for example, that 'Husband and Wife, though they have but one common concern, yet having different understandings, will unavoidably sometimes have different wills too'.[120] Much more worrying was the absence of conflict, as this implied that wives and other household members were 'subjected to the Absolute Dominion and Arbitrary Power of their Masters'. Indeed, subjection 'to the inconstant, uncertain, unknown, Arbitrary Will of another Man' was 'the *state of Slavery*' and only rightfully endured by 'Captives taken in a just war'.[121] Slaves were 'not capable of any Property' and 'cannot in that state be considered as any part of *Civil Society*': a state within which, as contemporaries well knew, women were especially vulnerable. Slavery in Massinger's *The city madam*, for example, was a social relationship defined by economic dependence on the one hand and subjection to an arbitrary power, or will, on the other. At the beginning of the play Lady Frugal and her two daughters are quintessential tyrants. This is reflected in their attitude towards their paternal uncle, Luke, who, due to his own profligacy, is financially dependant on Frugal and his household: as Lady Frugal tells her daughters Mary and Anne at the outset of the play, 'He is your slave, and as such use him' (1. 1. 103). It is a trope that re-emerges during marital negotiations between the daughters and their suitors. Encouraged by her mother, who has been assured by an astrologer of the 'rule, pre-eminence and absolute sovereignty in women', Anne explains that:

> I require first
> (And that since 'tis in fashion with kind husbands,
> In civil manners you must grant), my will
> In all things whatsoever, and that will
> To be obey'd, not argued.
> (2. 2. 85–7; 2. 2. 105–9)

This sets the tone for a stream of 'articles' that lead the suitors to conclude that they 'will not take us / For their husbands, but their slaves' (2. 3. 31).

Like *The parliament of women*, *The city madam* inverts gender roles in order to both critique the excesses of male behaviour – in this instance, the creation of tyrannous households – and satirise female foibles and vices. When the tables are turned and Luke replaces Frugal as master of the house, there is much hope that the wilful pride of the women will be curtailed. Lord Lacey explains to them that 'he that was your slave' is now 'by fate appointed / Your governor' and hopes this will instil the degree of order and decorum requisite of the 'wife and daughters of a knighted citizen' (3. 2. 96, 150). However, Luke's conception of freedom is that of Filmer's: what Locke mocks as '*A Liberty for every one*

---

[120] Locke, *Two treatises of government*, p. 321.   [121] Ibid., pp. 322–3, 284.

to do what he lists, to live as he pleases, and not to tied by any Laws'. The result is a vindictive and arbitrary government that quickly dispels any notions of reform and the establishment of *'Freedom of Men under Government'*: rules 'common to every one of that Society'.[122] As the play reaches a denouement, the new tyrant happily agrees to sell mother and her virginal daughters for human sacrifice in Virginia. In a surprisingly powerful conclusion, the New World provides a startling context for understanding the slavery of English women. At one end of the social spectrum they can be sold as commodities, either for human sacrifice or marriage to Amerindian kings against their wills. At the other, they figure among the 'condemn'd wretches / Forfeited to the law' – the 'Strumpets and bawds, / For the abomination of their life, / Spew'd out of their own country' – who 'are sent as slaves to labour there' (5. 1. 105–9, 112).

The problem of slavery was not confined to political treatises and dramatic satires. The slavery endured by Grace Allenson in Yorkshire after the Restoration likewise consisted of economic dependency and subjection to a will at once uncivil and tyrannous. Grace finally initiated a cause for marital separation after her husband, Charles, 'turned her out of doors' in York in 1676; at least three female witnesses, all of them 'spinsters' and ex- servants to the household, testified that the life of Grace had been one of 'slavery' and 'misery'.[123] In describing Grace's slavery they also articulated what they understood to be ideal, normal, or at least acceptable in terms of household governance. For both male and female witnesses this rested on the reciprocal benefits of civility, authority, and civil society. Spinster Sarah Dawson, a servant in the household in the later 1660s, was typical in describing the 'base currish ill-conditioned and snarling carriage' of Charles and his 'base language and opprobrious terms': attributes that merely reflected a 'cross furious passionate and strange disposition'. Lacking either affection or self-control, he was 'continually scolding, brawling, quarrelling . . . beating and kicking [Grace] . . . without any occasion given but merely upon words or fancies which he was pleased to make occasions himself'.[124] In contrast, Grace continually strove for what Maria Sparling, a twenty-nine-year-old servant, described as the 'civility and respect that behoves a wife to a husband'. No doubt striking the poses necessary to impress the court, Grace was invariably described as 'discreet respectful dutiful', of 'modest strict civil conversation', and given to 'as much obliging care, kindness, circumspection as any would well doe to a husband'.[125] John Goldborough, a vintner in York and until recently Allenson's steward, commented on her 'virtuous and modest behaviour and conversation'; her reputation as a 'submissive' and

---

[122] Locke, *Two treatises of government*, p. 284.
[123] BIHR, CPH 3264, 1676, depositions of Frances Turner, Sarah Dawson, Margaret Green, Maria Sparling.
[124] Ibid., deposition of Sarah Dawson.   [125] Ibid., deposition of Maria Sparling.

'good wife'; her 'industrious' attempts and 'constant endeavours' 'to please [Allenson]'. He also noted that in return she generally received 'brawling and chiding', 'ugly names', and a 'black face': 'notwithstanding she had meat and clothes and all things of that nature yet she wanted content quiet and satisfaction'.[126] Only Margaret Redmaine, who described herself as friend rather than servant, suggested a more robust and less ideal response on the part of Grace. As she put it, 'when her husband hath been chiding with her Grace gave bad language and tart replies as when he hath bid damn her she hath bid damn him and hath called her queen she hath replied and called him rogue'.[127]

Allenson's incivility excluded Grace from the wifely duties and rituals that ideally placed her at the civil centre of the house – in particular, the provision and consumption of food. It was recalled by a number of witnesses that 'many times [Grace] has lived privately with the children in the nursery not daring to go to dine with her said husband'. Similarly:

if she had ventured up to sit beside him, if he had wanted anything as a glass of beer or the like he would have knocked the maid up and upon such occasions she has heard her mistress very kindly say 'Honey I could have given you that' and he would reply 'God damn her he would have nought of her giving' . . . and then she came crying and sit by the kitchen fire.[128]

Allenson further encroached on her role by interfering during pregnancy – hauling her from bed, depriving her of rest, and placing her in physical danger – and transferring his affections from wife to maid. Margaret Green recalled Allenson shouting at Grace 'why did she stay God damn her he loved his maid (meaning Frances Hardy then a servant in the house) better than her'. It was noted that 'when her mistress had gone to supper with her master he would not let her cut him any meat but would make the said Frances Hardy help him'.[129] As a servant to the house, Richard Thackwray remembered hearing Allenson 'quarrel with his present maid Frances Hardy and she hath replied and wished him hanged whereof he hath taken no notice'. Now living as a linen weaver in the suburbs of the city, Thackwray suggested 'that in case his [Allenson's] wife had at any time when he was abusing her given him such a word he would have been past guiding'.[130] Usurpation of place was accompanied by a systematic campaign to undermine the authority of Grace with other household members. Margaret Green remembered that 'Mrs Allenson for some misdemeanours took her son Marmaduke a small box on the ears for which Mr Allenson in a very furious manner beat her and abused her most sadly.' She recalled how Allenson would 'stand in the door when the children came from school and if they wanted a button he never called any of the servants but fell a-beating her about it'. She

---

[126] Ibid., deposition of John Goldborough.   [127] Ibid., deposition of Margaret Redmaine.
[128] Ibid., deposition of Margaret Green.   [129] Ibid., deposition of Margaret Green.
[130] Ibid., deposition of Richard Thackwray.

also deposed that when Allenson and Hardy locked Grace out of his bedchamber 'she durst not for her life go into bed in any other room without his order'. As a result, she was 'forced to sit up two nights in the nursery . . . and this examinant sit up with her those two nights'.[131] Grace was not simply excluded from the civil society of dinner table and bedroom; she was reduced to the place of a child or servant.

The predicament of Grace confirms that the household was not a metaphor for commonwealth so much as its crucible. It was in the house that a person's awareness of – and participation in – place, conversation, civility, governance, and community were expected; and it was here that, as part of that process, freedom or slavery was experienced. The quality of that experience related, in turn, to whether the house was urban or rural. In *The city madam*, Mary Frugal described the uncivil ignomiqy of rural slavery and her plans to avoid it herself. She would not:

> Sit like a fool at home and eye your thrashers
> Then make provision for your slavering hounds
> When you come drunk from an alehouse after hunting,
> With your clowns and comrades as if all were yours,
> You the lord paramount, and I the drudge.
>
> (2. 2. 155–9)

It is an image that eerily anticipated William Poppleton's description of the Allenson house when the family lived in the North Riding village of Crake. He described how Allenson

would come home late at nights and bring . . . raggeyley fellows in his company such as were not fit company for his servants and would at such times Notwithstanding he had servants enough for that purpose would call and cause his wife to rise out of bed and come and give the said fellows meat.[132]

Neighbour Lucas Mawburne had also heard the stories. In Crake it was 'generally reported by many of the neighbours' that Allenson was 'a very ill conditioned and cruel husband' who 'called in country fellows who had been drinking with him to see what an obedient wife he had'. Even then, though, Allenson's tyranny was not admired: 'those fellows [would] have dissuaded him from making her come to them and told him that in case they should do so with their wives it would be past living for them'. It was also recognised, however, that if Grace 'had not submitted and complied to all his ill humours that he would have done her some mischief'.[133]

The exhibitionist role of 'lord paramount' adopted by Allenson in his country manor was different to, if not the antithesis of, his tyranny in York. His main

---

[131] Ibid., deposition of Margaret Green. [132] Ibid., deposition of William Poppleton.
[133] Ibid., deposition of Lucas Mawburne.

concern in the city was to regulate and curtail the interaction of his wife with civil society, reducing Grace to a state that observers perceived to be no less servile and slavish than public and ritualised subjugation. Sarah Dawson testified that when Grace 'at any time went abroad she usually asked his leave as those she had been a servant and if she had gone otherwise he was angry'. If this was unusual enough, then 'when she did ask leave he has many times denied her, in such manner that... her mistresses life was a continual slavery and misery and this examinant extremely wonders that a woman was able to endure what her mistress did'.[134] Goldborough noted that 'because Mrs Allenson had as [Allenson] pretended talked with Mr Hodgson about some business or other in his absence', Allenson 'was very angry with Mrs Allenson and did beat her'. Having beaten her, he then 'asked her what she had to do to discourse with him in his absence'.[135] Thackwray deposed that as a servant to Allenson he was 'discharged... for coming into the house at any time but meal times or when he had necessary business... to prevent him from observing or taking notice of his base carriage to his wife'.[136] Grace was equally concerned to prevent her problems becoming public knowledge. Frances Turner was one of several female witnesses to note that Grace 'did use all her endeavours to suppress conceal and hide his ill condition and aversion to her and could not endure that anybody should know thereof'.[137] Enforced segregation and secrecy explained, in turn, the absence of any 'common fame' in York against Allenson. Excluded from the civil society of either her husband or the wider public networks that characterised female company, Grace's only consolation was to 'privately [declare]' to her servants and friend 'the sadness of her condition and [lament] and [bewail] her misfortune'.[138]

'As private as they could'

At about the same time as Grace sought relief from her tyrannous husband, Mary Marvell also 'did bewail the condition'. Her problem was twofold. First, her marriage to Andrew Marvell was secret. Mary explained to the Court of Chancery in 1681 that she 'in private did live with [Marvell] as his wife, But the said Andrew Marvell her husband had reasons best known to himself to keep the marriage secret and not to call herself his wife'. As a result, 'she went by the name of Mrs Palmer which was her name when the said Marvell married her... and [she] at his request and desire did on all occasions conceal the said marriage and keep it as private as they could'.[139] Second, Marvell died suddenly in October 1678, leaving a negligible estate and no will and testament.

---

134 Ibid., deposition of Sarah Dawson.   135 Ibid., deposition of John Goldborough.
136 Ibid., deposition of William Thackwray.   137 Ibid., deposition of Frances Turner.
138 Ibid., deposition of Margaret Redmaine.   139 TNA, C6/242/13, statement of Mary Marvell.

One set of papers that Mary succeeded in salvaging from his private closet on Maiden Lane were the poems that formed the *Miscellaneous poems* of 1681. A bond of Marvell's for £500 proved more elusive. John Farrington – one of the co-partners of the ill-fated bank of Woollchurch Market – successfully argued in Chancery that, although the bond was in Marvell's name, it had belonged to Edward Nelthorpe, another partner of the bank and Marvell's closest friend. The subterfuge had been necessary because Nelthorpe was on the run from his creditors: with Nelthorpe also dead (Marvell and Nelthorpe died within a month of each other) the bond now rightfully belonged to the remaining partners of the bank and their creditors. The doubts cast by Farrington about whether or not the Marvells were legally married proved a useful tactic that discredited Mary in the eyes of both the court and posterity. As Farrington put it: 'nor is it probable that the said Andrew Marvell who was a Member of the house of Commons for many years together and very learned man would undervalue himself to intermarry with so mean a person'. At the time of their marriage, Mary was 'the widow of a Tennis Court Keeper in or near the City of Westminster who died in a mean condition'. Moreover, 'Andrew Marvell did not at any time in his lifetime own or confess that he was married to the said Mary or any other person nor did he cohabit with the said Mary at any time as a man and wife use to do.'[140] Mary conceded that 'the difference in their conditions might be (as the defendant believes it was) one reason why the said Mr Marvell was pleased to have the marriage kept private'. She also convincingly refuted the charge. Providing time and place of the marriage, she declared that 'although it be true that her former husband Palmer was a Tennis Court Keeper and did die in a mean condition . . . and though it be likewise true that the said Andrew Marvell was a Parliament man and a learned man, yet it doth not follow but he might marry this defendant as in truth he did, and so it appears in the register aforesaid'.[141] The issue was never again raised in court.

Mary's robust rebuttal of Farrington's insinuations has not prevented Annabel Patterson authoritatively observing that one of the two 'most important facts about Andrew Marvell' was that '(despite the misleading testimony of the *Miscellaneous poems*) he never married'.[142] The orthodoxy that this reflects stems in large part from Fred Tupper's initial interpretation of the Court of Chancery material. Tupper took the allegations of Farrington against Mary at face value and then hypothesised wildly about how a 'mean' housekeeper could come to pretend to be Marvell's wife.[143] It is an orthodoxy consistent with an older tradition of Whig hagiography that, in eulogising the 'dignity, honour, sense, genius, fortitude, virtue and religion' of Marvell, dismissed Mary as a mercenary

---

[140] Ibid., statement of John Farrington.   [141] Ibid., statement of Mary Marvell.
[142] Annabel Patterson, *Marvell: the writer in public life* (Harlow, 1999), p. 8.
[143] Tupper, 'Mary Palmer, alias Mrs Andrew Marvell', pp. 386–8.

housekeeper. In putting her name to the *Miscellaneous poems*, she was merely profiteering in a dishonest fashion from her dead master's reputation.[144] The social and patriarchal assumptions that constitute the Marvellian myth were, of course, the very ones that entailed the marriage should remain secret in the first place: assumptions with which Marvell, through his insistence on secrecy, was complicit even as he subverted them. In fact, the question of whether or not Mary and Andrew were legally married is unanswerable given that the register to which Mary refers in her deposition no longer exists. More importantly, it is a question that obscures the fact that the household on Great Russell Street was not a familial or conjugal institution. Formed as a hiding place following the bankruptcy of Nelthorpe, Farrington, and Thompson in 1675, it was a locus for kinship and friendship.[145] Far from enshrining the values of conjugal society it was expressly designed as a safe house for citizens. Farrington claimed to be a regular visitor to the house; Nelthorpe and Richard and Dorothy Thompson were itinerant lodgers; and Mary performed the role of housekeeper when others were present. It was on these grounds that, as Mary explained, she sometimes attended on her husband 'more like a servant than wife (which was the better to conceal their being man and wife)'. One consequence of this was that, as Farrington testified, 'the said Mr Marvell and [Mary] did not . . . diet together'. Mary 'did not sit at meals with the said Andrew Marvell and the complainant but eat her meals after they had done as servants use to do as this defendant hath seen'.[146] Even then, though, her public manner within the house was not always servile: certainly when only Marvell and Nelthorpe were at home for dinner 'she did very often and so often as she pleased set down with them at meals and eat her meal with them'. At other times, however, 'she not always set down with them at meals'.[147]

As a secret nexus for civil sociability, the house on Great Russell Street nicely illustrates the essential diversity of household forms during the period. Rather than economic production, its main function was the preservation of a community of 'friends': it was the means by which, even in trying circumstances, a 'sympathy of affections [could be] firmly united together'.[148] At its heart was the relationship between Marvell and Nelthorpe, Farrington describing 'a more than ordinary kindness and friendship between them' and Mary concurring that 'Mr Marvell was very intimate with Mr Nelthorpe and might be a relation to him though she cannot tell what'.[149] The motif of friendship that characterised

---

[144] Edward Thompson, *The life of that most excellent citizen and uncorrupted Member of Parliament, Andrew Marvell* (London, 1776), pp. 447, 489.

[145] TNA, C6/242/13, statement of Mary Marvell

[146] TNA C8/252/9, statement of John Farrington.

[147] TNA, C6/242/13, statement of Mary Marvell.

[148] Daye, *The second part of the English secretorie*, p. 408.

[149] Ibid., statement of John Farrington, Mary Marvell.

the house can be placed within a well-established tradition of civil sociability that Angel Daye described as the 'original of love' that 'grows by a sympathy of affections, of which affections virtue is said to be the whole and simple ground'. The correspondence of its householders was ripe with this particular friendship's conceits.[150] Just as Richard Thompson explained his desire to live 'the exquisite life', so his kinsman Sir Henry Thompson of York could ask Marvell to forgive 'my barbarous incivility' in 'leaving the town without my taking solemn leave of you' (the reason being an ill daughter).[151] Likewise the letters of Dorothy Thompson to the Braman household in Chichester – where Richard, her husband, hid during the spring of 1678 – insinuated the obligations of kinship, civility, and citizenship. In a letter dated 30th March 1678 she was 'infinitely sorry that I am so unfortunate as to want a habitation to bid you welcome to', especially after her sister and brother-in-law had fulfilled their duty as kin 'by doing a courtesy to these in affliction'. She was meticulous in presenting her 'service' to the extended network of 'brothers' and 'sisters' who constituted the community – not least 'Mr Farrington and his lady' and 'my sister Popple', wife of another of Marvell's close correspondents. She also apologised for having 'no news since Sunday last for I am remote from town so hear but as friends come and visit', although she did feel her husband should not return to London 'by reason it is hard to judge what will become of the parliament'.[152] In another letter she acknowledged 'my obligations both to you ['dear Brother'] and her sister ['your dearest'] for your kind cheering of my dear [her husband]' and commiserated that 'you have not received the satisfaction you desired from the Duke of Buckingham'. She added 'but we are not now to learn that noblemens' promises are oftener broken than kept'.[153]

Excluded from this community of friends and kin, Mary was inevitably isolated within a household in large part constituted by it. Just as the enforced privacy of Grace Allenson was tantamount to slavery, so the secrecy imposed on Mary condemned her to public effacement and servility. Although she rented and ran the house – Farrington conceding that there was 'reposed great trust in the honesty of the said Mary' – she did so as a servant rather than a social equal. Exclusion need not have precluded conjugal intimacy, however. Certainly, a marriage that traversed social distinctions was rare and ran the risk of antagonising friends.[154] Just as friends of Martha Thornton prevented her marrying her true love, Robert Calsey, so Catherine Chattey of Truro was torn between her engagement to Isaac Bennett and the knowledge that she 'would never marry without [my] friends consent'. Keeping the 'matter private' for as long as possible, she eventually reneged on her promise, prompting Isaac to call

---

[150] Ibid., p. 408.   [151] BJL, DDFA/39/26.   [152] TNA, SP29/402/166.
[153] TNA, SP29/401/232.   [154] Wrightson, *English society*, pp. 87, 77.

her a 'fool' and take her to court for breach of contract.[155] Marriages without the consent of friends nevertheless took place. The prospect of 'a voyage to sea' encouraged the London citizen Thomas Armeshouse to reveal in his will that, 'contrary to all my friends expectations', he was 'married to one Katherine Hughes a fellow servant with me in the house'. The 'great good affection I both now do and ever since I have known her have born unto her', plus 'the discharge of my own soul and conscience in the day of Judgement', led him to guarantee Katherine a third of his estate no matter his friends' opinion.[156]

The careful preparations of Armeshouse only highlight Marvell's lack of foresight and the subsequent vulnerability of Mary following his death. She recalled that 'whilst [she] was in great sorrow for her husband John Farrington prevailed with her to let him have the keys of the said lodgings and thereupon... Farrington and his agents abusing [her] too easy credulity and great trust' – and pretending 'great love and friendship' – 'did remove all the said trunks etc'. It was only going afterwards 'to look for her husband's estate and she finding no estate of her husband but a few books and pounds and papers of a small value' that she 'became sensible how greatly she had been injured or imposed upon by John Farrington'.[157] However, it was not only Mary Marvell but also Elizabeth, the wife of Edward Nelthorpe, who was excluded from the affairs of her husband at this crucial juncture. Elizabeth was an alderman's daughter, ward of the court of aldermen, and wealthy in her own right when she married Nelthorpe. Her impeccable civic credentials were no help in the vicious household politics that followed the deaths of Marvell and Nelthorpe. In a deposition that is unfortunately damaged, she described how, following the bankruptcy and the threat of commission against her husband, the Nelthorpe household was broken up and the location of the safe house kept secret from her. Even when Nelthorpe 'fell sick', Dorothy Thompson thought it 'not convenient to let her know where her husband lodged for that she might be compelled by the commissioners to discover them'. It was only twenty-four hours before his eventual death that Dorothy Thompson wrote a letter to her 'Dear cousin' explaining a sickness had come and abated, and even on the day he died Dorothy visited Elizabeth and assured her it was best she stayed away. Later that day she sent two letters in two hours of each other: one giving directions to the house, another saying Nelthorpe was dead. Elizabeth was convinced that the Thompsons 'falsely informed her of her husband's recovery and kept her ignorant of the place of his abode'. Friends or not, their motives were clear enough. 'If she had been with him he would have left his money and estate in her custody and management and not trusted the Thompsons therewith.'[158]

---

[155] DCRO, Chanter 11036 (Bundle), Bennett vs Bennett, 1662.
[156] TNA, Probate 91/99 1600, Thomas Armeshouse.
[157] TNA, C7/587/95, complaint of Mary Marvell.
[158] TNA, C10/216/74.

Although both Mary and Elizabeth were thoroughly outwitted in this domestic politics, their vulnerability was not simply the product of gendered or, indeed, social inequalities. On the contrary, it was Dorothy Thompson who, out of all the friends in the house on Great Russell Street, emerged as the person most politically adept: in the household itself; her friendship and kin-networks; and affairs of state. If Dorothy Thompson was, perhaps, exceptional in her political dexterity, she nevertheless indicates the kind of agency female citizens were capable of. The experiences of Mary Marvell and Grace Allenson suggest, in turn, the ever-present dangers of slavery and servility. Somewhere between the two lay a more conventional and recognised medium. In both prescription and practice female agency was public rather than private; communal rather than separate; and fully implicated in the practice of city commonwealth. The public conversations and associations of everyday sociability were defined by a powerful feminine presence. While the household was fully integrated into this society, it was also a political entity in which concepts and processes associated with commonwealth had not simply metaphorical but also practical purchase. Certainly the house was no refuge from the public exigencies of sociability and politics: indeed, women were most vulnerable socially when an undue privacy or secrecy was imposed upon them. The publicness of women, and their participation in and control over certain kinds of civil company and conversation, gave them direct and indirect influence over civic politics. This power emanated from their brokerage of reputation and opinion, especially of the honesty – sexual, religious, and economic – of family, friends, and neighbours; and through the translation of that influence, through networks of kin, friends, and communicants, into places and networks of civic authority. It also rested on the fact that men could be, in certain situations, as concerned about their sexual reputations as women. All of which suggests that female agency – or, as importantly, agency regarded by contemporaries as feminine – was a normal if sometimes problematic feature of patriarchal and political relations. The point is never better demonstrated than the predicaments and contradictions of Andrew Marvell. Attuned to the moral decrepitude of court, he nevertheless used libel, satire and scandal to expose its degradation of public and domestic virtue. A citizen fully reflective of his civility and honesty, he was nevertheless implicated in a relationship that was potentially scandalous in the eyes of both enemies and friends – one that entailed for his wife a damaging secrecy. With circles like these to square, it was hardly surprising that he only drank at home.

8   Calvinism, citizenship, and the English revolution

'Seducers of divers sorts'

Thomas Hobbes' *Behemoth, or the Long Parliament*, provided one of the more controversial accounts of the 'troubles' of the mid-seventeenth century. In a series of dialogues between an eyewitness and his pupil, Hobbes exposed and explained for a Restoration 'Public' 'the wickedness of that time'.[1] That Charles II refused to license it did not prevent the text circulating at court before its unauthorised publication during the renewed parliamentary crisis of the later 1670s.[2] Written to justify Hobbes' theory of political obligation and used, like Filmer's *Patriarcha*, to bolster the 'Tory' defence of church, state, and the Stuart succession, *Behemoth* diagnosed the ideological causes of the civil war. Moreover, unlike much subsequent historiography, Hobbes had no qualms in linking those ideas to agency and political practice, providing a holistic interpretation of the 'causes, pretensions, justice, order, artifice, and event' of his 'iniquitous' and 'foolish' countrymen's 'actions'.[3] To this end, he described a range of 'seducers' who had propagated 'certain opinions in divinity and politics' in order to 'corrupt' the 'people in general' into war against their monarch.[4] The lesson in 1680 was that, just as they had succeeded in destroying the monarch once before, so the same 'seducers' were on the verge of doing so again: England's troubles had not gone away.

Hobbes' seducers were of 'divers sorts'. They included the 'great number of men of the better sort, that had been so educated, as that in their youth having read the books written by famous men of the ancient Grecian and Roman commonwealths' they fell 'in love with their forms of government'. In 1640 they 'were chosen the greatest part of the House of Commons, or if they were not the greatest part, yet, by advantage of their eloquence, were always able to sway the rest'.[5] These aligned with 'the city of London and other great towns': bodies that, 'having in admiration the great prosperity of the Low Countries after they had revolted from their monarch', imagined a 'like change in government'

---

[1] Thomas Hobbes, *Behemoth, or the Long Parliament*, ed. Ferdinand Tonnies (London, 1939), p. ix.
[2] Ibid., pp. viii–xi.   [3] Ibid., p. 2.   [4] Ibid., pp.2–4.   [5] Ibid., pp. 2, 3.

would 'produce the like prosperity'. This alliance of republicans and citizens was joined by three sorts of men that 'longed for a war, and hoped to maintain themselves hereafter by the lucky choosing of a party to side with'. Personifying the social and economic flux of the previous 150 years, they included the downwardly mobile, the socially ambitious, and those 'that had able bodies, but saw no means how honestly to get their bread'.[6] Pride of place in Hobbes' gallery of seducers belonged, however, to three sorts of religious activist: Presbyterian, Papist, and those that 'declared themselves for a liberty of religion'. The Presbyterians were 'ministers, as they called themselves, of Christ; and sometimes, in their sermons to the people, God's ambassadors; pretending from a right from God to govern everyone in his parish, and their assembly the whole nation'. Less numerous were the Papists who 'did still retain a belief that we ought to be governed by the Pope, whom they pretended to be the vicar of Christ, and, in the right of Christ, to be the Governor of all Christian people'. While the Independents, Anabaptists, Quakers, 'and other divers sects . . . whose names and peculiar doctrines I do not well remember' held 'different opinions one from another', they all 'arose against his Majesty from the private interpretation of the Scripture, exposed to every man's scanning in his mother-tongue'.[7]

Hobbes was critical of the political conceits of all three sorts of religious ideologue. However, it was the Presbyterians who were most culpable because they had acted from positions of ostensible authority and trust. Hobbes explained that the 'duty' of the subject 'is a science, and built upon sure and clear principles, and to be learned by deep and careful study, or from masters that have deeply studied it'. Ministers were crucial to the process of inculcation: 'The people have one day in seven the leisure to hear instruction, and there are ministers appointed to teach them their duty.' The crucial question was 'how have those ministers performed their office?' It transpired that 'A great part of them, namely, the Presbyterian ministers, throughout the whole war, instigated the people against the King.' While 'independent and other fanatic ministers' subsequently jumped on the bandwagon, 'the mischief proceeded wholly from the Presbyterian preachers, who, by a long practised histrionic faculty, preached up the rebellion powerfully'. Their final aim was 'the State becoming popular' and 'politics . . . subservient to religion', so that 'they might govern, and thereby satisfy not only their covetous humour with riches, but also their malice with power to undo all men that admired not their wisdom'.[8] Nor did they preach into a vacuum. That 'the people in general were so ignorant of their duties' stemmed from the widespread perception that the subject 'was so much the master of whatsoever he possessed, that it could not be taken from him upon any pretence of common safety without his own consent'. This was in part the fault of common law, which steeped the people in 'precedents and customs'

---

[6] Ibid., p. 4.   [7] Ibid., pp. 2, 3.   [8] Ibid., p. 159.

rather than the 'rule of equity'.[9] As importantly, it reflected the social ubiquity of humanist language and platitudes. When Hobbes' pupil expostulated 'what silly things are the common sort of people, to be cozened as they were so grossly' by Parliament in 1648, Hobbes observed 'What sort of people, as to this matter, are not of the common sort?' For Hobbes it was a sad fact that 'The craftiest knave of all the Rump were no wiser than the rest whom they cozened', the majority believing that 'the same things which they imposed upon the generality, were just and reasonable'. He wondered: 'who can be a good subject to monarchy, whose principles are taken from the enemies of monarchy, such as were Cicero, Seneca, Cato ... and Aristotle of Athens?'[10]

The art of seduction implied, in effect, popular complicity, *Behemoth* arising with the consent of 'freeholders in the counties, and ... tradesmen in the cities and boroughs'.[11] The result was a malignant body of seducers and seduced – or representatives and represented – that was firmly embedded in the spatial and conversational resources of, among other things, England's corporate system. Hobbes was more aware than most that what followed was not a revolution against authority so much as a revolt by authority – freemen, burgesses, and citizens resisting their sovereign on the grounds that they were active participants in, and defenders of, commonwealth and public good. It was precisely such sentiments that godly ministers supplied and stoked. As Hobbes' patron, the Earl of Newcastle, also noted at the Restoration, corporations 'have done your Majesty more mischief in these late disorders with their lecturers than anything else has done'.[12] Just as for Hobbes they were 'worms in the bowels of a greater body', so Newcastle could see 'no reason why there should be so many, for why should tanners and shoemakers not be content to be governed by the same way that Lords, gentlemen, good yeomen and freeholders are'. If the civil wars had shown anything, it was 'that every corporation is a petty free state against monarchy', Newcastle recommending that 'your Majesty will be pleased to think of having all their charters forfeited'.[13] The need was all the more urgent given the apparent (and ongoing) propinquity of urban citizenship and religious militancy.

Hobbes and Newcastle anticipate the more recent emphasis on the confessional contexts of England's mid-century troubles. Historians are now generally agreed that it was rival forms of Protestantism, combined with a particularly virulent anti-Catholicism, which repeatedly transformed, or threatened to transform, constitutional disputes into partisan violence in the fifty years after

---

[9] Ibid., p. 4.   [10] Ibid., p. 158.   [11] Ibid., p. 121.
[12] Gloria Italiano Anzilotti, *An English Prince. Newcastle's Machiavellian political guide to Charles II* (Pisa, 1988), p. 136.
[13] Ibid.

1637.[14] That religious activism and conflict was particularly – though not, of course, exclusively – pronounced in urban settings has likewise intrigued religious and urban historians alike.[15] Although less studied, contemporaries likewise drew a strong correlation between urbanity and dissent and nonconformity in the decades after the Restoration.[16] Indeed, what might be termed the latent urbanity of confessional politics can be glimpsed at various moments of the revolutionary process – be they the election of Cromwell to the Short and Long Parliaments; the violence of the confessional crowd; or the recruitment of the New Model Army officer corps.[17] This is not to argue a deterministic link between citizenship and militant Protestantism: indeed, in the Irish Pale, where citizenship was quite as redolent of *honestas*, *civitas*, and *res*publicanism as its English equivalents, Catholicism proved the religion of civic preference.[18] Neither is it to imply that Protestant militancy was limited to boroughs and cities. It is to argue that there was a certain social and cultural logic as to why, in England as in Scotland, vernacular Calvinism should emerge as the most publicly vociferous and successful mode of civic worship in the decades after 1540 – especially among England's civic elites. This chapter suggests a certain resonance between Calvinism and citizenship as it has been defined in the previous chapters: a process of cultural symbiosis by which 'puritanism' became the dominant idiom through which the ideology of city commonwealth was expressed and enacted. It does so by focusing on the treatises and career of Edward Bowles, an English Presbyterian who both embodied the political conceits vilified by Hobbes and enjoyed an extremely productive relationship with the civic governors of revolutionary York. The next section considers the narrative of 'long reformation' that Bowles used to explain the crisis of the 1640s, suggesting its resonance for citizens in general and those in York in particular. Section two highlights some of the conceptual affinities between urban citizenship and Calvinism that underpinned this resonance. The final section examines the way in which the ideas and networks that constituted 'puritanism' mutated into the Restoration era, as well as the renewed concerns with episcopal and Catholic power that continued to lend it political efficacy.

---

[14] John Morrill, 'The religious context of the English civil war', in Cust and Hughes, *The English civil war*, pp. 159–76; Tim Harris, *Politics under the later Stuarts: party conflict in a divided society, 1660–1715* (Harlow, 1993).
[15] Patrick Collinson and John Craig, 'Introduction', in Collinson and Craig, eds., *The Reformation in English towns*, pp. 1–19; Slack, *From reformation to improvement*, ch. 2; Tittler, *Reformation and the towns*.
[16] Harris, *Politics under the later Stuarts*, pp. 11–12; Gary S. De Krey, *A fractured society: the politics of London in the first age of party, 1688–1715* (Oxford, 1985).
[17] Morrill, 'The making of Oliver Cromwell', pp. 19–48; Walter, *Understanding popular violence*, chs. 5, 6; Gentles, 'New Model Officer Corps', pp. 143–4.
[18] Lennon, *The lords of Dublin*.

'Instead of reforming, we were deforming'

Bowles wrote a series of pamphlets during the 1640s at first justifying war against the king and later calling for unity among the 'honest men' who initially supported what he described to George Monk as the 'good old cause'.[19] As chaplain to the household of Thomas Fairfax and head of the preaching Ministry established in York during the 1650s he was also an astute and effective political broker. While Hobbes' understanding of civil dissent was based on his system of 'scientific' analysis, for Bowles it served the greater good of Protestant teleology. In *Manifest truths*, an historical account of Anglo-Scottish relations, he included a 'brief touch of the method of Reformation in this Island'. He noted that 'It pleased God at the bringing of this Island out of Popery, to honour Scotland with a more full departure from Romish Idolatry and Superstition.' Although 'England wholly renounced their Doctrine, yet some dregs of discipline and superstitious Ceremonies remained'. For Bowles, the initial cause of England's comparative sluggishness was political, Elizabeth facing 'so much trouble for Holland, with Spain, and in Ireland, that her Council thought not fit to adventure upon the trouble of an alteration in this point'. The result was the survival of the medieval church polity, in particular episcopacy, Bowles acknowledging that 'many of our Reformers being Bishops, could not so well understand the convenience of their own abolition'. However, with the ascension of the Stuarts the structural survival of the pre-Reformation church became less a symptom and more the cause of reformatory tardiness. Under James the bishops 'fomented' his 'innate bitterness against Puritans'; under Charles, 'especially since the preferment of the late Archbishop of Canterbury, it hath been much worse with us': 'instead of reforming, we were deforming, and, instead of renouncing, returning to Rome apace'. That was not to say that 'England wanted not its honour in the eyes of God and good men; For God favoured it with men eminent in learning, able and earnest assertors of the Doctrine of the Gospel, against the Champions of Rome'. These included exponents of Calvinism like 'Whitaker, Reynolds, Jewel, Fulke, Perkins' as well as 'more practical Preachers and Writers': men who ensured that England, no matter the structural incongruities of its church, experienced what Bowles regarded to be 'a greater measure of the power of Godliness, then other reformed Churches'. Bowles perceived himself and his fellow reformers, now working through the agency of parliament, as the latest practitioners of the 'power of Godliness'.[20]

Bowles' narrative resonates with more recent accounts of England's Reformations – not least the 'British' and European contexts that gave the process breadth and the prospect of Catholic counter-reformation that gave it such

[19] David Scott, 'Politics, dissent and quakerism in York, 1640–1700' (unpublished D.Phil, University of York, 1990), p. 148.

[20] Edward Bowles, *Manifest truths* (1646), p. 24.

urgency. Likewise, his juxtaposition of 'bishops' and 'good men' reflected what is now seen as the 'paradoxical nature of the Elizabethan Church Settlement, with its peculiar arrested development in Protestant terms, and the ghost which it harboured of an older world of Catholic authority and devotional practice'.[21] At the heart of this paradox was the fact that a reformatory movement that by the 1570s was broadly Calvinist in nature – its exponents committed to the doctrine of predestination and convinced of 'the supremacy of scripture and preaching' – was nevertheless contained within the form of a pre-Reformation church. If 'one of the great puzzles of the English Reformation is why cathedrals survived without substantial alteration', then in the later sixteenth and early seventeenth centuries paradox became contradiction with the beginnings of a new 'Anglican synthesis' centred on England's cathedrals and the cultural legacies, and continuities, they embodied. What Diarmaid MacCulloch terms the 'Westminster Movement' (after its symbolic home of Westminster Abbey) refined a 'theology of episcopacy and a penchant for splendid liturgy which would make the first generation of Elizabethan bishops look askance'.[22] It also provided a context for the political ascendancy of Arminian or Laudian worship in the 1620s and 1630s: a mutation of Anglicanism that, as is well known, represented a direct assault on the doctrines and authority of Calvinist 'orthodoxy' and 'consensus'.[23] As Peter Lake has argued, this need not imply 'a static, monolithic, indeed conservative Calvinism under attack from a dynamic and innovative Arminianism'. The 'rise of Arminianism' that was one manifestation of 'Anglican synthesis' should not 'underplay the dynamism and, indeed, the potential instability of the English reformed synthesis'.[24] Bowles' 'good men' formed a complex, mutable, and often divided community of 'radical' and 'moderate' elements. Radicals included those 'who felt driven to give overt institutional form to their basic scripturalism, their drive to shepherd out the godly from the ungodly, to avoid popery and to render the fostering of a truly godly consciousness amongst the people the constitutive element in their concept of ecclesiastical order'. It certainly encompassed 'those who refused on principle to conform and those who went further and developed presbyterian or congregationalist platforms' as alternatives to episcopalianism. In contrast, moderates, who formed the majority of the puritan laity and clergy, 'felt able to avoid such overt gestures of disaffection and disobedience and to pursue their vision of true religion within the structures of the English church'. Indeed, until

---

[21] Diarmaid MacCulloch, *The later Reformation in England, 1547–1603* (Basingstoke, 2001), p. 85.
[22] Ibid., pp. 79, 85.
[23] Nicholas Tyacke, 'Puritanism, Arminianism, and counter-revolution', in Cust and Hughes, *The English civil war*, pp. 136–59; Morrill, 'The religious context', p. 165.
[24] Peter Lake, *The boxmaker's revenge: 'orthodoxy', heterodoxy', and the politics of the parish in early Stuart London* (Manchester, 2001), p. 407.

the unprecedented circumstances of the 1630s they were at once amenable to and often embedded within 'the power structures and hierarchies of the early Stuart church and state'.[25]

The tradition of 'good men' in which Bowles placed himself had long regarded cities and boroughs as crucial instruments in the quest for further reformation, whether as points from which to appropriate extant religious resources or, as Bowles preferred, as conduits for new forms of church government. It was no accident that 'it was in the urban context that such familiar features of reformation as town preachers, weekly lectures, and combinations of preachers, the tightening up of social discipline, the growing influence of Sabbatarianism, and the emphasis on godly learning, developed and flourished'.[26] As the most extensive sets of 'power structures and hierarchies' available to the English commons, common councils and corporations were an obvious tool of cultural change. Although 'some towns were slower than others', throughout Elizabeth's reign 'borough after borough witnessed, and suffered, the ascendancy of godly magistracy and ministry'.[27] London companies used their commercial muscle to supplement the process by sponsoring lectureships and endowing charities across the corporate system. That boroughs and cities often sub-divided into parochial units provided another layer of spatial resources to appropriate: parish livings for university-trained clergy and parish offices, such as parish clerk or churchwarden, for civic laity. Neither was it coincidental that resistance to reformation became a familiar feature of urban politics, reformers and their opponents jeopardising 'the civic values of peace and harmony which the early modern town was meant to embody'.[28] At stake was control of the very 'fictional personality' that distinguished urban citizenship from other forms of communal identity. As the journal of Londoner Thomas Juxon demonstrates, city commonwealths were ideal settings for well-placed and publicly motivated citizens to turn their personal 'consciences' into the public will of both their city commonwealths and the parliament in which they were represented.[29]

Bowles' narrative of interrupted Reformation was especially resonant in cathedral cities. Not only were the edifices of episcopacy – cathedrals, deaneries, choral chapters, church courts – a reminder of unfinished business. For citizens, they represented significant, alternative, and potentially dangerous forms of urban power. York was a case in point. Architecturally, the Minster dominated the city; politically, the Dean and Chapter exerted magisterial authority over a significant section of the city, constantly sparring with its corporate rival; culturally, the taverns, booksellers, and coffeehouses located in Minster Yard

[25] Ibid., p. 399.   [26] Collinson and Craig, 'Introduction', p. 11;
[27] Ibid. See also Wrightson and Levine, *Poverty and piety*, p. 212.
[28] Collinson and Craig, 'Introduction', p. 19; Hughes, 'Religion and society', pp. 58–84.
[29] Keith Lindley and David Scott, eds., *The journal of Thomas Juxon, 1644–1647*, ed. Keith Lindley and David Scott (Cambridge, 1999).

were a magnet for country and urbane gentry. Just as the church was the second largest landholder in the city after the corporation, so the endemic conflict between the two was a primary source of public contention throughout the seventeenth century. It is significant, then, that at the outbreak of civil war Bowles reconfigured episcopal sites and places as instruments of a Catholic conspiracy of international proportions, effectively reducing the larger politics of reformation to the microcosm of the city. He warned that '*Babel* is to be built, the *Architects* are the *Jesuits*, taking in some *Atheist Politicians* to their assistance, as *Surveyors of the work*'. To this end, '*Princes* must find the materials, as being made to believe that the work is designed for the House of their Kingdom, and the Honour of their Majesty'. While '*Papists*, with the rabble of *superstitious and ambitious Clergy*, are the *daily Labourers*', it was 'the profane and ignorant multitude' who 'are employed in the most servile works . . . as *natural brute beasts, made to be taken and destroyed*'.[30] For York citizens his words had an immediate topographical logic. Just as the 'Jesuit' William Laud and his 'ambitious' henchman Archbishop Neile had used the Minster and all its powers against the citizens, so the 'atheist politician' Sir Thomas Wentworth had turned the Council of the North, located in the King's Manor, into a site of urban dominance. Imperious in the city and untouchable in Privy Council, together they threatened the very destruction of city commonwealth and the liberties vested in it. In their hands, York was instead 'designed as a *Church* for the Papist Devotion, as a Palace for the Prelates ambition, as a Castle for the Princes power, and the rest have several baits by these cunning Anglers cast unto them, according to the variety of their dispositions'.[31]

This conception of an international struggle between proponents of 'tyranny and superstition' on the one hand and 'good men' on the other mapped almost perfectly onto the recent history of the city, not least because of the extent to which Calvinists had colonised sites of civic power. This reflected the further point that, in York, the most voracious and vociferous proponents of Reformation also constituted the 'better sort' of civic society.[32] Godly 'elect' and civic 'elite' households were often synonymous, clustering in the wealthy parishes in Micklegate and around Ouse Bridge, on the opposite side of the city to the Minster.[33] These were householders that, as was shown in chapter 4, were at once mercantile in nature and over-represented in civic government. Peter Lake has shown that in a contemporaneous London parish like St Katherine's Cree, Laudian opposition to Calvinist orthodoxy came from the 'chief men' within the parish.[34] In York, in contrast, it was prominent officers, inhabitants, and

---

[30] Bowles, *The mystery of iniquitie*, p. 2.   [31] Ibid., p. 2.
[32] Scott, 'Politics, dissent and quakerism', pp. 139–40; David Scott, *Quakerism in York, 1650–1720* (York, 1991).
[33] Withington, 'Urban political culture', pp. 225–7.
[34] Lake, *The boxmaker's revenge*, ch. 11.

dignitaries of the cathedral precinct that took that role. As a result, religious tensions peculiar to the 1630s overlay the perennial stand-offs between cathedral and city, York's civic elites taking a middle position between the 'common multitude' they were meant to govern and an alliance of clerics, gentry, magnates, and courtiers apparently intent on debasing their authority. The structure of religious conflict was embodied in the person of merchant Thomas Hoyle. A native of the West Riding, Hoyle completed his apprenticeship with Matthew Topham, a leader of York's first generation of puritans, in 1611, and swore his freedom a year later. Elected chamberlain in 1614, common councillor in 1619, sheriff in 1621, alderman in 1626, and one of the citizens' two parliamentary representatives in 1628, his ascent through the places of civic government was as rapid as his Baltic trading interests and local land investments were lucrative.[35] As a householder of St Martin's Micklegate, Hoyle lived in the most civic, godly, and mercantile parish in York. Embedded in an extensive set of friendly, familial, and commercial relationships, he served as a fulcrum of what Archbishop Neile termed the city's 'puritan party'.[36] And as a householder of elevated civic and godly conscience, he instigated reformatory policies within each of the tiers of parochial and civic government to which he was elected.

Hoyle was a key target of the archbishopric's attempts to break the city's puritans during the 1630s. The public settings for conflict were varied. It was Hoyle who negotiated the city's re-incorporation at the expense of the cathedral in 1632, probably as a reward for co-operating with Wentworth in the Council of the North in containing the plague. It was also Hoyle who represented the corporation in the ensuing controversy between city and cathedral over precedence in the Minster liberty – a struggle that culminated with a summons to the Privy Council and Laud informing the civic entourage 'that the clergy [were] fitter for government than the city'.[37] Simultaneously the ecclesiastical authorities attacked the puritan power-base in St Martin's parish. In 1632 Hoyle was among several senior parishioners charged with keeping their hats on in church and 'wilfully' and 'contemptuously' neglecting to kneel during worship.[38] However, the archbishopric's task was made difficult by the refusal of churchwardens to testify against their neighbours, their excuses inadvertently revealing the continental context of local politics. Two were 'by profession' merchants and so 'enforced to be much absent' on 'private affairs and employments' during their year in office. Travelling to Prussia and Holland during autumn, their return

[35] Claire Cross, 'A man of conscience in seventeenth-century urban politics: Alderman Hoyle of York', in John Morrill, Paul Slack, and Daniel Woolf, eds., *Public duty and private conscience in seventeenth-century England: essays presented to G. E. Aylmer* (Oxford, 1993), pp. 206–9.
[36] Charles Jackson, H. J. Morehouse, and S. Margerison, eds., *Yorkshire diaries and autobiographies in the seventeenth and eighteenth centuries* (Durham, 1878), p. 129.
[37] Cross, 'A man of conscience', p. 214.
[38] BIHR, CPH 1933, 1632/3, Office c. Churchwardens of Martin's Micklegate.

'after Christmas' was spent 'riding up and down the country' in order to sell 'commodities and merchandises and to treat and deal with such persons as were indebted'.[39] Closer to home, the tanner William Fairweather explained that for much of his term in office his 'eye sight was so dim' that 'he was advised by his physician not to go abroad or stir out of doors'.[40] When the Calvinist minister John Birchall was appointed to the living in 1634 the cathedral had new cause for concern. In 1634 Birchall was presented for failing to publish the Book of Sports and neglecting to follow the prayers and catechisms in the Book of Common Prayer. Instead he had instigated the kind of self-reflective and discursive worship anathema to Laudian ritual. During Divine Service he encouraged parishioners not to 'repeat of their vows and prayers either with or after the minister' but 'go along with him with their minds and intentions only'. Worst of all, he had 'taken upon you to dispute and determine in the pulpit points of controversy already decided by the church': namely predestination. It was alleged that 'after a long and tedious dispute and discourse on both sides you at last took [it] upon you to determine the same contrary to his Majesty's declaration'.[41]

The conflict centred, therefore, on both the relative powers of city and cathedral and the control of public place and conversation in a particular parish. However, a second case brought against Burchill two years later, in 1636, confirmed the ambiguity of publicness of domestic space suggested in the previous chapter. It transpired that Burchill and the Hoyles enjoyed a particularly close relationship: Hoyle not only secured the living for the young minister but also incorporated him into his household. This was a home that required the same attention to honesty and conversation as the larger community, and at its centre was Elizabeth Hoyle: a woman at once full of 'holy virtues' and free of 'wilful humour'. Conversationally 'she did even in regard of Moral things, but what a Civil and Moral man might have done'; as a person 'subjected . . . her will unto the will of God' in 'public, private, or secret'; and in her deportment showed 'wisdom', 'discretion', and 'judgement'.[42] Burchill, as a minister 'quick both in his tongue and in his mind', contributed to 'her presence, her counsel, her company, her prayers for the soul of her husband' and 'her Family'. He also consolidated the 'moral virtues' that defined 'her calling' in 'the City': as a woman with 'public duties' as well as private.[43] Where the former ended and the latter began was far from clear, and in 1636 Birchall was accused of assembling 'secretly by way of conventicle and in very unlawful manner' to 'utter a private or (extempore) conceived prayer of your own making'.[44] In response,

[39] BIHR, CPH 1978, 1633, Office c. Churchwardens of Martin's Micklegate, depositions of Edward Gillot and Samuel Brearey.
[40] Ibid., deposition of William Fairweather.
[41] BIHR, CPH 2010, 1634, Office c. John Burchill.
[42] John Birchall, *The non-pareil* (York, 1644), pp. 10, 12, 8.   [43] Ibid., p. 17, 15.
[44] BIHR, CPH 2123, 1636, Office c. John Birchill.

the minister explained that when 'Alderman Hoyle and his lady' decided to visit their recently purchased country house (in the nearby village of Colton) he 'went along with them to bear them company and to take the air'.[45] Family, kin and tenants 'came in unto the company' and, as 'the first time his wife and children were there', Hoyle requested that Birchall say a prayer.[46] Lasting a quarter of an hour, the prayer was 'made . . . in the house or parlour' of the house. It 'confessed sin and begged favour and grace for Christ's sake' and for 'a blessing upon the King's Majesty and the whole state of this land'.[47] Facing similar charges two decades earlier, John Etherington, the London boxmaker recently studied by Peter Lake, had argued that although the king could quite legitimately 'command a place and places for the publique worship of God', he could 'forbid none in private'. It remained the 'liberty that every Christian have' to worship and pray 'at all times and in all places, everywhere, even in our secret chambers'.[48] As Archbishop Neile well knew, however, the whole point of further reformation was that, just as 'honest' secret chambers should have public expression, so the secret chambers of others should be publicly reformed.

For Thomas Hoyle the 'publique calamities' that subsequently overtook the nation coincided with painful 'private crosses'.[49] In 1639 Elizabeth and Burchill died in quick succession. Two years later, Hoyle and another godly alderman, the merchant William Allenson, were elected to represent the city at the Long Parliament despite Stafford's claims of prior clientage. While the puritan party secured this particular place of public power, in York itself the spatial trinity of cathedral liberty, manor, and fortified garrison became the centre for their rival's dominance over not only urban but also provincial culture. Just as Charles established his council of peers in Minster Yard, so the Earl of Newcastle later appropriated the city as his northern headquarters. Perhaps more worrying for the citizenry was the success of Sir Henry Slingsby in taking control of the city militia: a command he had lobbied for, and which the citizens resisted, throughout the 1630s.[50] The fact that a borough or city became a royalist or parliamentary 'strong place' did not necessarily reflect the will of city commonwealth, still less the actions of its representatives in London. There was, instead, 'A new-come guest to the Town': a 1644 pamphlet surmised that the forceful occupation of York by Yorkshire gentry for 'the sword of King Charles' was really usurpation by 'an Howard, Dunbar, Evers' and other genteel Catholics: 'Hispaniolised and Jesuited Papists . . . all up in

---

[45] Ibid., response of John Burchill.   [46] Ibid., deposition of Samuel Hoyle.

[47] Ibid., deposition of Henry Hoyle.

[48] John Etherington, *The defence of John Etherington against Stephen Denison* (1641), pp. 22–3; Lake, *The boxmaker's revenge*, ch. 4.

[49] Birchall, *The non-pareil*, p. 7.

[50] Henry Slingsby, *The diary of Sir Henry Slingsby*, ed. D. Parsons (London, 1836), p. 76.

this business'.[51] The difficult relationship between John Hutchinson and the Nottingham citizenry suggests that any flavour of military occupation was feared by householders as an encroachment on the liberties and freedoms that city commonwealths embodied.[52] Without the requisite military resources that, in reality, only London possessed, the immediate preservation of those liberties required a pragmatic approach to allegiance that, while certainly reflective of the imperatives of place, was by no means a naïve or apolitical localism. On the contrary, negotiation and co-operation on the part of citizens were a quintessentially political response to extremely difficult circumstances. Likewise, armies that allayed civic fear of martial abuse, and were seen to respect the fundaments of commonwealth, enjoyed greater success. For example, the rapidity with which Fairfax subdued Cornwall was widely attributed to the civility of his soldiers: 'his army conquered not only by the sword [but also by] love, especially that county who were thought irreconcilable'.[53] The Scots in the north-west had the opposite effect, and Bowles warned them that 'if you love the Presbytery, reform the Army, for it is very scandalous'.[54]

Royalist control of York ended in September 1644, its fall precipitating the exile of the Earl of Newcastle to the continent and the appropriation by the citizens – the godly foremost among them – of cathedral, manor, and castle. Their representative presence in Parliament was complemented by alliances at home, a broadly defined 'honest' party assembling around two sources of 'Presbyterian' and 'Independent' patronage. This was the Fairfax faction – for whom Bowles and the Cokeian lawyer Sir Thomas Widdrington were prominent intermediaries – and 'friends' of Adam Baines, the Leeds attorney, soldier, and republican with close connections to Major General John Lambert. Presbyterians formed the civic majority, and included the powerful kinship network of the Thomson brothers, Henry and Leonard, as well as more moderate households. Both parties could retrace their civic influence to 15 January 1614 when Richard Baines, brother of Adam (and also neighbour and close friend of baker James Wright) was chosen alongside Thomas Hoyle as city chamberlain.[55] Flitting between the two factions was the dominant civic personality of the 1650s, Hoyle's son-in-law, the merchant Thomas Dickenson.[56] Both groupings were associated with the Micklegate quarter of town: Dickenson lived close to Fairfax's townhouse in the parish of St Martin's, while the merchant Bryan Dawson, an alderman and client of Adam Baines, resided close by in St Johns. The spatial proximity of godly and civic households merely reflected

[51] 'A new-come guest to the Town' (1644).
[52] Lucy Hutchinson, *Memoirs of the life of Colonel Hutchinson*, ed. N. H. Keeble (London, 1995), pp. 112–13, 143, 158, 361.
[53] Juxon, *Journal*, p. 110.   [54] Edward Bowles, *Manifest truths*, p. 41.
[55] *Register of the freemen of the city of York*, p. 62.
[56] YCA, B36, f. 208; BL Add MS 21417, f. 29.

the ideological insinuation of citizenship and Calvinism and the practical compatibility of orthodox and more independent forms of worship: a symbiosis that, as David Scott has shown, was unbroken by the Restoration and the episcopalian reaction.[57] It was no coincidence that Martin's' parishioners were most forward in serving in the militia after the defeat of royalists or more energetic, alongside other Micklegate inhabitants, in sitting on the distinctly reformatory juries that characterised the period.[58] That said, although godliness was less apparent in other city neighbourhoods it was by no means exclusive to the city's elites. Godly networks of kin and friends permeated the body of freemen as a whole, encompassing bakers, tailors, and brewers as well as merchants, mercers, and grocers.[59]

It was from the Micklegate quarter of the city that Bowles' preaching ministry found its greatest support. Erected in the old cathedral precinct – in the institutional, architectural, and symbolic places of episcopacy, and with the active support of the city's ruling elites – it marked a dramatic if temporary resolution to both the paradox of England's delayed reformation and the problem of civic–episcopal antagonism within the city. The logistics of this involved the citizenry removing the Minster's ornamental fabric; conveying houses and offices to godly ministers and laity; and purchasing the liberty of the Dean and Chapter.[60] All these policies were reversed in 1660. The preaching that the ministry instituted was the responsibility of four learned ministers referred to by Bowles as 'my fellow labourers in Christ'.[61] Three further measures intended to complement the speaking of the Word were never properly implemented: the rationalisation of the city's parochial structure into a local classis; the strict enforcement, by citizen militia if necessary, of the Sabbath; and the creation of a university for the 'North'. The spiritual concerns of ministry went hand in hand with an invigorated magistracy. Between 1654 and 1658 an average of £255 per annum was spent on the city workhouse, house of correction, and city gaols, accounting for 67 per cent of public spending over the five-year period.[62] The policies driving this investment – the most expensive public building project by the citizens before the eighteenth century – reached a climax during the mayoralty of the grocer Stephen Watson, at whose swearing Bowles gave the sermon. A 'Committee for the Poor' imported wool manufacturing into the city in order to encourage industry and relieve poverty.[63] Quarter-session business

---

[57] Scott, 'Politics, dissent, and quakerism', pp. 128, 139.
[58] YCA E87, May 1648; YCA, F7, F8; Withington, 'Urban political culture', pp. 147, 121.
[59] Withington, 'Urban political culture', pp. 167–68.
[60] YCA, E63, ff. 4, 5v, 6, 8–8v, 15v, 19v, 20–20v, 23, 24–25v, 27v, 71v, 76v–77, 80, 83v, 86v, 90, 92, 94–95v, 104v, 107v, 109v, 110v, 116, 121, 123v, 132; B37, f. 47v–8, 70v–71, 72v–73, 87v–88v, 91v.
[61] BIHR, York wills, July 1662, Edward Bowles.
[62] Calculated from YCA, C24–C28. See Withington, 'Urban political culture', p. 134.
[63] YCA, B37, ff. 82–3.

was dominated by presentments associated with the 'reformation of manners' (and, in 1657, the problem of recusants).[64] The citizens began to administer the orphans' school in Sherburn – recently wrested from the control of a local Catholic family by 'decree of chancery' – by appointing a person of 'honesty, ability and fitness' to the 'place of Governor'.[65] John Hewley, an Independent lawyer and subsequently 'Whig' MP for the city during the exclusion crisis, was made the city's legal counsel. The 'commonwealths arms' were 'set up in the counsel chamber'.[66] And a 'unanimous vote' was taken by both the aldermen and common councillors of the city decreeing that Bowles should receive £50 per annum 'out of the public revenue of the city' as a 'gratuity and respect of his Extraordinary pains in his Ministry'.[67] Nor were events in York unusual. Across the corporate system there existed a degree of reciprocity between city commonwealth and the 'commonwealth of England' that was expressed in tangible political and material gains for citizens, and articulated through the language of spiritual and social reform.[68] As Bowles explained in 1643, 'Puritans though they be thought a little factious and troublesome in the Church, yet they are good Common-wealths men, resolute asserters of publique liberty, that will pay roundly, and fight too, if need be.'[69] It is to the cultural affinities between citizenship and puritanism that we can now turn.

Honesty and circumspection

Peter Lake has usefully argued that Calvinist or 'puritan' orthodoxy as it had emerged in England by the seventeenth century took the form of a 'consistent conversation' between 'formal doctrine', 'practical divinity', and 'the responses and reactions' of the godly laity.[70] In its form, content, interlocutors, and locations this culture was unusually proximate to the proponents and ideology of commonwealth outlined in previous chapters. It echoed the profound sense of place and calling characteristic of civic culture. It emphasised the importance of self-reflective conversation, debate, and deportment. It accentuated demands for honesty, truth, and trust. It appealed to the Aristotelian imperative of meritorious aristocracy and the public good. And it invested in a *res*publican conception of the national polity. All of which suggests that Calvinism extrapolated a sense of governance and civility – both of the person and the community – which appealed to essential tenets of English citizenship. Put slightly differently,

---

[64] YCA, F7, f.373; Withington, 'Urban political culture', p. 220; Wrightson and Levine, *Poverty and piety*, p. 140–1.
[65] YCA, B37, f. 89.   [66] Ibid., f. 91.   [67] YCA, B37, f. 84.
[68] Ian Roy, 'The English republic, 1649–1660: the view from the town hall', in Helmut G. Koenigsberger, ed., *Republiken und republikanismus im Europa der fruhen Neuzeit* (Munich, 1988), pp. 236–7.
[69] Bowles, *Plaine English*, 15.   [70] Lake, *The boxmaker's revenge*, p. 409.

it was through the paradigm of godliness that crucial tenets of city commonwealth were amplified, appropriated, and, at moments like the 1650s, taken to their practical extremes. That these tenets were encased in scriptural terms, publicly implemented and enforced, and suborned to the will of 'the godly' was, in turn, a source of division and conflict both locally and nationally. Controlling corporate souls was ultimately a contested and exclusionary business.

The civic ascendancy of 'puritanism' during the mid-seventeenth century was based on sociological, political, and military factors. However, there was also a degree of intersection and overlap between Calvinist and civic discourse that encouraged conversation even among citizens of more 'moderate' persuasion. The idea of the Christian's 'double calling' was a case in point. As we saw in chapter 4, William Perkins adopted a traditional concept of civic culture and gave it a Calvinist twist. A Christian possessed not one but two callings: a 'particular calling, as he follows this or that trade of life'; and their 'general calling, as he is a Christian': what the Jacobean London minister Stephen Denison described as 'the most honourable calling in the world'.[71] Both vocational types required the cultivation of personal dispositions and virtues and an appropriate fit between place and person. However, while particular callings placed people according to their social 'skills' and 'abilities', general callings positioned everyone 'in heavenly places'. Styled by Lake the archetypal puritan preacher, Denison used 'the double calling' as a relentless and surprisingly democratic tool of social criticism by which each person was accountable to their places and the common good they constituted.[72] On the one hand, it was 'not sufficient to seem to be a good Christian, but we must be good Magistrates, or good Masters, or good husbands, or good wives, or good servants, or good children', so glorifying 'in the rank wherein God hath set us'. On the other hand, while 'many proud worldlings are lifted up, and exalt themselves above poor Christians, because they have borne all offices that Christians have not', the calling of a Christian was 'worth ten thousand of yours; yea indeed yours is not worthy to be compared of'.[73] Taken together, 'this double calling' required constant exertion on the part of the person, for although 'a true child of God, may for a time be overtaken with idleness . . . idleness doth not reign in him'. It also served 'to discover many to be no true Christian'. These included 'many of our gentry, which follow no calling but spend their precious time idly and scandalously. Secondly, our common beggar, which cast off all labour, and live by begging. Thirdly, usurers which cast off their lawful callings and live by

---

[71] Stephen Denison, *An exposition upon the first chapter of the second epistle of Peter* (1622), pp. 71, 30.
[72] Lake, *The boxmaker's revenge*, p. 76; Paul Seaver, *Wallington's world: a puritan artisan in seventeenth-century London* (London, 1985).
[73] Denison, *An exposition*, p. 37.

usury. Fourthly, stage players, and cheaters, and drunkards and harlots, with many others, which follow no lawful employment.'[74]

For the city parishioners that Denison addressed, this map of 'particular callings' and their malcontents fitted extremely snugly onto the symbolic topography of citizenship and its antitheses. It also gave the classically Aristotelian middle position of citizens – between gentry on the one hand and the beggars, usurers, and itinerants on the other – a degree of moral vindication. In this sense, the contrast between 'the spiritual mutuality and charity of the godly' and 'the atomised, sinful individualism of the wider society' was directly transferable onto civic identities. Thomas Calvert, for example, a fellow preacher of Bowles in York, extrapolated a complex set of meanings from the metaphor of *The wise merchant, or the peerless pearl*, a sermon given before the Company of Merchants in 1650 and belatedly published ten years later. On the one hand, a merchant's particular calling depended on 'counsels' derived not from 'the lusts of natural and carnal men' but 'divine counsel, to be honest and upright'. To become a 'wise and holy merchant' was 'not to neglect your Trade, but to advance it': grace did 'not destroy our wits in natural things and civil, but promote them, raise them higher, regulate them better' and ultimately ensure 'profit'.[75] On the other hand, Calvert depicted a person's Christian calling in mercantile terms: the relationship between the Saints and Christ was one of 'purchase', 'bargains', 'diligence', 'travel', 'merchandise', 'possession', 'commodity' as well as 'wit' and 'judgement'.[76] That some people fused their general and particular callings and some did not was, in turn, exclusionary. Denison recalled with admiration how his mercantile patron, Mrs Elizabeth Juxon, jettisoned her 'profit, pleasure, credit, ease, liberty, and the liking of carnal friends' for godliness. 'Whereas in her carnal state, her carnal neighbours respected her; afterwards, when they observed this godly change in her, they ceased to give her that respect that was due to her' as the wife of a prosperous merchant and citizen.[77] He also warned 'Masters', 'Masters of Families', 'ancient people', and 'chief men in Parishes' that, 'though they would take it in great scorn if a Minister should turn them back from the sacrament', they were guilty of profanity – and liable to exclusion from communion – 'as well as any other'.[78] That said, it was one thing to acknowledge that God 'respects no mans person or greatness'; it was quite another for godly laity to ignore the calling and authority of their minister. As Lake has shown, the logic of callings could be quite as unsettling for 'moderate' puritan preachers as 'masters of families' when

[74] Ibid., pp. 70–1.
[75] Thomas Calvert, *The wise merchant, or the peerless pearl* (York, 1660), pp. 35–6.
[76] Ibid., pp. 5–7, 30.
[77] Stephen Denison, *The monument or tombstone, or a sermon preached . . . at the funeral of Mrs Elizabeth Juxon* (1620), pp. 44–5.
[78] Stephen Denison, *The doctrine of both the sacraments* (1621), p. 143.

appropriated by the more general godly community. As John Etherington put it: 'such gifts of God, as to prophecy, if in a man of the lowest degree, place, or calling in the Church of God, Shepherd, Clown, Carpenter, or other, ought not to be despised or envied at for his low estate, or meanness of his person sake'.[79] On the contrary, it justified agency outwith ministerial and social authority.

Calvinist conceptions of place and calling recognised and talked to the term's civic inferences even as they appropriated and extenuated them. The same was true of *honestas*, or what Denison regarded as virtuous Christianity. He told his readers to '*Add to your faith virtue*' and that 'By virtue we are to understand an honest and good life, or a universal practice of all those graces which God hath put in us.' Indeed, '*every Christian should labour to be truly virtuous, to be of good life and conversation*'. Just as God was 'more glorified by deeds than words', so the virtuous life allowed Christians to at once 'reprove . . . viciousness' and 'convince the wicked' without risking the charge of 'mere hypocrisy'.[80] Denison acknowledged that 'Many of the heathens were virtuous, some excelled for justice, others for fortitude, others for temperance, others for prudence' and certain virtues corresponded with classical definitions. A 'temperate person', for example, should not only quit 'the drunkenness and gluttony of the time' but also 'apparel himself according to his sex, according to his place, according to the most modest fashion of his country'. In terms reminiscent of Cicero, *The city madam*, or the Cambridge burgess Thomas French, Denison bewailed the confusions of fashion and lack of distinction 'between a Gentlewoman and a Lady . . . a Citizen and a Courtier'. However, because heathen virtues 'were not added to faith, therefore they were but glittering sins': 'Virtue without faith is no better than Cain's sacrifice: it may give satisfaction to men but is an abomination to God.' Like Robert Horne in contemporaneous Ludlow, Denison agreed with humanists that 'wisdom is the principal thing'; and, like Horne, he gave the concept a godly twist. He meant not 'worldly wisdom, much less sinful craft and subtlety' or 'bear literal knowledge in the brain' but rather 'an holy experimental knowledge wrought in the hearts of the elect by the holy Ghost'.[81]

Godly virtue required, in effect, the same degree of self-reflection as *honestas*. As Denison put it: '*Let a man examine himself*' in 'the truth of his knowledge . . . his faith . . . his repentance . . . his charity'. Because 'every man's conscience is best known to God himself . . . every communicant should examine himself' and his 'secret sins'. The assumed rationality of the process was reflected in the fact that, 'because none of these can examine themselves', children, madmen, fools, and idiots were excluded from the sacrament.[82] It likewise contributed to the Presbyterian contempt for 'our Almanac men' and

---

[79] Etherington, *The defence of John Etherington*, p. 12.
[80] Denison, *The exposition*, pp. 45, 46–7.   [81] Ibid., pp. 51, 49.
[82] Denison, *The doctrine of both the sacraments*, pp. 144, 149.

the astrological commentaries that became such an influential feature of public discourse during the civil war. As Bowles commented, 'that such and such positions and conjunctions in Planets, should infer what the dispositions, actions, events of rational and freemen should be, is easily said and hardly proved by Scripture or reason, I mean in words at length and not in figures'. He insisted that it was 'not conjunctions, but corruptions in men' that caused 'evil times'.[83] Rational self-examination prevented what Denison described as a 'floating knowledge, swimming in the brain' and ensured a 'working knowledge, residing in the heart'. This knowledge was to be sustained by 'hard labour in the use of means, as in hearing, in reading, meditations, in the use of the sacrament, in conference, in keeping faith and in good conscience'.[84] It was also a triumph of discourse. As Bowles put it, the 'whole counsel of Christ' and 'the moulding of men by the force of outward rules and precepts, into a kind of Gospel conversation, is not acceptable or lasting, unless the heart be inwardly changed, and renewed by spiritual ingrafture'.[85] Social reformation required, in effect, 'personal reformation': though 'men frame and fancy what new moulds and devices they will for bettering the times, till men and manners be better it will not be'. The conundrum was that reformed self-governance was a social and cultural process: the person had to be taught to want to be good. The only possible answer was familiar to humanists: 'where we have Laws, we want Magistrates, or at least Magistrates want wisdom, will, courage, fidelity, or something necessary to put them in execution' – not by 'words and writings, but real amendments, for nothing else will do it'.[86]

In establishing a knowing reciprocity between personal and public reformation the minister – with his calling, his pulpit, and his rhetoric – exerted interpretative and discursive authority.[87] As Bowles reiterated in 1655, 'Divine Institution and Blessing are the main advantages in hearing the Word, not the gifts of the speakers, or the capacity of the Hearers.'[88] However, for all its ambitions of social ubiquity, personal reformation, like place and calling, also depended on comparison with others who were incapable or unwilling to cultivate appropriate dispositions. Just as Calvinist predestination distinguished between saints and reprobates, so practical virtue was an exclusive and distinctive attribute. As Denison put it, 'The angry person must especially labour for patience, the lascivious for charity, the ambitious for humility, the niggard for liberality'; in this way they could 'justly condemn the common multitude' who were 'prone to bless themselves' for the 'one good quality in them'.[89] Such

---

[83] Edward Bowles, *Good counsel for evil times* (1648), p. 2.
[84] Denison, *The doctrine of both the sacraments*, p. 149; *The monument or tombstone*, p. 2.
[85] Bowles, *Good counsel*, p. 2.   [86] Ibid., pp. 9, 20.
[87] Lake, *The boxmaker's revenge*, p. 54.
[88] Edward Bowles, *The dutie and danger of swearing* (York, 1655), Av.
[89] Denison, *The exposition*, p. 43.

exclusions were taken further still by the deregulated and unauthorised conversations of those most willing to engage in 'Gospel conversation'. A recurring feature of Etherington's *Defence* was the importance of godly company – a notion of rational and voluntary sociability in which 'to read, hear, and understand the word of God'. These were conversations much more autonomous (and exclusive) than that prescribed by either Denison or Bowles. When 'sociates' of Denison lured Etherington 'into their company' to test what Diarmaid MacCulloch has called his 'God talk', Etherington claimed that then, as always, his 'speech was not in any manner of teaching or expounding . . . but in the way of reasoning and answering'.[90] What Etherington did confess was that 'I have not been . . . so conversant and sociable with the profane multitude of the world as I have been with the sober and well-disposed, the wise in heart.' He had 'desired to converse with such especially above all other whatsoever I have come to talk and confer together of the word of God . . . and so daily as opportunity might permit . . . I have done in society with such persons'.[91] It was the same practices of intense but also exclusive company that for Bowles characterised the war-effort against the king. The Cavaliers were defeated by 'Men that fasted, prayed, that have too sweet counsel together, and walked in the House of God in company, that have loved and been willing to die together'.[92] Conversely, one of the great crimes of the Laudian regime was that it had deprived men of the power and means to learn and articulate such judgement. Through control of 'the Pulpit and Press', they kept 'the people from the key of knowledge by disgracing and discountenancing preaching, silencing painful Ministers, putting down Lectures' and forbidding 'all discourse of Religion . . . upon occasional meetings'. Instead of 'plain English', 'The Schools, the Press, the Pulpit, began to speak Latin apace' and 'Ignorance and Profanity' were 'generally countenanced in the Kingdom'.[93] As Thomas Hoyle and his neighbours could testify, Laudian 'superstition' worked against not simply Protestantism but also civil conversation.

The obligations of place and calling; the cultivation of the reflective, virtuous, and conversational person; the inextricability of personal and public improvement: here was a repository of ideals and practices that – whatever their appropriations and enclosures – were familiar to Calvinists and citizens alike. As symbiotic was the attribute closest to Bowles' heart: the practice of honesty, trust, and truth, and their centrality to the public good. The very titles of his pamphlets and sermons suggest as much. *The mystery of Iniquitie* and *Plaine English* (both 1643) 'proved' the existence of a Catholic-Absolutist conspiracy in the highest echelons of English society and suggested the grounds

---

[90] Etherington, *The defence of John Etherington*, p. 10;
[91] Ibid., pp. 7–8.   [92] Bowles, *Good counsel*, p. 11.
[93] Bowles, *Mystery of iniquitie*, pp. 13, 15.

on which the ensuing political crisis could be resolved 'honestly'. While *Manifest truths* (1646) established the true nature of parliament's recent dealings with the Scots, *Good counsel for evil times* (1648) called for unity among the 'honest' but increasingly fractious godly who, having defeated the king, were now intent on destroying each other. Finally, *The duty and danger of swearing* (1655) defended the appropriate use of a speech-act that epitomised the social necessity of trust. Dedicated to the York citizenry, it reflected Bowles' general conviction that 'Humane societies cannot subsist without evidences of truth, and mutual belief among men.'[94] Indeed for Bowles, the civil war and its aftermath were one long haemorrhaging of honesty. In the early 1640s men who 'deceived their trust' shattered that 'mutual belief' within the polity: it was left for 'honest and engaged men' to impose 'an honest and honourable peace' on a king who was 'too true to his own ends, and to the persons promoting them'.[95] By the second half of the decade, the prospect of peace and 'Truth among us' faced a new threat: the implosion of precisely that coalition of 'conscience and honesty' that had pursued the conflict in the first place.[96] The honest quest for truth had become 'licentious, lawless, boundless': predicated on the assumption 'that everyone whose brain is big of some new conceit, or the transmigration of an old error, should have the Midwifery of a Toleration to produce and propagate it'.[97] Bowles lamented that 'if men will run away with the sound of words, instead of the sense of them, and single out an expression in Scripture, and urge it against the evidence of several plain places, speaking the contrary, it argues an Heretical disposition, more addicted to opinion than truth'.[98] Not only had the initial prospect of 'Popery and Tyranny' given way to an equally dangerous 'Babel of Confusion': the very bonds of 'truth and fidelity' that preserved 'human societies' were under renewed threat.[99]

'Honesty' for Bowles reflected, in the first instance, a straightforward commitment to reformation. An 'honest' peace between king and parliament in 1643 would have sought to establish 'true Religion in purity and plenty . . . extirpate Popery and superstition, lay the grounds of a painful pious Ministry, and to that end cast out those scandalous seditious persons': the bishops.[100] On these grounds, the extent of dishonesty in 1643 was wide indeed: 'It consists of Papists, Protestants, viz. the King, Prelates, Courtiers, and Cavaliers, the dissolute Gentry, the superstitious Clergy, the profane and ignorant people' and some 'Anabaptists and Brownists'. Together they threatened to engulf 'Puritans' – a label freed by Bowles from its pejorative connotations to denote 'Lovers of Protestant Religion, with the desire of Reformation, friends to the Parliament,

---

[94] Bowles, *Duty and danger*, p. 7.   [95] Edward Bowles, *Plaine English* (1643), pp. 13, 20.
[96] Bowles, *Manifest truths*, p. 22.   [97] Bowles, *Good counsel*, p. 16.
[98] Bowles, *Duty and danger*, p. 10.
[99] Bowles, *Mystery of iniquitie*, p. 9; *Good counsel*, p. 16; *Duty and danger*, p. 15.
[100] Bowles, *Plaine English*, pp. 10–11.

and native Liberty of the Subject'.[101] Described in these terms, the position of England's 'honest men' clearly resonated with its citizens and burgesses, once again appropriating that middle place between the 'high way' of court, cathedral, and gentry and the 'herd of profane ignorant people'.[102] The geography of subsequent political allegiances likewise suggested synonymy between honest Protestantism and citizenship. Bowles noted that 'Profanity hath made a general aversion to Reformation, and ignorance, with the help of that hath furnished the King with an Army against the Parliament, fetched from the barren Mountains of Wales, Cornwall, and the North.'[103] Cumberland and Westmorland were 'particularly disadvantageous to this Cause', their lack of co-operation stemming not so much from the innate disaffection of its commonalty as the lack of 'care taken to engage them'. They also formed the least incorporated and urbanised province of England, and Bowles argued that it was the absence of civic resources, in conjunction with 'arbitrary Impositions' of especially Scottish troops, which had encouraged not so much royalism as militant localism among the unreformed Westmorland commons in 1646.[104] It was on precisely these grounds that he spent the 1650s attempting to establish a centre of learning and preaching in the provincial capital of York – not simply for the edification of its citizens but the northern commons in general.

However, honesty for Bowles was also an ideal of social and virtuous behaviour that was essentially humanist in nature. That monarchy and episcopacy were institutions that could no longer be trusted was a case in point. Both were types of place uniquely prone to appropriation by private will and purpose. As he argued in 1643, 'If any here think or say, there is a great deal of reason his Majesty should grant what may be for the safety of the Kingdom, or his own safety: I answer my question is concerning will, not concerning reason.' Although it might be reasonable to assume a Prince should actively want 'to be ruler of a rich and free people . . . we many times find that Princes present their subjects to themselves in the same relation as the land to the sea'. As 'it is in France', which had seen the long-term degradation of civic autonomy, so now it was for an English monarch in which 'every abasement of a privilege in them is an advancement of a prerogative in me, the emptying their purses fills my coffers'. While monarchy reduced the people's safety to 'his gracious Majesty's will', there remained 'no way to judge men's wills and dispositions, but their former actions and present preparations'. Strafford and other counsellors had demonstrated that this was 'a generation that are extremely set for liberty only, that themselves may be licentious, and very hot against arbitrary government, till themselves have . . . a share in it'. Indeed, 'when I consider

---

[101] Bowles, *Mystery of iniquitie*, p. 25.
[102] Bowles, *Plaine English*, p. 13; *Mystery of iniquitie*, p. 30.
[103] Bowles, *Mystery of iniquitie*, p. 13.   [104] Bowles, *Manifest truths*, pp. 31–34.

the disposition of many men about his Majesty' it must be 'doubted whether he will, so whether he can . . . yield to things so much for our advantage, and for the disadvantage of his great Guard'. 'The truth is, though it sounds like a Paradox, where few can be trusted more must': with 'men very subject to be corrupted by honour and authority . . . let the Law and Rule be made as plain and certain as may be'.[105] Episcopacy presented an even worse structural problem: a set of 'places which have been the dens of superstition, the dungeons of ignorance, the sinks of profanity' and 'from whom little other can be expected'. In these circumstances, public trust was impossible, and Bowles wondered 'What an apish disposition hath possessed our Gentry, what an asinine disposition our Commonalty, which if not timely shaken off will make for the worst of France to be ruled by horses instead of men.'[106]

The public mediation of private wills was, of course, a central tenet of civic culture and the freedoms it protected. Another was that a degree of *honestas* was required on the part of the person to act on behalf of the public good – not merely in established positions of power and authority, but also in the larger public debates that quickly developed in the early 1640s. Bowles conceptualised what was essentially a notion of *honestas* with the term 'circumspect'. Writing in 1648, he wondered what it meant for a Christian 'to walk circumspectly'. He acknowledged that circumspection implied precision, exactness, and diligence: an 'honest walking' based on faith that was virtuous, strong, without sin. However, the term also 'seems to imply something more, and that is walking wisely'. Wisdom was the recognition that 'there are divers actions, as time, place, company, person, and such like, which have a strong influence into actions, sometimes to alter the very nature of them'.[107] In adopting such an explicitly humanist – indeed Machiavellian – notion of wisdom, Bowles may have been unusual. For Thomas Calvert as for Robert Horne, wisdom was 'the Book of God's continual study and meditation': 'Christ's fools are wiser than the World's Doctors'.[108] For Bowles, in contrast, a circumspect Christian 'must look to the circumstances of his actions, as to set them off with the best advantage as may be'. Indeed, 'it is the part of wisdom to reduce knowledge to profitable and seasonable action, And happy is he that can walk thus circumspectly'.[109] Circumspection encouraged self-reflective Christians to augment their calling through discreet and considered words and deeds. As a mode of behaviour it was more than akin to the kind of *honestas* expected of citizens in their civic and commercial dealings, as well as perfectly suited to the difficult circumstances that the parliamentary coalition found itself in after the second civil war. As such, it is unsurprising that the sermon in which Bowles developed the idea was

---

[105] Bowles, *Plaine English*, pp. 15, 14.   [106] Ibid., pp. 18, 25.
[107] Bowles, *Good counsel*, p. 26.   [108] Calvert, *The wise merchant*, p. 12.
[109] Bowles, *Good counsel*, pp. 26–7.

delivered to one common council of citizens, in York, and commissioned for publication by another, in London. It also explains why Sir Thomas Wharton could comment in 1660 that Bowles was 'a very wise man, understanding men and business more than any . . . of his calling'.[110]

Bowles' conflation of honesty, circumspection, and citizenship was never more apparent than in his sermon at the mayoralty of York citizen Stephen Watson, when he confronted that most problematic and contested of discursive acts: the swearing of oaths. For Bowles, confusion over swearing was symptomatic of a more general public malaise – a society 'mourning under . . . the rash vain Oaths of profane and licentious men' and 'deliberate promissory Oaths and Covenants so frequently violated'.[111] The false appropriations were many. Swearing and oaths symbolised an irreconcilable royalism. The 'frequent drinking of healths, not so much of good fellowship, as of faction, which were . . . continued in Taverns, but are now got into private houses, and public streets . . . are ready to fill us with drunkenness, and dash us one against another'.[112] They signified an affective gentility: the 'kind of gallantry and gracefulness of speech to interlace it with Oaths and Execrations' was 'so exceeding vain and vile, that they will study new fashioned Oaths, as well as clothes, and so go down to destruction in the right mode'. They epitomised the widespread absence of circumspection, Bowles noting that 'those that swear in common conversation' did so 'not in judgement, they do it so frequently, so slightly, that their understanding cannot exercise any deliberate act about it'. In fact, neither 'nature nor custom which is the second nature' excused the fact that 'some places are so profane, that swearing is become the very dialect of the Town or Family where they dwell'.[113] They suggested the practical limits of the state as currently constituted. Whereas Hobbes regarded oaths as the preserve of sovereignty, Bowles, a subscriber to the Solemn League and Covenant, regarded enforced loyalty 'exceeding dangerous'. Although 'Governors are ready to think it their great security to establish themselves by Oaths, Covenants, and engagements', in this time of 'quick revolution . . . men will not be bound, much less the Almighty by such cords as these'.[114] Finally, the wholesale condemnation of oaths by certain sectarians perfectly encapsulated the interpretative laxity of the age. This was a time when 'there is no truth so clear and fundamental, but it meets with them that doubt it, and deny it, and no error so ridiculous, and unreasonable, but finds them that will embrace and maintain it'.[115] In fact, a sensitive, historicised and humanist reading of the

[110] Scott, 'Politics, dissent and quakerism', p. 142.
[111] Bowles, *Duty and danger*, pp. 19, 21.
[112] Ibid., p. 22.   [113] Ibid., p. 12.   [114] Ibid., p. 19.
[115] Richard Garbutt, *A demonstration of the resurrection* (1656), Preface.

Bible showed that, whether as an 'assertory oath . . . to evidence the truth' or a 'promissory oath to engage the truth', swearing signified the 'interposing of the Name of God' and 'imports that he sees and knows our appeal'.[116]

It was on this basis that oaths sustained a more general culture of honesty. On the one hand, they consolidated bonds of 'truth and fidelity' upon which civil society depended: 'if it be generally looked upon as unworthy to break a man's word or promise . . . much more unworthy is it to recede from a promise strengthened and seconded with an Oath'. On the other hand, they demanded a degree of *honestas* from those who used them: the onus on the person was to swear 'in righteousness, in a lawful and just matter' and with 'judgement, that is, wisely discerning the occasion and ordering the circumstances of his oath'.[117] As Calvert put it, they enabled men to 'use our natural love, civil and friendly trust in men with whom we have to do', forming 'the bonds of civil fellowship and communion'.[118] They were, in effect, the mainsprings of freedom. The great shame was the 'number of them that swear but not in judgement, is exceeding great; alas, how few are there that understand an oath, and fewer that consider it'. A priority of civic magistrates in 1655 was, therefore, the 'punishing unlawful oaths, preventing unnecessary oaths, and duly regulating those which are lawful and necessary'. Likewise 'the Oaths taken by inferior Officers, by Tradesmen in Companies and Corporation' were 'too much used and too little observed among them'. In the short term, penalties rather than promises were better suited to make men perform their obligations.[119] More important in the long term was the cultivation by citizens of a knowing and practical honesty: to act, that is, like Calvinists and citizens. As Bowles put it, 'let us be exceeding circumspect' in the taking of oaths, 'well weighing what we do and with what intention, and once engaged, not to study evasions but executions of trust and promise'. Within city commonwealths the highest ranking office-holders were 'tacitly obliged to understand the duty of your places and expressly bound to execute them to the *utmost* of your skill and power, which is great, and hard to be performed'.[120] In their counsel, aldermen and common councillors should assist rather than hinder, while freemen in general were required to be 'exceeding circumspect': 'think not it is left to your private determination, what is just and good government; you must take it as you find it'. Moreover, in their capacity as jurors all freemen were sworn '*not to present for hatred and malice* nor your private opinion and mistaken charity'. In short, it was requisite for freemen to '*Take heed of yourselves, and keep yourselves diligently*': '*In all things that I have said unto you be circumspect*'.[121]

---

[116] Bowles, *Duty and danger*, pp. 8–9.   [117] Ibid., pp. 15, 9.
[118] Calvert, *The wise merchant*, p. 40.   [119] Bowles, *Duty and danger*, p. 19.
[120] Ibid., p. 21.   [121] Ibid., p. 22.

'A quick and regular motion in their own sphere'

Bowles' concern for honesty carried obvious appeal for citizens: constitutive of civic practice, it was also a powerful and critical way of talking about kings and their counsellors. In 1643 he bellowed, 'Hear, O people, Consider that you are considerable or might be, if good counsel would be taken . . . your right is much, and your power no less, if you would know the one and use the other.' Then as now he was 'from the monster of Democracy. Rather, that which I call the people for, is but a quick and regular motion in their own sphere' and 'to do that which Parliament hath sometimes called them for'.[122] City commonwealths were one particular 'sphere', the *res*publican infrastructure of parliament and law that they constituted another; and both had originally served as conduits for the civic humanism that characterised English and Scottish political theory in the second half of the sixteenth century. In this respect, Bowles' resistance to what he perceived to be the tyranny and Catholicism of the king was essentially retrospective – a reclaiming of civic, *res*publican, and humanist territory. He explained that the 'freedom of John Knox and George Buchanan . . . I could well consent it was revived, so it be rightly bestowed, as by them it was, against the Popery of the then Queen, and the self-interests of great men in public works, and against the tyranny in Princes'. Buchanan had tutored the young James VI of Scotland in the rights of kingship; for Bowles it was evident enough that 'King Charles deserves a severer Schoolmaster than ever King James had'.[123] In the same vein, Bowles looked to the conciliar kingship of Edward VI – 'whose wisdom and virtue was beyond his years' – and the 'prudent counsel' of Elizabeth I as appropriate precedents for current public action.[124] The close involvement of Scottish Covenanters in the very existence of the Long Parliament had reconstituted the relationship between English and Scottish reformers, who conceived themselves as 'yoke-fellows' pitted against 'his Majesties intention to enslave his Kingdom'.[125] That was not to say, as certain Scottish writers argued, that the war should instigate full unification: like a true *res*publican Bowles noted that 'the customs and constitutions of the Kingdoms, and the dispositions of the people' were too different for that.[126] However, it was certainly the case that the 'mutual preservation' of their people as 'good *Subjects*, though not *slaves*' made the 'continuation and confirmation of this Union' essential.[127]

Bowles appealed, therefore, to the commonwealth – those public 'spheres', rights, and persons long present within the polity – as a safeguard of Reformation from a corrupt, private, and wilful court. Just as 'temporal tyranny is a great step to Ecclesiastical', so the civil war represented the 'great division betwixt the

---

[122] Bowles, *Plaine English*, p. 25.   [123] Bowles, *Manifest truths*, p. 20.   [124] Ibid., p. 23.
[125] Bowles, *Plaine English*, p. 5.   [126] Bowles, *Manifest truths*, A2.
[127] Bowles, *Mystery of iniquitie*, p. 11; *Manifest truths*, A2.

friends and enemies of reformation, betwixt men that loved their own liberty, and men that loved the public liberty'.[128] Foot-draggers within the parliamentary cause were vulnerable to the same critique: he condemned opponents to the New Model Army for making 'it their great business to cross this work (so little did they value the public good in respect of their own conceits, wills, and interests)'.[129] Military organisation aside, it was not public innovation so much as civic and civil renovation at which Bowles aimed: the reclamation of the 'people's good', 'whose proper Representative is the *Parliament*'.[130] War was necessary because 'The King hears no other language than Gracious Sovereign, Your Sacred Majesty': 'the intoxications of Rome, backed with continual evil Counsels' had sought to replace 'our safety and liberty' for the 'Deity of a King'.[131] That Bowles laced his *res*publicanism with the conceits of aristocracy further enhanced its attractions and resonance for civic elites. As he observed in 1646, insofar as church government was concerned 'Aristocracy is the most even Government, if faction can be avoided'. Likewise, 'if there be a necessity of Rulers, for the conservation of Liberty (as there is) there is an equal necessity for preserving the authority of those Rulers, especially employing their endeavours for public good, as the Parliament doth'.[132] Parliaments (and councils) represented the people and secured their good, but they were not the people's 'servants': 'If the Rulers be servants, the people are Masters; whereas the truth is, the Magistrate serves the good of the people.' Although 'it be fit that all exorbitant usurpation, and arbitrary dominion of Rulers have a seasonable stop, lest public Liberty suffer, yet must it be done without debasing those in authority, whose honour and esteem with the people, is necessary to the order and conservation of the whole'.[133] He commented in 1648 that 'those dreams of parity in civil affairs is unequal and impossible': like natural bodies, civil and politic bodies' required 'a predominant element to determine it'. As tellingly, those 'that are now for equality while they are inferior, would be for superiority when things are equal; if the Vine and the Olive were taken away, the Bramble will rule over the trees: for somebody will'.[134]

For certain citizens at least, the force of Bowles' rhetoric lay, then, in the familiarity of its ideals and the accentuation of their civil elements. The world as described by London citizen Nehemiah Wallington 'was an almost exact replication of that pumped out for thirty years in the pulpit and press by Denison'.[135] Likewise the journal of Thomas Juxon, second son of Denison's patrons, John and Elizabeth Juxon, reveals a close affinity with the principles elucidated by Bowles. Writing in London between 1644 and 1647, Juxon

[128] Bowles, *Plaine English*, p. 4; *Good counsel*, p. 11.   [129] Bowles, *Manifest truths*, p. 12.
[130] Ibid., p. 20; *Plaine English*, p. 13.   [131] Ibid., p. 6; *Mystery of iniquitie*, p. 11.
[132] Bowles, *Manifest truths*, pp. 64, 72.   [133] Ibid., p. 20.
[134] Bowles, *Good counsel*, p. 17.   [135] Lake, *The boxmaker's revenge*, p. 390.

enunciated a civic humanism that included the imperative of the public good, the dangers of private interest, and an aristocratic notion of political participation based on 'citizenship, public virtue, and true nobility'.[136] This was matched by a conception of honesty that signified at once a reformatory intent tending towards godliness; the personal capacity for 'ingenuity' and wisdom; and the imperative of self-effacement in the light of both the public good and God's providential will in human affairs. Such values can certainly be traced to his civic and Calvinist education. Juxon attended Merchant Taylor's School between the ages of five and seven, lived in his father's household between seven and sixteen, was apprenticed to William Allott, a liveryman in the Merchant Taylors' Company, for nine years, and gained his freedom by patrimony in 1637. The result was a 'soundly educated, literate, and informed individual with some knowledge of Latin and French, the classics and history, and an intellectual curiosity ready to feed on the great array of published news, information and controversy during the unprecedented press freedom of the early 1640s'.[137] At the outbreak of war he was fully active in the higher echelons of mercantile and civic society and in 1647 he married into the Somerset landed elite. If this was the 'final seal of his social respectability' then his gentility remained distinctly civic. Juxon retained a profound distrust of the lords as an estate as well as a deep aversion to various manifestations of the 'dissolute gentleman' against whom 'honest citizens' defined themselves. These included 'malignant' Cavaliers as well as 'reformadoes' attached to the regiments of Essex and Manchester who attacked 'honest' and 'true-hearted citizens' in the summer of 1647.[138] Indeed, while Juxon was fully immersed in the politics of parliament and common council, he regarded an autonomous city militia as the most appropriate outlet for his civic energies. As Hobbes might have put it: that a minister like Bowles could 'seduce' citizens was in large part because he already spoke their language.

While the discursive affinities between Calvinism and citizenship were one reason for the eventual success of the 'parliamentary power', the intensity and scale of the conversation carried obvious dangers. Printed appeals to the judgement, honesty, and discretion of 'indifferent observers' were, by their nature, indiscriminate, implying civil and civic dispositions even among those without place and office. That even Presbyterian propagandists like Bowles used ostensibly feminine techniques like rumour, scandal, and 'common fames' to shape 'opinion' and justify actions inevitably extended the participatory and symbolic parameters of 'the public' still further.[139] As Bowles confessed in 1643, 'there are very few that look upon the wheels and springs, the weights and lines, which move and act the things we see and hear'. He was himself 'very far from a Statesman, my years will not allow me experience, my parts insight,

---

[136] Juxon, *Journal*, p. 32.   [137] Ibid., pp. 1–2.   [138] Ibid., pp. 166–7.
[139] See above, ch. 7.

my calling leisure, nor my acquaintance intelligence, all which are necessary thereto'. However, 'I never yet shut my eyes to light, nor my ears to truth, I have not been indigent in observing and comparing the actions and proceedings of men'. This age of 'freedom of speaking' presented the perfect opportunity 'to give an account of my thoughts concerning the hinges upon which these troubles now move'.[140] However, by 1646, with the 'honest party' that had opposed the king now riven by faction and interests, the time for opinion and talk was over. In 'this 'quarrelsome age . . . Men in trust and Authority should take care that the People may rather have the advantage, then the knowledge of their proceedings'.[141] It was on the same grounds that Bowles warned common councillors 'You also take an Oath of *secrecy*, in which there is a snare, be careful that you be not taken in it, but let prudence and conscience set a watch before the door of your lips.'[142]

Attempts to re-enclose discourse were matched by constitutional caution and the conviction that, with the bishops abolished, institutional meddling was as wilful and dangerous as was evil counsel. As Bowles advised in 1648, 'No violent or sudden change of Civil Government according to the Ideas and chimeras in the minds of more witty than wise men is likely to better these times.' The 'fancies of men' did not justify regicide. Just as the 'weight of Kingdoms is too great to be turned by the weak engine of human invention', so 'God uses to suit providences and spirits of men to great works when he intends them'.[143] The same ambivalence was expressed by Bowles' patron, Thomas Lord Fairfax, who wished the king's execution 'from time be blotted quite' but also acknowledged that 'if the Power divine permitted this / His Will's the Law and ours must acquiesce'.[144] While Cromwell reconciled himself to acting God's 'great works', Fairfax did not. Lucy Hutchinson recalled that 'persuaded by his wife and her Presbyterian chaplains', the general 'threw up his commission at such a time, when it could not have been done more spitefully and ruinously to the whole Parliament interest'.[145] Royalists likewise interpreted the suicide of a 'melancholic' Hoyle in 1650 as the ultimate expression of a damaged conscience.[146] Although republicans like John Milton regarded this disavowal as illogical and hypocritical, it was nevertheless consistent with the *res*publican (as opposed to republican) principles that had led Presbyterians like Bowles to foment war in the first place. It was a *res*publicanism that also encapsulated the majority position of the many common councils which initially supported the parliamentary defence of their liberties and religion, but which were far from

---

[140] Bowles, *Plaine English*, pp. 2–3.   [141] Bowles, *Manifest truths*, A2.
[142] Bowles, *Duty and danger*, p. 21.   [143] Bowles, *Good counsel*, p. 17.
[144] Peter Davidson, *Poetry and revolution: an anthology of British and Irish verse 1625–1660* (Oxford, 2001), pp. 356–7.
[145] Hutchinson, *Memoirs of the life of Colonel Hutchinson*, p. 240.
[146] Cross, 'A man of conscience', pp. 206–7.

comfortable with the unleashing of unprecedented 'chimeras', 'inventions', and 'fancies'. Indeed, the regicide was never more 'blotted' than in the civic minutes of York, where evidence that the citizens had co-operated in proclaiming the abolition of monarchy was subsequently scrubbed from civic record.[147]

Bowles' predicament in 1649 was inherent to humanist and Protestant reformers alike. As Lake has shown, it was not that a Jacobean controversialist like Etherington was opposed to the doctrines of Denison but that he learnt and practised them too well. Likewise humanists who propagated civility and citizenship were inevitably vulnerable to the slings and arrows of appropriation: as the grammar school-educated John Lilburne repeatedly demonstrated, it was one thing to take the proverbial horse to water, quite another to dictate how it drank. This was never more so than in the 1640s, when householders of England's city commonwealths found a massively enlarged public in which to express and position themselves. In such circumstances it is perhaps unsurprising that, for many civic elites, the commonwealth platform elucidated by Bowles rang many more bells than the republican 'fancies', democratic 'monsters', licentious 'Libertinism', or Hobbesian 'state' that also gathered at the trough after 1642. Just as Bowles and Fairfax refused to condone regicide, so they abetted Restoration – and the removal of the ministry from York Minster – ten years later, aligning with 'constitutional royalists' in order to avert the sectarian tyranny and libertarian mayhem that Lambert threatened.[148] In the final analysis, the prospect of 'settling' an Aristotelian mixed polity of commons, lords, and king was worth jeopardising the 'good old cause'. It was, after all, what they had originally fought for.

Honest distinctions

Restoration did not resolve religious politicking. Even as the Presbyterians turned on their Independent allies, so both were confronted by a resurgent episcopacy. As late as January 1661, a long and careful entry in the civic minutes of York reiterated the need for preachers 'on the Pavement and at other churches'. It also confirmed support for Bowles and his 'fellow labourers in Christ'. Although the public funding of the ministry was no longer possible, there were those 'in the country as well in the city . . . very willing and ready to contribute toward their maintenance'. It was 'thought fit', therefore, that the 'sundry persons in this city' who had offered to organise 'subscriptions and collect the monies' should be sanctioned by the court of aldermen.[149] Only two months later, however, Thomas Bradley elucidated some uncomfortable political realities to the citizenry in his coronation sermon. He explained that he

---

[147] YCA, B36, f. 222.   [148] Phil Withington, 'Views from the bridge', pp. 140–1.
[149] YCA, B37, ff. 84v, 147.

would have 'made thy prayers to sound beyond the walls of London and thy fame to ring in the princes ears and in the stately palaces of Westminster and Whitehall'. However, it now transpired 'that thou did intend and desire not only willingly to forfeit thy Prince's favour but in a way of defiance to exacerbate to affront and to provoke Majesty': 'to disoblige those noble persons, which were most willing and able to do thou good'. He referred to the attempts of local gentry to seize control of the city's magisterial and parliamentary resources, and the citizens' resistance to those encroachments. Having brandished the rhetorical stick, he concluded with a conciliatory carrot, observing that he knew 'the miscarriage of this business was not the act of the whole congregation the body of this famous and loyal city'. Rather it was the fault of 'some of the greener heads jeroboams counsellors Rumpers lately crept in to the counsel in corrupted times and not yet purged out'. That purge, he implied, would come soon enough. In the meantime, 'it is neither just nor reasonable that the whole corporation consisting of grave, wise and more sober citizens should suffer or be worse thought of'.[150] The age of partisan politics had arrived.[151]

Inscriptions on two separately owned copies of the same 1661 almanac (both of which survive in Cambridge University Library) nicely illustrate how the old division between episcopates and reformers quickly re-emerged to dominate the politics of settlement. George Wharton's *Calendarium Carolinum* was a work of Cavalier propaganda grafted onto an astrological format. His eulogies to monarchy and its recent martyrs framed twelve chapters – one for each month of the year – which supplied basic lunar information as well as space for the reader to write their own entries. Two versions of Wharton's almanac were published each year: one with a Latin inscription on the front, and one with an English inscription. A reader of the Latin edition of 1661 fulfilled the author's ideological expectations, faithfully recording in a neat and efficient hand the business of the Restored court and, in particular, the itinerary of the royal coronation that climaxed with the ceremony in St Paul's on 23 April 1661.[152] Wharton's six-line stanza for April ends: 'We reverence both the cassock and the gown: / But Charles His Presence *Consecrates* the Town'. This particular reader accordingly noted the movements of the king between his trip to Windsor on 15 April (in order to re-establish the ceremonial order of Knights of Bath) and his crowning in London eight days later. He also jotted down the marriage of the Duke of York in February and the death of his 'dear brother', the Dean of St Paul's, in August. However, a second reader's inscriptions on a different copy of the same edition (with the frontispiece removed) suggest a contrasting sensibility. Wharton's prefatory poem about the 'Martyrs and *Saints*, my

---

[150] Leeds Sheepscar, NH 2848, Thomas Bradley to Sir Metcalfe Robinson, 24 April 1661.
[151] Halliday, *Dismembering the body politic*, ch. 4.
[152] George Wharton, *Calendarium Carolinum* (1661). The copy is CUL, Hhh. 453.

Kalendar displays' was, for example, heavily annotated. In particular, the lines 'Triumphant *Charles*, Blessed *Strafford*, Glorious Laud, / I celebrate; as Martyrs without *Fraud*' were crossed out and replaced with 'Cromwell not [Laud, / I celebrate . . .]'.[153] January saw the reader practising the alphabet and February was illustrated with a satirical cartoon of a Cavalier/gallant with a large nose. Most interestingly, the entry for April was not the coronation itinerary but the forenames of three of the four parliamentary representatives elected by the London citizens for the 'settlement' parliament.

Accounts of the London election, held at the Guildhall on the morning of 19 March 1661, illuminate the significance of this last inscription. It so happens that sixty-three letters posted from London describing the vote and its outcome survive because they were intercepted by the Secretary of State before reaching their respective destinations.[154] The letters were diverse: just as correspondents ranged from business partners to family, kin, and friends and lived in all corners of England, so their content combined 'news . . . concerning the public' with a variety of private and commercial concerns.[155] That said, they displayed three characteristics. First, over four-fifths of the letters had an urban address and as many as two-thirds were intended for inhabitants of an incorporated city or borough. Of the twenty-three incorporated destinations, six letters were meant for Newcastle, four each for Ipswich and York, three for Norwich, Coventry, and Chesterfield, and two for Derby, Gloucester, Chester, and Salisbury. They reflected, that is, opinion that was closely connected to the corporate system. Second, the letters by and large presented the election as a triumph for 'honest men' and the 'honest party' in the face of what Stephen Offley described as burgeoning 'Episcopasia' and what most other correspondents termed the 'episcopal party'.[156] Honesty was used to convey the godly credentials of both the four elected representatives – it was generally agreed that 'for their judgement as we use to distinguish men two of them are presbyterians and two independents' – and the unusually large number of citizens who turned out to elect them.[157] However, correspondents also linked it to qualities of 'circumspection', 'judgement', 'excellent parts', 'moderation', 'wisdom', 'fitness', 'ability', 'goodness', 'oratory', 'knowledge', and the 'public good': virtues that were implicitly lacking from the episcopal party.[158] Third, the letters looked to make the London elections a 'precedent' for the rest of the country. Richard Royle told 'my friend Mr Thomas Gibbons' in Wolverhampton that 'you and the honest men so use your judgement to choose sober and moderate

---

[153] The copy is CUL, Adams.8.66.23 (1).   [154] TNA, SP29/32/82–145.
[155] TNA, SP29/32/94.   [156] TNA, SP29/32/145.
[157] TNA, SP29/32/82, 83, 85, 86, 93, 94, 95, 96, 100, 102, 104, 106, 107, 108, 109, 117, 120, 121, 122, 123, 124, 126, 131, 135, 136, 139, 140, 141.
[158] TNA, SP29/32/97, 85, 113, 83, 100, 92, 109, 120, 141, 87, 95, 96, 120, 122.

men for parliament men from the example of this place'. Although 'here so far there have been many parties yet honest sober men appeared this day as one man and God hath given there desire and I hope the land will have the fruits of it'.[159] Writing to his father in Newcastle, Thomas Cooper likewise hoped that the fact that London had 'elected four famous and honest citizens to represent them in the next parliament . . . will be presidential to the whole kingdom'. If it was, then a 'well-grounded settlement may follow in order to the happiness of his Majesty[,] the security of religion in its power and purity[,] and the establishment of our civil rights upon firm foundations'.[160] And Edward Bowles, who had more intercepted letters addressed to him than anyone else, was told that 'my Lord Fairfax thanks you for your care and pains'; that 'Captain John Jones your old tobacco friend' had been elected; and that all four were 'chosen as unanimously as ever I saw'. There had never been 'such a general union of Presbyterians Independents and Anabaptists all crying down the episcopal party who went away some cursing, some swearing, others wishing they had never come there'. Here at last was an opportunity 'for love and truth' so long as 'the countries and corporations would follow the example of the city in their choice'.[161]

In the event, interference in the postal service was one of several techniques that the royal administration was able to bring to bear on the elections, especially those in incorporated boroughs. Other forms of influence included the prospect of *quo warranto* for recalcitrant common councils, royal letters of recommendation for particular burgesses, polemical fireworks from the pulpit, the stigmatisation of anti-episcopates as 'fanatics', sustained pressure from local gentry, and the propagation of popular royalism that was epitomised by the coronation ceremony. Here was a carefully choreographed and much-publicised ceremony that at once re-incorporated the commonwealth into the king's two bodies, confirmed the bishops and lords in their spiritual and temporal estates, and engendered a sense of political sublimation that *res*publicans like Bowles, or indeed republicans like Milton, could only dream of. If all of these pressures were brought to bear on a city as 'homogeneal' and well-connected as York, then it is unsurprising that the impact nationally was the dominance of the 'episcopal party' and their allies in the early months of the settlement parliament.[162] As is well known, the result was a series of retributive, punitive, and exclusionary legislation that made the settlement quite as exclusive in confessional terms as the reformers of the 1640s and 1650s ever did. Nonconformity and corporations were particular (and related) concerns for a parliamentary settlement that became an 'incubus' for episcopacy rather than a framework

---

[159] TNA, SP29/32/85.   [160] TNA, SP29/32/126.   [161] TNA, SP29/32/103.
[162] YCA, B38, ff. 150, 152, 154v–55, 156, 157, 159–59v, 160v.

for reconciliation. It was precisely this appropriation of the political process that turned John Locke from being a proponent of magisterially enforced civil worship into the most eloquent defender of private conscience and public toleration.[163] Likewise within city commonwealths the civic Calvinism that had characterised the better sort of citizen in the first half of the century transmuted into a culture of civic dissent – an 'orthodox nonconformity' that was also an important element of the critical 'whiggish' public to emerge in the 1670s. Certainly it was no coincidence that when the Cavalier parliament was finally dissolved in 1679, the 'Whig' candidates elected in York to the three 'exclusion' parliaments that followed represented the dissenting and nonconformist elements among the freemen and their households. The traditional but also deeply problematic alliance of 'honest' and 'good' men had re-formed under a new name.

Bowles died in August 1662. The good old cause, which he expected to be buried with him, did not; or rather it survived and mutated through the complex networks that have already been adumbrated in previous chapters. A key figure in this respect was the second Duke of Buckingham, whose marriage to Fairfax's daughter and heir, Mary, in 1657 was an intriguing clue as to the kind of mutation that would take place. Buckingham replaced Fairfax (and Lambert) as the dominant titular influence within the locality after 1660. Already an acquaintance of Andrew Marvell, Buckingham also became friends with the generation of York merchants who came to civic prominence in the years after the Restoration – in particular Marvell's friends, Henry and Edward Thompson.[164] Marvell tutored Mary Fairfax and would have known Bowles personally. Both he and Sir Henry Thompson senior were friends of Dr Witty, a moderate Episcopalian who did much to salve the local (if not national) tensions between city and cathedral after 1660.[165] That Witty witnessed Bowles' will and its codicil in 1661 suggests the enduring significance of pre-Restoration alignments as well as the moderate church settlement that 'honest men' had hoped to achieve by reneging on the good old cause.[166] Bowles was perceived by Wharton, another of Marvell's 'friends', as the man most likely 'to bring Episcopal men and Presbyterians to such a condensation in things which are not absolutely necessary, as that there be no jarrings, but all agree for public and peace'.[167] Although Bowles refused to join the restored Dean and Chapter in late 1660, he and the citizenry clearly envisaged the development of more consensual and co-operative religious culture within the city. The perceived lurch to 'Episcopasia' on the one hand and 'fanaticism' on the other made this impossible.

[163] Mark Goldie, 'John Locke and Anglican royalism', *Political Studies*, 31, 1983, pp. 61–85.
[164] BJL, DDFA/39/4.   [165] BJL, DDFA/39/26.
[166] BIHR, York wills, July 1662, Edward Bowles.
[167] Scott, 'Politics, dissent and quakerism', p. 142.

However, the same groupings that had instigated the restoration process also looked to reverse its religious consequences. While the households of Fairfax, Widdrington, and Hoyle had presided over a militant civic puritanism, so those of Buckingham, Marvell, the Thompsons, and Hewley now publicly nurtured its dissenting and nonconformist progeny. They did so at court, parliament, and law; in printed and scribal literature; and within the domestic, civic, parochial, and commercial settings of city commonwealth. Likewise Bowles' mid-century role as broker between magnate and citizenry was perpetuated in York by another cleric, Tobias Conyers. In the course of the 1660s Conyers became chaplain to Buckingham; the minister of choice for the resolutely mercantile and godly parishioners of St Martin's; and the 'dear friend', and political ally, of Sir Henry Thompson.[168] Regarded as the main intermediary of Buckingham's interest in the city, in the by-election in 1673 he went 'about from alehouse to alehouse and to taverns to treat the people and to assure them that his Grace is absolutely for Sir Henry'.[169] By the 'exclusion crisis' of 1680, York was once more divided between city commonwealth on the one hand and its 'pricks and goads' on the other. The royal governor Sir John Reresby observed that 'the loyal party in York is much inferior in number to the factious' ('loyalty' denoting support for the Duke of York, 'factious' with attempts to exclude him from the succession). Reresby explained that 'the first [loyal party] consists of the gentry, clergy, officers, and dependants of the Church, militia officers and soldiers, and about a fourth part (as is computed) of the citizens'. The second [factious party] encompassed 'the Mayor and whole magistracy (two aldermen only excepted), the sheriffs and most of the common council, and the rest of the city'. National partisan allegiances had transposed almost exactly onto local urban distinctions: while citizens tended towards the 'Whig' position of exclusion, the garrison, gentry, and cathedral were steadfastly 'Tory'. Prominent among the 'contrivers' who 'industriously maintained' this 'nice difference' was Sir Henry Thompson senior and his brother, Edward Thompson ('a close sensible fellow'). They were aided by three nonconformist lawyers: Sir John Hewley; 'Alderman [Robert] Waller, a rich attorney, very spiteful but open'; and 'one Rokesby, a lawyer rich and well versed in his calling, that steers them in their proceedings as to point of law'. It was, finally, a 'party' very much rooted in the sociability and obligations of urban freedom. As Reresby conceived it, 'a great many in such a body . . . either from fear or interest join with the strongest, and several there have confessed that they dare not act according to their judgements (viz. for the government) for fear of being undone in their trade'. Indeed, it is now come to that, that there is not only a separation of interests, but few

168 BL Add MSS 28051, f. 26; BIHR, PR/Y/MG 19, f. 365; BIHR, York wills, July 1683, Henry
    Thompson.
169 BL Add MSS 28051, f. 26.

do buy of, or have any commerce but with those of their own principle'.[170]
For all Reresby's hostility it was clear that York's 'homogeneal and essential
members' – not to mention their 'permanent and local interest' – were alive,
well, and an integral feature of national politics. It was equally clear that,
as Hobbes and the Restoration public well knew, the cords connecting civic,
national, and civic politics were frayed but uncut.

---

[170] Reresby, *Memoirs*, pp. 579–80.

Conclusion

In autumn 1674, verses circulated *On the Lord Mayor and Court of Aldermen presenting the late King and Duke of York each with a copy of their Freedom.*[1] The libel was attributed to Andrew Marvell. Whether he wrote them or not is less important than the fact that, in terms of their content and intent, he (and his friends) clearly could have done so. Marvell was hardly averse to satirising the Stuarts. He was also fully acquainted with the political and idiomatic contexts that, in this instance, informed the satirist's pen: indeed, his friend Richard Thompson sat on the committee charged with costing the presentation of the freedom to the Duke of York.[2] The poet's initial objection to the presentation was that 'you Addle-Brain'd Citts' had wasted money on 'Diamonds and Gold' when 'your Orphans want Bread to feed on'. As importantly, neither Charles nor James was worthy of enfranchisement. The king 'ne'er knew not he / How to serve or be free'. Since being 'bound' as monarch in 1661, he had 'every Day broke his Indentures': instead of learning his trade he wasted all his time 'Revelling, Drinking and Whoring'. A bad apprentice, he was also profligate. Although his 'Masters' – the public – had 'Intrusted him with Cash', he had spent and borrowed so 'his Creditors' were 'all left in Sorrow'. He 'molested the neighbours', kept 'Company lewd', and left only 'Debts / And the Bastards he gets' in his wake. His appetites – and those of his soldiers – threatened to turn 'All your Wives' into 'Strumpets'. Moreover,

> His word nor his Oath
> Cannot bind him to Troth,
> He values not Credit nor Hist'ry,
> And tho' he has serv'd now
> Two Prentiships through,
> He know's not his Trade, nor his Mist'ry.[3]

---

[1] 'Upon his Majesties being made free of the city', in Margoliouth, *Poems and letters*, vol. 1, pp. 181–4.
[2] CLRO, Rep 80, f. 129.
[3] Ibid., p. 183.

265

For all Charles' dishonesty and incivility, the enfranchisement was not all bad. In an abrupt (and typically Marvellian) shift in tone, line eighty saw the citizens commended on their 'fortunate choice' of a monarch whose 'virtues exceed all his vices' – indeed, enfranchisement might well contribute to his further civilisation. The same could not be said for James. Sketched in the *Advice to a painter* (likewise attributed to Marvell) as a man wondering that subjects 'dare to contradict my Will / And think a Prince o'th Blood can e'er do ill', here was a prince implacably advancing 'The Government of France / With a Wife of Religion Italian'.[4] Faced with a future monarch bent on destroying 'their Liberties and Laws / Their Parchment Presidents, their dull Records' it was suggested that the box in which his freedom was to be presented had better uses. It could be appropriated as a 'Box of pills' for his syphilis; a ballot box for 'A new Duke to choose'; a box to hold 'the Cross with the Dagger' in case citizens had to resist James with force. Whichever was preferred, its current use merely confirmed that the citizens 'for Slaves are decreed' – that 'You in Chains offer your freedom'.

In admonishing the Stuarts, Marvell's verses invoked many of the constitutive features of commonwealth, freedom, and citizenship as they have been described in previous chapters. Most notable, perhaps, was the idea that the values that ideally defined citizens were a vantage point from which to judge not simply gentry and nobility but also monarch and heir to the throne. The Stuarts were not civil enough, honest enough, hardworking enough, skilled enough, creditable enough, socialised enough, or virtuous enough to warrant enfranchisement. Like Luke in *The city madam*, their wills were 'still the same'. The *honestas* required of this most civil of civil societies, and which was so lacking at court, was at once personal and social: dispositions that married self-reflection and discretion with an astute appreciation of place, company, conversation, and performance. Moreover, they were qualities that did not stop with the council chamber, but rather characterised all domestic, neighbourly, and commercial company and conversations of male and female citizens alike. In this way, city commonwealths formed an economic, patriarchal, and religious community in which incivility in one realm had profound consequences for distinctions, reputation, and credit in another – the positions and conversations of civic governance included. This fusion of personal and social morality – and the creation of a regulated and sharply defined self – was married to an equally powerful sense of place: a tangible culture of possession, ownership, and inclusion that made even the inclusion of the monarch a contingent and political process.

In both respects, the previous 130 years witnessed a process of structural and behavioural urbanisation: the expansion of a corporate system of city

---

[4] *Advice to a painter* (1679), p. 1; 'Upon his Majesties being made free', p. 184.

commonwealths. This fecundity of place allowed the promulgation of civic and civil values that served as a template for the political, social, and economic practice of citizens; informed more general conceptions of civil society; and addressed, in particular, the role of 'the commons' – or middling sort – within it. In these ways urbanisation was constitutive of developments that traditionally delineate the 'early modern' as a distinctive period in English history: not least commercialisation, state-formation, the transformation of 'the public sphere', and the intensified politics of patriarchy, religion, and class. However, it also complicates those narratives in terms of their antecedents, agents, contexts, resistance, and meanings. In particular, it offers a counterpoint to the narrative of sovereign state and private subject found in writers like Jonson, Bacon, Hobbes, Baines, Brady, and Barbon. This genealogy was, perhaps, the most radical dynamic of seventeenth-century political culture: certainly regimes that came closest to behaving like 'a state' – in the 1630s, 1650s, 1680s – provoked violent and successful opposition within the commonwealth at large. However, the very potency of this opposition points to the survival and, indeed, consolidation of an institutional and symbolic space that can slip as easily through the fingers of historians as be dismissed by proponents of *Leviathan* or 'universal monarchy'. This was a space located somewhere between household and sovereignty, and colonised by both; that was redolent with the common and public good, and contested and appropriated accordingly; that transmuted into eighteenth-century civil society.

The very centrality of this space to local and national politics explains, perhaps, its occasional invisibility in the historiography. With so many intersections, overlaps, and legacies, the very fact of English urbanity outwith the parameters of court and country house can be lost. This peculiar ambiguity was never better demonstrated than by a seventeenth-century coin now held at the Marischal Museum in Aberdeen.[5] In terms of its metal content and design the coin is consistent with unites minted for the Commonwealth between 1649 and 1660. Likewise the inscription of the George Cross on a shield surrounded by the words 'THE COMMONWEALTH OF ENGLAND' is formulaic. What is unusual about this particular coin is that the words 'GOD WITH US 1646' are inscribed on the reverse side: that is, it was minted three years before the execution of the king. In the absence of any retooling, the most likely explanation is that is that a 'die-sinker' erroneously punched in the figure 9 upside-down (although research has failed to locate any other recorded specimens). If the error was noticed at once, and the offending die re-cut or destroyed, it may be that very few coins struck from it were released into circulation.[6] However,

---

[5] The coin's registration number is ABDUA 47318.
[6] N. M. McQ. Holmes, 'A Commonwealth unite dated 1646', *Numismatic Circular*, 111, 6, 2003, p. 311.

this book suggests that, long before 1646, notions of city and national commonwealth were the predominant frame of reference for English citizens and freemen. Householders like the York baker James Wright, Cambridge fish merchant Thomas French, and Ludlow weaver John Bradford would have recognised the coin and its signification. The coin's inscription may have been hasty, but it was by no means unthinkable.

Bibliography

PRIMARY SOURCES

MANUSCRIPT SOURCES

Berkshire County Record Office (BCRO)

WO/01/1 and WO/AL   Wokingham Charters

Borthwick Institute of Historical Research (BIHR)

CPH   Consistory Court papers
D/C   Dean and Chapter Court papers
P Q 42.74 (library) St John's, York parish register
PR Y/J 1   St John's, York parish register
PR Y/J 17   St John's, York churchwarden's account
PR.Y/MG 19   St Martin's and Gregory's churchwardens account
Y/MB 34   St Michael le Belfrey churchwarden's account
Y/HTG 15   St Trinity Goodramgate constable's accounts
York wills

British Library (BL)

Add MSS 12497   Papers of Robert Cecil
Add MSS 35831   Papers of William Cecil
Add MS 21417–27   Papers of Adam Baines
Add MSS 28051   Papers of Thomas Osborne

Brymor Jones Library (BJL)

DDMM   Papers of Thompson-Lawley family

Cambridgeshire County Record Office (CCRO)

City Shelf C, Books 7 and 8   Common Day Books
City Box II, 9   Orders 1608–11

Corporation of London Record Office (CLRO)

Microfilm MCFP/552   Commons Journal
Rep 80, 82   —

Devonshire County Record Office (DCRO)

Chanter 11036 (Bundle)   Cornish depositions

East Sussex Record Office (ESRO)

Accession N 2936   Trial of Suzanne Swapper and Anne Taylor

Herefordshire County Record Office (HCRO)

HD4/2/17   Cases of instance, early 17th century

Huntingdon Record Office (HRO)

HB28   George Morrit's Book

Leeds Sheepscar (LS)

NH 2443   Robinson papers

Marischal Museum, Aberdeen

ABDUA 47318   1646 Commonwealth coin

North Yorkshire County Record Office (NYCRO)

NYRO, ZTP I   Wills, administrations, and settlements

Post Office Record Office (PORO)

PO 94/12   Letter book of Colonel Whitley

Shropshire Archives (SA)

LB2   Ludlow corporate minutes
LB7   John Bradford c. Corporation of Ludlow
LB 17   Ludlow guild records
LB Fiche 1, 2–3   Freemen lists
SRRC Q63   Copies of charters and grants to the town of Ludlow,
                   ed. W. Felton

The National Archive (TNA)

ASSI 45	Northern Assizes
C6	Chancery
C7	—
C10	—
E134	Exchequer
E179	Hearth Tax
STAC 8	Star Chamber
Probate 91/99	Wills c.1600
SP16	State Papers
SP29	—

Tyne and Wear Archive, Newcastle-upon-Tyne (TWA)

GU/GP	Guild records, Goldsmiths and pewtherers
GU/BS	Guild records, Barber surgeons
MD/NC/2/2	Common Council minutes

York City Archives (YCA)

B Series	City house-books
C Series	Chamberlains' accounts
E Series	Poor rate records, militia musters
F Series	Quarter session records

PRINTED SOURCES (CONTEMPORARY AND EDITIONS)

Alberi, Eugenio, ed., 'Relazioni dInghilterra di Giovanni Micheli', in *Relazioni degli Amabasciatori Veneti al Senato*, series 1, vol. II (Firenze, 1840)

An exact collection of all remonstrances, declarations, votes, orders, ordinances, proclamations, petitions, messages, answers, and other remarkable passages between the King's most excellent Majesty and his High Court of Parliament (1643)

Annals of Windsor. being a history of the castle and town, 2 vols., ed. Robert Richard Tighe and James Edward Davis (London, 1858)

Anonymous, 'A discourse of the names and first causes of the institution of cities', in John Stowe, *A survey of London* (1603)

— *Thomas of Woodstock, or, Richard the Second, part one/Anon*, ed. Peter Corbin and Douglas Sedge (Manchester, 2002)

— *The Reformado* (1642)

— *A new-come guest to the town* (1644)

— *The parliament of women* (1684)

Aristotle, *The politics, and The constitution of Athens*, ed. Stephen Everson (Cambridge, 1996)

Atkins, Richard, *Original and growth of printing collected out of history and the records of the kingdom* (1664)

Aubrey, John, *Brief lives: a selection based upon existing contemporary* portraits, ed. Richard Barber (Wallop, 1975)

Bacon: Francis, *Francis Bacon: a critical edition of the major works*, ed. Brian Vickers (Oxford, 1996)

Bacon, Nathaniel, *The annalls of Ipswich: the lawes, customes, and government of the same* (1664), ed. William H. Richardson (1884)

— *An historical discourse of the uniformity of the government of England* (1647)

Barbon, Nicholas, *An apology for the builder: or a discourse shewing the cause and effects of the increase in building* (1685)

Birchall, John, *The non-pareil* (York, 1644)

Blount, Thomas, *Glossographia, or, a dictionary interpreting all such hard words* (1656)

Bohun, Edmund, *Freedom of the press: four tracts with the diary of Edmund Bohun* (London, 1975)

Boulton, Edmond, *The cities advocate* (1628)

— *The cities great concern* (1674)

Bowles, Edward, *Plaine English* (1643)

— *The mystery of iniquitie* (1643)

— *Manifest truths* (1646)

— *Good counsel for evil times* (1648)

— *The dutie and danger of swearing* (York, 1655)

Brady, Robert, *An historical treatise of cities and burghs, or boroughs* (1690)

Bulloker, John, *An English expositer: teaching the interpretation of the hardest words used in our language* (1616)

Butcher, Richard, *The survey and antiquity of the town of Stamford in the county of Lincoln* (1717)

Calvert, Thomas, *The wise merchant, or the peerless pearl* (York, 1660)

Carew, Richard, *The survey of Cornwall*, ed. F. E. Halliday (London, 1954)

Cavendish, *An English Prince: Newcastle's Machiavellian political guide to Charles II*, ed. Gloria Italiano Anzilotti (Pisa, 1988)

Dalton, Michael, *The country justice*, 5th edition (1635)

Davidson, Peter, *Poetry and revolution: an anthology of British and Irish verse 1625–1660* (Oxford, 2001)

Daye, Angel, *The English secretorie* (1586)

— *The second part of the English secretorie* (1635)

De-Lanne, Thomas, *The present state of London* (1681)

Denison, Stephen, *An exposition upon the first chapter of the second epistle of Peter* (1622)

— *The monument or tombstone, or a sermon preached . . . at the funeral of Mrs Elizabeth Juxon* (1620)

— *The doctrine of both the sacraments* (1621)

Dod, John and Cleaver, Robert, *A Godlie forme of householde government* (1612)

Donne, John, *Pseudo-martyr* (1610)

Drake, Francis, *Eboracum* (1736)

Etherington, John, *The defence of John Etherington against Stephen Denison* (1641)

Faraday, M. A., 'The Ludlow poll-tax return of 1667', *Shropshire Archaeological Society*, 59, 1971–2

Fichte, Johann Gottlieb, *Addresses to the German nation* (1808), ed. George Armstrong Kelly (London, 1968)

Filmer, Robert, *Patriarcha: or the natural power of kings* (1680)

Foreman, Simon, *The autobiography and personal diary of Dr Simon Foreman the celebrated astrologer 1552–1602*, ed. James Orchard Halliwell (London, 1849)

Fulwood, William, *The enemie of idlenesse: teaching a perfect platforme how to indite epistles and letters of divers sorts* (1593)

Gale, Peter, *An inquiry into the ancient corporate system of Ireland and suggestions for its immediate restoration and general extension* (London, 1834)

Garbutt, Richard, *A demonstration of the resurrection* (1656)

Grey, William, *Chorographia, or a survey of Newcastle-upon-Tyne* (1649)

Heath, James, *Flagellum: or the life and death, birth and burial of O. Cromwell the late usurper* (1669)

Hobbes, Thomas, *Leviathan*, ed. Richard Tuck (Cambridge, 1992)

— *Decameron physiologicum: or, ten dialogues of natural philosophy* (1678)

— *Behemoth, or the Long Parliament* (1679), ed. Ferdinand Tonnies (London, 1939)

Horne, Robert, *The Christian governor in the common-wealth and private families* (1614)

Hutchinson, Lucy, *Memoirs of the life of Colonel Hutchinson*, ed. N. H. Keeble (London, 1995)

Jackson, Charles et al., eds., *Yorkshire diaries and autobiographies in the seventeenth and eighteenth centuries* (Durham, 1878)

James VI and I, *King James VI and I: selected writings*, ed. Neil Rhodes, Jennifer Richards, and Joseph Marshall (Aldershot, 2003)

— *A counter-blaste to tobacco* (1604)

— *The workes of the most high and mightie prince, James* (1616)

Jonson, Ben, *Bartholomew fair*, ed. G. R. Hibberd (London, 1977).

— 'Discoveries', in Ian Donaldson, ed. *Ben Jonson: the Oxford authors* (Oxford, 1985)

— *The alchemist*, ed. Alvin B. Kernan (New Haven, 1974)

Juxon, Thomas, *The journal of Thomas Juxon, 1644–1647*, ed. Keith Lindley and David Scott (Cambridge, 1999)

Lilly, William, *The last of the astrologers: Mr William Lilly's history of his life and times from the year 1662 to 1681*, edited and introduced by Katharine M. Briggs (London, 1974)

Locke, John, *Two treatises of government*, ed. Peter Laslett (Cambridge, 1988)

Maitland, Frederick William and Bateson, Mary, eds., *The charters of the borough of Cambridge* (Cambridge, 1901)

Manship, Henry, *The history of Great Yarmouth*, ed. Charles John Palmer (1854)

Marvell, Andrew, *The poems and letters of Andrew Marvell*, 2 vols., ed. H. M. Margoliouth (Oxford, 1927)

— *An account of the growth of popery* (1676)

— *Advice to a painter* (1679)

Massinger, Philip, *The city madam*, ed. Cathy Shrank (London, 2004)

Middleton, Thomas, *A chaste maid in Cheapside* (1613), ed. Alan Brissenden (London, 1968)

— *The triumphs of truth* (1616)

— *Honourable entertainments, composed for the service of this noble city* (1621)

— *Hengist, King of Kent; or the Mayor of Queenborough* (1619) (Washington, 1938)

Milton, John, *John Milton: a critical edition of the major works,* ed. Stephen Orgel and Jonathan Goldberg (Oxford, 1991)

Monckton, Philip, *The Monckton papers*, ed. E. Peacock, *Miscellanies of the Prohibition Society,* XVI (1884)

More, Thomas, *Utopia*, ed. George M. Logan and Robert M. Adams (Cambridge, 1998)

Morison, Richard, *A remedy for sedition* (1536)

Morrell, J. B., *The biography of the common man of the city of York as recorded in his epitaph* (London, 1948)

Mulcaster, Richard, *Positions concerning the training up of children* (1581)

— *The first part of the elementaries* (1582)

Nashe, Thomas, 'Nashe's Lenten Stuff', in *The unfortunate traveller and other works,* ed. J. B. Steane (Harmondsworth, 1985), 394

Nedham, Marchamont, *Mercurius Britanicus*, 92, 28 July–4 August 1645

Palmer, William Matlock, ed. *Cambridgeshire subsidy rolls 1250–1695* (Norwich, 1912)

Parker, Henry, *Observations upon some of his Majesties late answers and expresses* (1642)

Pepys, Samuel, *The diary of Samuel Pepys*, 10 vols., ed. R. C. Latham and W. Matthews (London, 1995)

Phillips, Edward, *New world of words* (1658; 1695; 1706)

Reading charters, acts and orders 1253–1911, ed. C. Fleetwood Pritchard (Reading, 1913)

Register of the freemen of the city of York, II, 1559–1759, ed. Francis Collins (Durham, 1900)

Reresby, John, *The memoirs of Sir John Reresby: the complete text and a selection from his letters*, ed. Andrew Browning, 2nd edition, preface and notes by Mary M. Geiter and W. A. Speck (London, 1991)

Scott, William, *An essay on drapery: or, the complete citizen* (1635)

Shakespeare, William, *The Oxford Shakespeare: the complete works,* ed. Stanley Wells and Gary Taylor (Oxford, 1994)

Sharp, Andrew, ed., *The English Levellers* (Cambridge, 1998)

Sheppard, William, *Of corporations, fraternities, and guilds* (1659)

Slingsby, Henry, *The diary of Sir Henry Slingsby*, ed. D. Parsons (London, 1836)

Smith, Thomas, *A discourse of the commonweal of this realm in England* (1549), ed. Mary Dewar (Charlottesville, 1969)

— *De Republica Anglorum: the maner of governement or policie of the realme of England* (1583)

Speed, John, *The theatre of the empire of Great Britain* (1611, 1616)

Steen, Sarah Jane, *Ambrosia in an earthen vessel: three centuries of audience and reader response to the works of Thomas Middleton* (New York, 1993)

Thompson, Edward, *The life of that most excellent citizen and uncorrupted Member of Parliament, Andrew Marvell* (London, 1776)

Wharton, George, *Calendarium Carolinum* (1661) in Cambridge University Library: Hhh. 453; Adams.8.66.23 (1).

Widdrington, Thomas, *Analecta Eboracensia: some remains of the ancient city of York collected by a citizen of York*, ed. C. Caine (London, 1897)

Williams, Roger, *A key into the language of America* (1643)

Wilson, Thomas, *The art of rhetorique* (1563)

— *The state of England anno. dom. 1600*, ed. F. J. Fisher (Camden Misc. XVI, 1936)

UNPUBLISHED DISSERTATIONS CITED IN TEXT

Chynoweth, John, Gentry of Tudor Cornwall (Exeter, 1994)
Rees Jones, Sarah, 'Property, tenure and rents: some aspects of the topography and
    economy of medieval York' (York, 1987)
Scott, David, 'Politics, dissent and quakerism in York, 1640–1700' (York, 1990)
Shepard, Alexandra Jane, 'Meanings of manhood in early modern England with specific
    reference to Cambridge, c. 1560–1640' (Cambridge, 1998)
Wilson, B. M., 'The corporation of York, 1580–1660' (York M. Phil, 1967)
Withington, P. J., 'Urban political culture in later seventeenth-century England: York,
    1649–1689' (Cambridge, 1998)

SECONDARY SOURCES

Allridge, Nick, 'Loyalty and identity in Chester parishes, 1540–1640', in Susan Wright,
    ed., *Parish, church and people: local studies in lay religion, 1350–1750* (London,
    1988)
Amussen, Susan Dwyer, *An ordered society: gender and class in early modern England*
    (Oxford, 1988)
Archer, Ian W., *The pursuit of stability: social relations in Elizabethan London* (Cam-
    bridge, 1991)
—'The nostalgia of John Stowe', in David L. Smith, Richard Strier, and David
    Broughton, eds., *The theatrical city: culture, theatre, and politics in London, 1576–
    1649* (Cambridge, 1995)
—'Politics and government, 1540–1700', in Peter Clark, ed., *The Cambridge urban
    history of Britain, volume II, 1540–1840* (Cambridge, 2000)
—'Popular politics in the sixteenth and early seventeenth centuries', in Paul Griffiths
    and Mark Jenner, eds., *Londinopolis: essays in the cultural and social history of
    early modern London* (Manchester, 2000)
Barry, Jonathan, 'Introduction', in Jonathan Barry, ed., *The Tudor and Stuart town: a
    reader in urban history, 1530–1688* (Harlow, 1990)
—'Bourgeois collectivism? Urban association and the middling sort', in Jonathan Barry
    and Christopher Brooks, eds., *The middling sort of people: culture, society and
    politics in England, 1550–1800* (Basingstoke, 1994)
—'Civility and civic culture in early modern England: the meanings of urban freedom', in
    Peter Burke, Brian Harrison, and Paul Slack, eds., *Civil histories: essays presented
    to Sir Keith Thomas* (Oxford, 2000)
Barton, Anne, 'Falstaff and the comic community', in Anne Barton, *Essays, mainly
    Shakespearean* (Cambridge, 1994)
Bearman, Robert, 'Introduction', in Robert Bearman, ed., *The history of an English
    borough: Stratford-upon-Avon, 1196–1996* (Sutton, 1996)
Bergeron, David M., 'Middleton's moral landscape: *A chaste maid in Cheapside* and
    The triumphs of truth', in *'Accompaninge the players: essays celebrating Thomas
    Middleton, 1580–1980* (New York, 1980)
Birtles, Sara, 'Common land, poor relief and enclosure: the use of manorial resources
    in fulfilling parish obligations, 1601–1834', *P&P*, 165, November 1999

Borsay, Peter, *The English urban renaissance: culture and society in the provincial town, 1660–1770* (Oxford, 1989)

——'The English urban renaissance: the development of provincial urban culture *c*.1680–*c*.1760', in Peter Borsay, ed., *The eighteenth century town: a reader in English urban history, 1688–1820* (Harlow, 1990)

——'Introduction', in Peter Borsay, ed., *The eighteenth century town: a reader in English urban history, 1688–1820* (Harlow, 1990)

Bourdieu, Pierre, *Language and symbolic power*, edited and introduced by J. B. Thompson (Cambridge, 1991)

Braddick, Michael J., 'State formation and social change in early modern England: a problem stated and approaches suggested', *Social History*, 16, 1991

—— *State formation in early modern England c.1550–1700* (Cambridge, 2000)

Branaman, Ann, 'Goffman's social theory', in Charles Lemert and Ann Branaman, eds., *The Goffman reader* (Oxford, Blackwell, 1997)

Brewer, John, *The sinews of power: war, money and the English state, 1688–1783* (London, 1989)

Brooks, C. W. *Pettyfoggers and vipers of the commonwealth: the 'lower branch' of the legal profession in early modern England* (Cambridge, 1986)

——'Apprenticeship, social mobility and the middling sort, 1550–1800', in Jonathan Barry and Christopher Brooks, eds., *The middling sort of people: culture, society and politics in England, 1550–1800* (Basingstoke, 1994)

Brunton, D. and Pennington, D.H. *Members of the long parliament* (London, 1968)

Bryson, Anna, *From courtesy to civility: changing codes of conduct in early modern England* (Oxford, 1998)

Capp, Bernard, *When gossips meet: women, family and neighbourhood in early modern England* (Oxford, 2003)

Carlin, Norah, 'Liberty and fraternities in the English revolution: the politics of London artisans' protests, 1635–1659', *International Review of Social History*, 39, 1994

Certeau, Michel de, *The practice of everyday life*, trans. Steven F. Randall (California, 2002)

Chakravorty, Swapen, *Society and politics in the plays of Thomas Middleton* (Oxford, 1996)

Clark, Peter and Slack, Paul, 'Introduction', in Peter Clark and Paul Slack, eds., *Crisis and order in English towns, 1500–1700* (London, 1972)

—— *English towns in transition, 1500–1700* (Oxford, 1976)

——'"The Ramoth-Gilead of the good": urban change and popular radicalism at Gloucester 1540–1640', in Jonathan Barry, ed., *The Tudor and Stuart town: a reader in English urban history, 1530–1688* (Harlow, 1990)

—— *British clubs and societies, 1580–1800: the origins of an associational world* (Oxford, 2000)

Colclough, David, '"The muses recreation": John Hoskyns and the manuscript culture of the seventeenth century', *Huntingdon Library Quarterly*, 61, 3 & 4

Collinson, Patrick, 'The monarchical republic of Queen Elizabeth I', *Bulletin of the John Rylands Library*, 69, 1987

—— *The birthpangs of Protestant England: religious and cultural change in the sixteenth and seventeenth centuries* (Basingstoke, 1988)

—— *De Republica Anglorum; or history with the politics put back* (Cambridge, 1990)

Collinson, Patrick and Craig, John, 'Introduction' in Patrick Collinson and John Craig, eds., *The Reformation in English towns, 1500–1640* (Basingstoke, 1998)

Crawford, Patricia, '"The poorest she": women and citizenship in early modern England', in Michael Mendle, ed., *The Putney debates of 1647: the army, the Levellers and the English state* (Cambridge, 2001)

Cromartie, Alan, 'The constitutionalist revolution: the transformation of political culture in early Stuart England', *P&P*, 163, May 1999

Cross, Claire, 'A man of conscience in seventeenth-century urban politics: Alderman Hoyle of York', in John Morrill, Paul Slack, and Daniel Woolf, eds., *Public duty and private conscience in seventeenth-century England: essays presented to G. E. Aylmer* (Oxford, 1993)

Cust, Richard and Hughes, Ann, 'Introduction: continuities and discontinuities in the English civil war', in Cust and Hughes, eds., *The English civil war* (London, 1997)

Daunton, M. J., *Progress and poverty: an economic and social history of Britain, 1700–1850* (Oxford, 1995)

D'Cruze, Shani, 'The middling sort in eighteenth-century Colchester: independence, social relations and the community broker', in Jonathan Barry and Christopher Brooks, eds., *The middling sort of people: culture, society and politics in England, 1550–1800* (Basingstoke, 1994)

De Krey, Gary S., 'The London Whigs and the exclusion crisis reconsidered', in A. L. Beier, David Cannadine, and James M. Rosenheim, eds., *The first modern society: essays in English history in honour of Lawrence Stone* (Cambridge, 1989)

— *A fractured society: the politics of London in the first age of party, 1688–1715* (Oxford, 1985)

Dean, D. M., 'London lobbies and parliament: the case of the brewers and coopers in the parliament of 1593', *Parliamentary History*, 8/2, 1989

— 'Parliament and locality', in D. M. Dean and N. L. Jones, eds., *The parliaments of Elizabethan England* (Oxford, 1990)

Dennison, Patricia, 'Timothy Pont's portrayal of towns', in Ian C. Cunningham, ed., *The nation survey'd: Timothy Pont's maps of Scotland* (East Linton, 2001), pp. 125–38

Dyer, Alan, 'Crisis and revolution: government and society in Stratford, 1540–1640', in Robert Bearman, ed., *The history of an English borough: Stratford-upon-Avon 1196–1996* (Sutton, 1996)

— 'Small market towns, 1540–1700', in Peter Clark, ed., *The Cambridge urban history of Britain, Volume II, 1540–1840* (Cambridge, 2000)

Eastwood, David, *Government and community in the English provinces 1700–1870* (Basingstoke, 1997)

Elias, Norbert, *The civilizing process*, trans. Edmund Jephcott (Oxford, 2000)

Ellis, Joyce, 'A dynamic society: social relations in Newcastle-upon-Tyne, 1660–1760', in Peter Clark, ed., *The transformation of English provincial towns, 1600–1800* (London, 1984)

Elsky, Martin, *Authorising words: speech, writing and print in the English Renaissance* (Ithaca, 1989)

Elton, G. R., *The Tudor constitution: documents and commentary*, 2nd edition (Cambridge, 1995)

Evans, John T., *Seventeenth-century Norwich: politics, religion, and government, 1620–1690* (Oxford, 1979)

—'The decline of oligarchy in seventeenth-century Norwich', *JBS*, 14, 1974

Everitt, Alan, *The local community and the Great Rebellion* (London, 1969)

Faraday, Michael, 'The Ludlow poll-tax return of 1667; *Shropshire Archaeological Society*, 59, 1971–2

— *Ludlow 1085–1660: a social, economic, and political history* (Chichester, 1991)

Fletcher, Anthony, *Tudor rebellions* (London, 1968)

Fox, Adam, 'Rumour, news and popular political opinion in Elizabethan and early Stuart England', *HJ*, 50, 1997

—'Religious satire in English towns, 1570–1640', in Patrick Collinson and John Craig, eds., *The Reformation in English towns, 1500–1640* (Basingstoke, 1998)

— *Oral and literate culture in England 1500–1700* (Oxford, 2000)

Freist, Dagmar, *Governed by opinion: politics, religion and the dynamics of communication in Stuart London, 1637–1645* (London, 1997)

Galley, Chris, *The demography of early modern towns: York in the sixteenth and seventeenth centuries* (Liverpool, 1998)

Gauci, Perry, *The politics of trade: the overseas merchant in state and society, 1660–1720* (Oxford, 2001)

Gaustad, Edwin S., *Liberty of conscience: Roger Williams in America* (Michigan, 1991)

Gentles, Ian, 'The New Model Officer Corps in 1647: a collective portrait', *Social History*, 22, 2, 1997

Gillespie, Raymond, 'The origins and development of an Ulster urban network, 1600–41', *Irish Historical Studies*, 24, 93, 1984

— *Colonial Ulster: the settlement of East Ulster 1600–1641* (Cork, 1985)

Gilpin, W. Clark, *The millenarian piety of Roger Williams* (Chicago, 1979)

Goldie, Mark, 'John Locke and Anglican royalism', *Political Studies*, 31, 1983

Goose, Nigel, 'Household size and structure in early Stuart Cambridge', in Jonathan Barry, ed., *The Tudor and Stuart town: a reader in English urban history, 1530–1688* (Harlow, 1990)

Gowing, Laura, *Domestic dangers: women, words, and sex in early modern London* (Oxford, 1996)

— *Common bodies: women, touch, and power in seventeenth-century England* (New Haven, 2003)

Gregory, Annabel, 'Witchcraft, politics, and good neighbourhood in early seventeenth-century Rye', *P&P*, 133, 1991

Griffiths, Paul, *Youth and authority: formative experiences in England 1560–1640* (Oxford, 1996)

—'Secrecy and authority in late sixteenth and seventeenth-century London', *HJ*, 40, 4, 1997

Gurr, Andrew, *The Shakespearian playing companies* (Oxford, 1996)

Guy, J. A., *The public career of Thomas More* (Brighton, 1980)

— *Tudor England* (Oxford, 1988)

Habermas, Jürgen, *The structural transformation of the public sphere*, trans. Thomas Burger and Frederick Lawson (Cambridge, 1992)

Halliday, Paul D., *Dismembering the body politic: partisan politics in England's towns, 1650–1730* (Cambridge, 1998)

Harris, Tim, *Politics under the later Stuarts: party conflict in a divided society, 1660–1715* (Harlow, 1993)

Heal, Felicity, *Hospitality in early modern England* (Oxford, 1990)

Heller, Herbert Jack, *Penitent brothers: grace, sexuality, and genre in Thomas Middleton's city comedies* (Newark, 2000)

Herrup, Cynthia, *The common peace: participation and the criminal law in seventeenth-century England* (Cambridge, 1987)

Hindle, Steve, 'The shaming of Margaret Knowsley: gossip, gender, and the experience of authority in early modern England', *Continuity and Change*, 9 (3), 1994

— 'The keeping of the public peace', in Paul Griffiths, Adam Fox, and Steve Hindle, eds., *The experience of authority in early modern England* (Basingstoke, 1996)

— 'A sense of place? Becoming and belonging in the rural parish, 1550–1650', in Alexandra Shepard and Phil Withington, eds., *Communities in early modern England: networks, place, rhetoric* (Manchester, 2000)

— *The state and social change in early modern England, c. 1540–1640* (Basingstoke, 2000)

Hirst, Derek, *The representative of the people? Voters and voting in England under the early Stuarts* (Cambridge, 1975)

Holmes, N. M. McQ., 'A Commonwealth unite dated 1646', *Numismatic Circular*, 111, 6, 2003

Houlbrooke, Ralph, ed., *English family life, 1576–1716: an anthology from diaries* (Oxford, Blackwell, 1989)

Houston, R. A., *The population history of Britain and Ireland, 1550–1750* (Cambridge, 1992)

Howell, Roger, 'Neutralism, conservatism and political alignment in the English Revolution: the case of the towns, 1642–9', in John Morrill, ed. *Reactions to the English civil war* (London, 1982)

— 'Newcastle and the nation: the seventeenth-century experience', in Jonathan Barry, ed., *The Tudor and Stuart town: a reader in English urban history, 1530–1688* (Harlow, 1990)

Hoyle, R. W., *The pilgrimage of grace and the politics of the 1530s* (Oxford, 2001)

Hughes, Ann, 'Coventry and the English revolution', in R. C. Richardson, ed., *Town and countryside in the English revolution* (Manchester, 1992)

— 'Religion and society in Stratford-upon-Avon, 1619–1638', *Midland History*, 1994

— 'Gender and politics in Leveller literature', in Susan Amussen and Mark Kishlansky, eds., *Political culture and cultural politics in England: essays presented to David Underdown* (Manchester, 1995)

— 'The king, parliament and the localities during the English civil war', in Richard Cust and Ann Hughes, eds., *The English civil war* (London, 1997)

Hunt, Margaret R., *The middling sort: commerce, gender, and the family in England 1680–1780* (Berkeley, 1996).

Hunter, R. J., 'Towns in the Ulster plantation', *Studia Hibernia*, 11, 1971

Ingram, Martin, 'From reformation to toleration: popular religious cultures in England, 1540–1690' in Tim Harris, ed., *Popular culture in England, c.1500–1850* (Basingstoke, 1995)

Innes, Joanne and Rogers, Nicholas, 'Politics and government, 1700–1840', in Peter Clark, ed., *The Cambridge urban history of Britain, Volume II, 1540–1840* (Cambridge, 2000)

Jenner, Mark S. R. and Griffiths, Paul, 'Introduction', in Mark S. R. Jenner and Paul Griffiths, eds., *Londinopolis: essays in the cultural and social history of early modern London* (Manchester, 2000)

Keeler, Mary F., *The long parliament* (Philadelphia, 1954)

Kermode, Jenny, *Medieval merchants: York, Beverley and Hull in the later middle-ages* (Cambridge, 1998)

Kishlansky, Mark, *Parliamentary selection: social and political choice in early modern England* (Cambridge, 1986)

Knights, Mark, *Politics and opinion in crisis, 1678–1681* (Cambridge, 1994)

Kupperman, Karen, *Providence Island, 1630–1641: the other puritan colony* (Cambridge, 1993)

Kussmaul, Ann, *A general view of the rural economy of England, 1538–1840* (Cambridge, 1990)

Lake, Peter, *The boxmaker's revenge: 'orthodoxy', 'heterodoxy', and the politics of the parish in early Stuart London* (Manchester, 2001)

Lamburn, David, 'Politics and religion in early modern Beverley', in Patrick Collinson and John Craig, eds., *The Reformation in English towns, 1500–1640* (Basingstoke, 1998)

Langford, Paul, *A polite and commercial people: England, 1727–1783* (Oxford, 1989)

Lennon, Colm, *The life of Richard Stanihurst the Dubliner, 1547–1618* (Blackrock, 1981)

— *The lords of Dublin in the age of reformation* (Dublin, 1989)

MacCulloch, Diarmaid, 'Kett's rebellion in context', *P&P*, 84, 1979

— *Suffolk and the Tudors: politics and religion in an English county, 1500–1600* (Oxford, 1986)

— *The later reformation in England, 1547–1603* (Basingstoke, 2001)

McMillin, Scott and MacLean, Sally-Beth, *The Queen's Men and their plays* (Cambridge, 2000)

McRae, Andrew, *God speed the plough: the representation of agrarian England, 1500–1600* (Cambridge, 1996)

—'"On the famous voyage": Ben Jonson and civic space', in Andrew Gordon and Bernhard Klein, eds., *Literature, mapping and the politics of space in early modern Britain* (Cambridge, 2001)

Maitland, F. W., *Township and borough* (Cambridge, 1898)

Manley, Lawrence, *Literature and culture in early modern London* (Cambridge, 1997)

Martin, Jeanette, 'Leadership and priorities in Reading during the Reformation', in Patrick Collinson and John Craig, eds., *The Reformation in English towns, 1500–1640* (Basingstoke, 1998)

Martin, Julian, *Francis Bacon, the state, and the reform of natural philosophy* (Cambridge, 1992)

Mason, Roger, *Kingship and the commonweal: political thought in Renaissance and Reformation Scotland* (East Linton, 1998)

Mayhew, Graham, *Tudor Rye* (Falmer, 1987)

Mendelson, Sara and Crawford, Patricia, *Women in early modern England* (Oxford, 1998)

Mendle, Michael, *Dangerous positions: mixed government, the estates of the realm, and the making of the answer to the XIX propositions* (Alabama, 1985)

Moody, T. W., *The Londonderry plantation, 1609–1641: the City of London and the plantation in Ulster* (Belfast, 1939)

Morrill, J. S., *The revolt of the provinces: conservatives and radicals in the English civil war* (Harlow, 1980)

—'The making of Oliver Cromwell', in J. S. A. Adamson and J. S. Morrill, eds., *Oliver Cromwell and the English revolution* (Harlow, 1990)

— 'The religious context of the English civil war', in Richard Cust and Ann Hughes, *The English civil war* (London, 1997)

Muldrew, Craig, *The economy of obligation* (Basingstoke, 1998)

—'From a "Light Cloak" to an "Iron Cage": historical changes in the relation between community and individualism', in Alexandra Shepard and Phil Withington, eds., *Communities in early modern England: networks, place, rhetoric* (Manchester, 2000)

Neale, J. E., *The Elizabethan House of Commons* (London, 1949)

Norbrook, David, *Writing the English republic: poetry, rhetoric and politics, 1627–1660* (Cambridge, 1999)

—"Words more than civil": republican civility in Lucy Hutchinson's "The life of John Hutchinson"', in Jennifer Richards, ed., *Early modern civil discourses* (Basingstoke, 2003)

Ohlmeyer, Jane and O'Ciardha, Eammon, *The Irish statute staple books, 1596–1687* (Dublin, 1998)

Palliser, D. M., *Tudor York* (Oxford, 1979)

Patterson, Annabel, *Marvell: the writer in public life* (Harlow, 1999)

Patterson, Catherine F., *Urban patronage in early modern England: corporate boroughs, the landed elite, and the crown, 1580–1640* (Stanford, 1999)

Pearl, Valerie, *London and the outbreak of the Puritan revolution: city government and national politics, 1625–1643* (Oxford, 1961)

Peltonen, Markku, *Classical humanism and republicanism in English political thought, 1570–1640* (Cambridge, 1995)

— 'Political philosophy', in Markku Peltonen, ed., *The Cambridge companion to Bacon* (Cambridge, 1996)

Perkins, William, *The works of that famous and worthy minister of Christ in the University of Cambridge* (1626)

Phythian Adams, Charles, *Desolation of a city: Coventry and the urban crisis of the late middle ages* (Cambridge, 1979)

—'An agenda for English local history', in Charles Phythian Adams, ed., *Societies, cultures, and kinship, 1580–1850* (London, 1996)

Pincus, Steve,'"Coffee politicians does create": coffeehouses and Restoration political culture', *Journal of Modern History*, 67, 4, December 1995

Plumb, J. H., *The growth of political stability in England 1675–1725* (London, 1967)

Pocock, J. C. A., *The Machiavellian moment: Florentine political thought and the Atlantic republican tradition* (Princeton, 1975)

— *Virtue, commerce, and history: essays in political thought, chiefly in the eighteenth century* (Cambridge, 1985)

— *The ancient constitution and the feudal law: a study of English historical thought in the seventeenth century* (Cambridge, 1987)

Pryde, George Smith, *The burghs of Scotland: a critical list* (Oxford, 1965)

Rappaport, Steve, *Worlds within worlds: structures of life in sixteenth-century London* (Cambridge, 1989)

Reed, Michael, 'London and its hinterland, 1600–1800: the view from the provinces', in Peter Clark and B. Lepetit, eds., *Capital cities and their hinterlands in early modern Europe* (Aldershot, 1996)

Reynolds, Susan, *An introduction to the history of English medieval towns* (Oxford, 1977)

Rhodes, Neil, *Elizabethan grotesque* (London, 1980)

Richards, Jennifer, *Rhetoric and courtliness in early modern literature* (Cambridge, 2003)

Robinson, Philip, *The plantation of Ulster: British settlement in an Irish landscape, 1600–1670* (Dublin, 1984)

Rollison, David, *The local origins of modern society: Gloucestershire, 1500–1800* (London, 1992)

Roper, Lyndal, '"The common man", "the common good", "common women": gender and meaning in the German Reformation commune', *Social History*, 12, 1987

Rowse, A. L., *Tudor Cornwall: portrait of a society* (Basingstoke, 1969)

Roy, Ian, 'The English republic, 1649–1660: the view from the town hall', in Helmut G. Koenigsberger, ed., *Republiken und republikanismus im Europa der fruhen Neuzeit* (Munich, 1988)

Rublack, Ulinka, *The crimes of women in early modern Germany* (Oxford, 1999)

Sacks, David Harris, 'The corporate town and the English state: Bristol's "little businesses", 1625–1641', in Jonathan Barry, ed., *The Tudor and Stuart town: a reader in English urban history, 1530–1688* (Harlow, 1990)

— *The widening gate: Bristol and the Atlantic, 1450–1700* (Berkeley, 1991)

—'Ports, 1540–1700', in Peter Clark, ed., *The Cambridge urban history of Britain, Volume II, 1540–1840* (Cambridge, 2000)

Scott, David, *Quakerism in York, 1650–1720* (York, 1991)

Scott, Jonathan, *England's troubles: seventeenth-century English political instability in European context* (Cambridge, 2000)

Scribner, Bob, 'Is a history of popular culture possible?', *History of European Ideas*, 10, 1989

—'Communities and the nature of power', in Robert Scribner, ed., *Germany: a new social and economic history* (London, 1996)

Seaver, Paul, *Wallington's world: a puritan artisan in seventeenth-century London* (London, 1985)

Shagan, Ethan, H., 'Rumours and popular politics in the reign of Henry VIII', in Tim Harris, ed., *The politics of the excluded, c.1500–1850* (Basingstoke, 2001)

— *Popular politics and the English Reformation* (Cambridge, 2003)

Sharpe, J. A., *Defamation and sexual slander in early modern England: the church courts in York* (York 1980)

Shepard, Alexandra Jane, 'Meanings of manhood in early modern England with specific reference to Cambridge, c.1560–1640' (unpublished Ph.D. thesis, University of Cambridge, 1998)

—'Contesting communities? "Town" and "gown" in Cambridge, c.1560–1640' in Alexandra Shepard and Phil Withington, eds., *Communities in early modern England: networks, place, rhetoric* (Manchester, 2000)

—'Manhood, credit and patriarchy in early modern England, c.1580–1640', *P&P*, 167, 2000

Shrank, Cathy, 'The state', in Terence Ball, James Farr, and Russell L. Hanson, eds., *Political innovation and conceptual change* (Cambridge, 1989)

—'Rhetorical constructions of a national community: the role of the King's English in mid-Tudor writing', in Alexandra Shepard and Phil Withington, eds., *Communities in early modern England: networks, place, rhetoric* (Manchester, 2000)

—'Civil tongues: language, law, and reformation', in Jennifer Richards, ed., *Early modern civil discourses* (Basingstoke, 2003)

—*Writing the nation in Reformation England* (Oxford, 2004)

—'Civility and the city in *Coriolanus*', *Shakespeare Quarterly*, 54 (2003).

Slack, Paul, *The impact of plague in Tudor and Stuart England* (London, 1985)

— *Poverty and policy in Tudor and Stuart England* (London, 1988)

— *From Reformation to improvement: public welfare in early modern England* (Oxford, 1999)

—'Great and good towns, 1540–1700', in Peter Clark, ed., *The Cambridge urban history of Britain, volume II, 1540–1840* (Cambridge, 2000)

—'Perceptions of the metropolis in seventeenth-century England', in Peter Burke, Brian Harrison, and Paul Slack, eds., *Civil histories: essays presented to Sir Keith Thomas* (Oxford, 2000)

Smail, John, *Origins of middle-class culture: Halifax, Yorkshire, 1660–1780* (Ithaca, 1994)

Smith, Richard M., '"Modernisation" and the corporate medieval village community in England: some sceptical reflections', in Alan R. H. Baker and Derek Gregory, eds., *Explorations in historical geography* (Cambridge, 1984)

Sommerville, J. P., *Politics and ideology in England, 1603–1640* (Harlow, 1986)

Stoyle, Mark, *Loyalty and locality: Popular allegiance in Devon during the English civil war* (Exeter, 1994)

Sullivan, Ceri, *The rhetoric of credit: merchants in early modern writing* (London, 2002)

Sullivan, Garrett A., *The drama of landscape: land, property, and social relations on the early modern stage* (Stanford, 1998)

Sweet, Rosemary, *The writing of urban histories in eighteenth-century England* (Oxford, 1997)

Tadmor, Naomi, 'The concept of the household-family in eighteenth-century England', *P&P*, 151, 1996

— *Family and friends in eighteenth-century England: household, kinship, and patronage* (Cambridge, 2001)

Thirsk, Joan, *Economic policy and projects: the development of a consumer culture in early modern England* (Oxford, 1978)

Thompson, E. P., *The making of the English working class* (New York, 1966)

Tittler, Robert, 'The incorporation of the boroughs, 1540–1558', *History*, 62, 204, 1977

—'Elizabethan towns and the "points of contact": parliament', *Parliamentary History*, 8, 2, 1989

— *Architecture and power: the town hall and the English urban community, c.1500–1640* (Oxford, 1991)

— *The Reformation and the towns in England: politics and political culture, c.1540–1640* (Oxford, 1998)

— *Townspeople and nation: English urban experiences, 1540–1640* (Stanford, 2001)

Todd, Margot, *Christian humanism and the puritan social order* (Cambridge, 1987)

Tuck, Richard, 'Civil conflict in school and town, 1500–1700', in Brian Mains and Anthony Tuck, eds., *Royal Grammar School, Newcastle-upon-Tyne: a history of the school in its community* (London, 1986)

— *Philosophy and government, 1572–1651* (Cambridge, 1993)

Tupper, Fred S., 'Mary Palmer, alias Mrs Andrew Marvell', *Publications of the Modern Language Association*, 53, 2, 1938

Turner, James Grantham, 'Pepys and the private parts of monarchy', in Gerald MacLean, ed., *Culture and society in the Stuart Restoration: literature, drama, history* (Cambridge, 1995)

Tyacke, Nicholas, 'Puritanism, Arminianism, and counter-revolution', in Richard Cust and Ann Hughes, eds., *The English civil war* (London, 1997)

Underdown, David, *Fire from heaven: life in an English town in the seventeenth century* (London, 1993)

Vickery, Amanda, 'Golden age to separate spheres? A review of the categories and chronology of English women's history', *HJ*, 36, 1993

Victoria County History, Berkshire; Hertfordshire

Vries, Jan De, *European urbanization, 1500–1800* (London, 1984)

Walter, John, *Understanding popular violence in the English revolution: the Colchester plunderers* (Cambridge, 1999)

Walzer, Michael, 'Citizenship', in Terence Ball, James Farr, and Russell L. Hanson, eds., *Political innovation and conceptual change* (Cambridge, 1989)

Weinbaum, Martin, *British borough charters, 1307–1660* (Cambridge, 1943)

Williams, Penry, 'Government and politics in Ludlow, 1590–1642', *Transactions of the Shropshire Archaeological Society*, 56, 1957/8

— *The later Tudors: England 1547–1603* (Oxford, 1995)

Wilson, Kathleen, *The sense of the people: politics, culture and imperialism, 1715–1785* (Cambridge, 1995)

Withington, Phil, 'Citizens, community and political culture in Restoration England', in Alexandra Shepard and Phil Withington, eds., *Communities in early modern England: networks, place, rhetoric* (Manchester, 2000)

— 'Two renaissances: urban political culture in post-Reformation England reconsidered', *HJ*, 44, 1, 2001

— 'Views from the bridge: revolution and restoration in seventeenth-century York', *P&P*, 170, 2001

Withington, Phil and Shepard, Alexandra, 'Introduction', in Alexandra Shepard and Phil Withington, eds., *Communities in early modern England: networks, place, rhetoric* (Manchester, 2000)

Wood, Andy, 'Custom, identity and resistance: English free miners and their law', in Paul Griffiths, Adam Fox, and Steve Hindle, eds., *The experience of authority in early modern England* (Basingstoke, 1996)

— 'Beyond post-revisionism? The civil war allegiances of the miners of the Derbyshire "Peak Country"', *HJ*, 40, 1997

— 'The place of custom in plebeian political culture: England, 1550–1800', *Social History*, 22, 1, January 1997

— *The politics of social conflict: the Peak country, 1520–1770* (Cambridge, 1999)

Woodward, Donald, *Men at work: labourers and building craftsmen in the towns of northern England, 1450–1750* (Cambridge, 1995)

Wrightson, Keith, *English society, 1580–1680* (London, 1982)

—'Estates, degrees, and sorts: changing perceptions of society in Tudor and Stuart England', in Penelope Corfield, ed., *Language, history and class* (Oxford, 1991)

—'"Sorts of people" in Tudor and Stuart England', in Jonathan Barry and Christopher Brooks, eds., *The middling sort of people: culture, society and politics in England, 1550–1800* (Basingstoke, 1994)

—'Northern identities', in *Northern Review*, 2, 1995

— *Poverty and piety in an English village: Terling, 1525–1700* (Oxford, 1995)

—'The politics of the parish in early modern England', in Paul Griffiths, Adam Fox, and Steve Hindle, eds., *The experience of authority in early modern England* (Basingstoke, 1996)

—'The family in early modern England: continuity and change', in Stephen Taylor, Richard Conners, and Clyve Jones, eds., *Hanoverian Britain and empire: essays in memory of Philip Lawson* (Woodbridge, 1998)

— *Earthly necessities: economic lives in early modern Britain* (Yale, 2000)

Wrightson, Keith and Levine, David, *The making of an industrial society: Wickham, 1560–1765* (Oxford, 1991)

Wrigley, E. A., 'Urban growth and agricultural change: England and the continent in the early modern period', *Journal of Interdisciplinary History*, 15, 4, 1985.

Zwicker, Steven N., 'Virgins and whores: the politics of sexual misconduct in the 1660s', in Conal Condren and A. D. Cousins, eds., *The political identity of Andrew Marvell* (Aldershot, 1990)

Index

Index

triumphs of truth, The 201
Tuck, Richard 123, 163
Tudor politics 4
Tupper, Fred 225
Turner, Frances 224
tyranny 66, 68, 73, 237

Ulster 18, 64
urban domesticity *see* households
urban freedom 30
  and city commonwealth 89, 93
  and civil society 190–194
  economy of 159–194
urban migration 30
urban mobility 36
urban political culture 12
urbanisation 267
  and *commonweal* 25–37
  and urbanity 3–8
urbanity 3–8, 13, 18, 20, 233, 267
Utopia (More) 53

values 266, 267
Venice 7
virtue 55, 60, 163, 246, 247
vocation *see* calling
voices *see* fames
voluntary associations 190
Vox militaris 153

Wales 16, 18
Walker, Isabel 207
Waller, Robert 263
Wallington, Nehemiah 255
Walsall (Staffordshire) 32
Walters, John 181
Walwyn, William 152
Warter, John 134
Warwick 44
Wash 35
Waterford 20
Watson, Henry 177
Watson, Stephen 242, 252
way of the world, The (Congreve) 215
wealth *see* Cambridge, wealth; Ludlow,
  wealth
Welburne, Christopher 188
Welburne, Frances 200
Wentworth, Thomas 237
Westminster Assembly of Divines 120
Westminster Movement 235
Westmorland 30, 37, 250
Wexford 20
Wharton, George 259
Wharton, Thomas 252

Whitchurch (Hampshire) 17
White, Thomas 182, 218
Whitely, Ann 201
Widdrington, Thomas 59, 159–160, 189, 241,
  263
Wildman, John 80, 92, 166, 167, 180, 192
will
  city madam, The (Luke) 165
  civic conversations 140, 142
  General Council of the Army debate
    166–167
  mediation of 119, 164, 167
  place and person 115–118
  private 73, 76, 81
William of Nassau 131
Williams, Penry 69
Williams, Roger 128, 137, 140
Wilson, Kathleen 194
Wilson, Thomas 11, 12, 113, 114, 143
Windsor 9, 47, 150, 259
Winthrop, John 137
Wintringham, Anne 132, 133, 135
wisdom 118, 140, 251
Wistow 131, 132
witchcraft 195
Witham 35
Witton, Thomas 174
Wokingham 17
Wood, Andy 87
Wood, George 177–179
Wood, Toby 93
Woodcock, Martin 187
Woodstock (anon) 68
Woollchurch Market bank 192, 225
Wright, Elizabeth 135
Wright, James 14–15, 92, 99, 119, 154, 190,
  241
Wrightson, Keith 31, 68, 86
  economy of freedom 160, 163, 194
written communication 142–143

yeomen 168, 169
York
  Ainsty 189
  apprenticeship 30
  citizens 98
  citizens in parliament 65
  civic ceremonial 131, 133, 134
  civic practice 97
  civic representation 92
  common land and corporate leases 180
  corporate power 97
  corporate system 8, 20, 21, 38–40, 83
  defamation 204
  elections 44

Lightning Source UK Ltd.
Milton Keynes UK
172591UK00001B/48/P